Sand
Chronicles

Shojo Beat

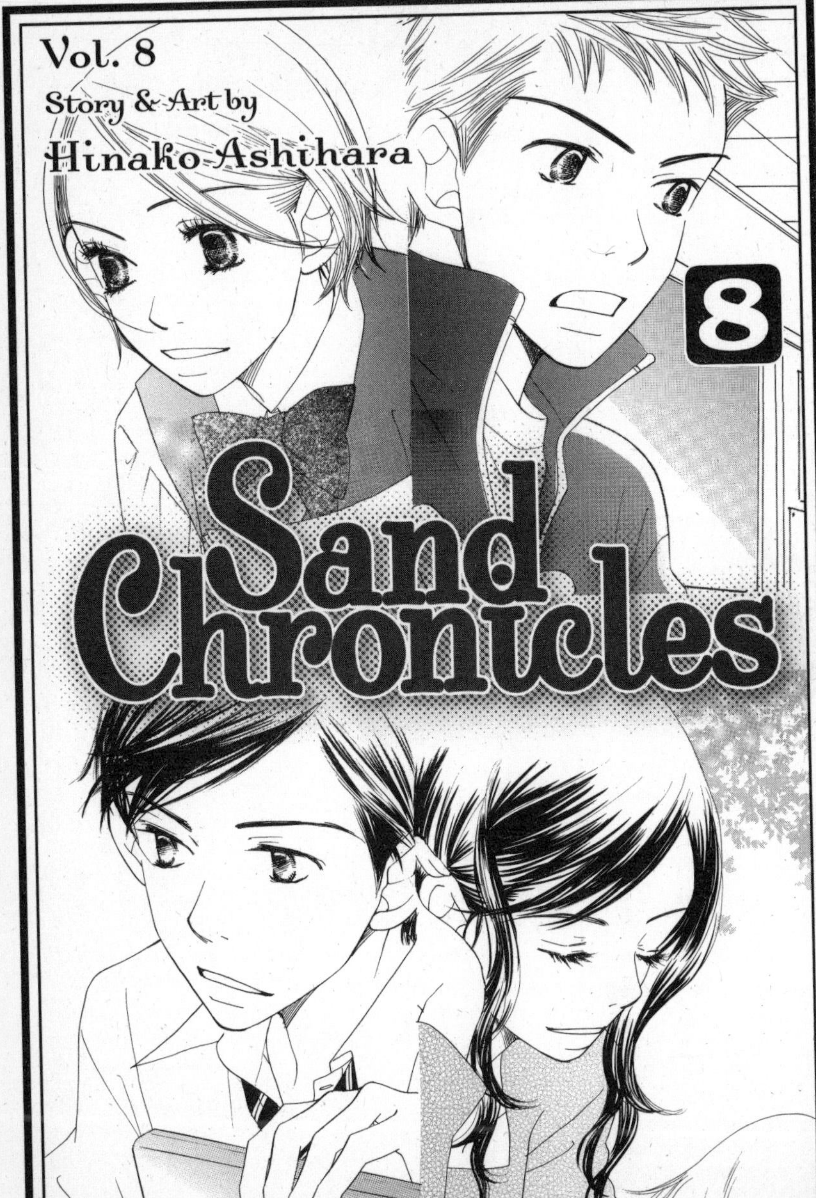
Vol. 8
Story & Art by
Hinako Ashihara
8
Sand Chronicles

Sand Chronicles

Volume 8

Contents

Story thus far...

After her parents' divorce, Ann moves to rural Shimane with her mother. When Ann's mother commits suicide, Ann's new friends, Daigo and wealthy siblings Fuji and Shika, are a great support to her. But then Ann moves back to Tokyo to live with her father... In the end, it isn't distance or time that tears Ann and Daigo apart—it's their emotions.

After breaking up with Daigo, Ann moves on with her life. She graduates from college and gets a job working at a corporation. While commuting home late one night, she meets an elite businessman who is the polar opposite of Daigo. They plan to marry, but when Ann challenges her fiancé over his lack of compassion, he breaks off the engagement. Thrown off balance again, Ann sets out on a journey to visit the Nima Sand Museum, which she visited with her mother shortly before her mother committed suicide...

Main characters

Shika Tsukishima
Fuji's younger sister. Currently studying abroad in Canada.

Fuji Tsukishima
Fuji was in love with Ann for a long time but is now dating his cousin.

Daigo Kitamura
Daigo is teaching elementary school in Okayama.

Ann Minase
Ann lives with her father, his new wife and her little half sister.

WINTER, AGE 26: PRAYER

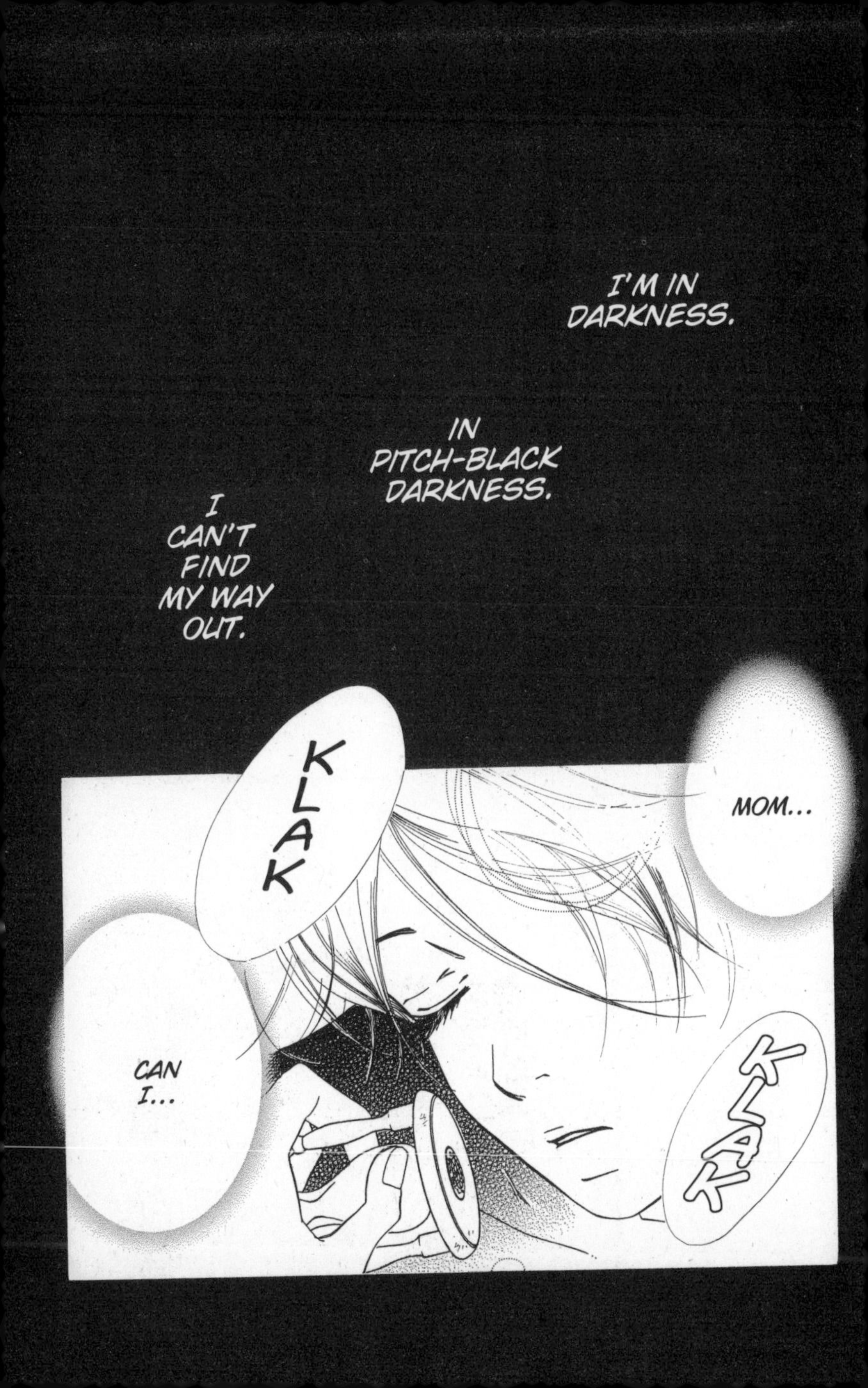
I'M IN DARKNESS.
IN PITCH-BLACK DARKNESS.
I CAN'T FIND MY WAY OUT.
MOM...
KLAK
KLAK
CAN I...

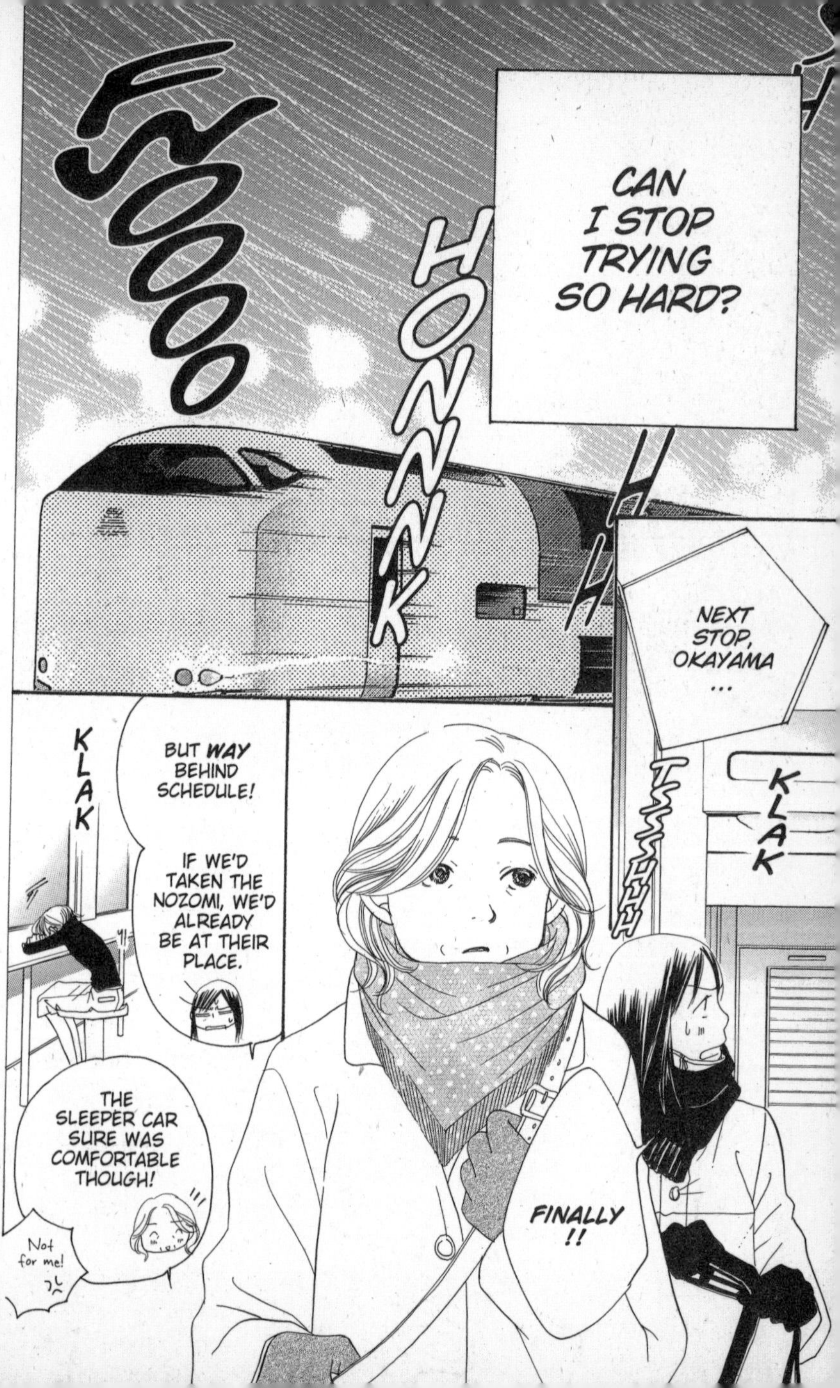
CAN I STOP TRYING SO HARD?
HONNNK
NEXT STOP, OKAYAMA ...
KLAK
FINALLY !!
KLAK
BUT WAY BEHIND SCHEDULE!
IF WE'D TAKEN THE NOZOMI, WE'D ALREADY BE AT THEIR PLACE.
THE SLEEPER CAR SURE WAS COMFORTABLE THOUGH!
Not for me!

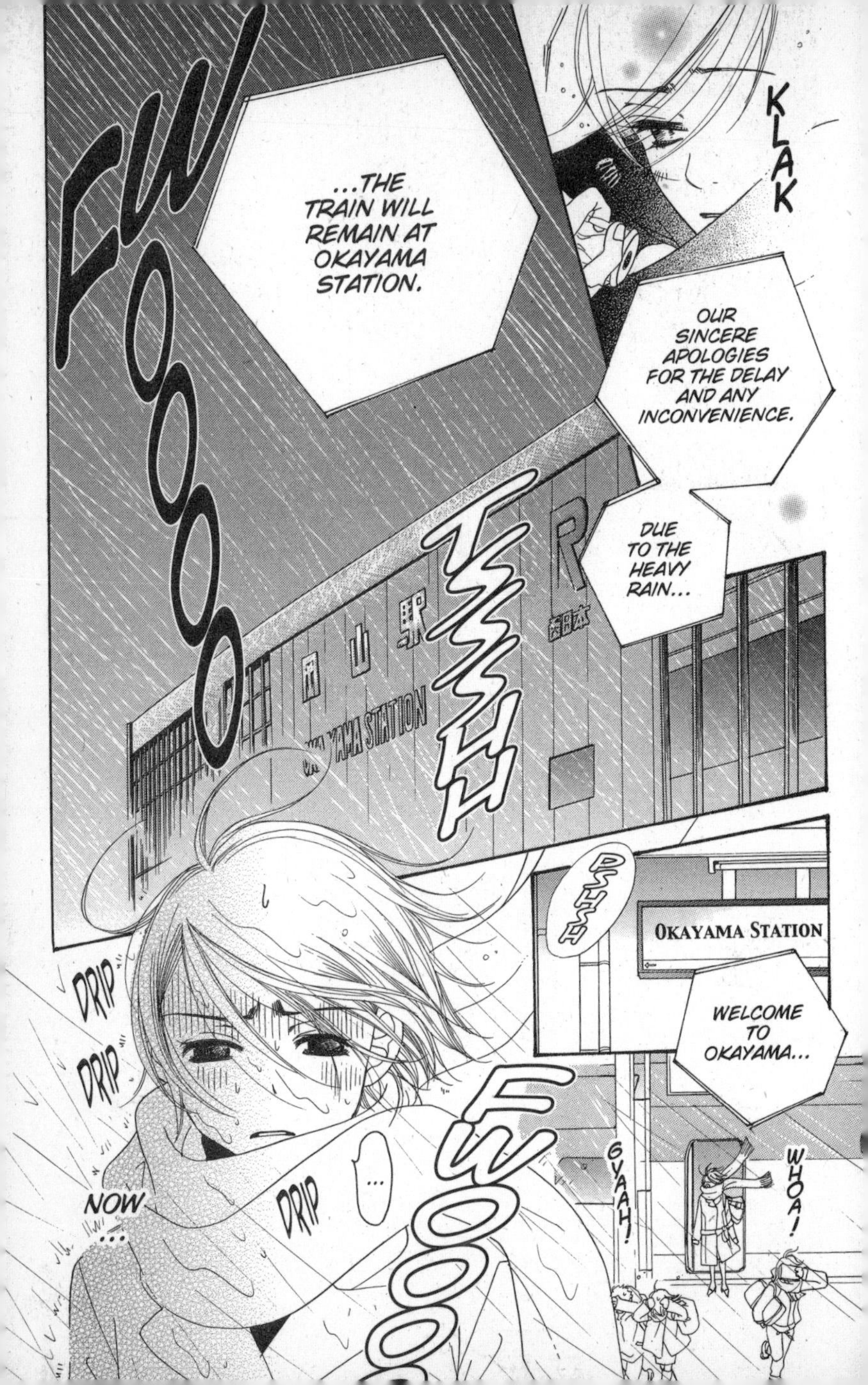
KLAK
DUE TO THE HEAVY RAIN...
...THE TRAIN WILL REMAIN AT OKAYAMA STATION.
OUR SINCERE APOLOGIES FOR THE DELAY AND ANY INCONVENIENCE.
FWOOOOO
TSSHHH
OKAYAMA STATION
WELCOME TO OKAYAMA...
PSHHH
OKAYAMA STATION
WHOA!
GYAAH!
FWOOOO
...
DRIP
DRIP
DRIP
NOW...

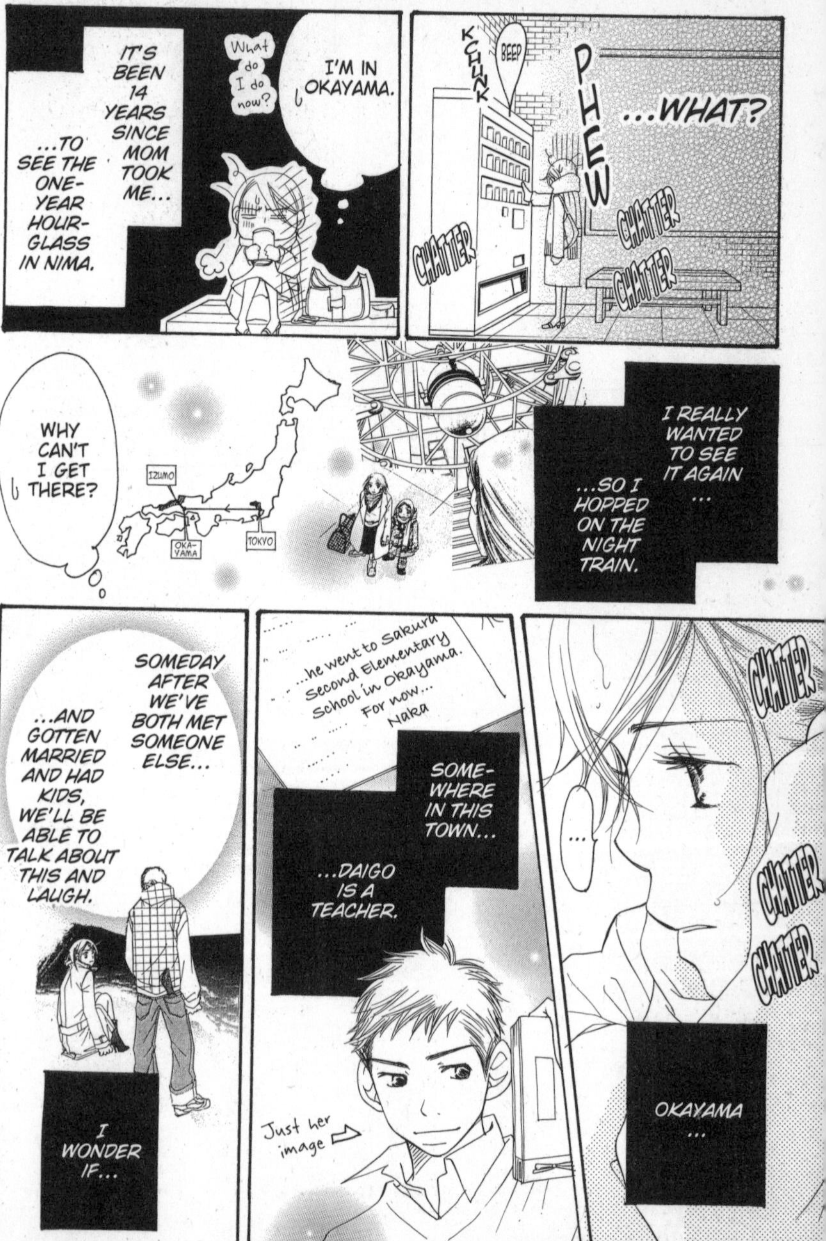
KCHUNK
BEEP
PHEW
...WHAT?
CHATTER
CHATTER
CHATTER
I'M IN OKAYAMA.
What do I do now?
IT'S BEEN 14 YEARS SINCE MOM TOOK ME...
...TO SEE THE ONE-YEAR HOURGLASS IN NIMA.
I REALLY WANTED TO SEE IT AGAIN...
...SO I HOPPED ON THE NIGHT TRAIN.
WHY CAN'T I GET THERE?
IZUMO
OKA-YAMA
TOKYO
CHATTER
...
CHATTER
CHATTER
OKAYAMA...
...he went to Sakura Second Elementary School in Okayama. For now... Naka
SOMEWHERE IN THIS TOWN...
...DAIGO IS A TEACHER.
Just her image
SOMEDAY AFTER WE'VE BOTH MET SOMEONE ELSE...
...AND GOTTEN MARRIED AND HAD KIDS, WE'LL BE ABLE TO TALK ABOUT THIS AND LAUGH.
I WONDER IF...

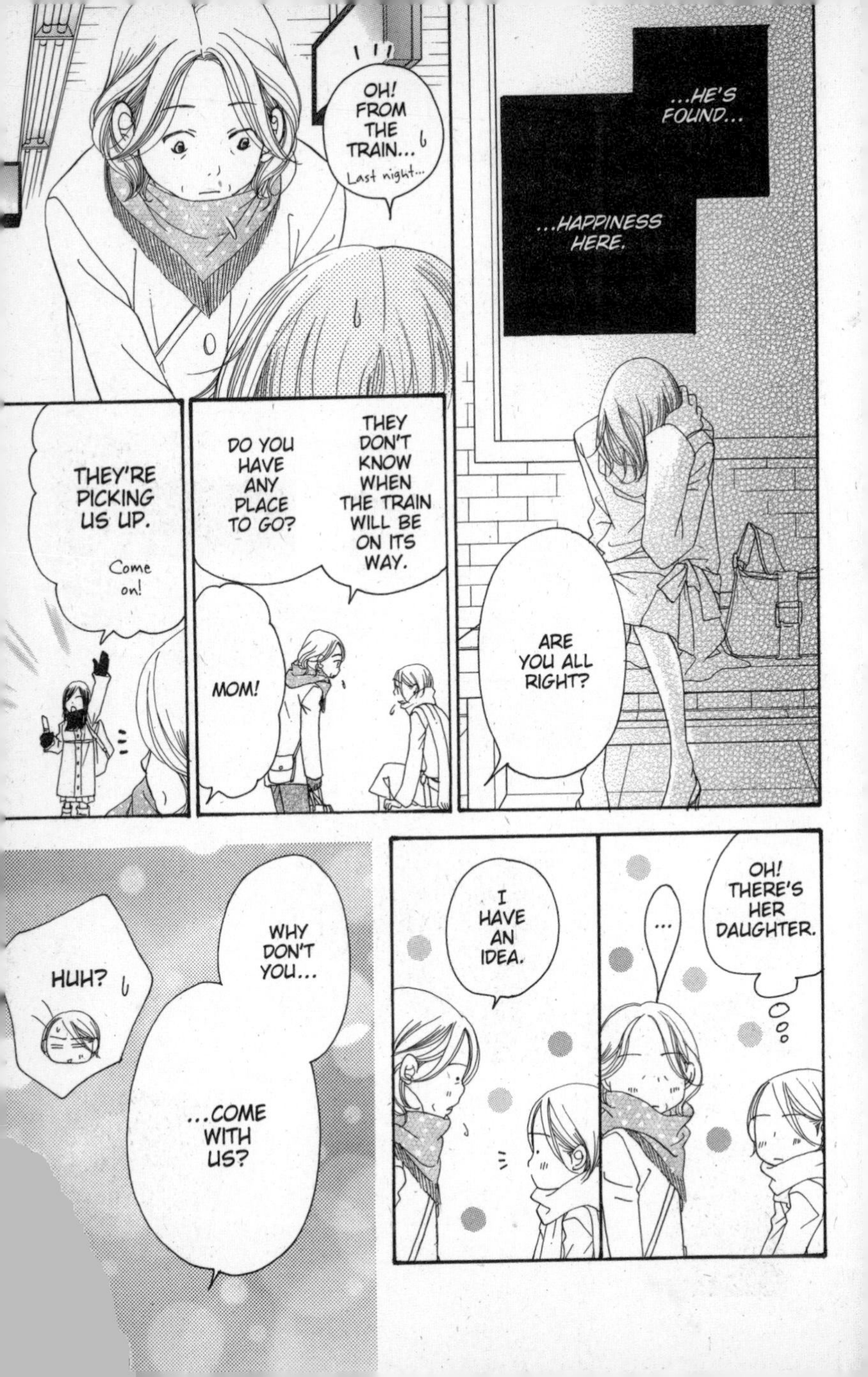
...HE'S FOUND...
...HAPPINESS HERE.
ARE YOU ALL RIGHT?
OH! FROM THE TRAIN...
Last night...
THEY DON'T KNOW WHEN THE TRAIN WILL BE ON ITS WAY.
DO YOU HAVE ANY PLACE TO GO?
MOM!
THEY'RE PICKING US UP.
Come on!
OH! THERE'S HER DAUGHTER.
...
I HAVE AN IDEA.
WHY DON'T YOU...
...COME WITH US?
HUH?

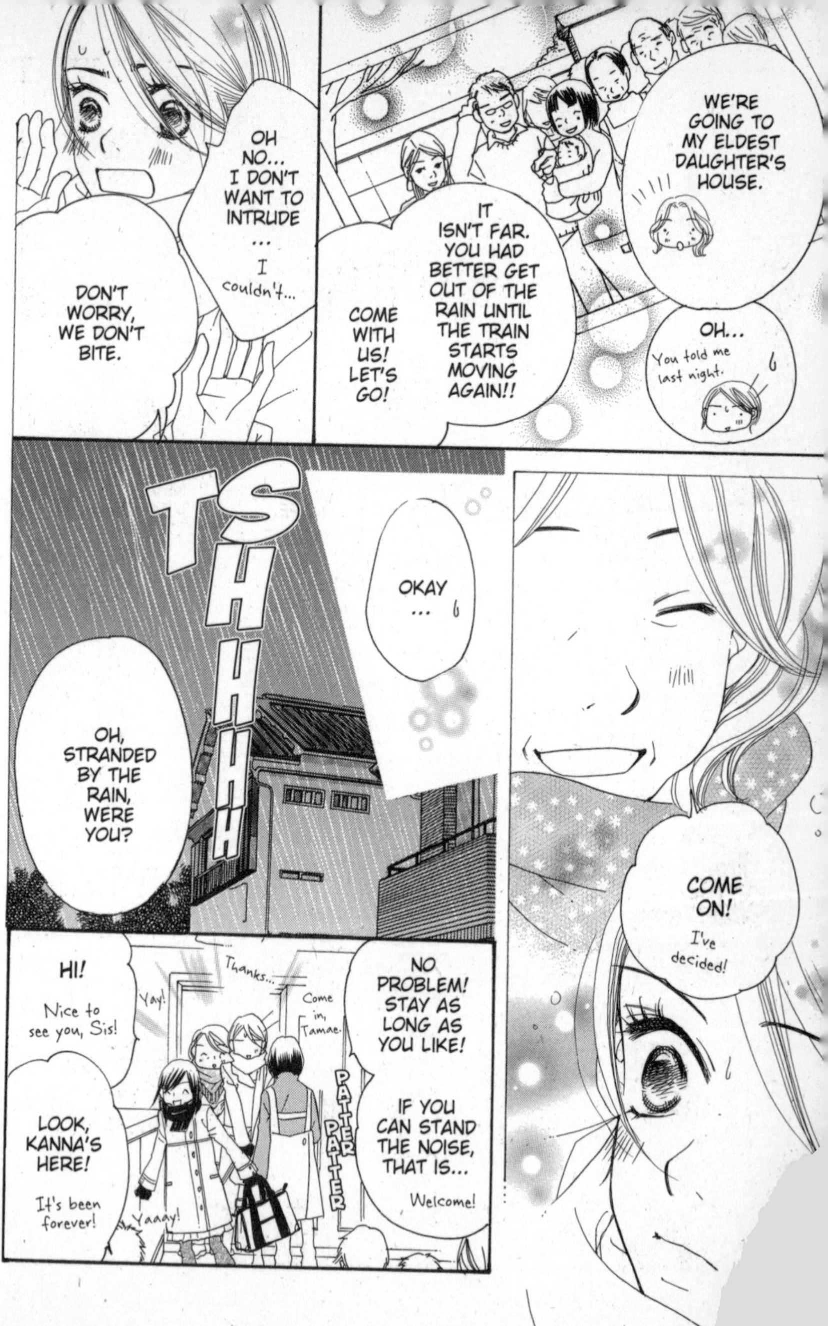
WE'RE GOING TO MY ELDEST DAUGHTER'S HOUSE.
OH... You told me last night.
IT ISN'T FAR. YOU HAD BETTER GET OUT OF THE RAIN UNTIL THE TRAIN STARTS MOVING AGAIN!!
COME WITH US! LET'S GO!
OH NO... I DON'T WANT TO INTRUDE... I couldn't...
DON'T WORRY, WE DON'T BITE.
COME ON! I've decided!
OKAY...
TSHHHHHH
OH, STRANDED BY THE RAIN, WERE YOU?
NO PROBLEM! STAY AS LONG AS YOU LIKE!
IF YOU CAN STAND THE NOISE, THAT IS...
Welcome!
PATTER PATTER
Come in, Tamae.
Thanks...
Yay!
HI! Nice to see you, Sis!
LOOK, KANNA'S HERE! It's been forever!
Yaaay!

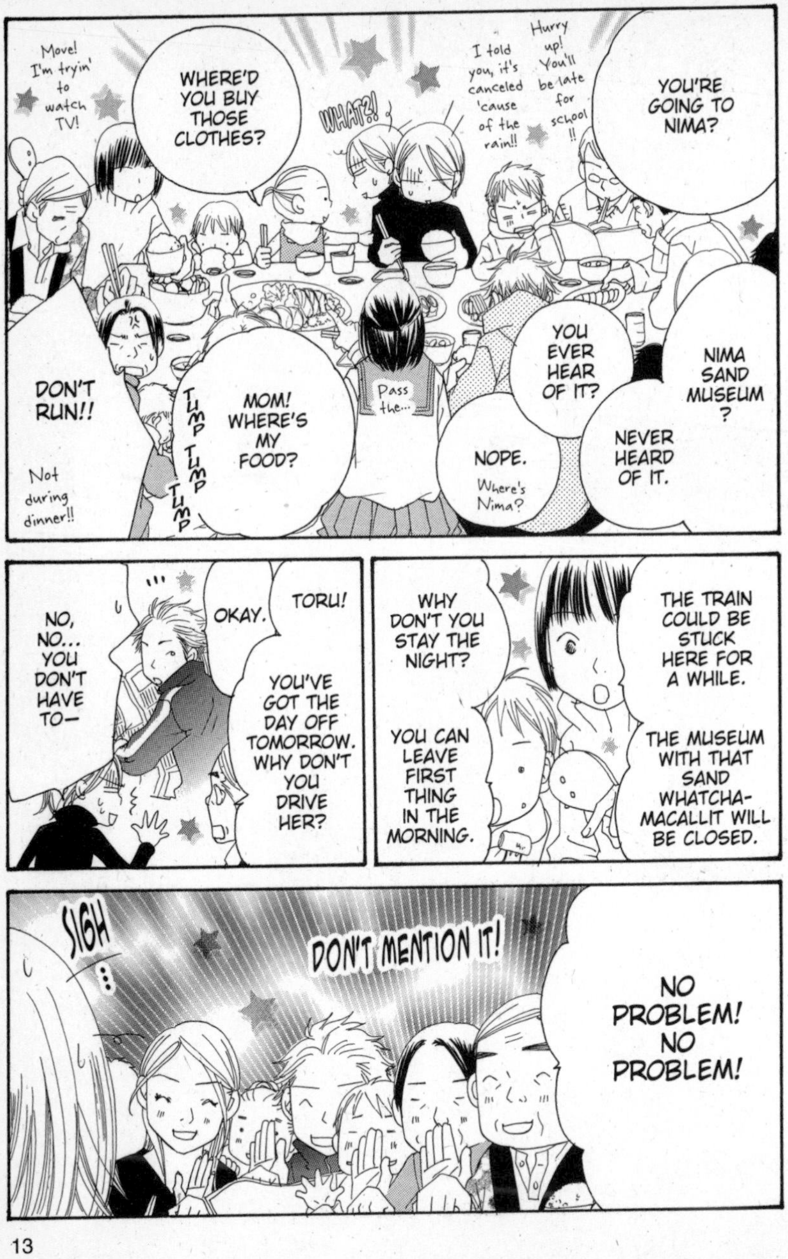
YOU'RE GOING TO NIMA?
Hurry up! You'll be late for school !!
I told you, it's canceled 'cause of the rain!!
WHAT?!
WHERE'D YOU BUY THOSE CLOTHES?
Move! I'm tryin' to watch TV!
NIMA SAND MUSEUM ?
YOU EVER HEAR OF IT?
NEVER HEARD OF IT.
NOPE.
Where's Nima?
Pass the...
MOM! WHERE'S MY FOOD?
TUMP TUMP TUMP
DON'T RUN!!
Not during dinner!!
THE TRAIN COULD BE STUCK HERE FOR A WHILE.
THE MUSEUM WITH THAT SAND WHATCHA-MACALLIT WILL BE CLOSED.
WHY DON'T YOU STAY THE NIGHT?
YOU CAN LEAVE FIRST THING IN THE MORNING.
TORU!
YOU'VE GOT THE DAY OFF TOMORROW. WHY DON'T YOU DRIVE HER?
OKAY.
NO, NO... YOU DON'T HAVE TO—
NO PROBLEM! NO PROBLEM!
DON'T MENTION IT!
SIGH...

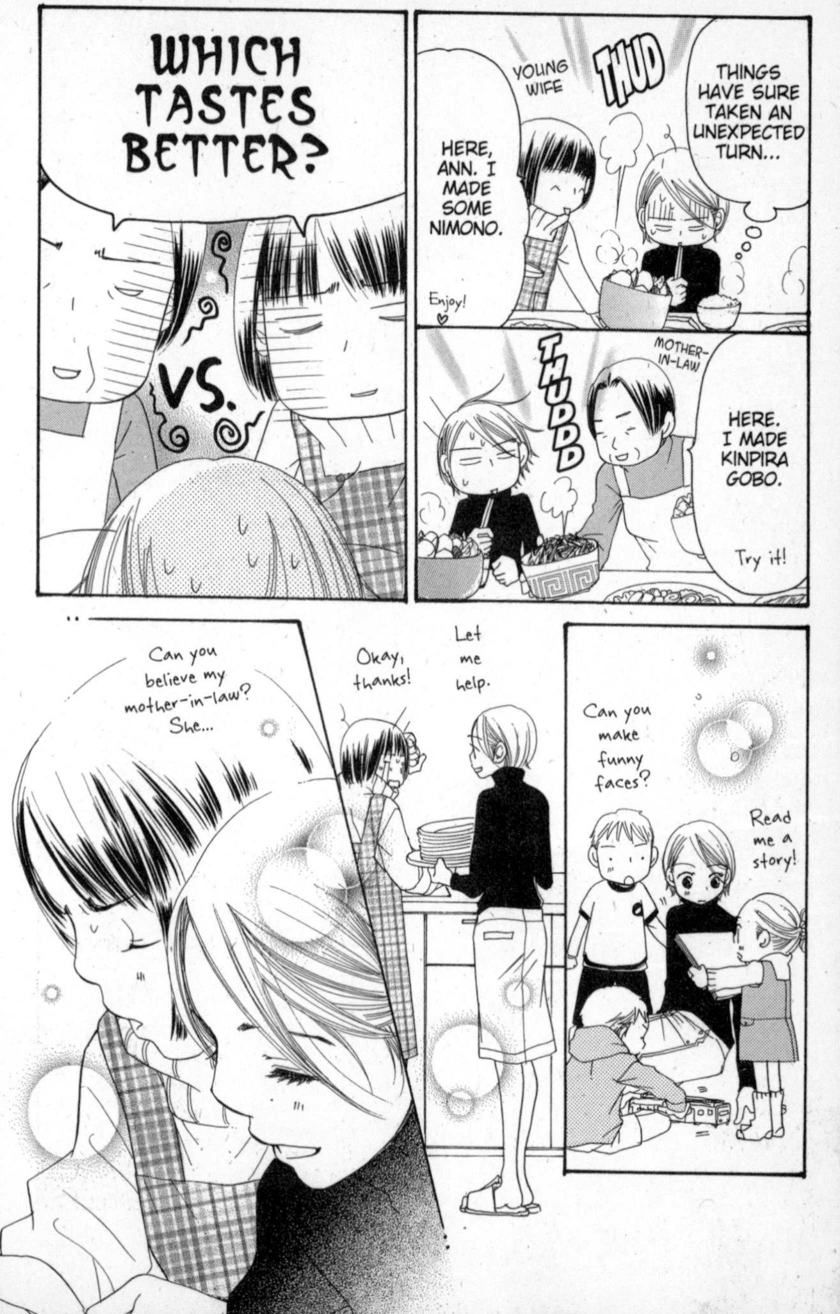
THINGS HAVE SURE TAKEN AN UNEXPECTED TURN...
THUD
YOUNG WIFE
HERE, ANN. I MADE SOME NIMONO.
Enjoy!
HERE. I MADE KINPIRA GOBO.
MOTHER-IN-LAW
Try it!
THUDDD
WHICH TASTES BETTER?
VS.
Can you make funny faces?
Read me a story!
Let me help.
Okay, thanks!
Can you believe my mother-in-law? She...

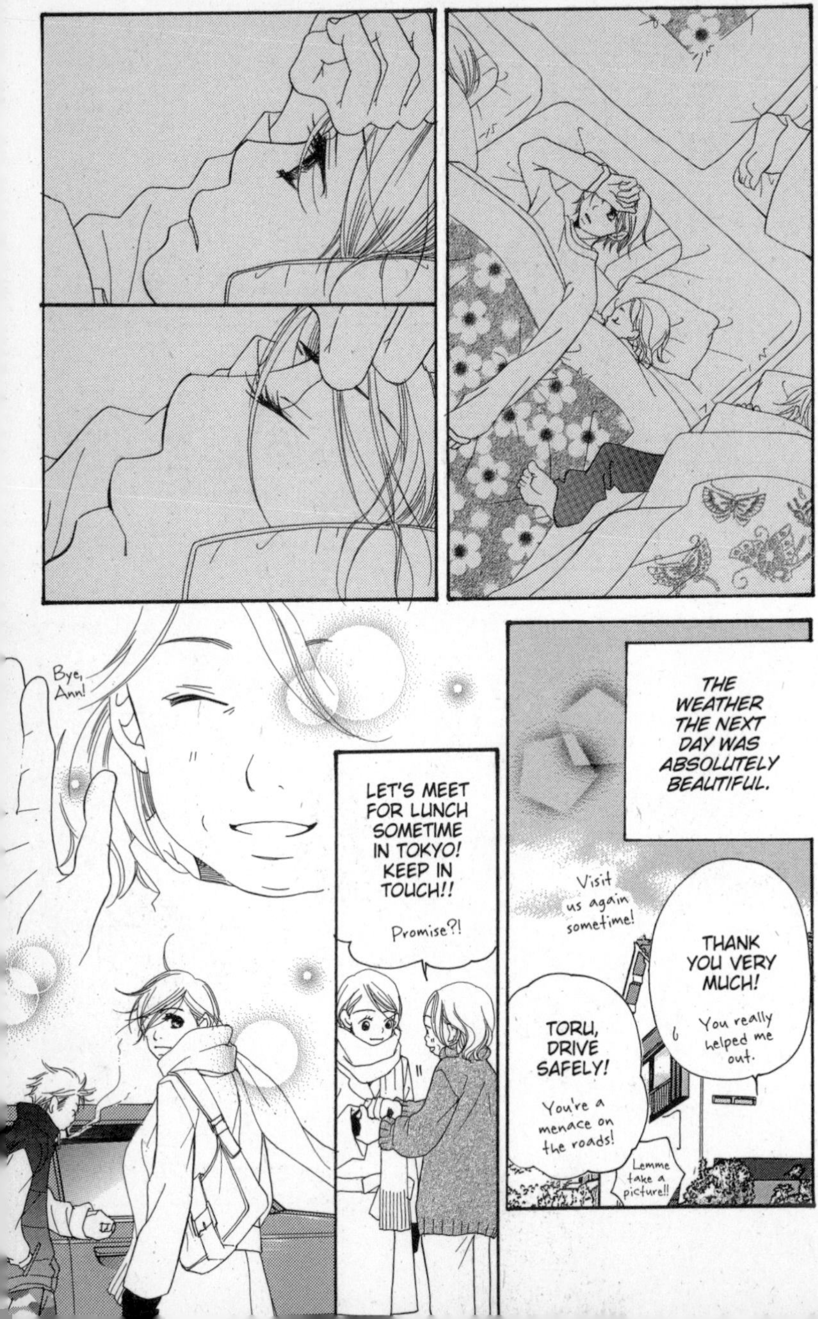
THE WEATHER THE NEXT DAY WAS ABSOLUTELY BEAUTIFUL.
Visit us again sometime!
THANK YOU VERY MUCH!
You really helped me out.
TORU, DRIVE SAFELY!
You're a menace on the roads!
Lemme take a picture!!
LET'S MEET FOR LUNCH SOMETIME IN TOKYO! KEEP IN TOUCH!!
Promise?!
Bye, Ann!

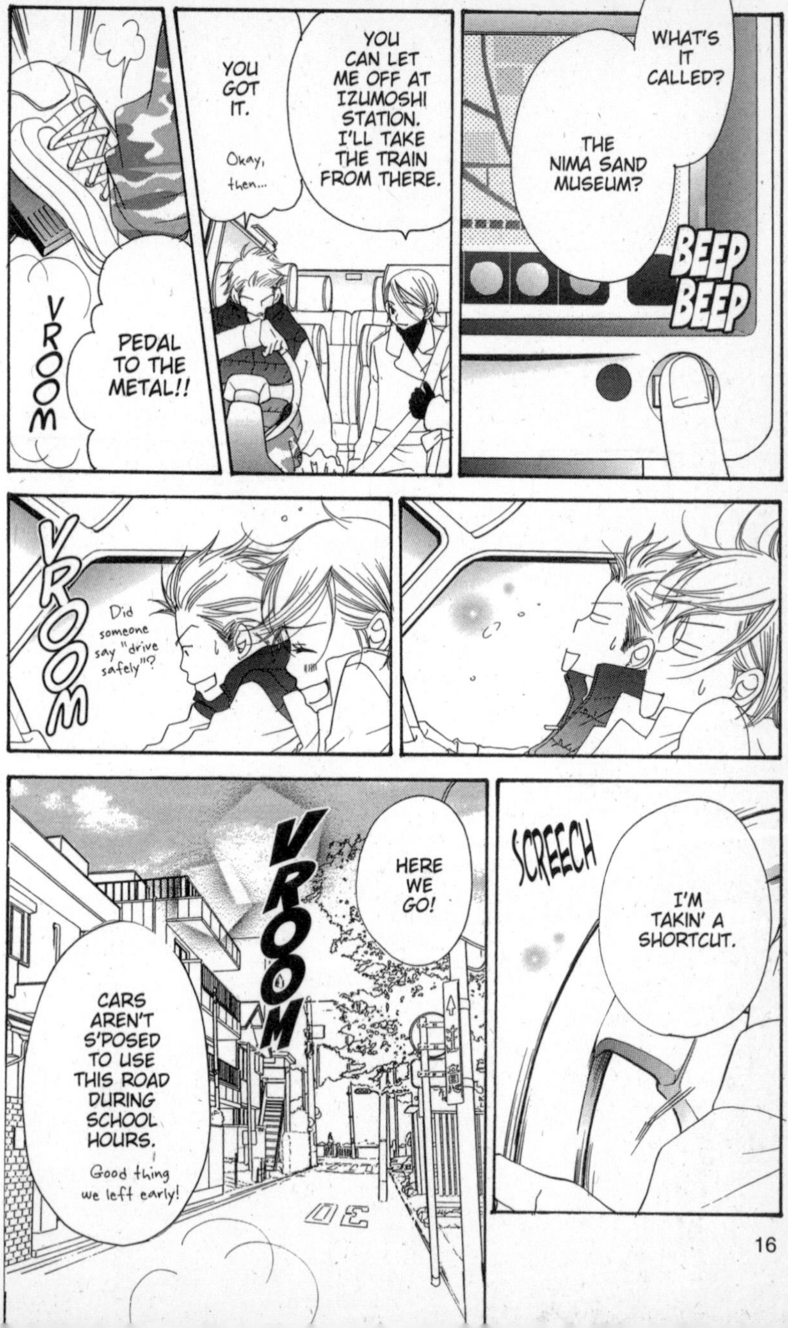
WHAT'S IT CALLED?
THE NIMA SAND MUSEUM?
BEEP BEEP
YOU CAN LET ME OFF AT IZUMOSHI STATION. I'LL TAKE THE TRAIN FROM THERE.
YOU GOT IT.
Okay, then...
PEDAL TO THE METAL!!
VROOM
VROOM
Did someone say "drive safely"?
SCREECH
I'M TAKIN' A SHORTCUT.
HERE WE GO!
VROOM
CARS AREN'T S'POSED TO USE THIS ROAD DURING SCHOOL HOURS.
Good thing we left early!

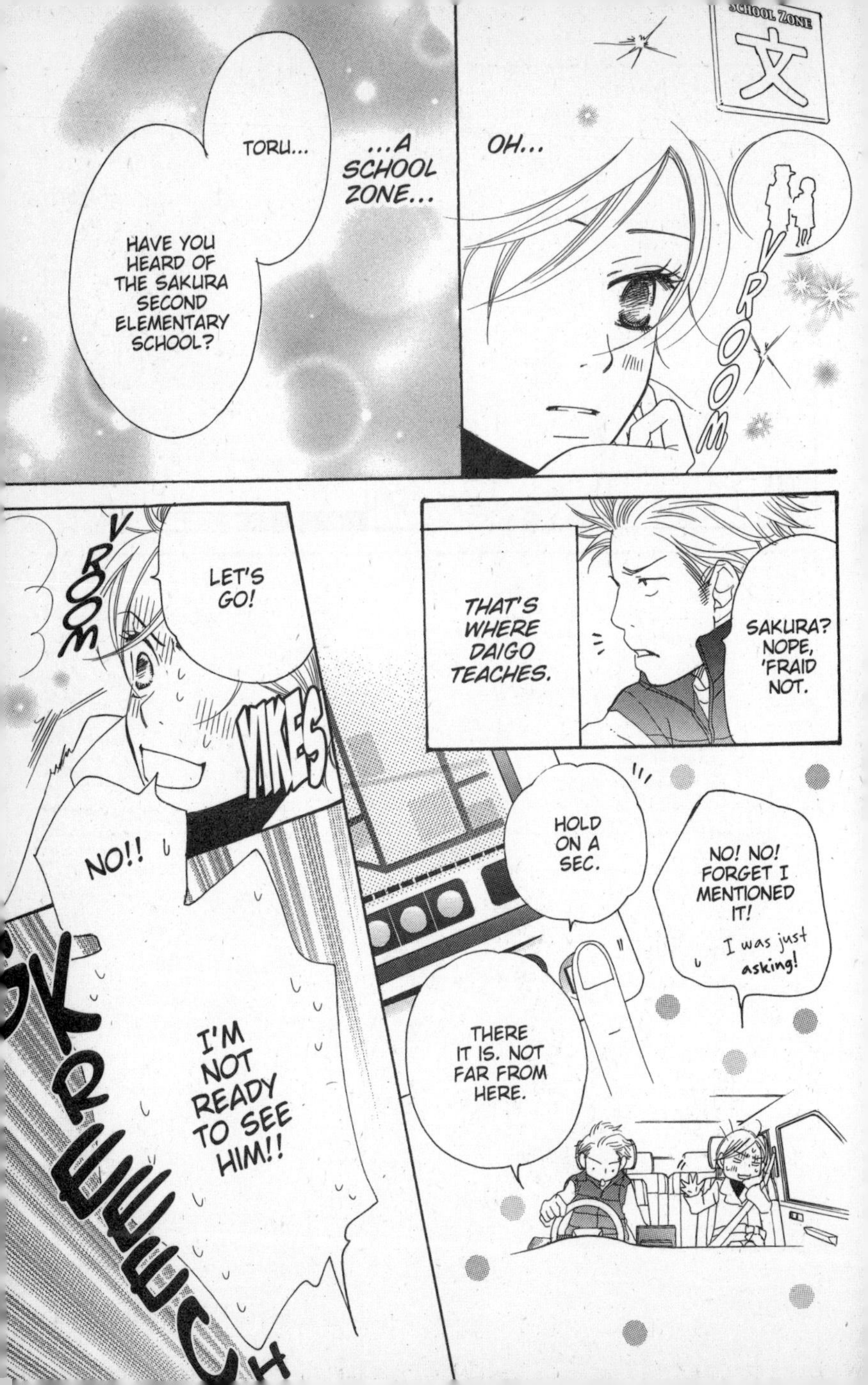
SCHOOL ZONE
文
OH...
VROOM
...A SCHOOL ZONE...
TORU...
HAVE YOU HEARD OF THE SAKURA SECOND ELEMENTARY SCHOOL?
SAKURA? NOPE, 'FRAID NOT.
THAT'S WHERE DAIGO TEACHES.
NO! NO! FORGET I MENTIONED IT!
I was just asking!
HOLD ON A SEC.
THERE IT IS. NOT FAR FROM HERE.
VROOM
LET'S GO!
YIKES
NO!!
I'M NOT READY TO SEE HIM!!
SKREEECH

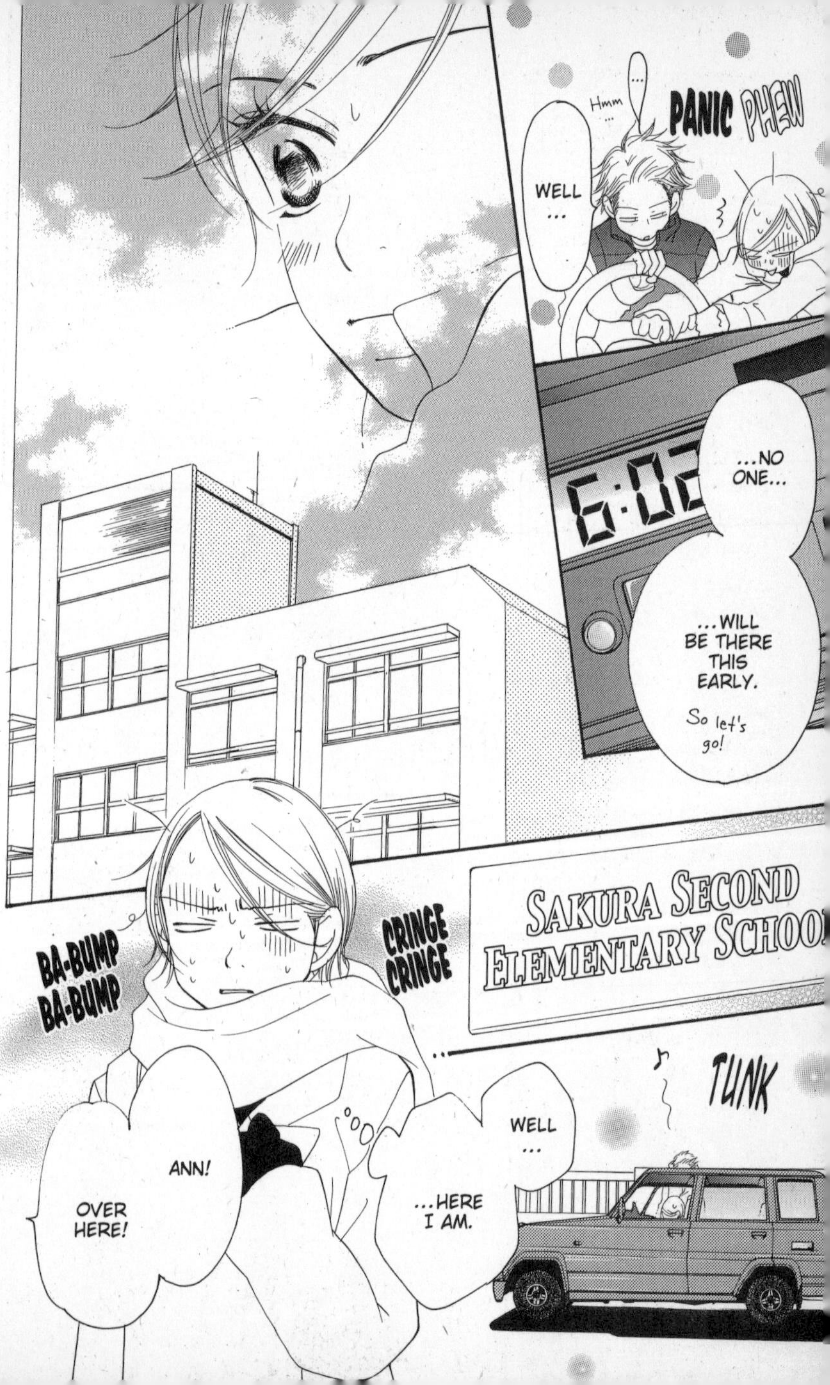
Hmm ...
...
WELL ...
PANIC PHEW
6:0
...NO ONE...
...WILL BE THERE THIS EARLY.
So let's go!
SAKURA SECOND ELEMENTARY SCHOO
CRINGE CRINGE
BA-BUMP BA-BUMP
TUNK
WELL ...
...HERE I AM.
ANN!
OVER HERE!

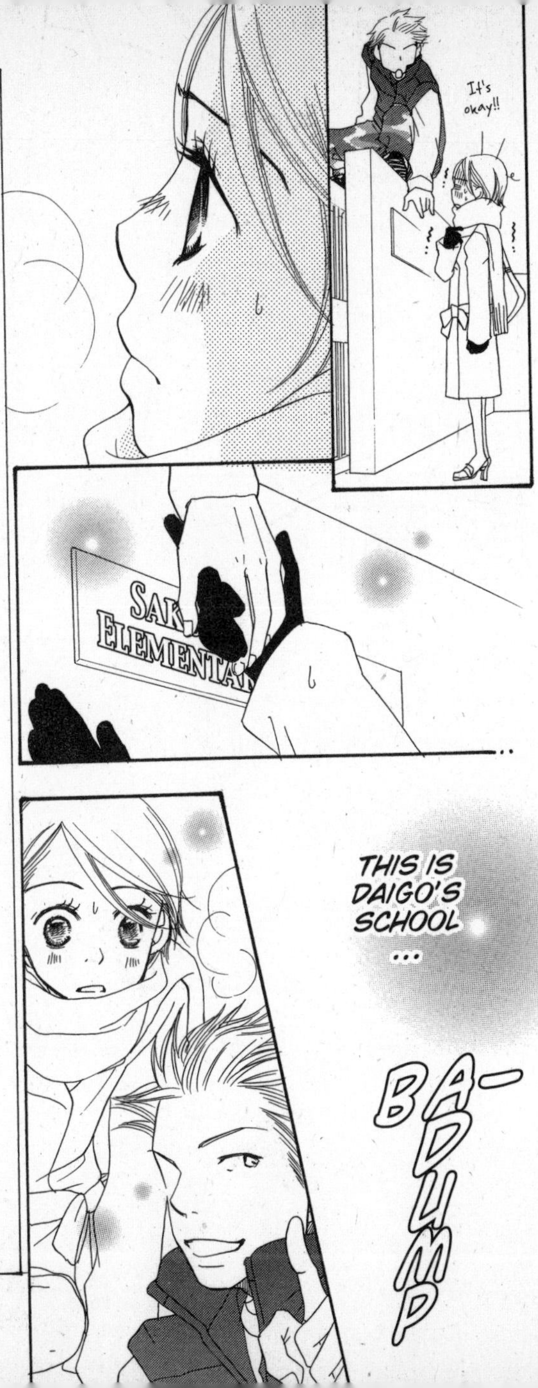
It's okay!!
SAK
ELEMENTA
THIS IS DAIGO'S SCHOOL ...
BA-DUMP

~Winter, Age 26: Prayer-

Welcome to volume 8! Thanks for reading! This chapter feels like the end to me. The next chapter is an epilogue. The main story comes to an end with this volume—but I've written some extra material for *Betsucomi*. It turned out to be pretty long. I know it's a little (a lot!) like cheating, but altogether the series will reach ten volumes. I hope you'll read them all!

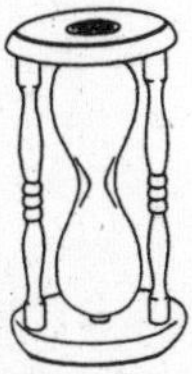

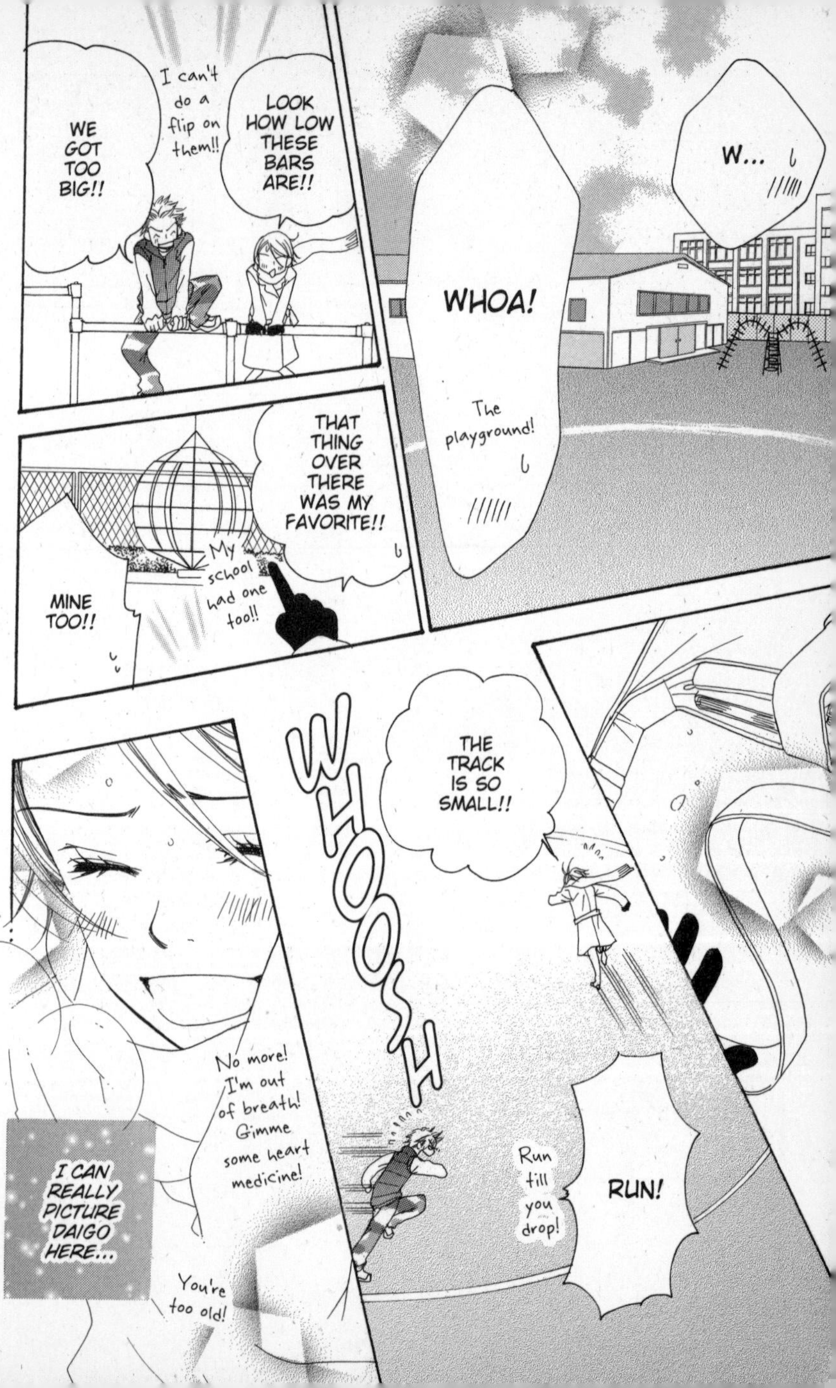
W...
WHOA!
The playground!
LOOK HOW LOW THESE BARS ARE!!
I can't do a flip on them!!
WE GOT TOO BIG!!
THAT THING OVER THERE WAS MY FAVORITE!!
My school had one too!!
MINE TOO!!
RUN!
Run till you drop!
THE TRACK IS SO SMALL!!
WHOOSH
No more! I'm out of breath! Gimme some heart medicine!
You're too old!
I CAN REALLY PICTURE DAIGO HERE...

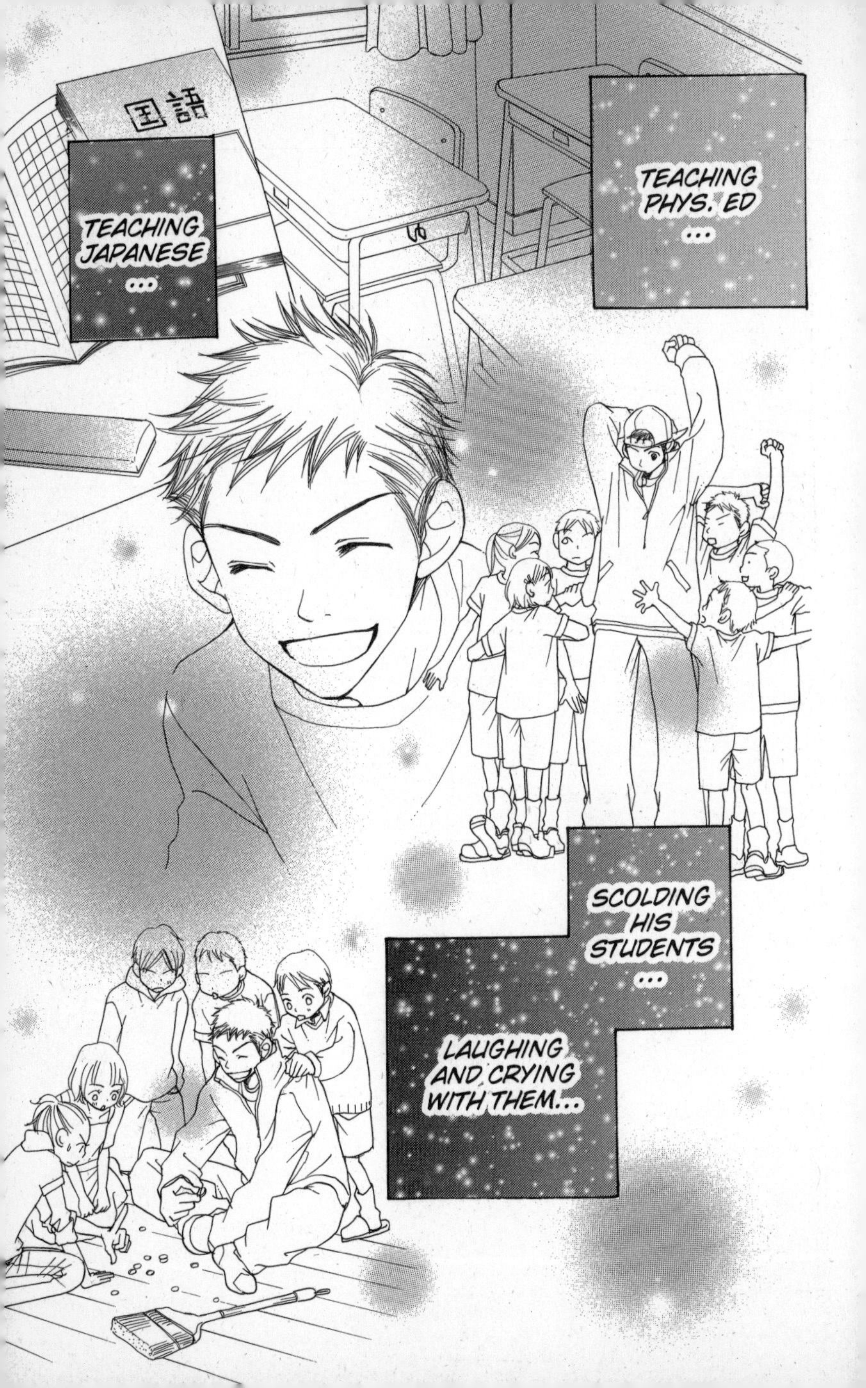
TEACHING PHYS. ED ...
国語
TEACHING JAPANESE ...
SCOLDING HIS STUDENTS ...
LAUGHING AND CRYING WITH THEM...

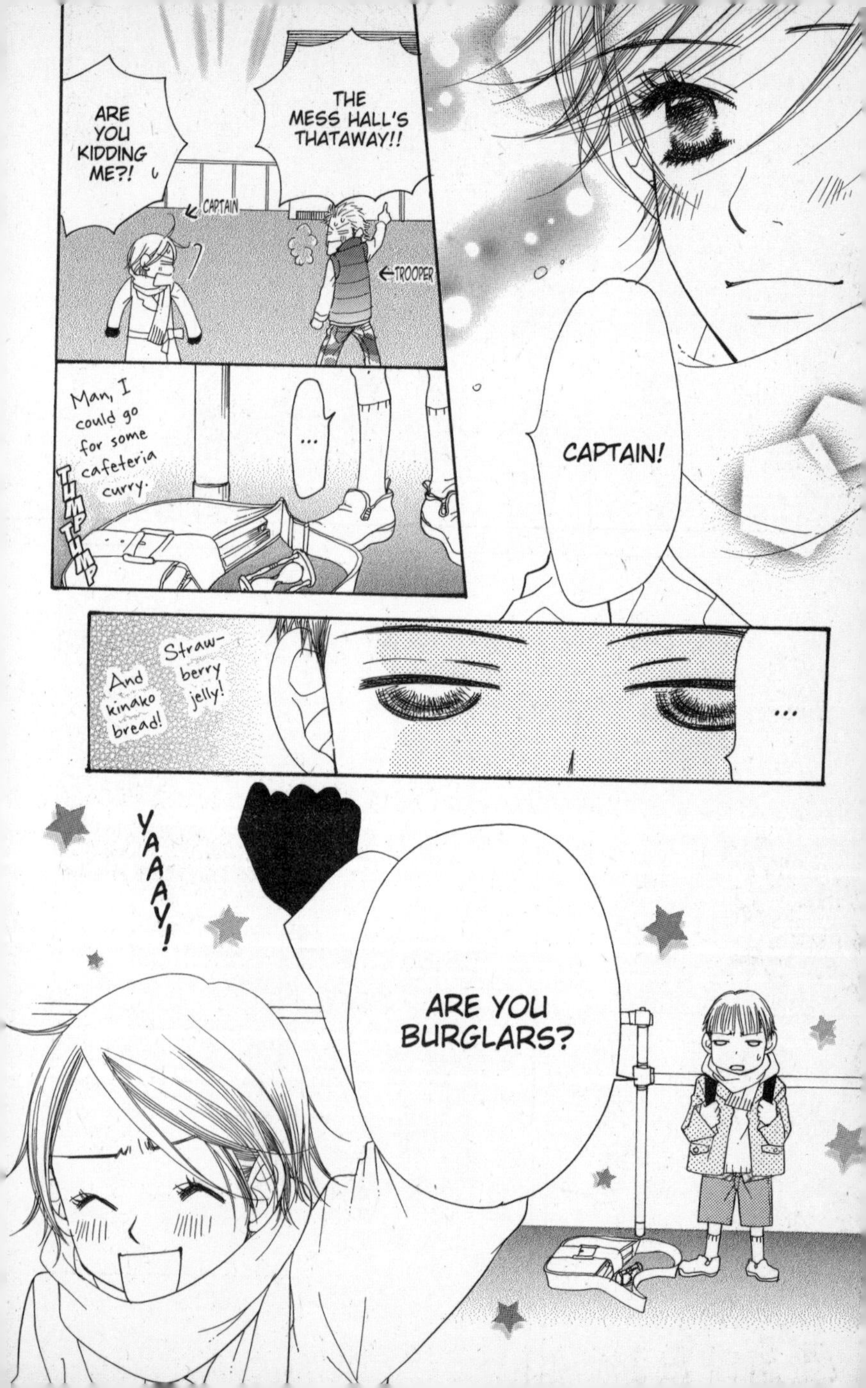
CAPTAIN!
THE MESS HALL'S THATAWAY!!
ARE YOU KIDDING ME?!
CAPTAIN
TROOPER
...
Man, I could go for some cafeteria curry.
TUMP TUMP TUMP
...
Straw-berry jelly!
And kinako bread!
ARE YOU BURGLARS?
YAAAAY!

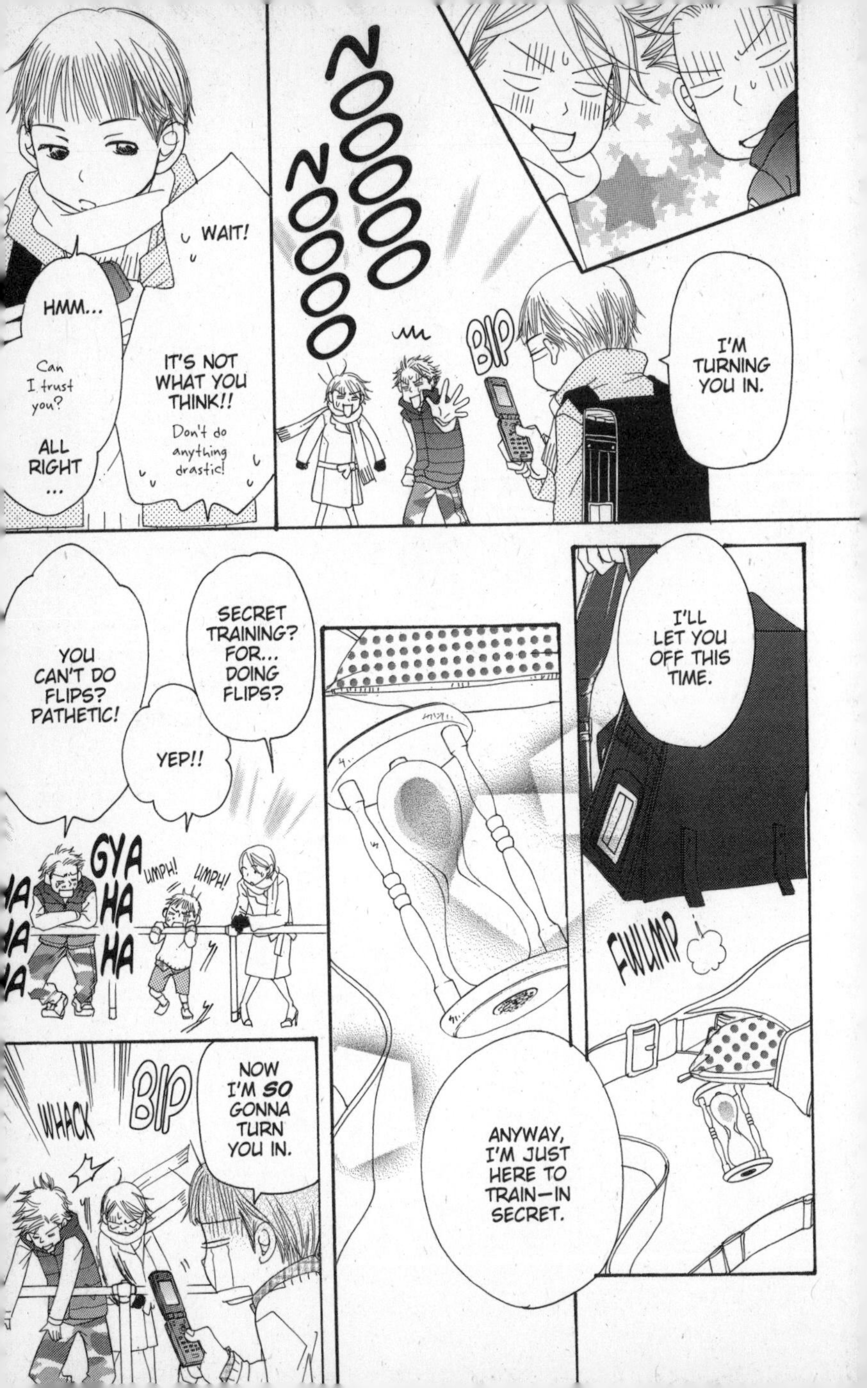
I'M TURNING YOU IN.
BIP
NOOOOO
NOOOO
WAIT!
IT'S NOT WHAT YOU THINK!!
Don't do anything drastic!
HMM...
Can I trust you?
ALL RIGHT ...
I'LL LET YOU OFF THIS TIME.
FWUMP
ANYWAY, I'M JUST HERE TO TRAIN—IN SECRET.
SECRET TRAINING? FOR... DOING FLIPS?
YEP!!
YOU CAN'T DO FLIPS? PATHETIC!
UMPH!
UMPH!
GYA HA HA
HA HA HA
NOW I'M SO GONNA TURN YOU IN.
BIP
WHACK

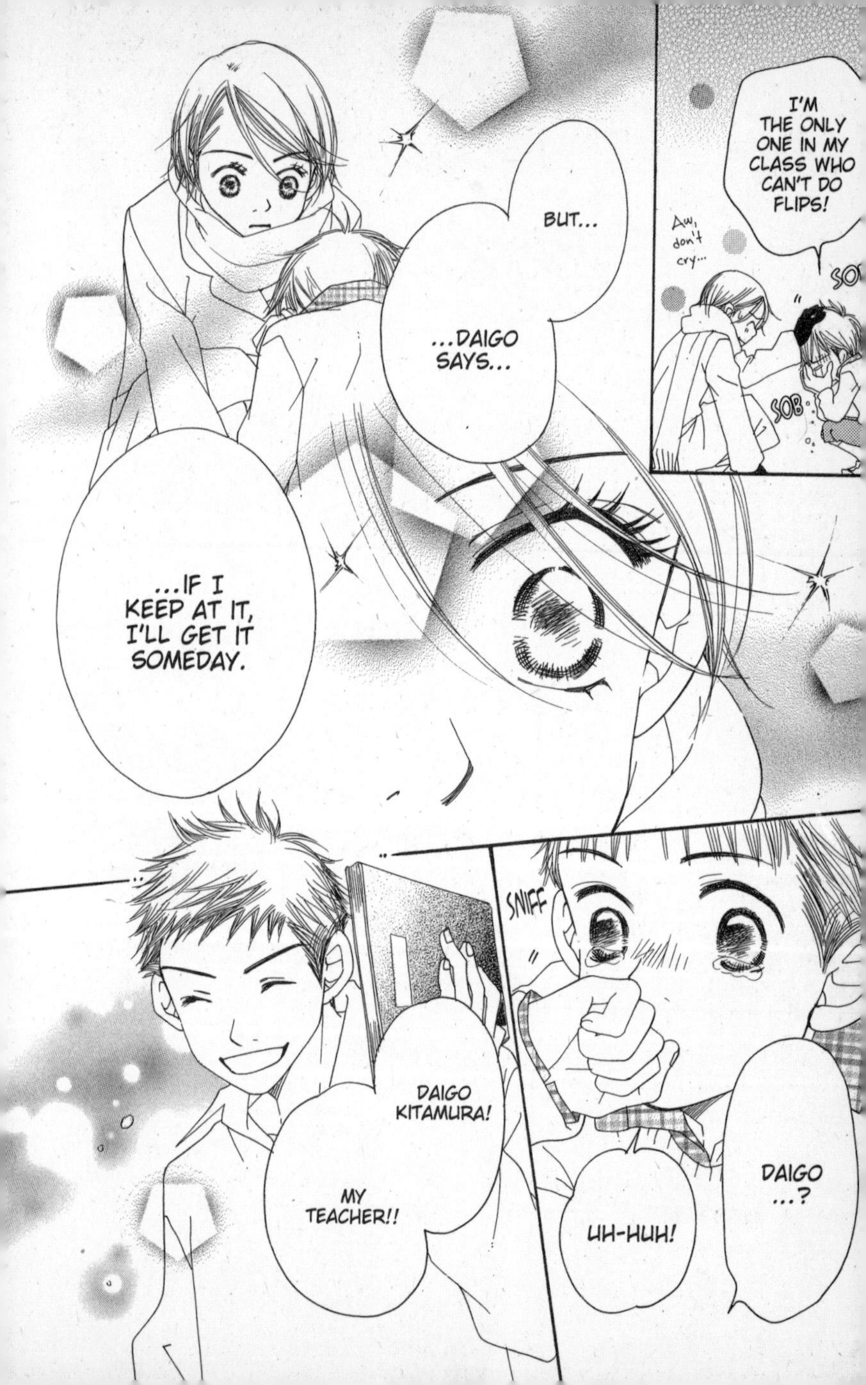
I'M THE ONLY ONE IN MY CLASS WHO CAN'T DO FLIPS!
Aw, don't cry...
SOB
BUT...
...DAIGO SAYS...
...IF I KEEP AT IT, I'LL GET IT SOMEDAY.
SNIFF
DAIGO ...?
UH-HUH!
DAIGO KITAMURA!
MY TEACHER!!

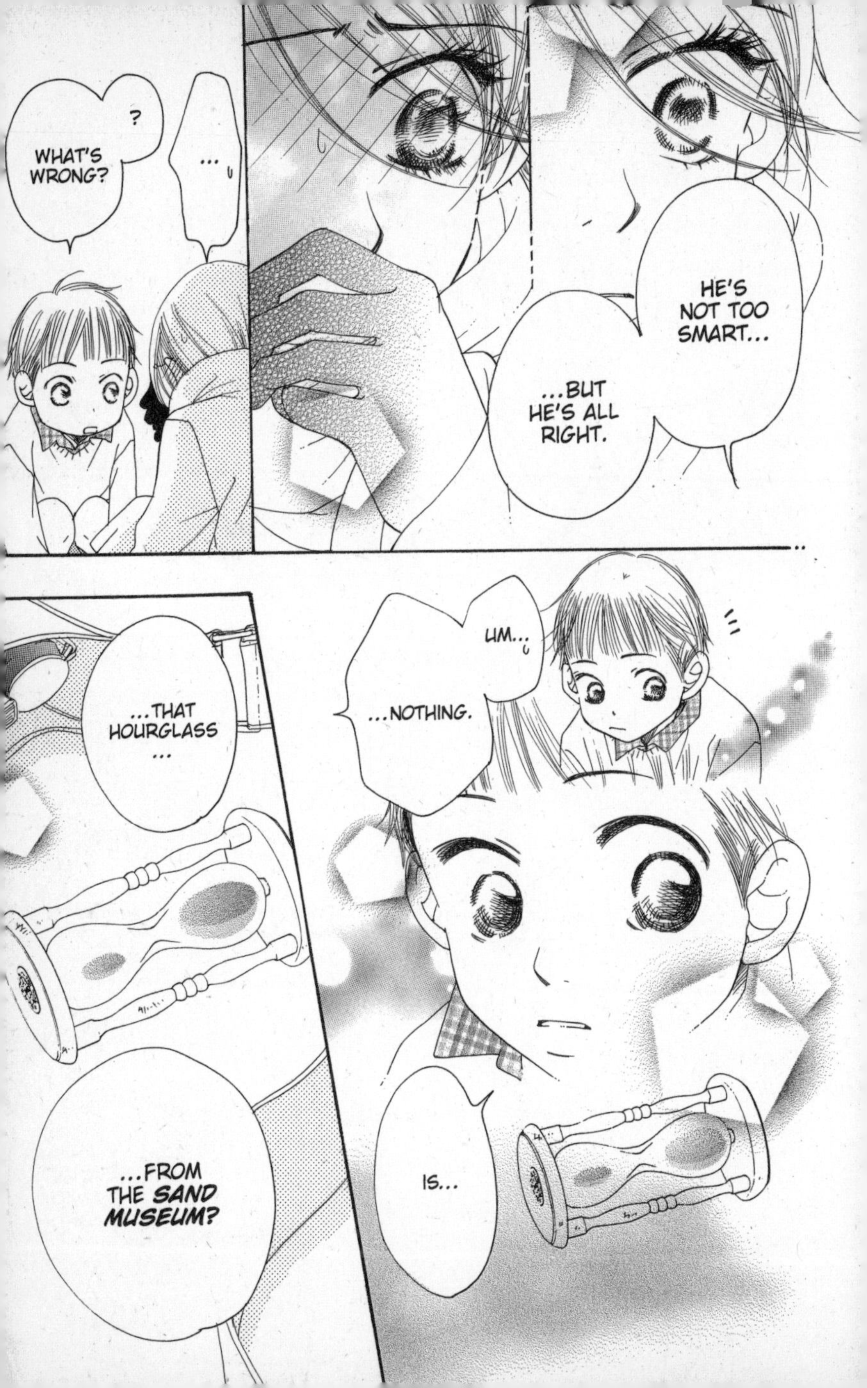
HE'S NOT TOO SMART...
...BUT HE'S ALL RIGHT.
...
? WHAT'S WRONG?
UM...
...NOTHING.
IS...
...THAT HOURGLASS ...
...FROM THE *SAND MUSEUM?*

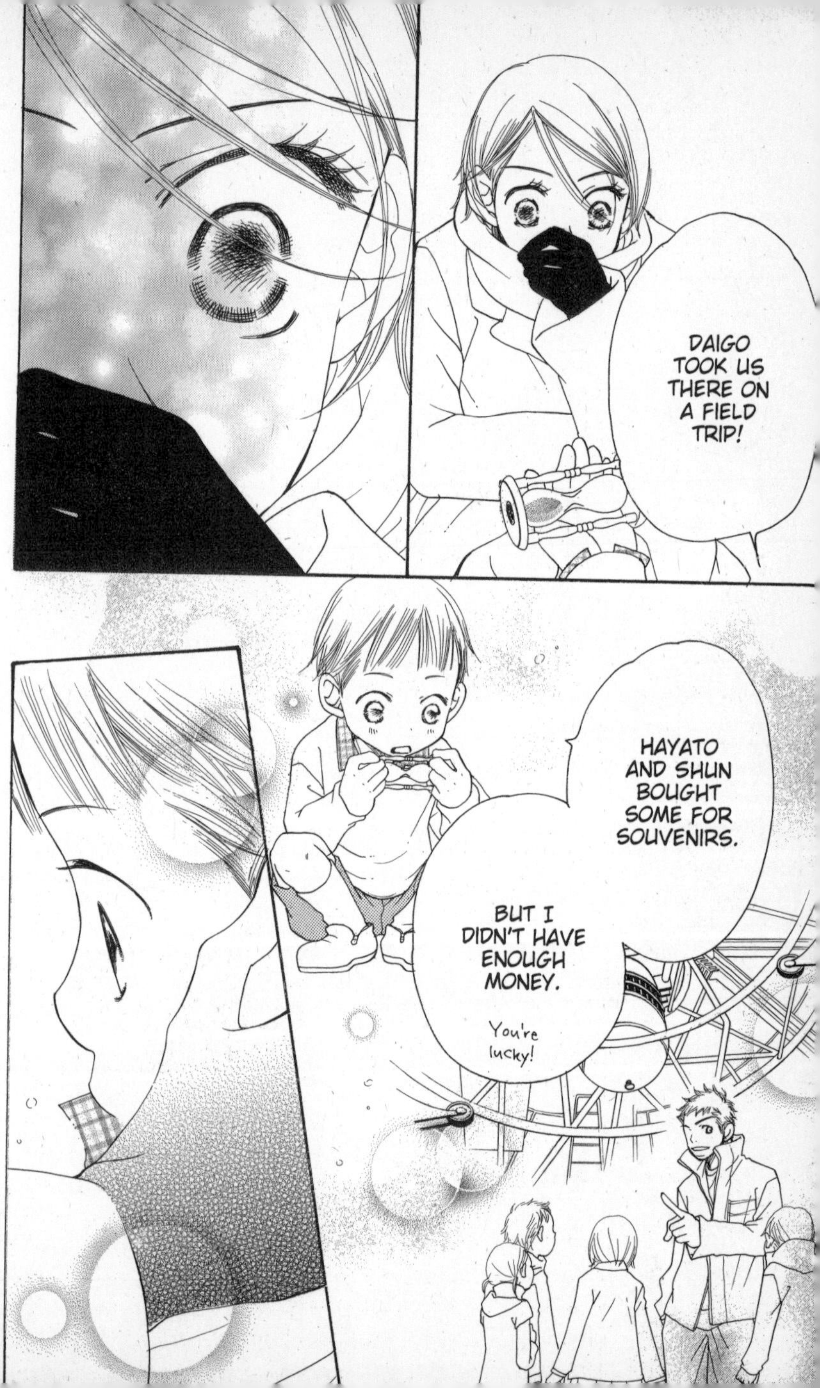
DAIGO TOOK US THERE ON A FIELD TRIP!
HAYATO AND SHUN BOUGHT SOME FOR SOUVENIRS.
BUT I DIDN'T HAVE ENOUGH MONEY.
You're lucky!

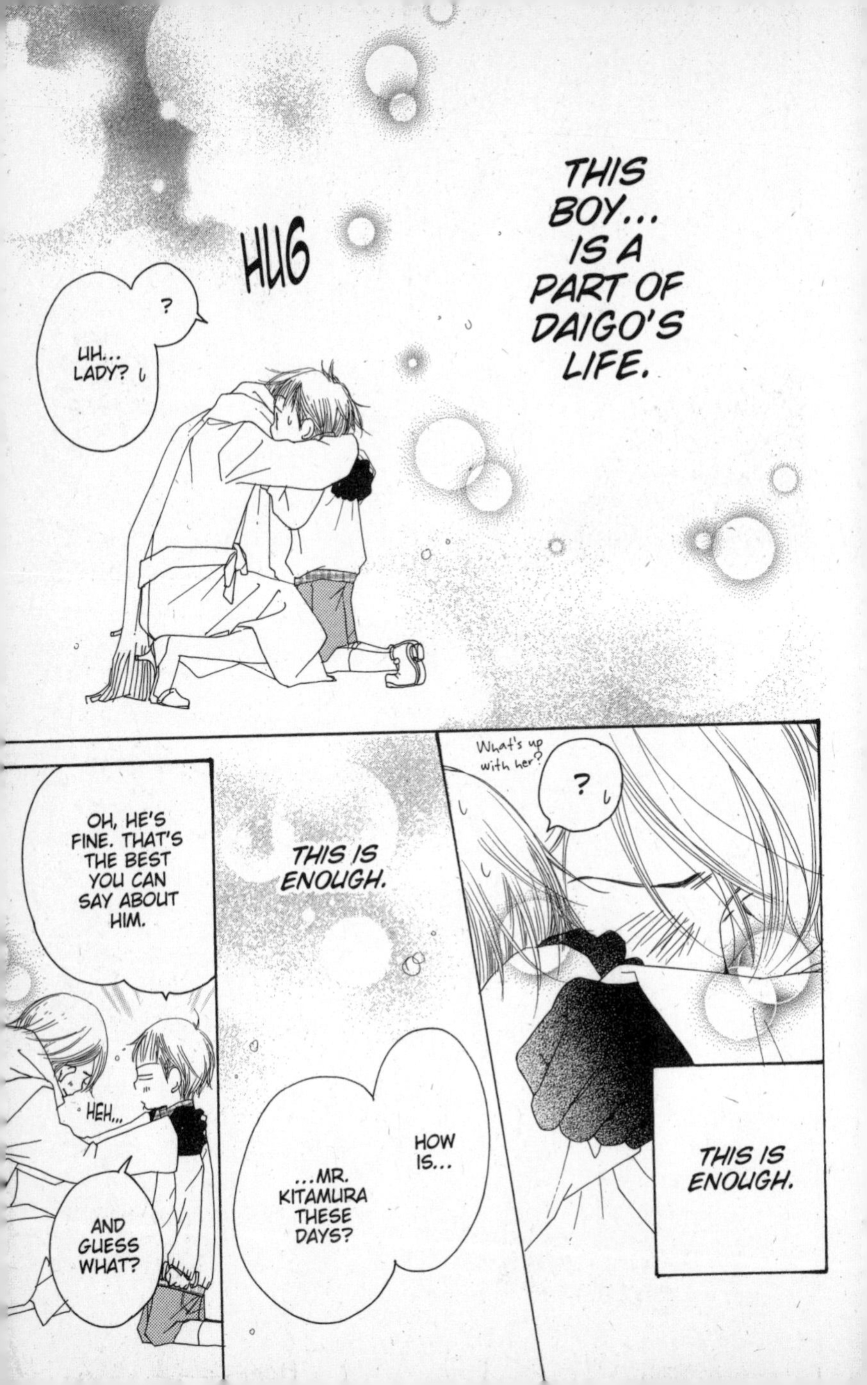
THIS BOY... IS A PART OF DAIGO'S LIFE.
HUG
?
UH... LADY?
What's up with her?
?
THIS IS ENOUGH.
THIS IS ENOUGH.
HOW IS... ...MR. KITAMURA THESE DAYS?
OH, HE'S FINE. THAT'S THE BEST YOU CAN SAY ABOUT HIM.
HEH...
AND GUESS WHAT?

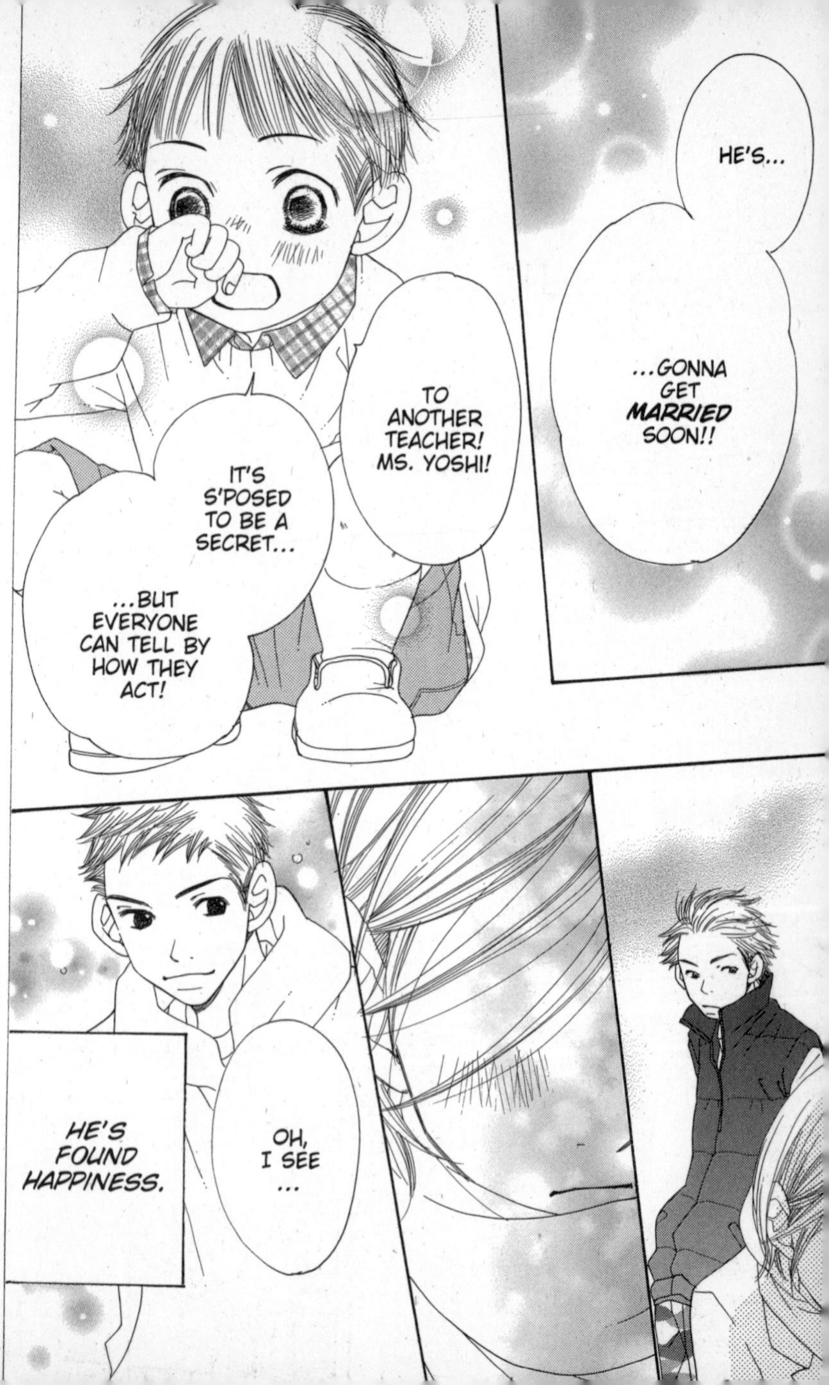
HE'S...
...GONNA GET **MARRIED** SOON!!
TO ANOTHER TEACHER! MS. YOSHI!
IT'S S'POSED TO BE A SECRET...
...BUT EVERYONE CAN TELL BY HOW THEY ACT!
OH, I SEE ...
HE'S FOUND HAPPINESS.

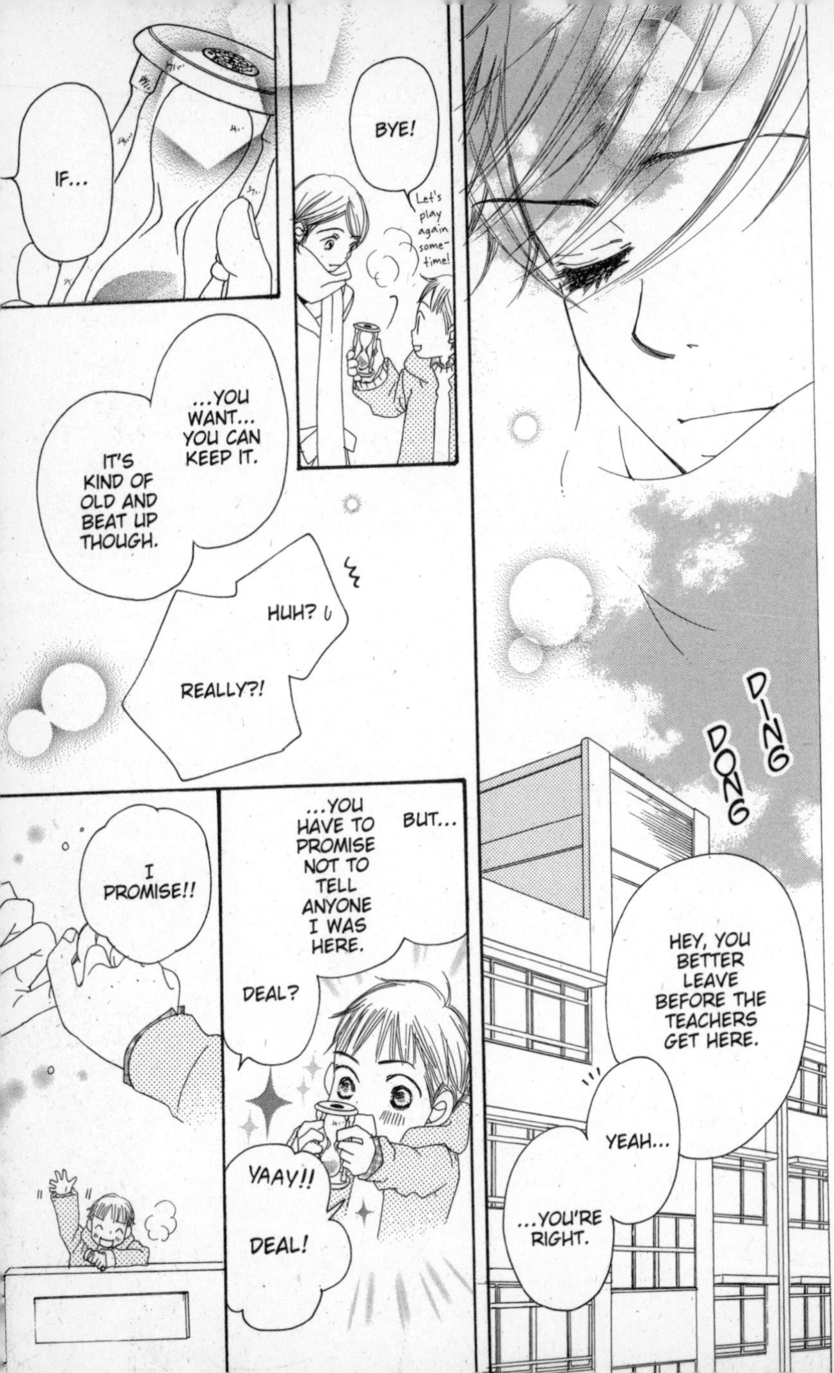
DING DONG
HEY, YOU BETTER LEAVE BEFORE THE TEACHERS GET HERE.
YEAH...
...YOU'RE RIGHT.
BYE!
Let's play again some-time!
IF...
...YOU WANT... YOU CAN KEEP IT.
IT'S KIND OF OLD AND BEAT UP THOUGH.
HUH?
REALLY?!
BUT...
...YOU HAVE TO PROMISE NOT TO TELL ANYONE I WAS HERE.
DEAL?
YAAY!!
DEAL!
I PROMISE!!

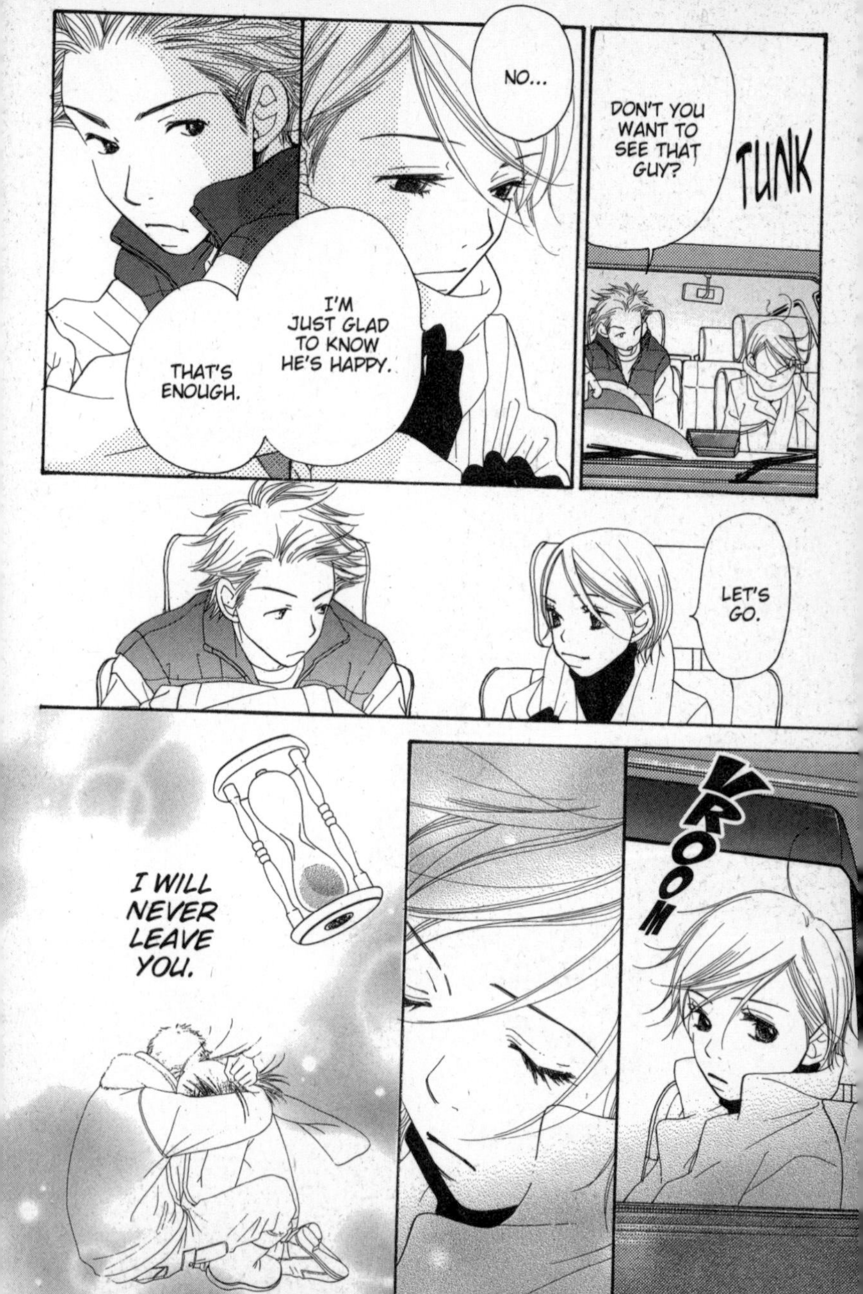
DON'T YOU WANT TO SEE THAT GUY?
TUNK
NO...
I'M JUST GLAD TO KNOW HE'S HAPPY.
THAT'S ENOUGH.
LET'S GO.
VROOM
I WILL NEVER LEAVE YOU.

...THERE'S NOTHING LEFT...

NOW

...

...TO REMEMBER HIM BY.

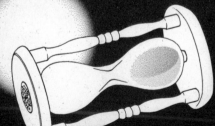

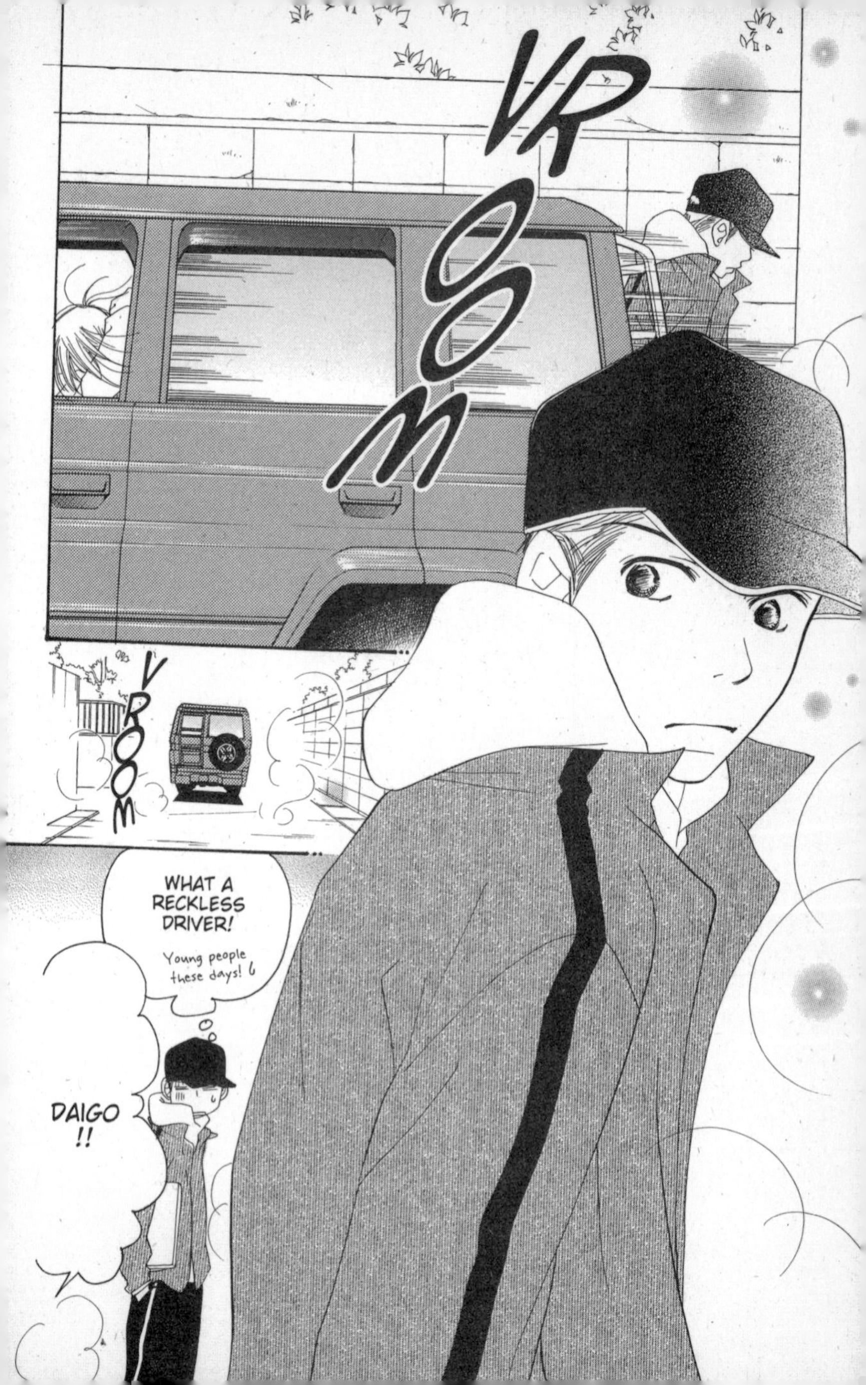
VROOM
VROOM
WHAT A RECKLESS DRIVER!
Young people these days!
DAIGO!!

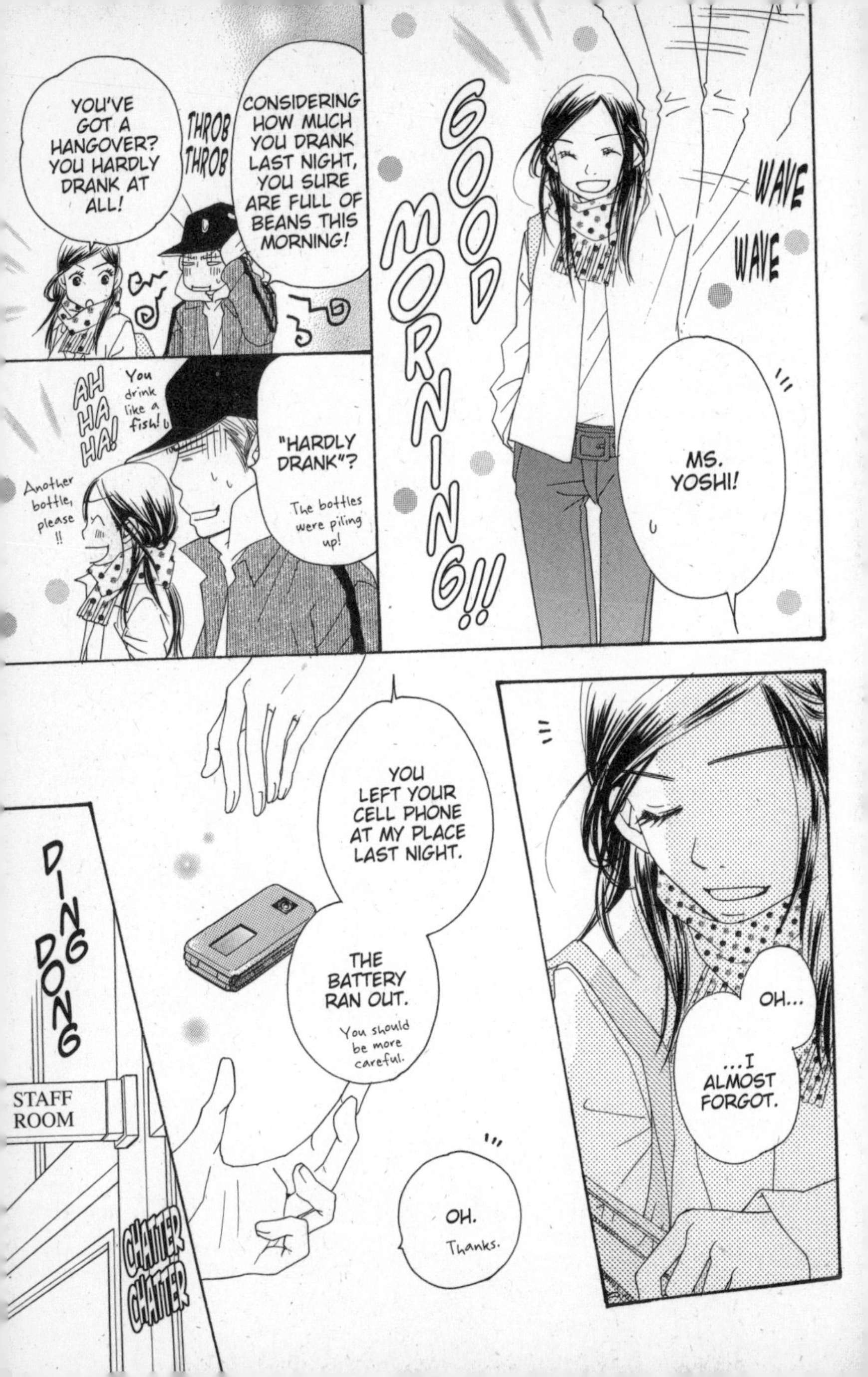
WAVE
WAVE
GOOD MORNING!!
MS. YOSHI!
CONSIDERING HOW MUCH YOU DRANK LAST NIGHT, YOU SURE ARE FULL OF BEANS THIS MORNING!
THROB THROB
YOU'VE GOT A HANGOVER? YOU HARDLY DRANK AT ALL!
"HARDLY DRANK"?
The bottles were piling up!
You drink like a fish!
AH HA HA!
Another bottle, please!!
OH...
...I ALMOST FORGOT.
YOU LEFT YOUR CELL PHONE AT MY PLACE LAST NIGHT.
THE BATTERY RAN OUT.
You should be more careful.
OH.
Thanks.
DING DONG
STAFF ROOM
CHATTER CHATTER

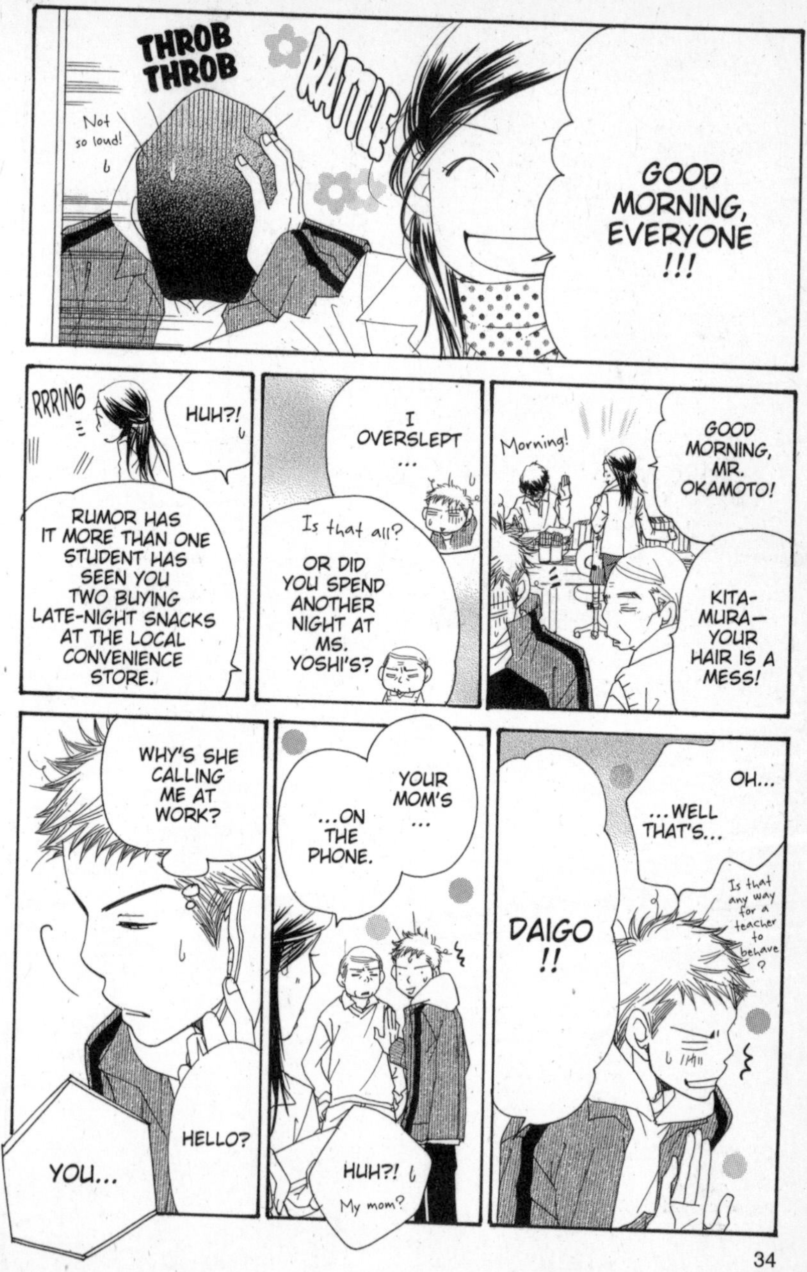
GOOD MORNING, EVERYONE!!!
RATTLE
THROB THROB
Not so loud!
GOOD MORNING, MR. OKAMOTO!
Morning!
KITA-MURA— YOUR HAIR IS A MESS!
I OVERSLEPT...
Is that all?
OR DID YOU SPEND ANOTHER NIGHT AT MS. YOSHI'S?
HUH?!
RRRING
RUMOR HAS IT MORE THAN ONE STUDENT HAS SEEN YOU TWO BUYING LATE-NIGHT SNACKS AT THE LOCAL CONVENIENCE STORE.
OH...
...WELL THAT'S...
Is that any way for a teacher to behave?
DAIGO!!
YOUR MOM'S...
...ON THE PHONE.
HUH?!
My mom?
WHY'S SHE CALLING ME AT WORK?
HELLO?
YOU...

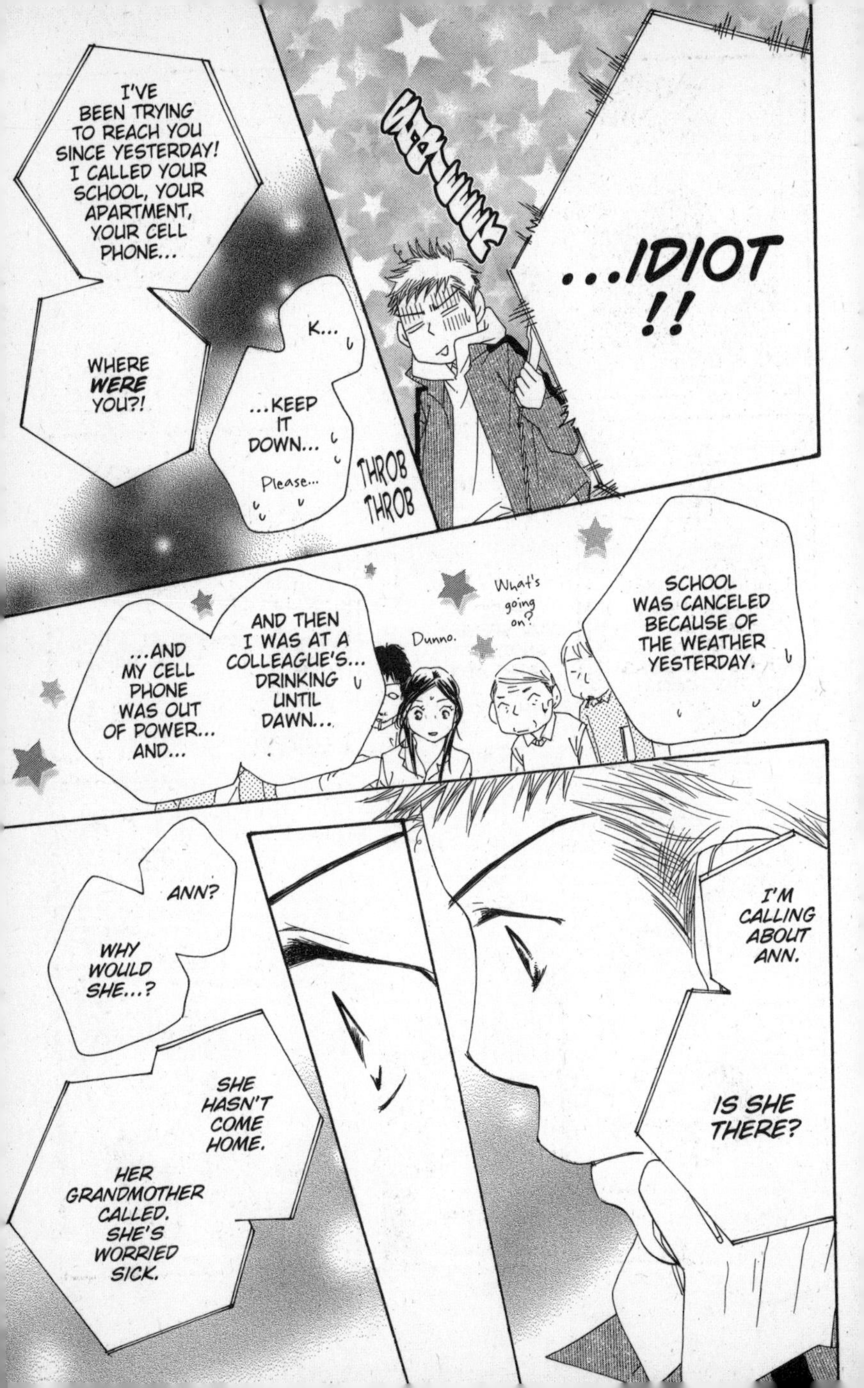
...IDIOT !!
THROB THROB
I'VE BEEN TRYING TO REACH YOU SINCE YESTERDAY! I CALLED YOUR SCHOOL, YOUR APARTMENT, YOUR CELL PHONE...
K...
WHERE WERE YOU?!
...KEEP IT DOWN...
Please...
SCHOOL WAS CANCELED BECAUSE OF THE WEATHER YESTERDAY.
What's going on?
Dunno.
AND THEN I WAS AT A COLLEAGUE'S... DRINKING UNTIL DAWN...
...AND MY CELL PHONE WAS OUT OF POWER... AND...
I'M CALLING ABOUT ANN.
IS SHE THERE?
ANN?
WHY WOULD SHE...?
SHE HASN'T COME HOME.
HER GRANDMOTHER CALLED. SHE'S WORRIED SICK.

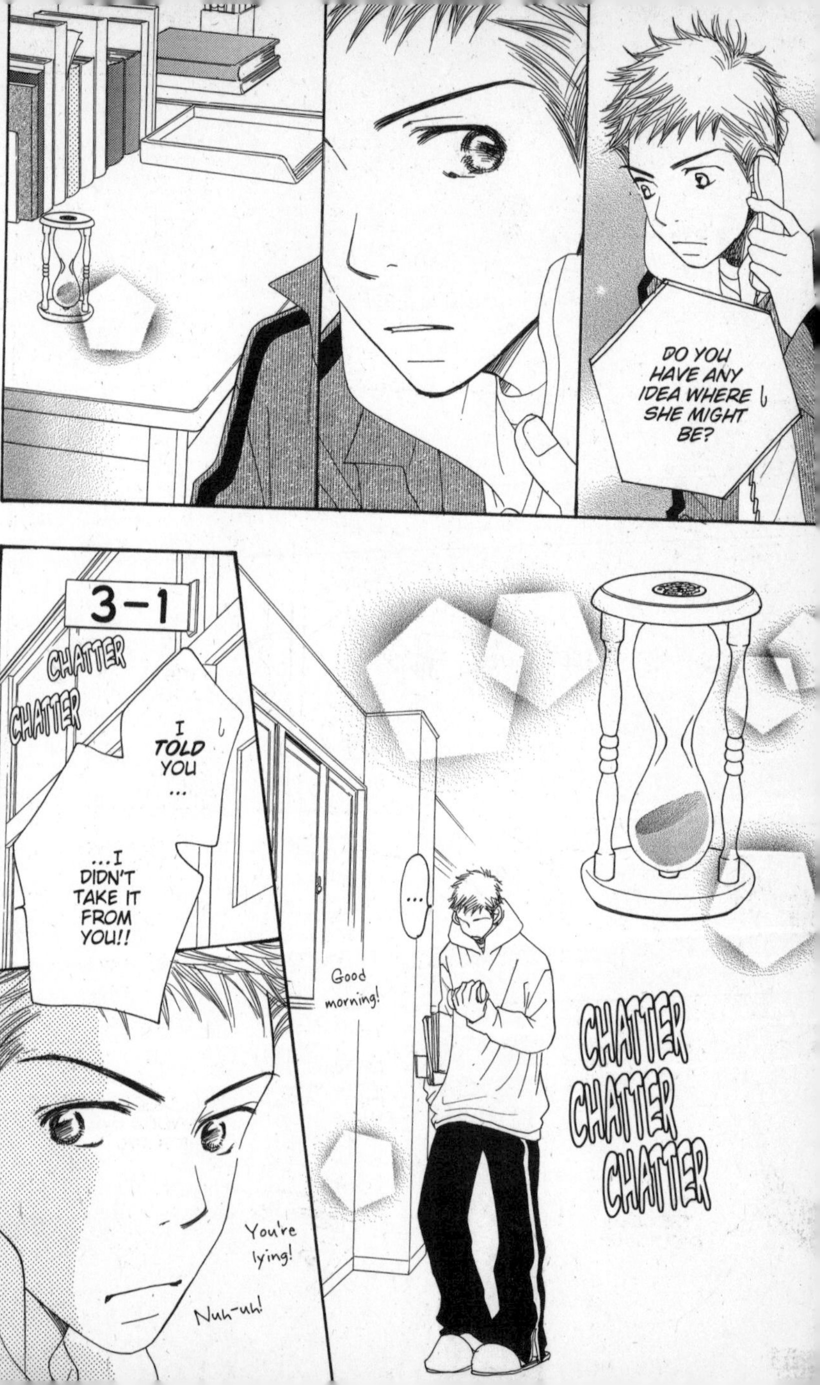
DO YOU HAVE ANY IDEA WHERE SHE MIGHT BE?
CHATTER CHATTER CHATTER
...
Good morning!
3-1
CHATTER
CHATTER
I TOLD YOU ...
...I DIDN'T TAKE IT FROM YOU!!
You're lying!
Nuh-uh!

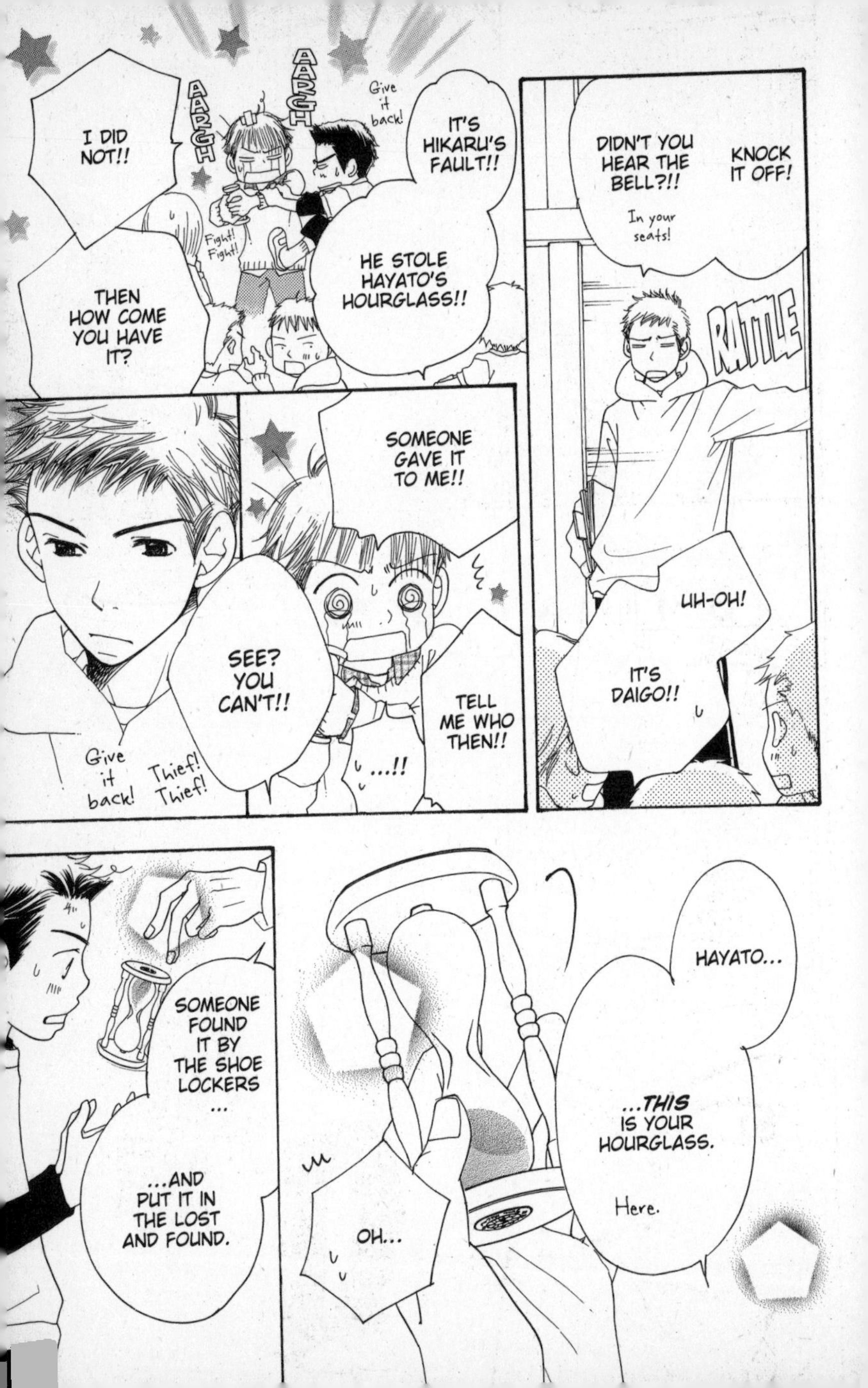
KNOCK IT OFF!
DIDN'T YOU HEAR THE BELL?!!
In your seats!
RATTLE
UH-OH!
IT'S DAIGO!!
Give it back!
IT'S HIKARU'S FAULT!!
AARGH
AARGH
HE STOLE HAYATO'S HOURGLASS!!
I DID NOT!!
Fight! Fight!
THEN HOW COME YOU HAVE IT?
SOMEONE GAVE IT TO ME!!
TELL ME WHO THEN!!
...!!
SEE? YOU CAN'T!!
Give it back!
Thief! Thief!
HAYATO...
...THIS IS YOUR HOURGLASS.
Here.
OH...
SOMEONE FOUND IT BY THE SHOE LOCKERS...
...AND PUT IT IN THE LOST AND FOUND.

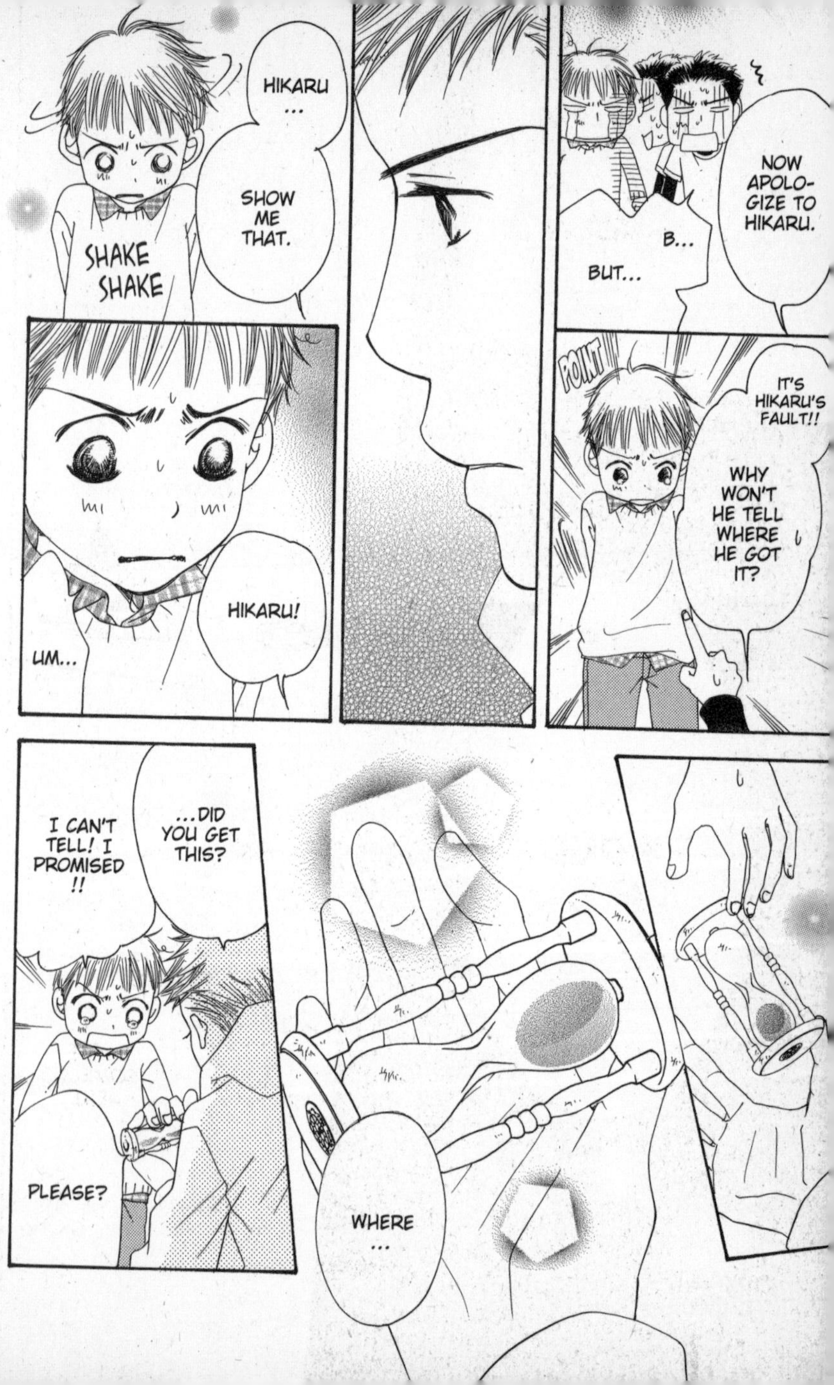
NOW APOLOGIZE TO HIKARU.
B...
BUT...
POINT
IT'S HIKARU'S FAULT!!
WHY WON'T HE TELL WHERE HE GOT IT?
HIKARU ...
SHOW ME THAT.
SHAKE SHAKE
HIKARU!
UM...
WHERE ...
...DID YOU GET THIS?
I CAN'T TELL! I PROMISED!!
PLEASE?

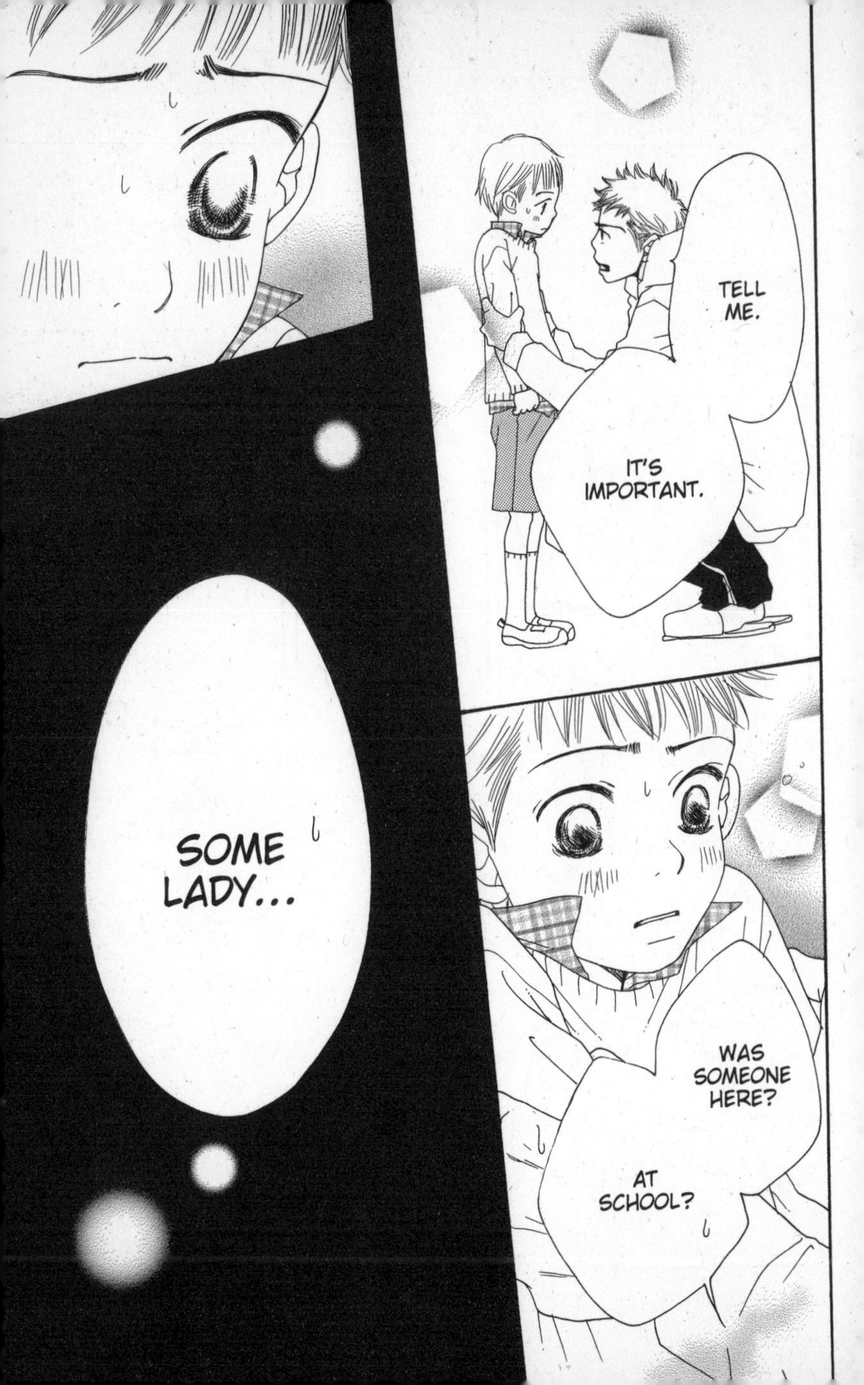
TELL ME.
IT'S IMPORTANT.
WAS SOMEONE HERE?
AT SCHOOL?
SOME LADY...

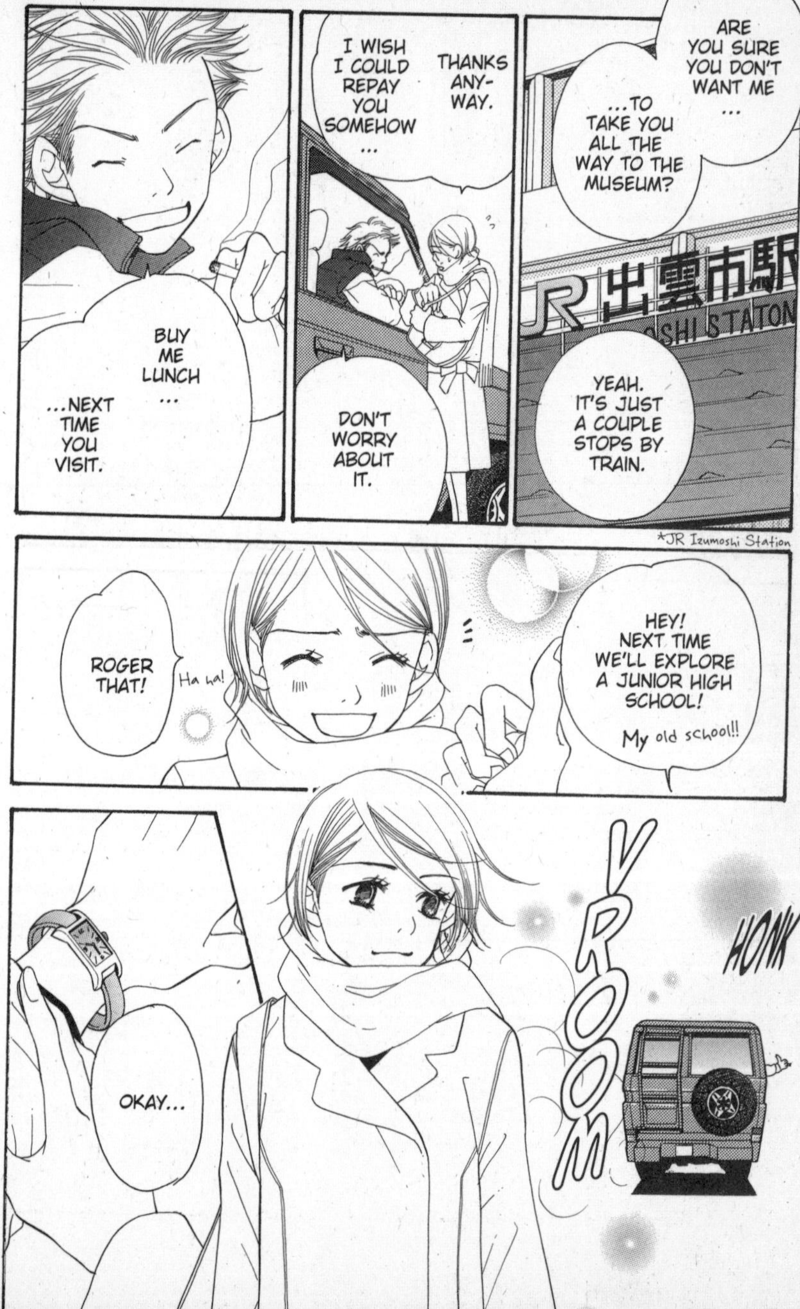
ARE YOU SURE YOU DON'T WANT ME ...
...TO TAKE YOU ALL THE WAY TO THE MUSEUM?
JR 出雲市駅
OSHI STATON
YEAH. IT'S JUST A COUPLE STOPS BY TRAIN.
THANKS ANYWAY.
I WISH I COULD REPAY YOU SOMEHOW ...
DON'T WORRY ABOUT IT.
BUY ME LUNCH ...
...NEXT TIME YOU VISIT.
HEY! NEXT TIME WE'LL EXPLORE A JUNIOR HIGH SCHOOL!
My old school!!
Ha ha!
ROGER THAT!
HONK
VROOM
OKAY...

*JR Izumoshi Station

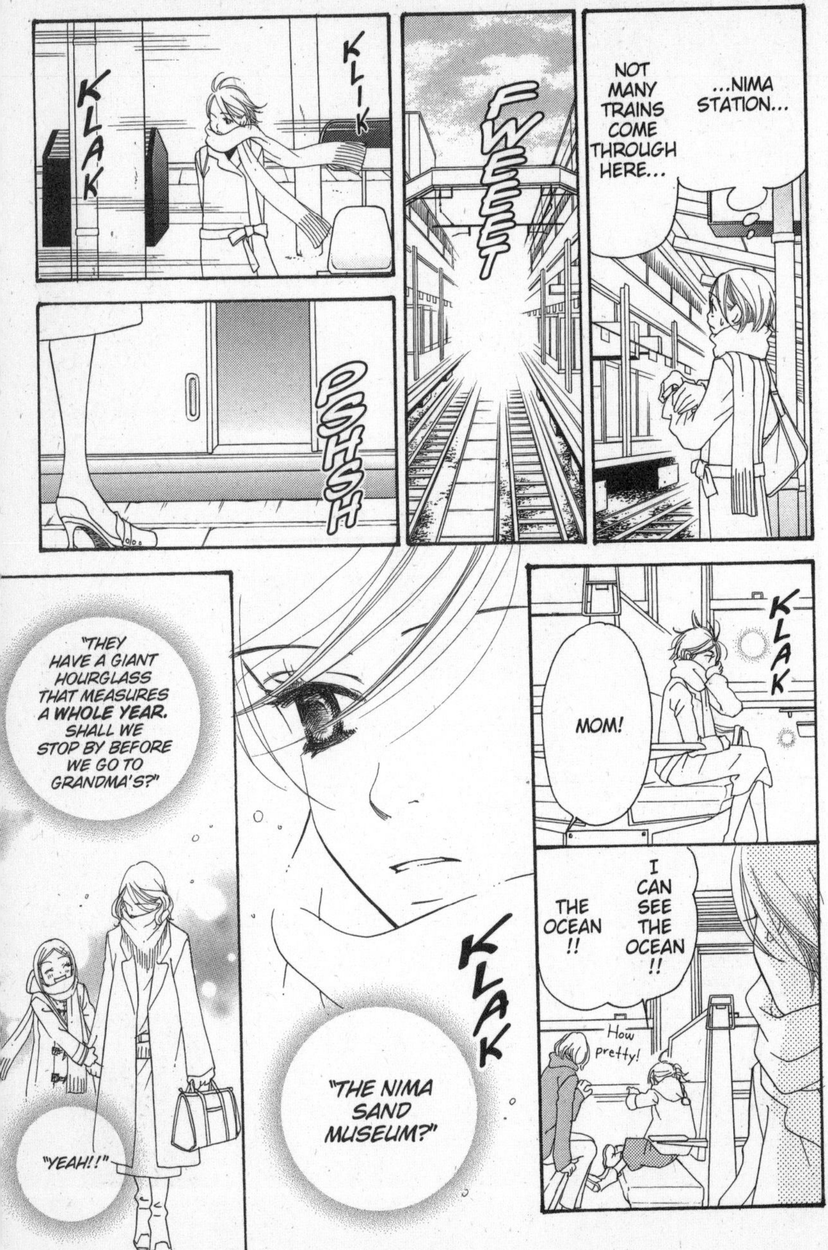
...NIMA STATION...
NOT MANY TRAINS COME THROUGH HERE...
FWEEET
KLIK
KLAK
PSHSH
KLAK
MOM!
I CAN SEE THE OCEAN!!
THE OCEAN!!
How pretty!
KLAK
"THE NIMA SAND MUSEUM?"
"THEY HAVE A GIANT HOURGLASS THAT MEASURES A WHOLE YEAR. SHALL WE STOP BY BEFORE WE GO TO GRANDMA'S?"
"YEAH!!"

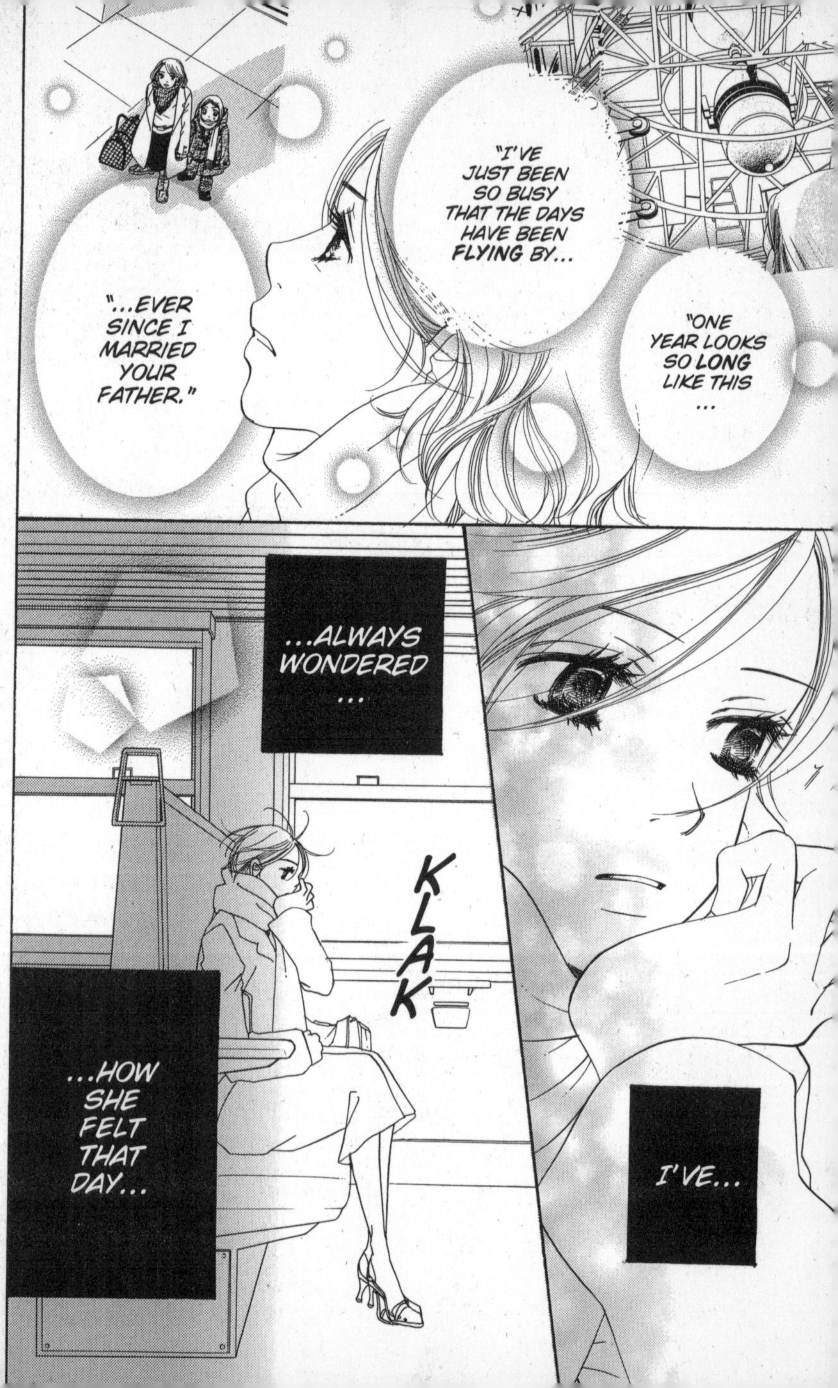
"I'VE JUST BEEN SO BUSY THAT THE DAYS HAVE BEEN FLYING BY...
"ONE YEAR LOOKS SO LONG LIKE THIS ...
"...EVER SINCE I MARRIED YOUR FATHER."
I'VE...
...ALWAYS WONDERED ...
KLAK
...HOW SHE FELT THAT DAY...

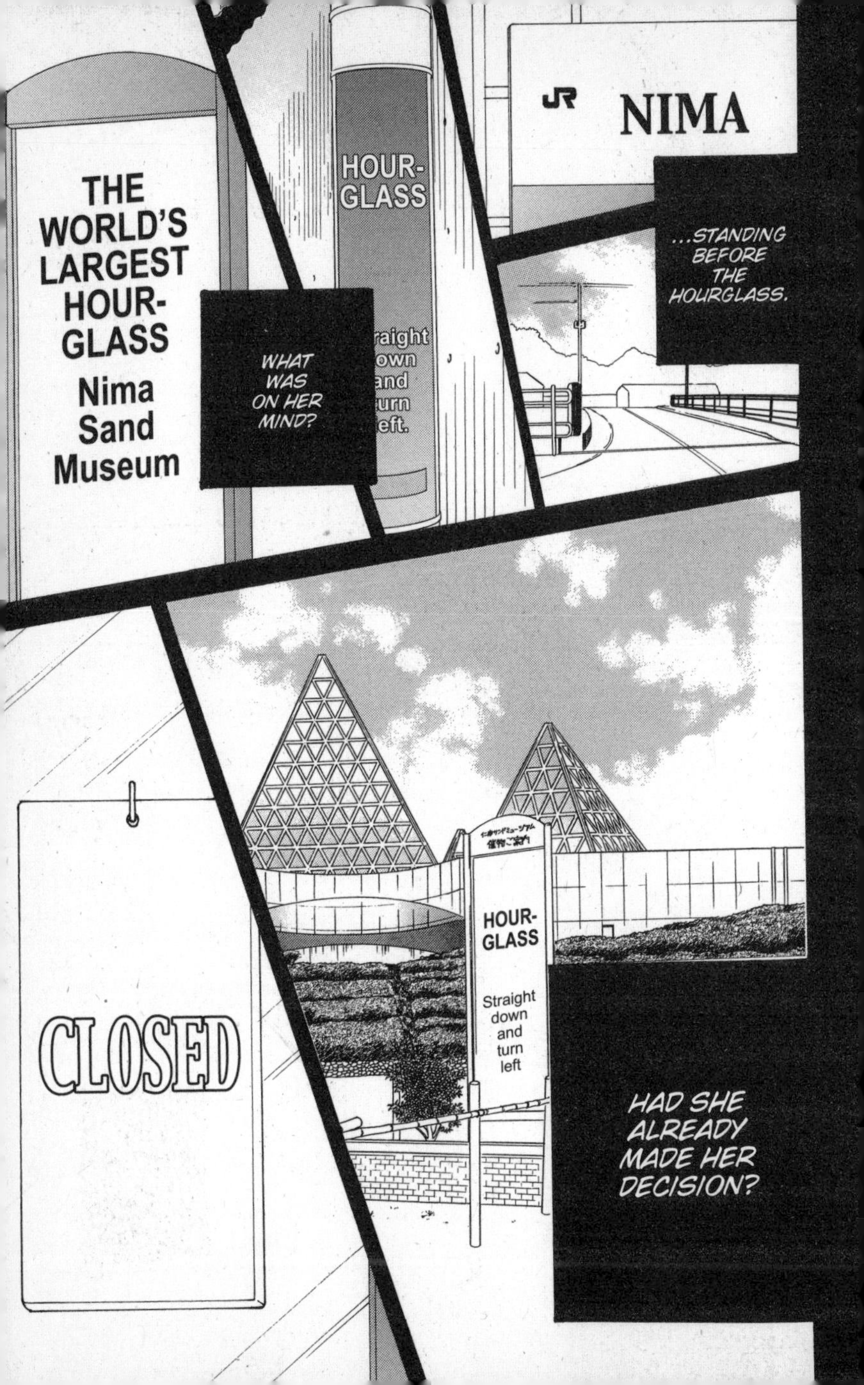
JR
NIMA
...STANDING BEFORE THE HOURGLASS.
HOUR-GLASS
WHAT WAS ON HER MIND?
THE WORLD'S LARGEST HOUR-GLASS
Nima Sand Museum
HOUR-GLASS
Straight down and turn left
HAD SHE ALREADY MADE HER DECISION?
CLOSED

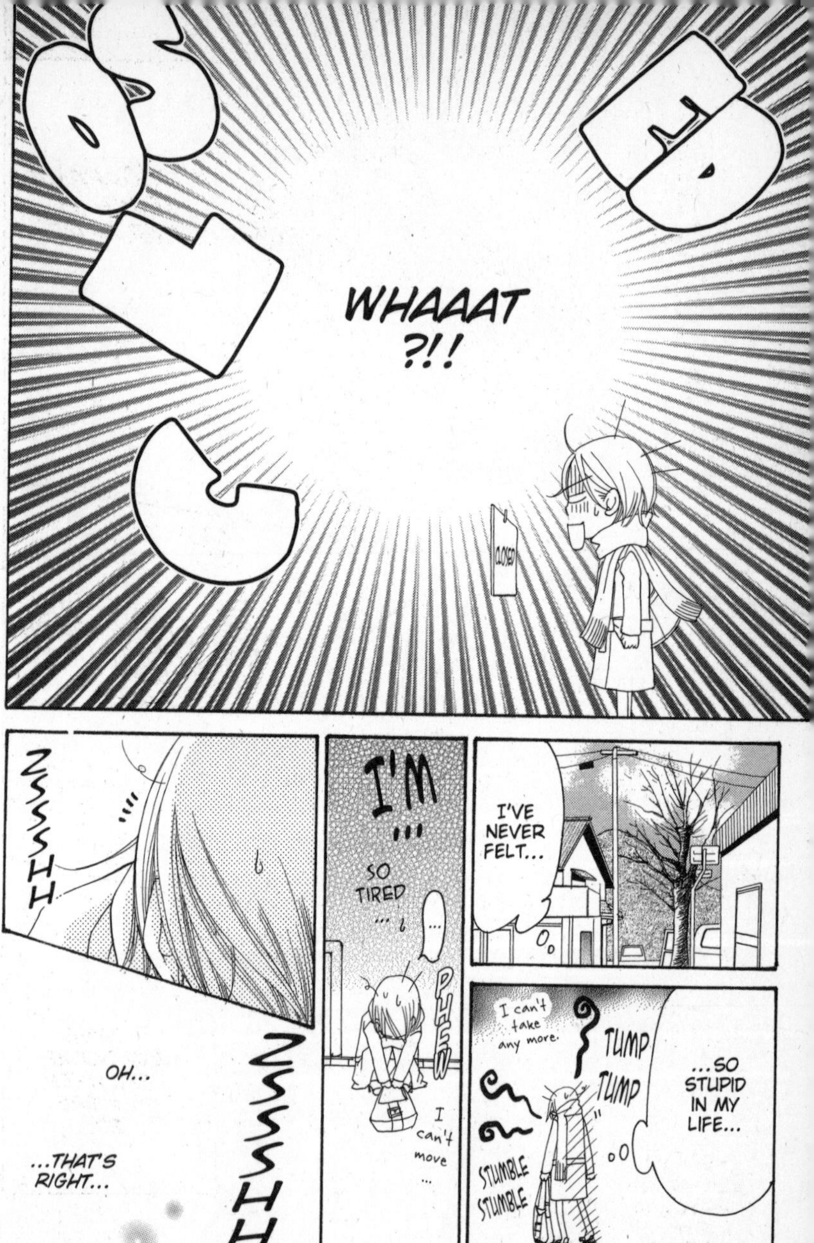
WHAAAT
?!!
I'VE NEVER FELT...
...SO STUPID IN MY LIFE...
I can't take any more.
TUMP
TUMP
STUMBLE
STUMBLE
I'M...
SO TIRED...
...
PHEW
I can't move...
OH...
...THAT'S RIGHT...

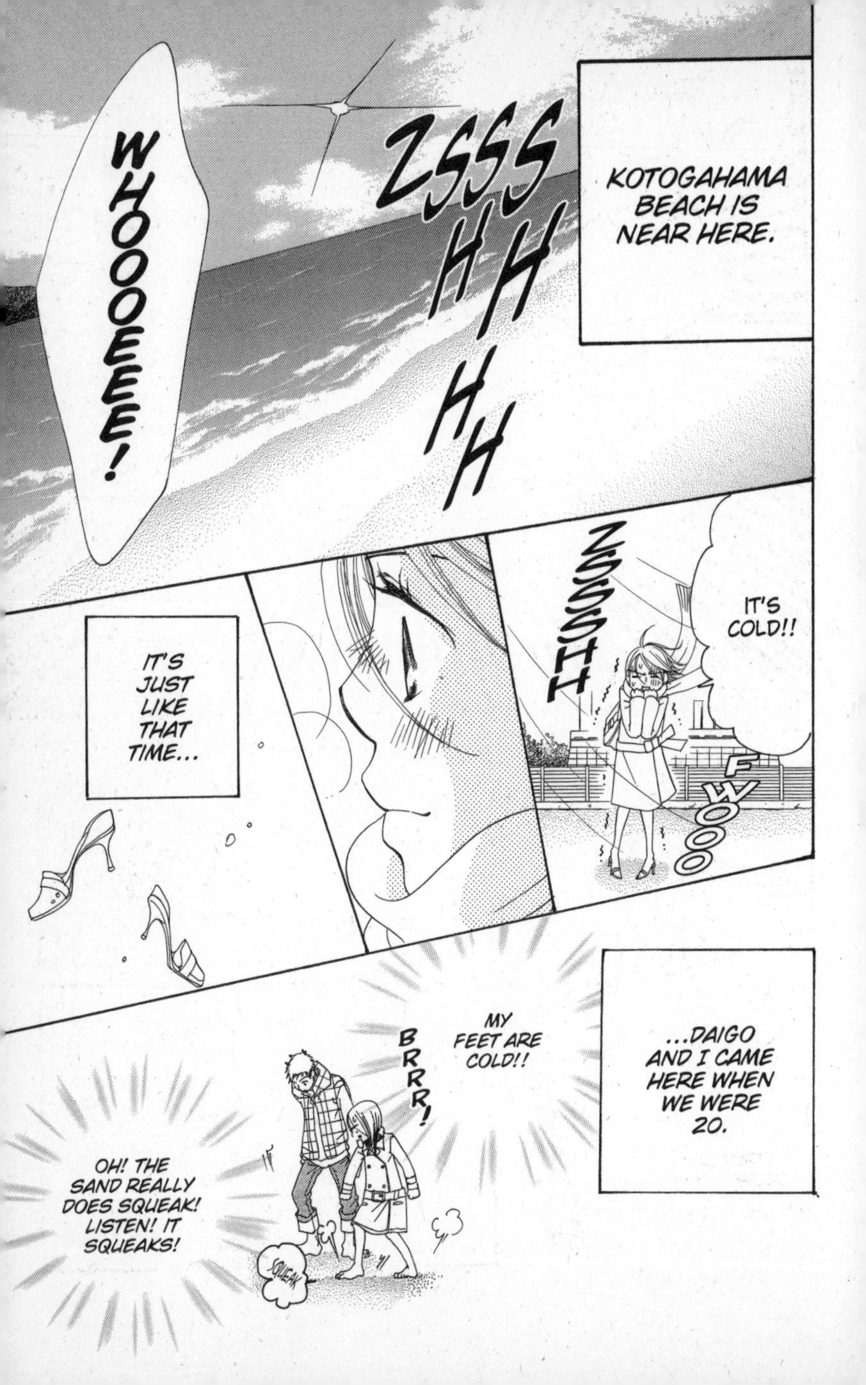
KOTOGAHAMA BEACH IS NEAR HERE.
ZSSSHHHH
WHOOOEEEE!
IT'S COLD!!
ZSSSHH
FWOOOO
IT'S JUST LIKE THAT TIME...
...DAIGO AND I CAME HERE WHEN WE WERE 20.
MY FEET ARE COLD!!
BRRR!
OH! THE SAND REALLY DOES SQUEAK! LISTEN! IT SQUEAKS!
SQUEAK

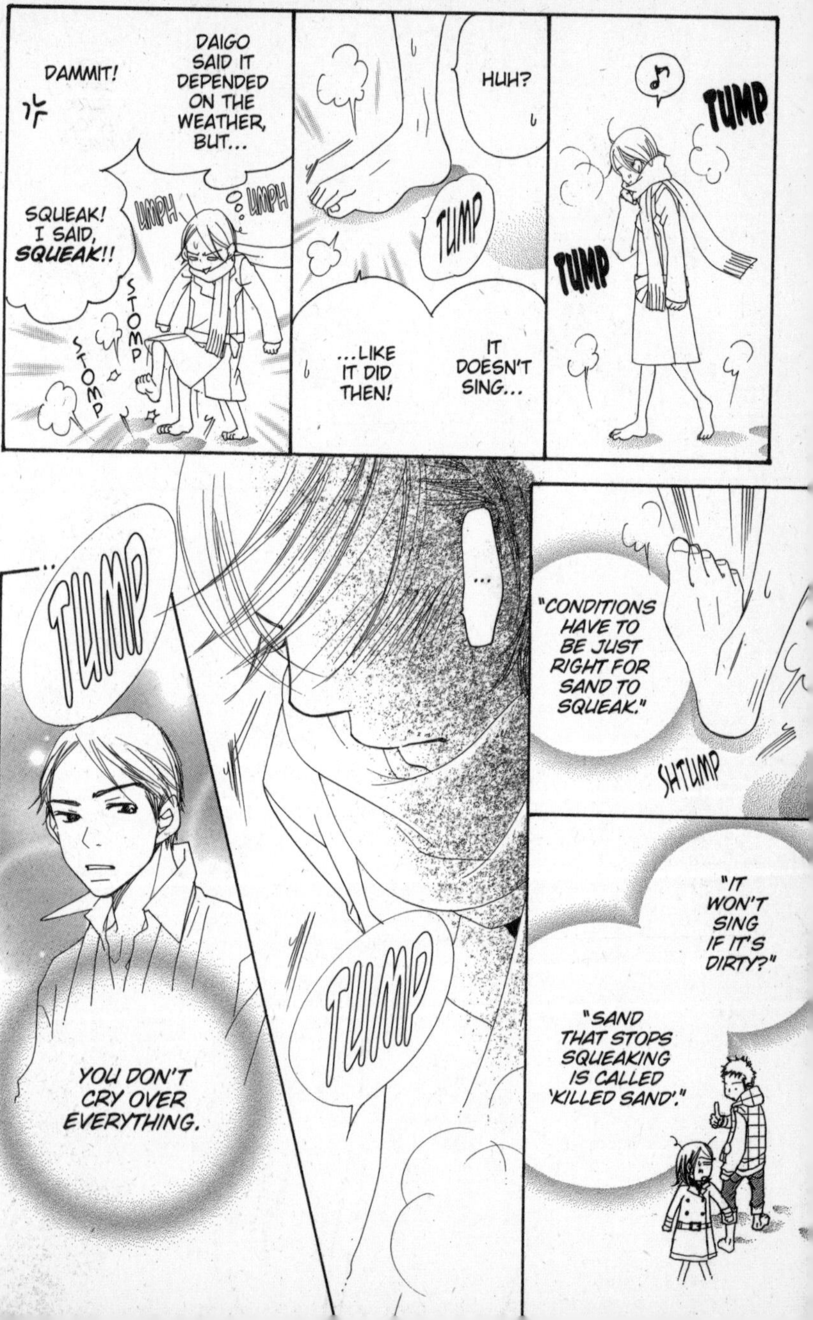
♪
TUMP
TUMP
HUH?
TUMP
IT DOESN'T SING...
...LIKE IT DID THEN!
DAIGO SAID IT DEPENDED ON THE WEATHER, BUT...
DAMMIT!
UMPH
UMPH
SQUEAK! I SAID, **SQUEAK!!**
STOMP
STOMP
"CONDITIONS HAVE TO BE JUST RIGHT FOR SAND TO SQUEAK."
SHTUMP
"IT WON'T SING IF IT'S DIRTY?"
"SAND THAT STOPS SQUEAKING IS CALLED 'KILLED SAND'."
...
TUMP
...
TUMP
YOU DON'T CRY OVER EVERYTHING.

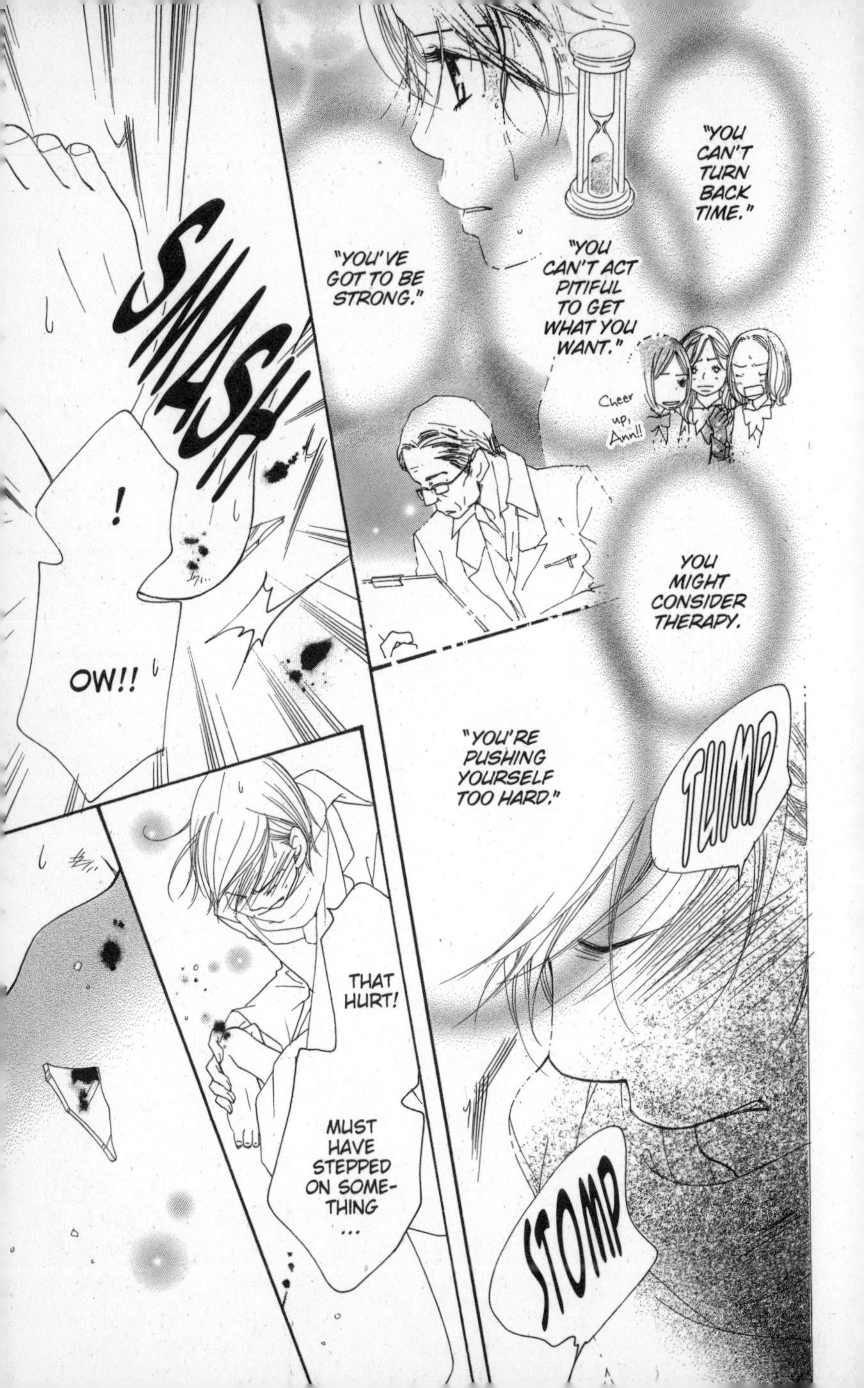
"YOU CAN'T TURN BACK TIME."
"YOU CAN'T ACT PITIFUL TO GET WHAT YOU WANT."
Cheer up, Ann!!
"YOU'VE GOT TO BE STRONG."
YOU MIGHT CONSIDER THERAPY.
"YOU'RE PUSHING YOURSELF TOO HARD."
TUMP
STOMP
SMASH
!
OW!!
THAT HURT!
MUST HAVE STEPPED ON SOME-THING ...

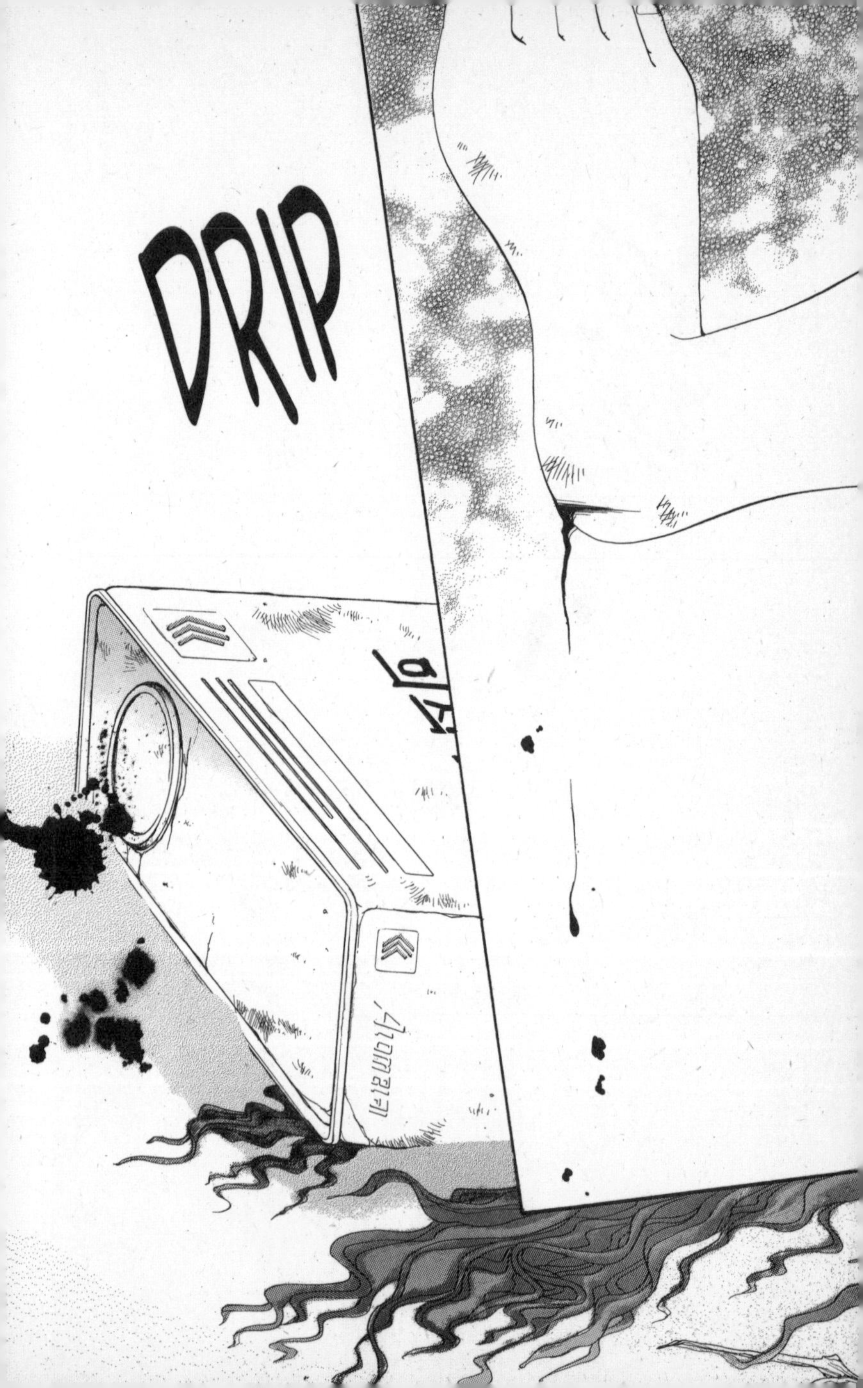
DRIP

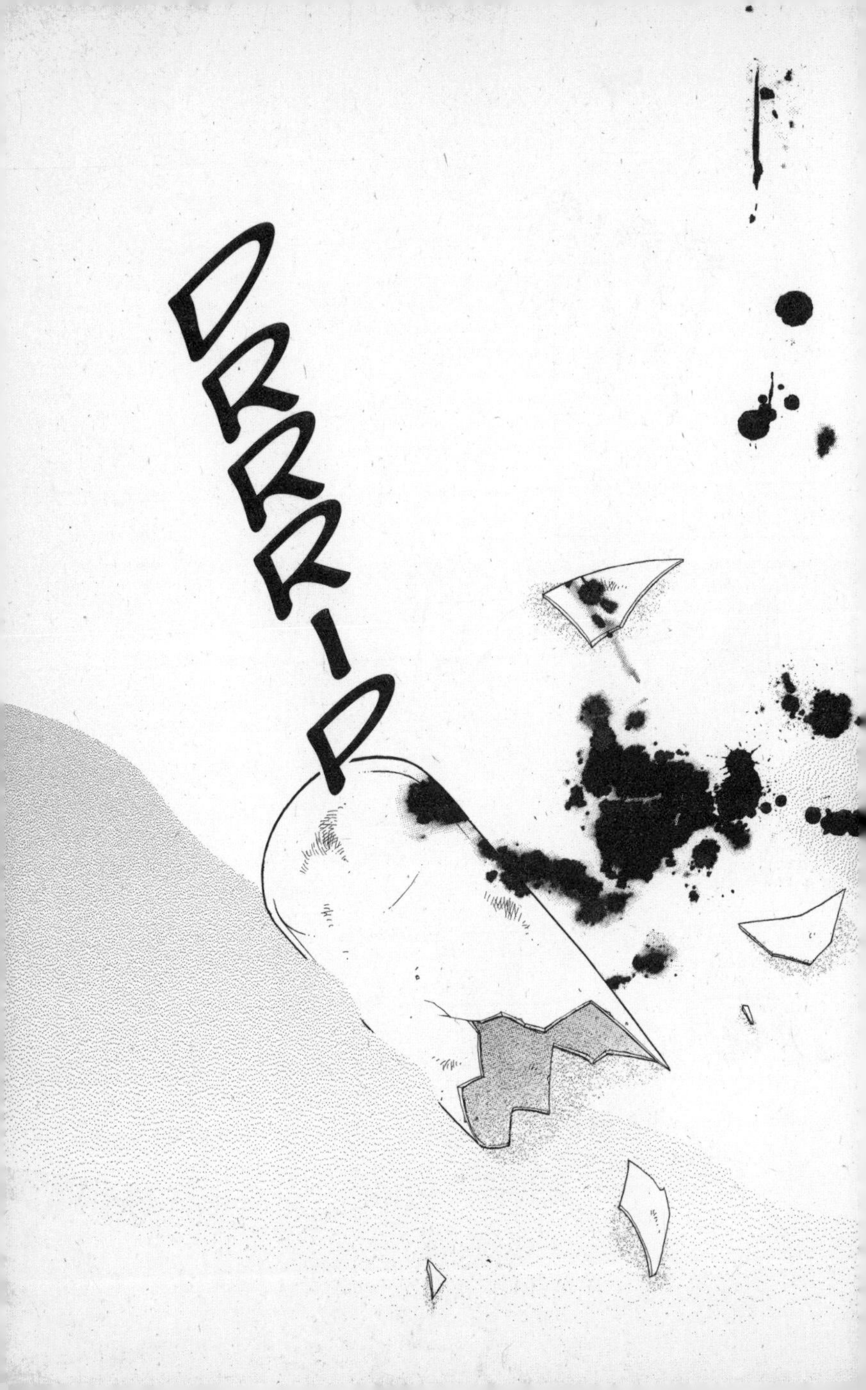
DRRRIP

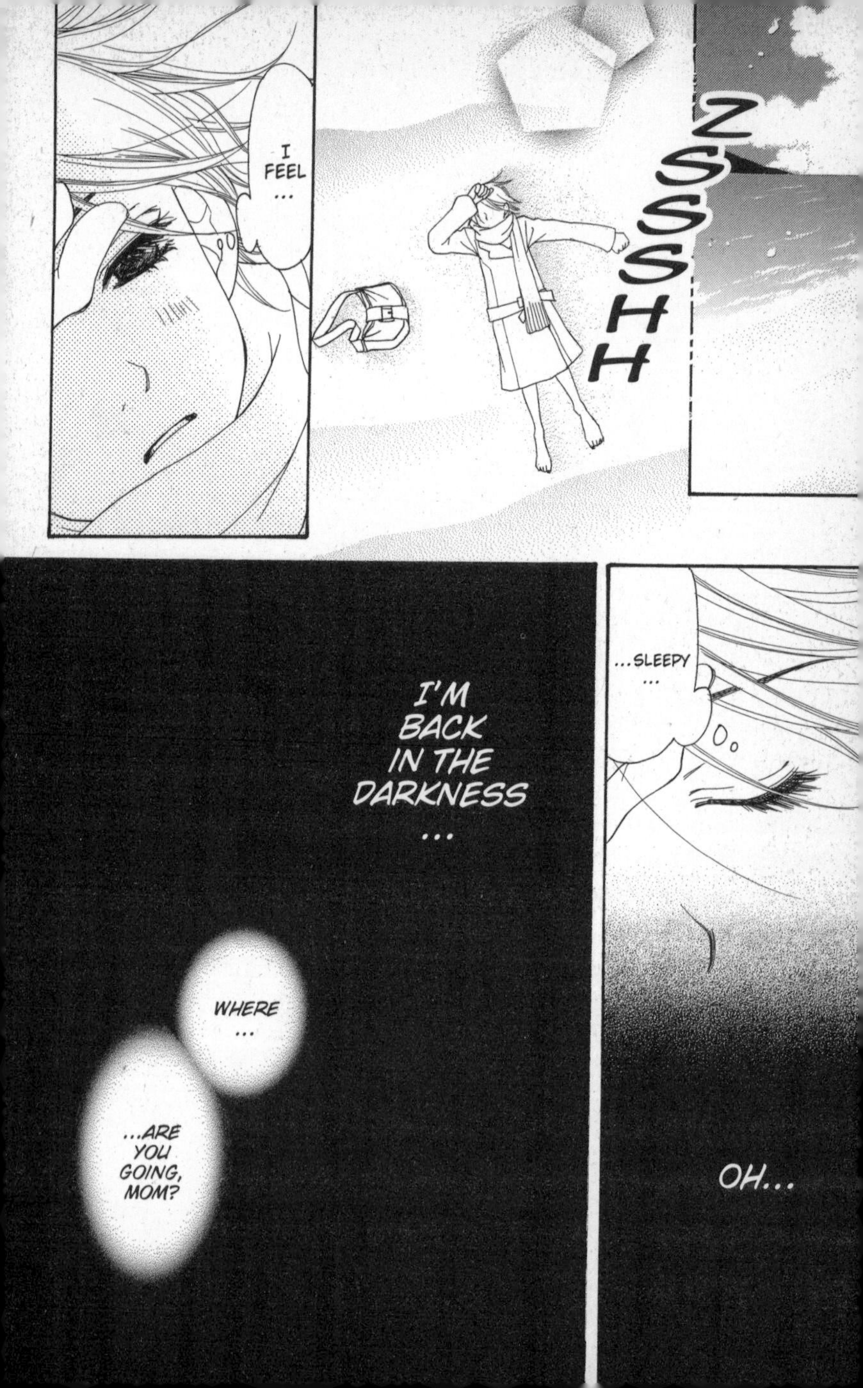
ZSSSHH
I FEEL ...
...SLEEPY ...
OH...
I'M BACK IN THE DARKNESS ...
WHERE ...
...ARE YOU GOING, MOM?

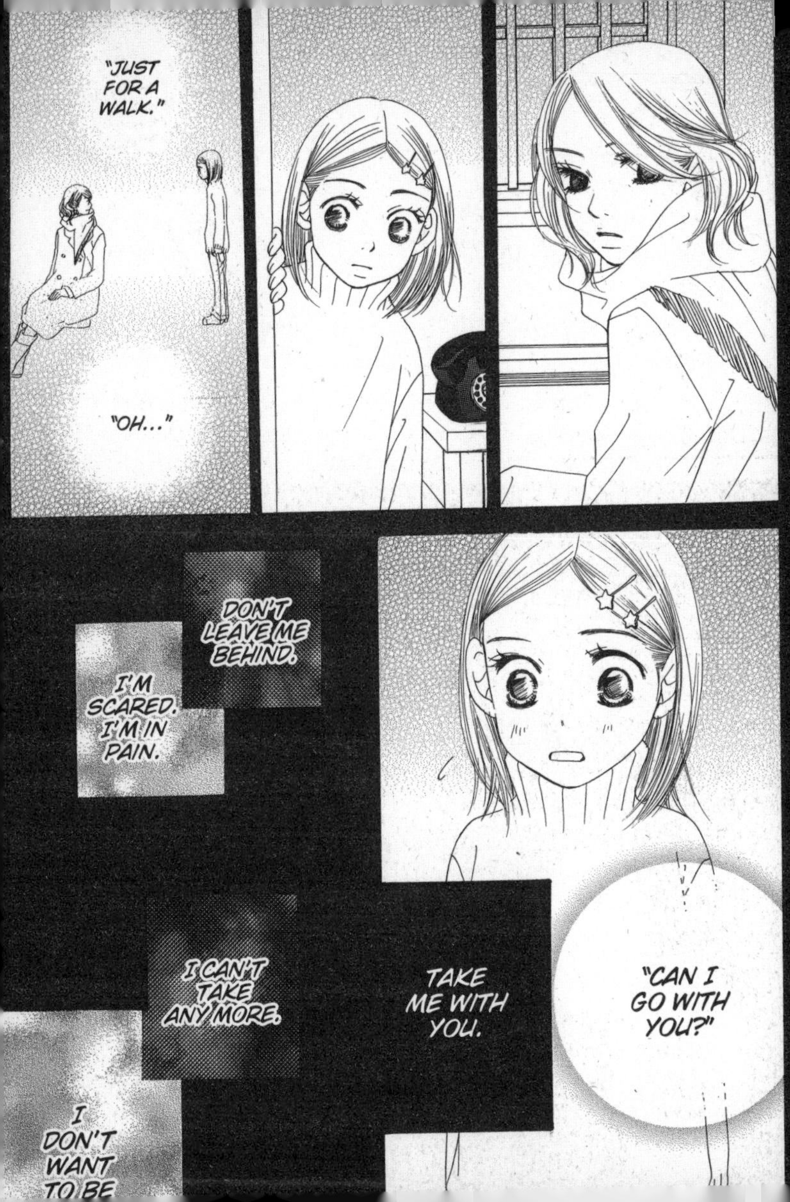
"JUST FOR A WALK."
"OH..."
"CAN I GO WITH YOU?"
TAKE ME WITH YOU.
DON'T LEAVE ME BEHIND.
I'M SCARED. I'M IN PAIN.
I CAN'T TAKE ANY MORE.
I DON'T WANT TO BE

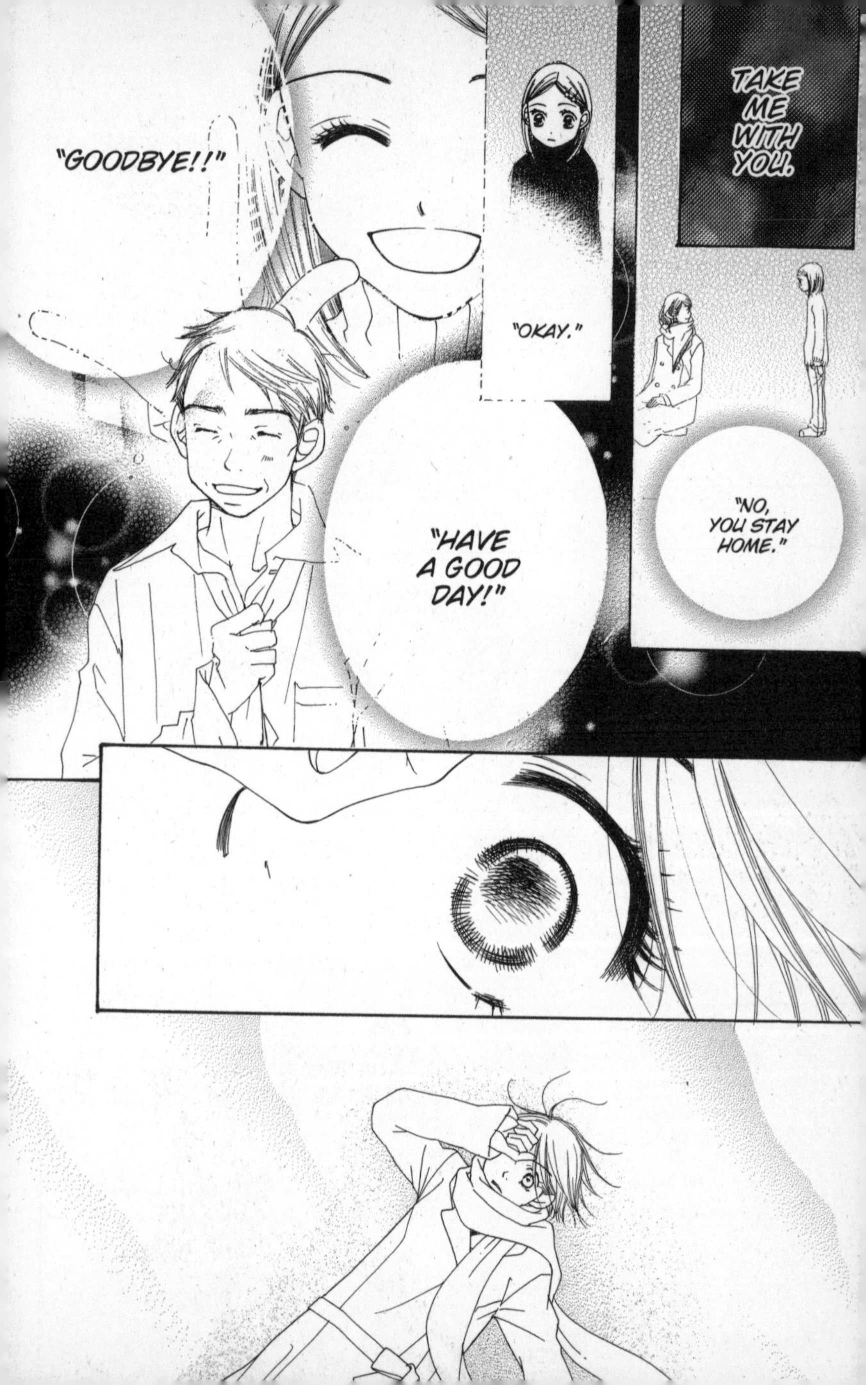
TAKE ME WITH YOU.
"NO, YOU STAY HOME."
"OKAY."
"HAVE A GOOD DAY!"
"GOODBYE!!"

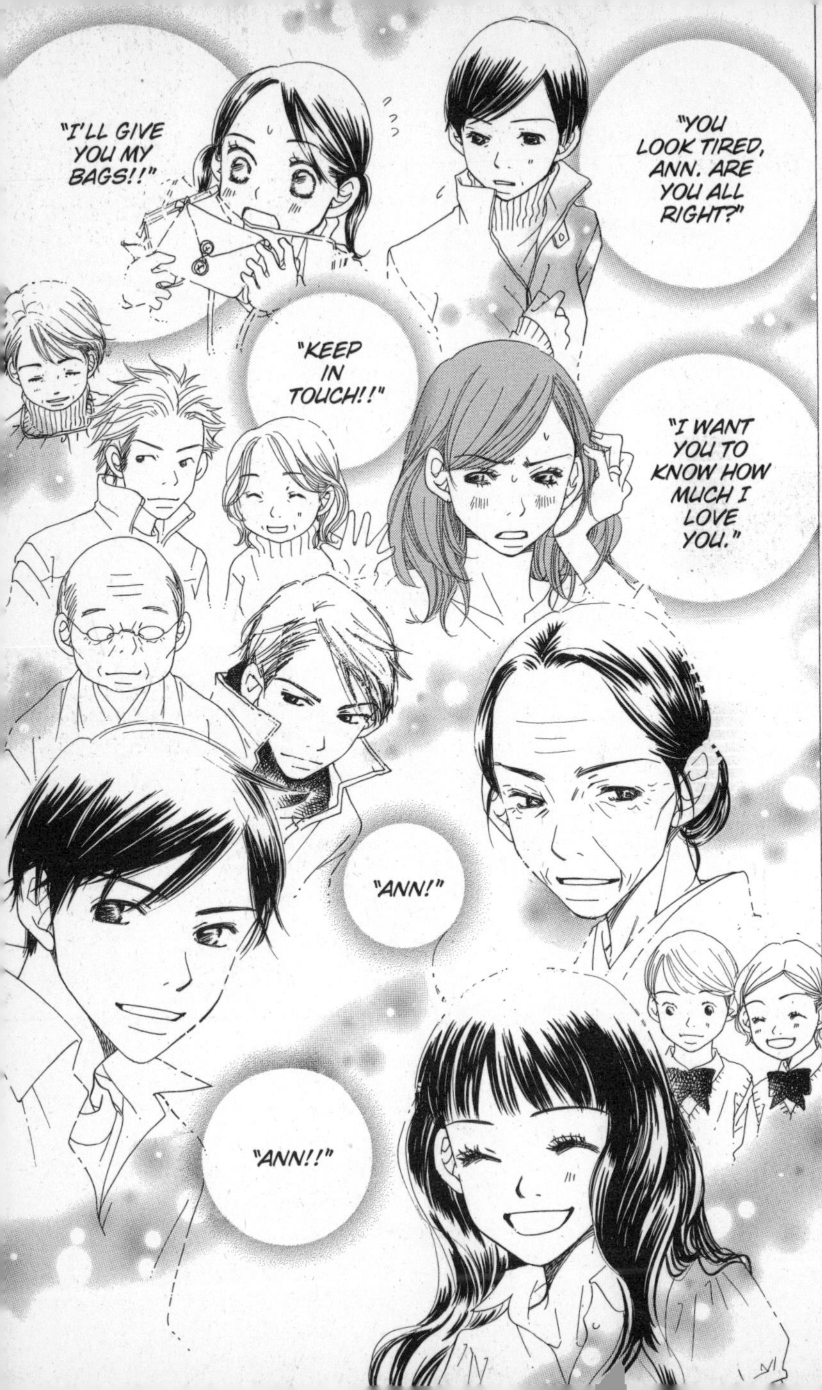
"YOU LOOK TIRED, ANN. ARE YOU ALL RIGHT?"
"I'LL GIVE YOU MY BAGS!!"
"I WANT YOU TO KNOW HOW MUCH I LOVE YOU."
"KEEP IN TOUCH!!"
"ANN!"
"ANN!!"

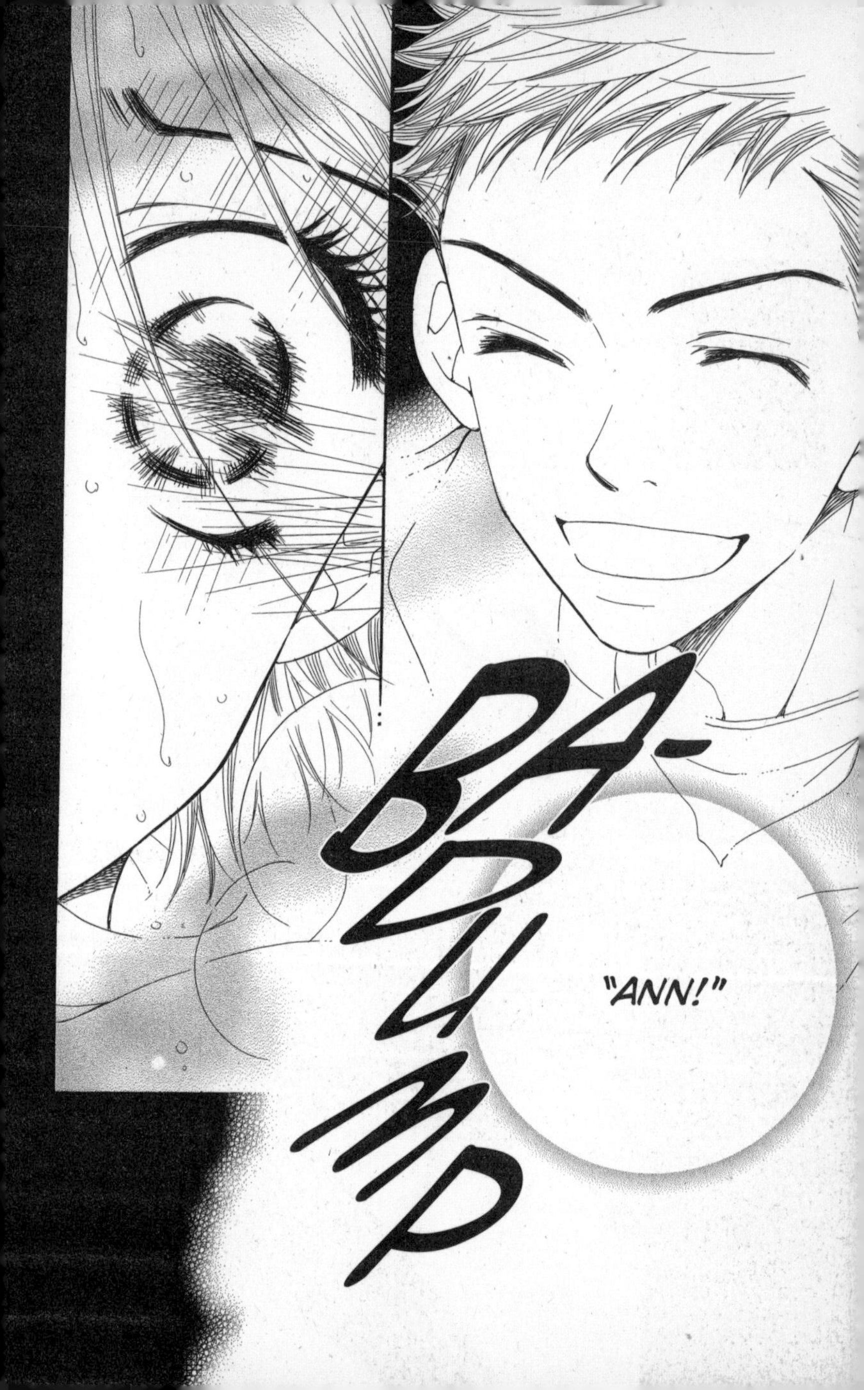
BA-BUMP
"ANN!"

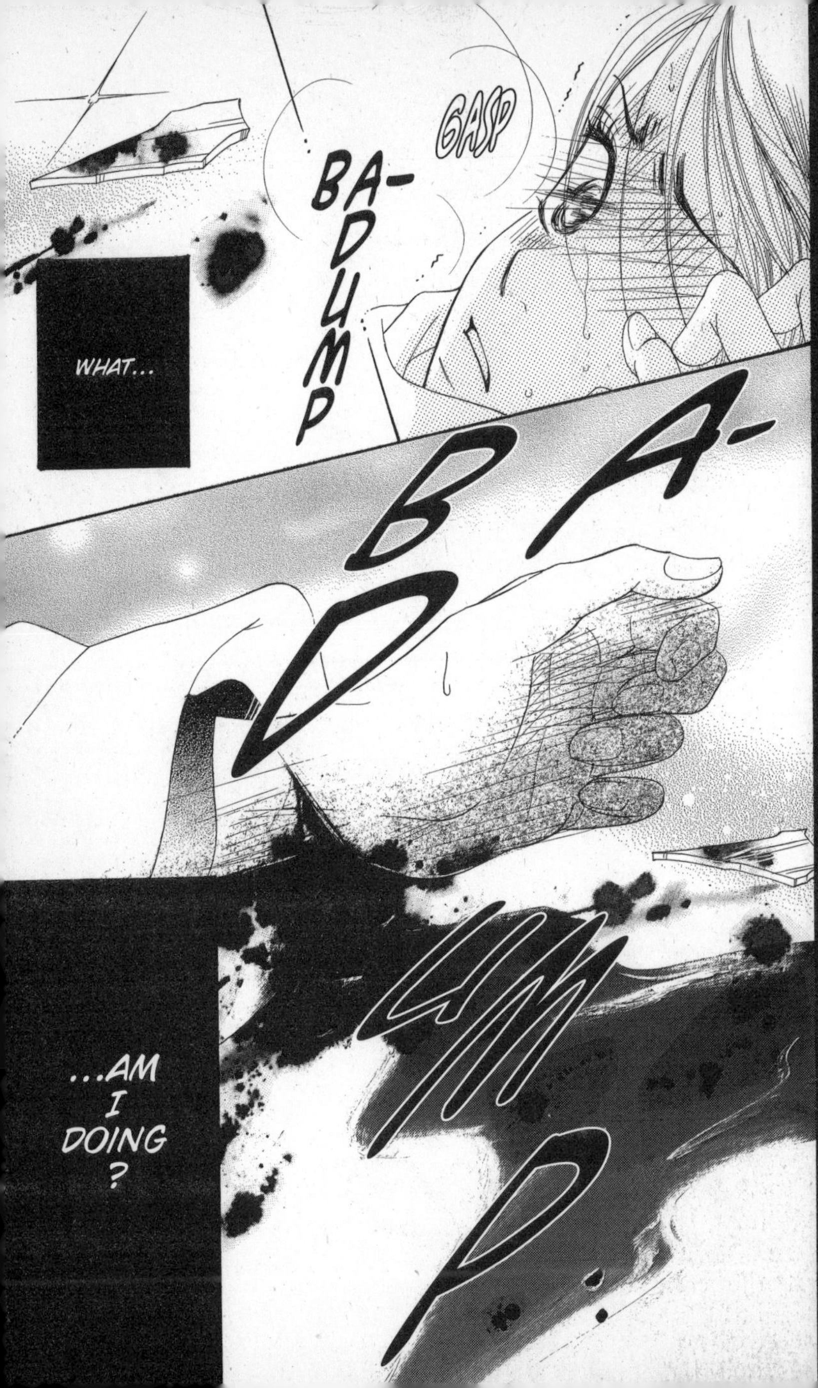
GASP
BA-DUMP
WHAT...
BA-DUMP
...AM I DOING?

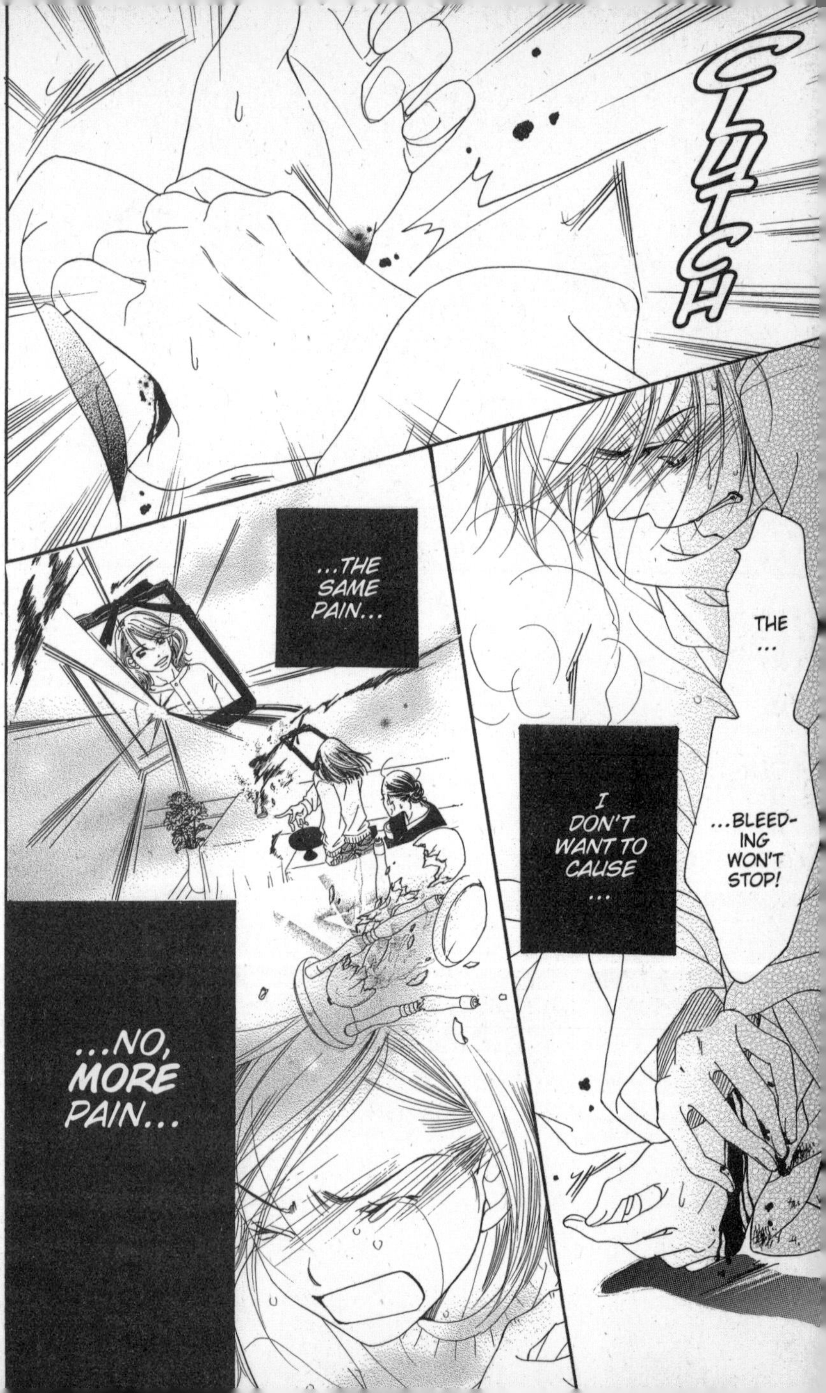
CLUTCH
THE ...
...BLEED-ING WON'T STOP!
I DON'T WANT TO CAUSE ...
...THE SAME PAIN...
...NO, MORE PAIN...

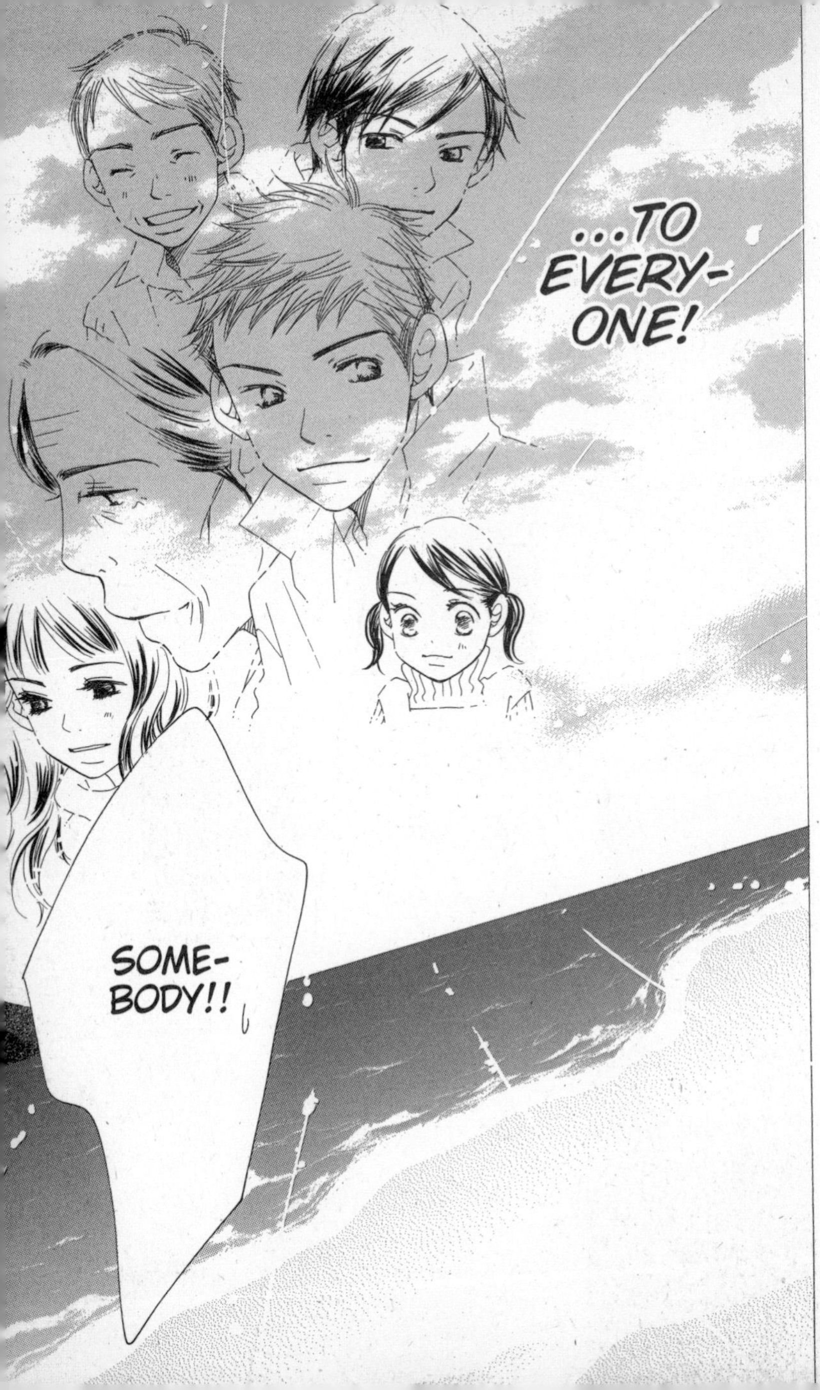
...TO EVERY-ONE!
SOME-BODY!!

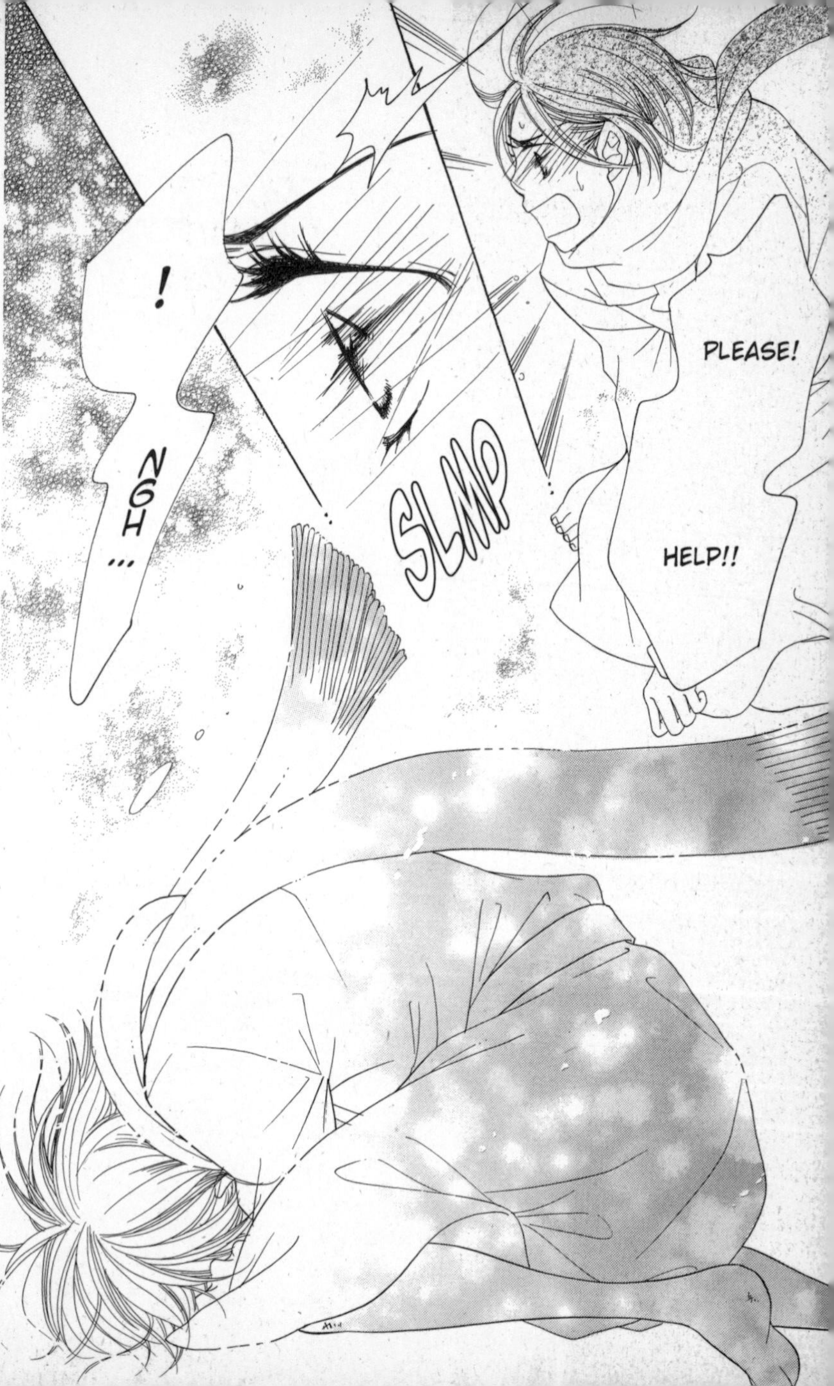
PLEASE!
HELP!!
SLMP
!
NGH...

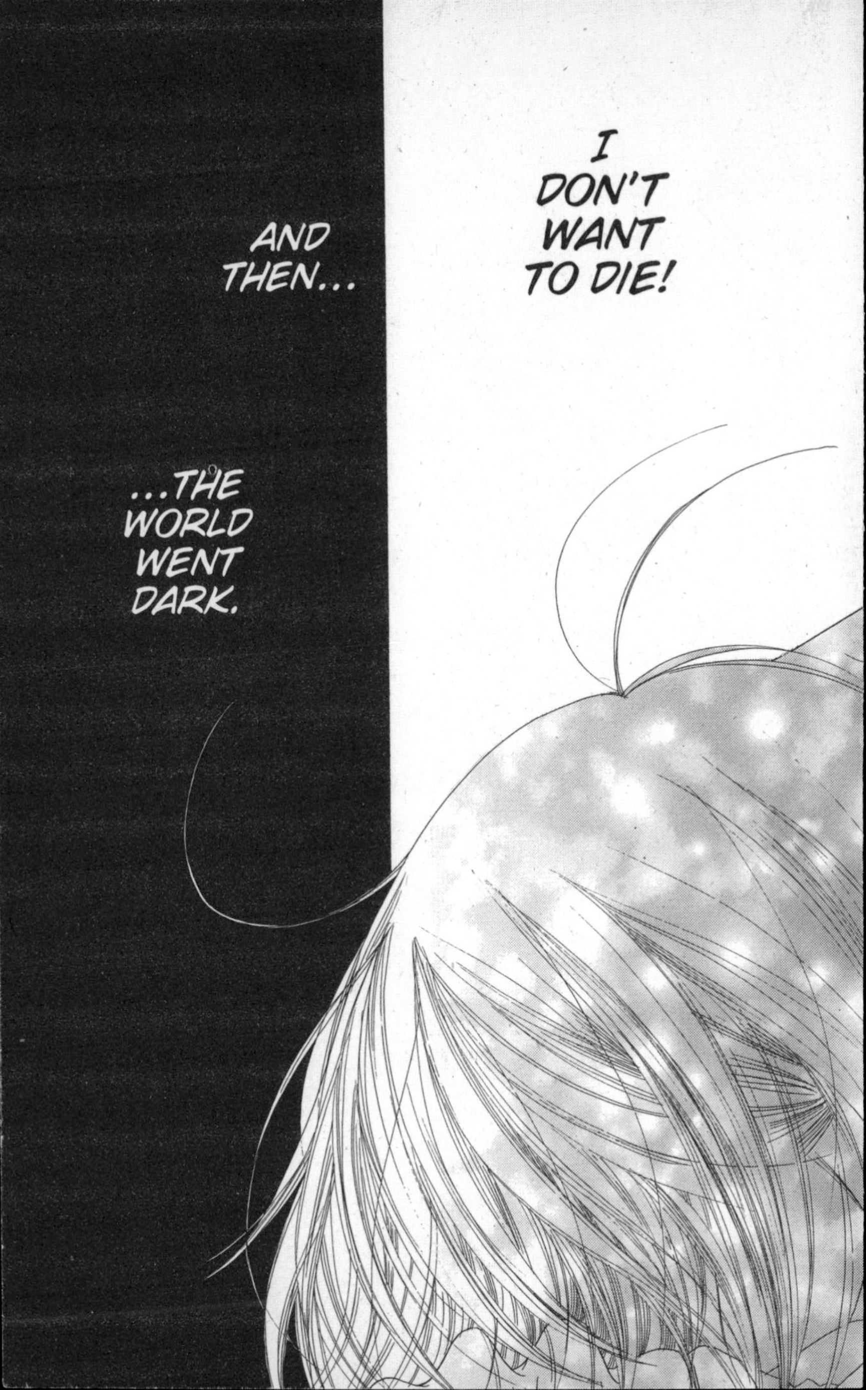
I DON'T WANT TO DIE!
AND THEN...
...THE WORLD WENT DARK.

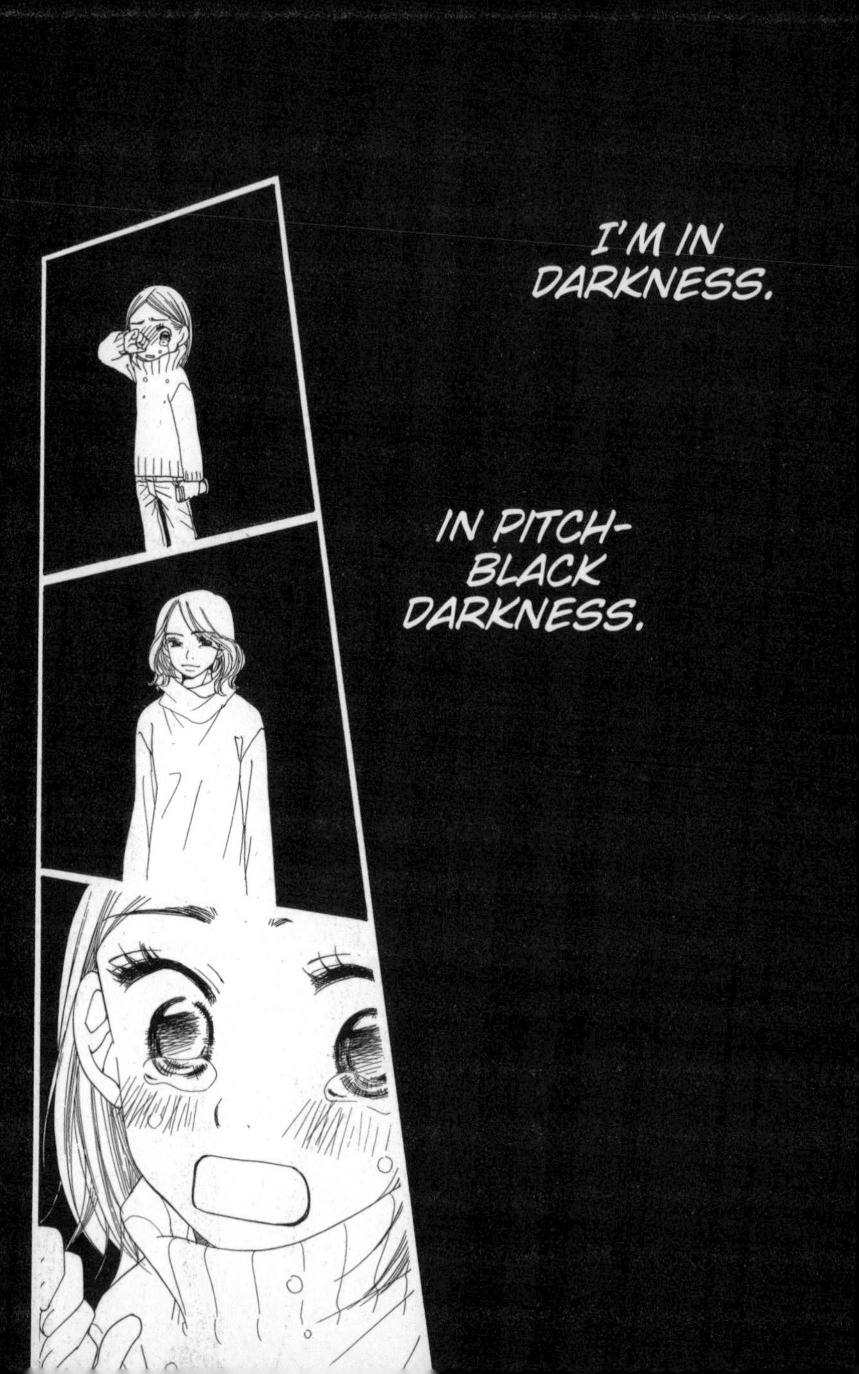
I'M IN DARKNESS.
IN PITCH-BLACK DARKNESS.

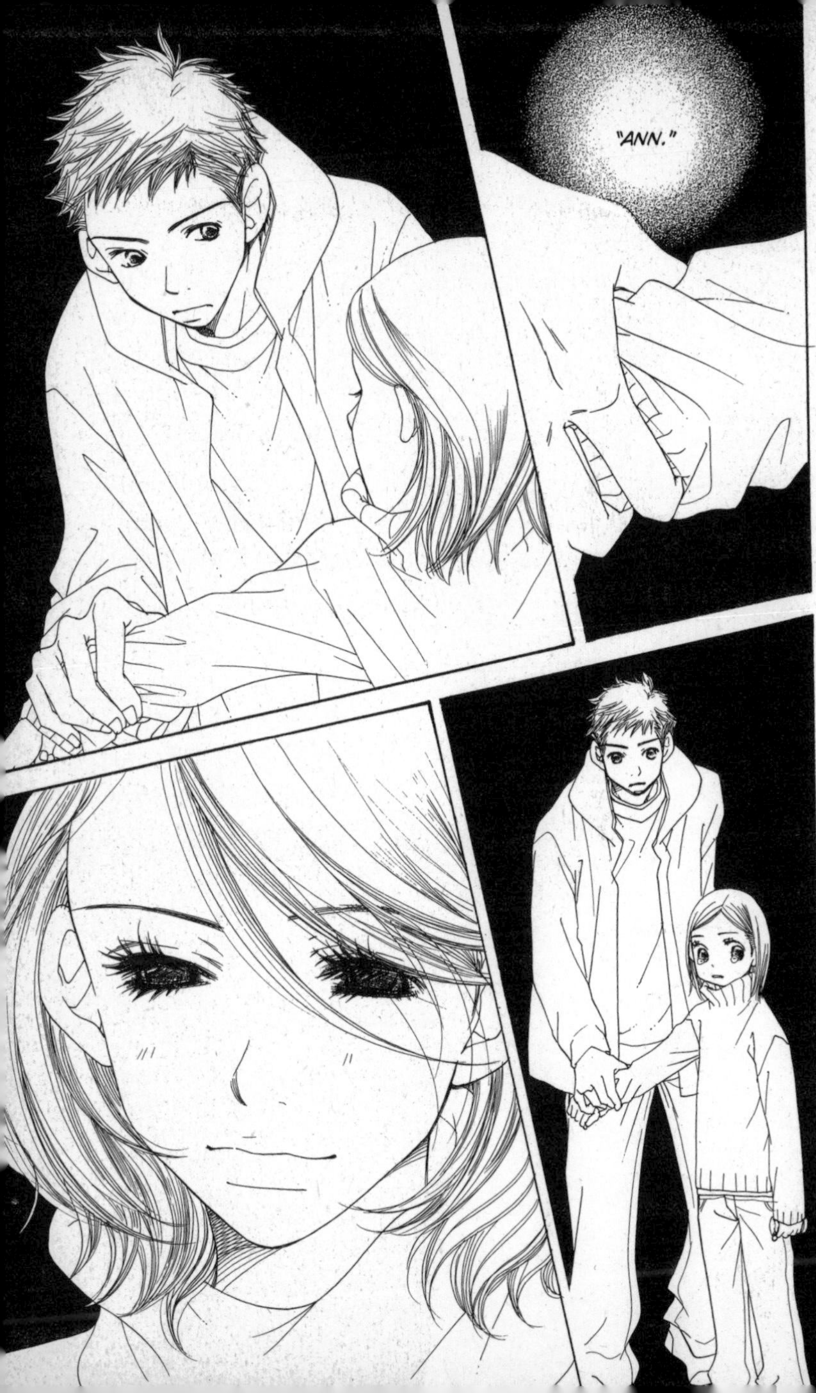
"ANN."

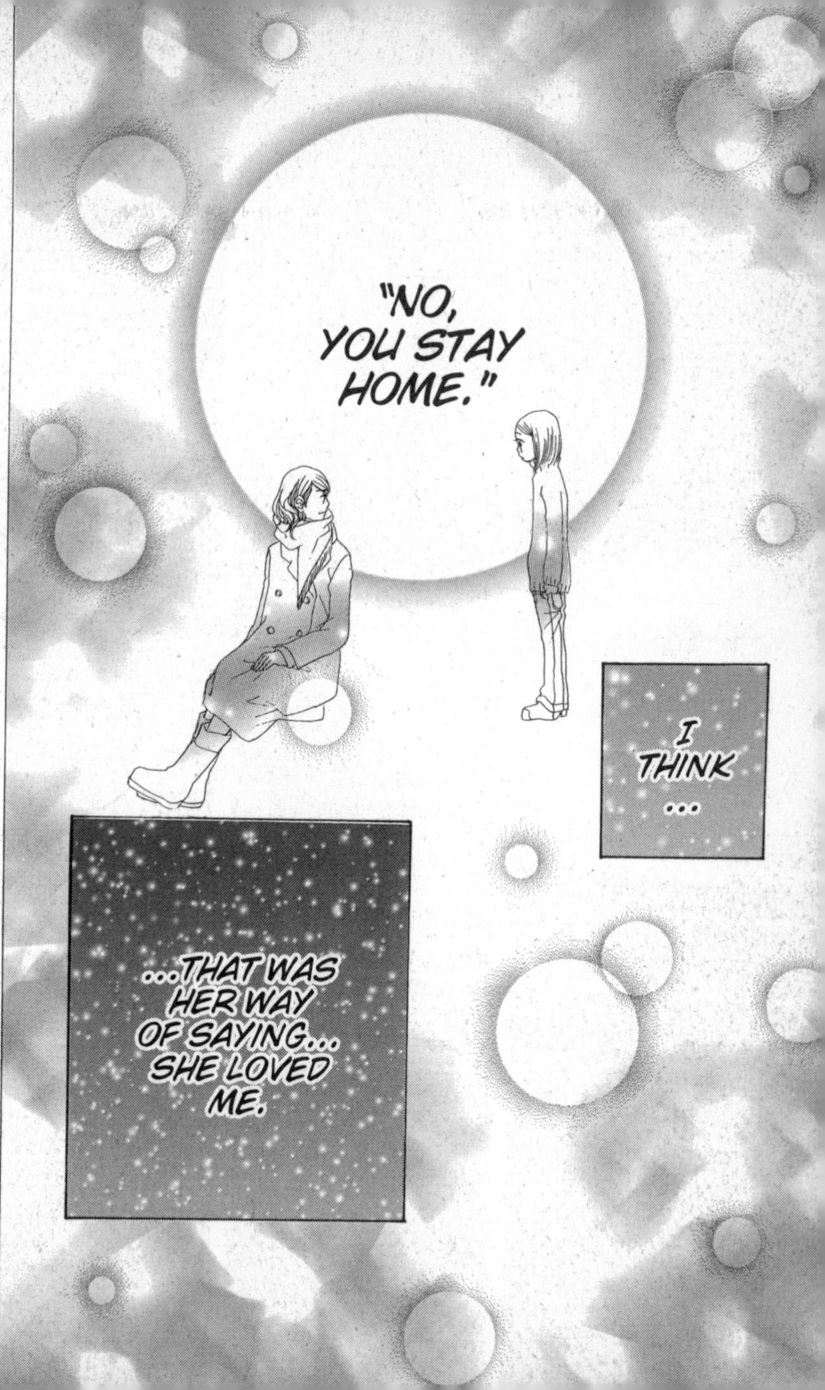
"NO, YOU STAY HOME."
I THINK...
...THAT WAS HER WAY OF SAYING... SHE LOVED ME.

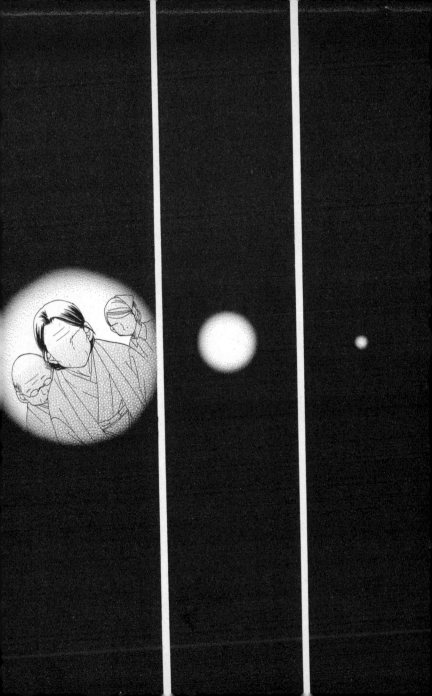

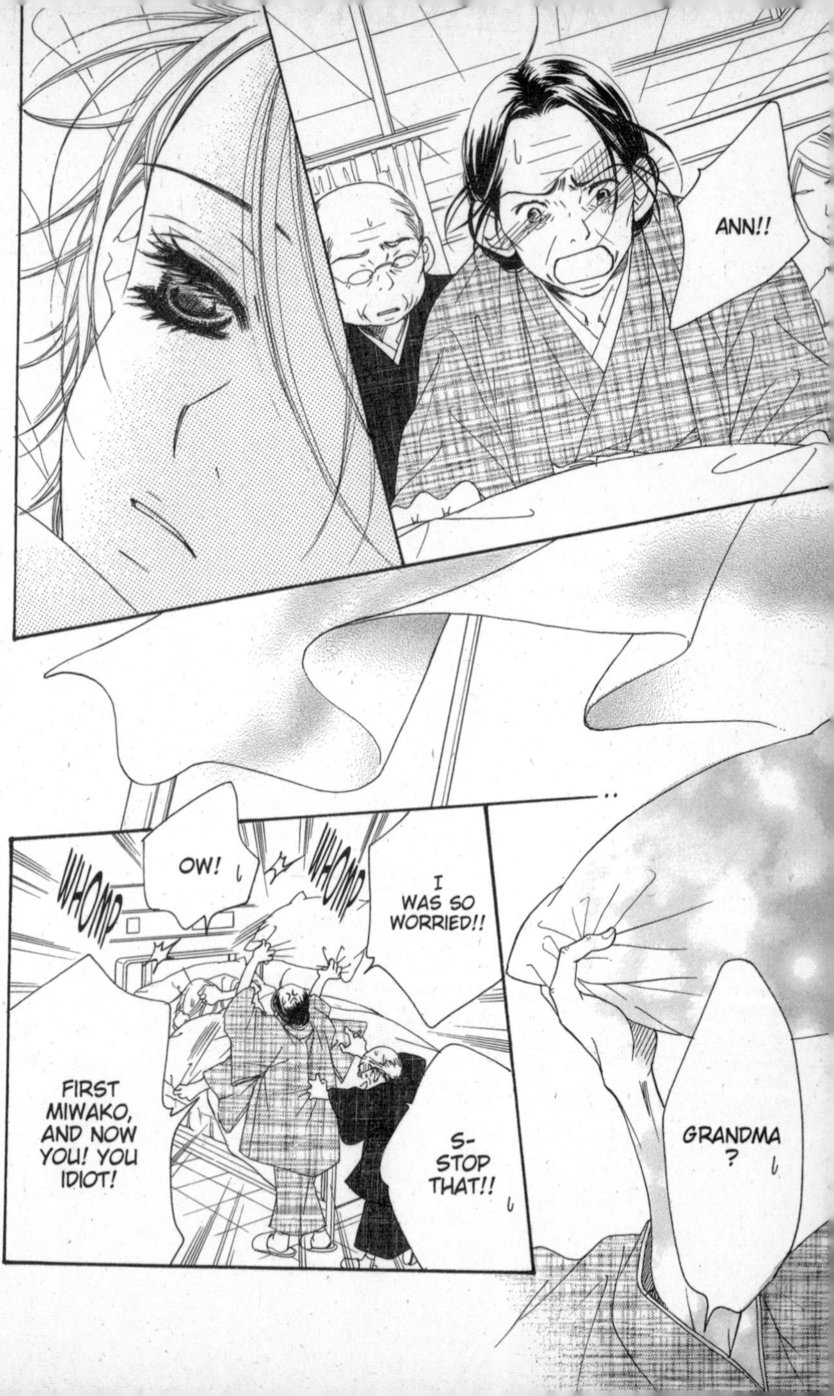
ANN!!
GRANDMA?
WHOMP
I WAS SO WORRIED!!
OW!
WHOMP
S-STOP THAT!!
FIRST MIWAKO, AND NOW YOU! YOU IDIOT!

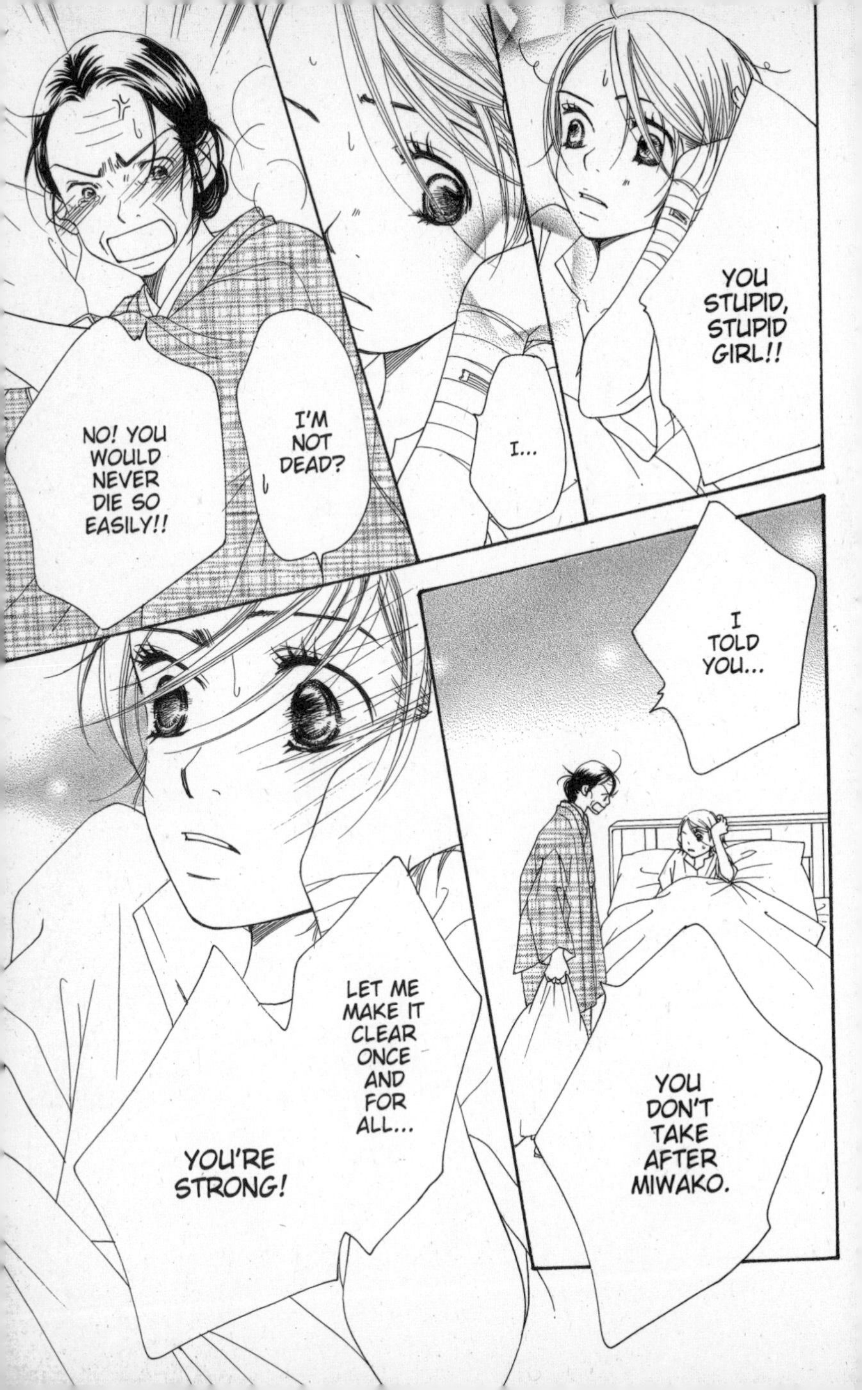
YOU STUPID, STUPID GIRL!!
I...
I'M NOT DEAD?
NO! YOU WOULD NEVER DIE SO EASILY!!
I TOLD YOU...
YOU DON'T TAKE AFTER MIWAKO.
LET ME MAKE IT CLEAR ONCE AND FOR ALL...
YOU'RE STRONG!

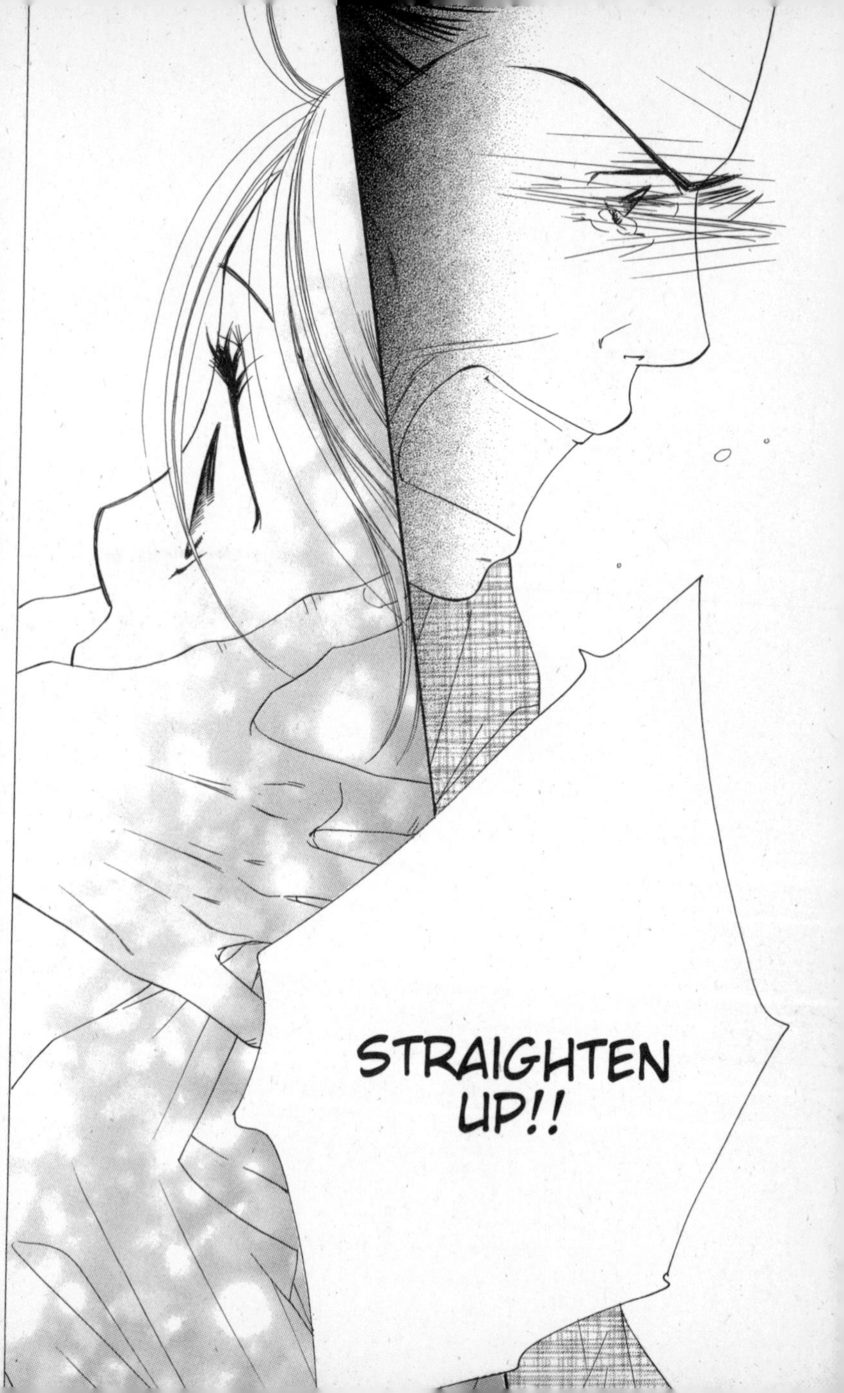
STRAIGHTEN UP!!

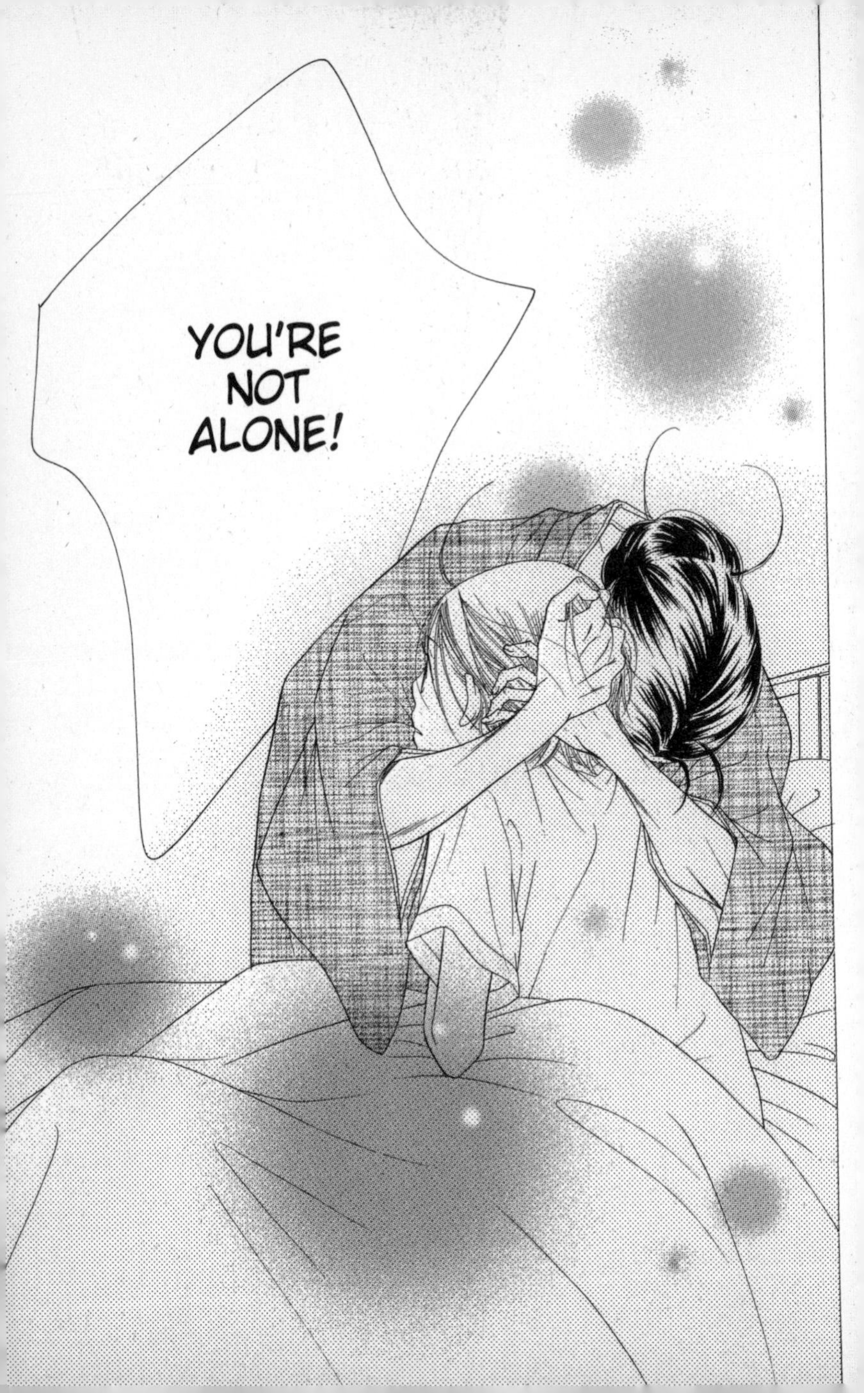
YOU'RE NOT ALONE!

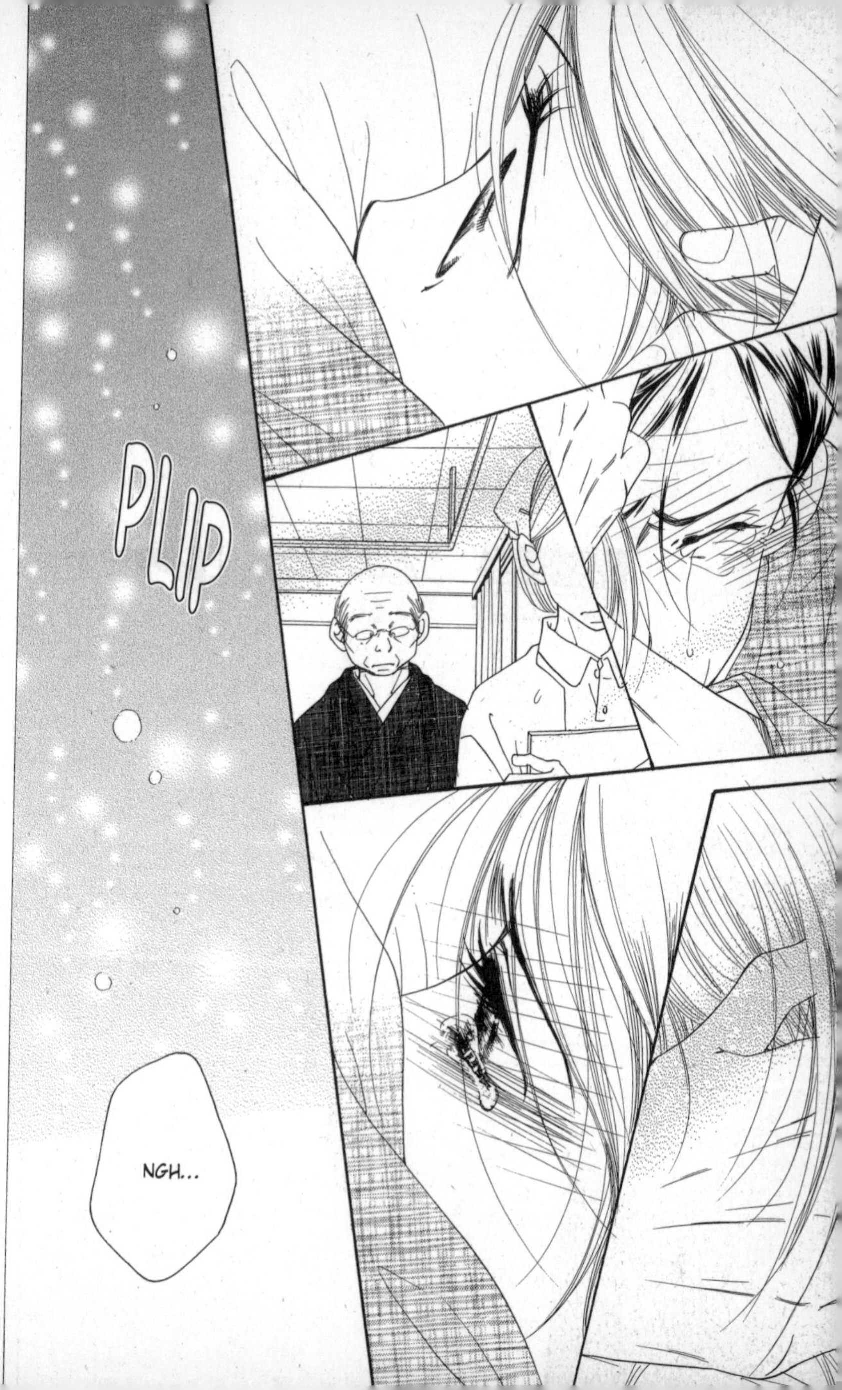
PLIP
NGH...

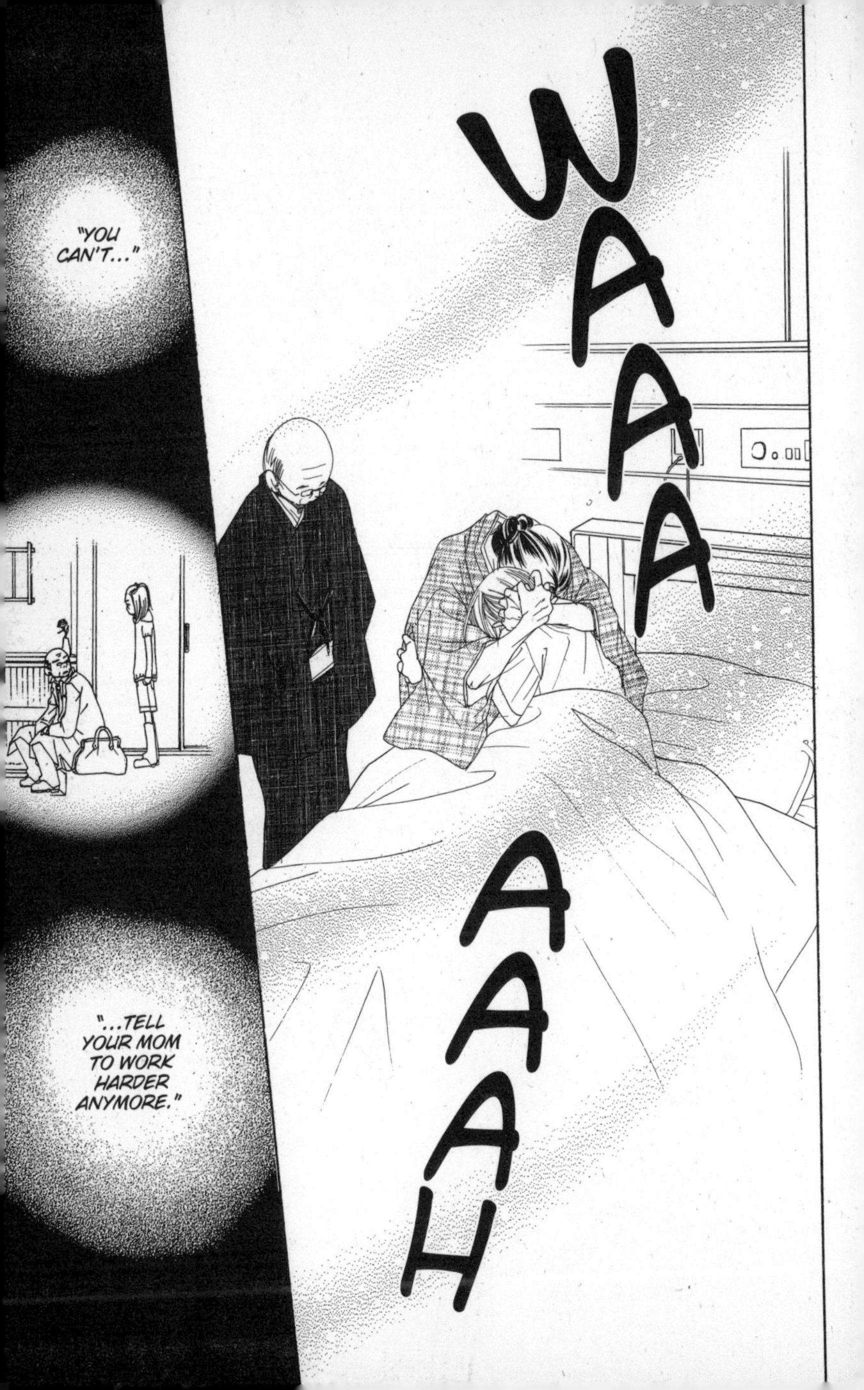
WAAAAAAH
"YOU CAN'T..."
"...TELL YOUR MOM TO WORK HARDER ANYMORE."

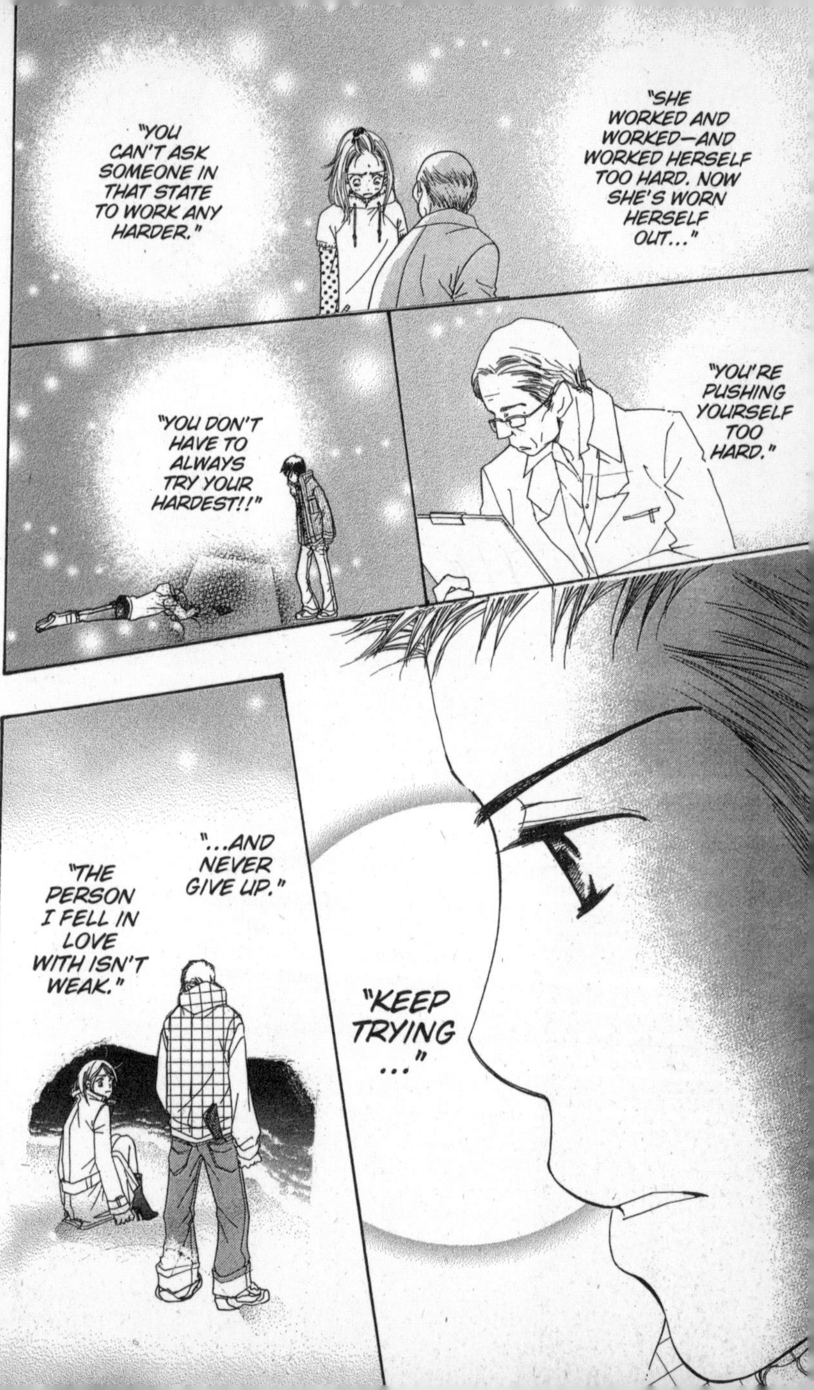
"SHE WORKED AND WORKED—AND WORKED HERSELF TOO HARD. NOW SHE'S WORN HERSELF OUT..."
"YOU CAN'T ASK SOMEONE IN THAT STATE TO WORK ANY HARDER."
"YOU'RE PUSHING YOURSELF TOO HARD."
"YOU DON'T HAVE TO ALWAYS TRY YOUR HARDEST!!"
"KEEP TRYING..."
"...AND NEVER GIVE UP."
"THE PERSON I FELL IN LOVE WITH ISN'T WEAK."

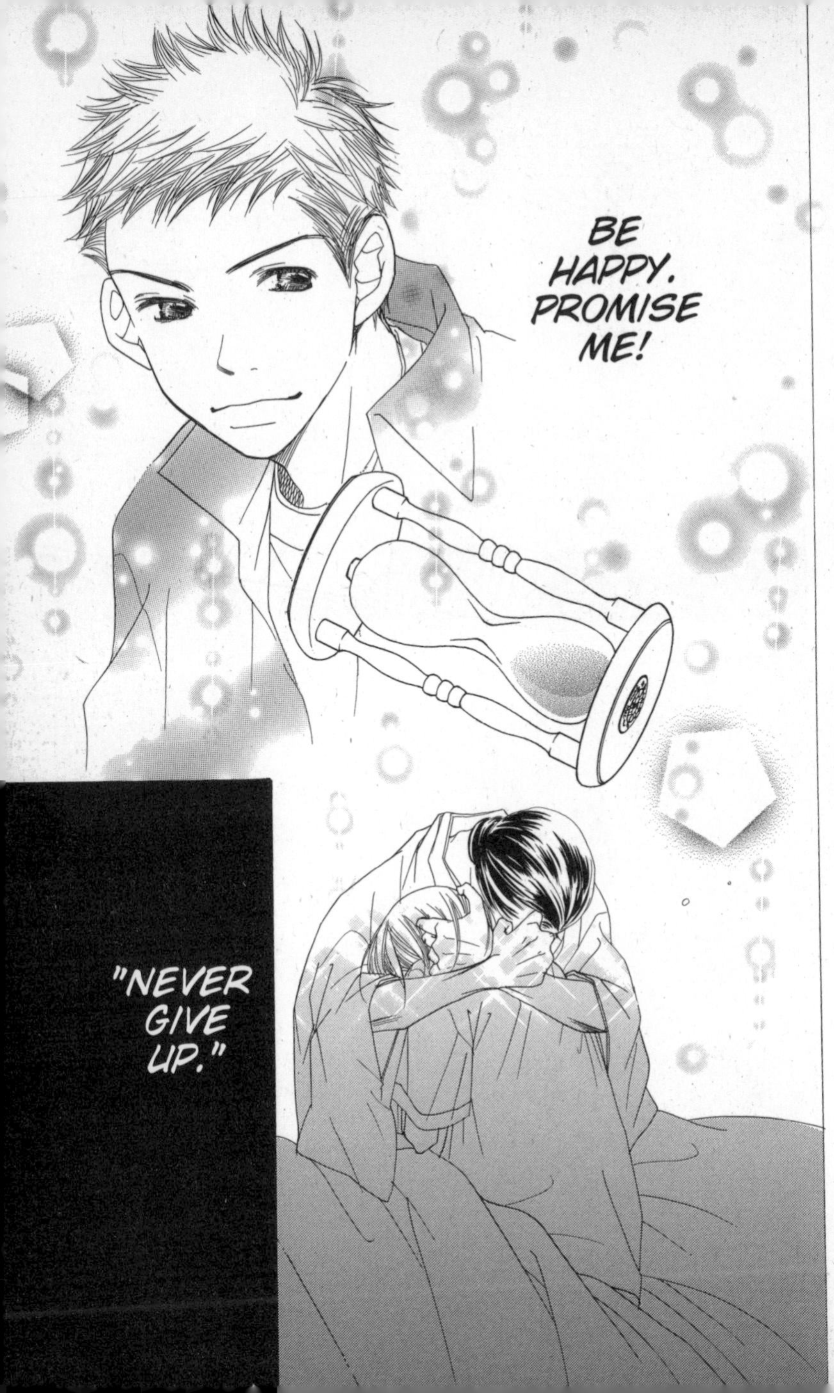
BE HAPPY. PROMISE ME!
"NEVER GIVE UP."

I
WON'T
GIVE
UP.

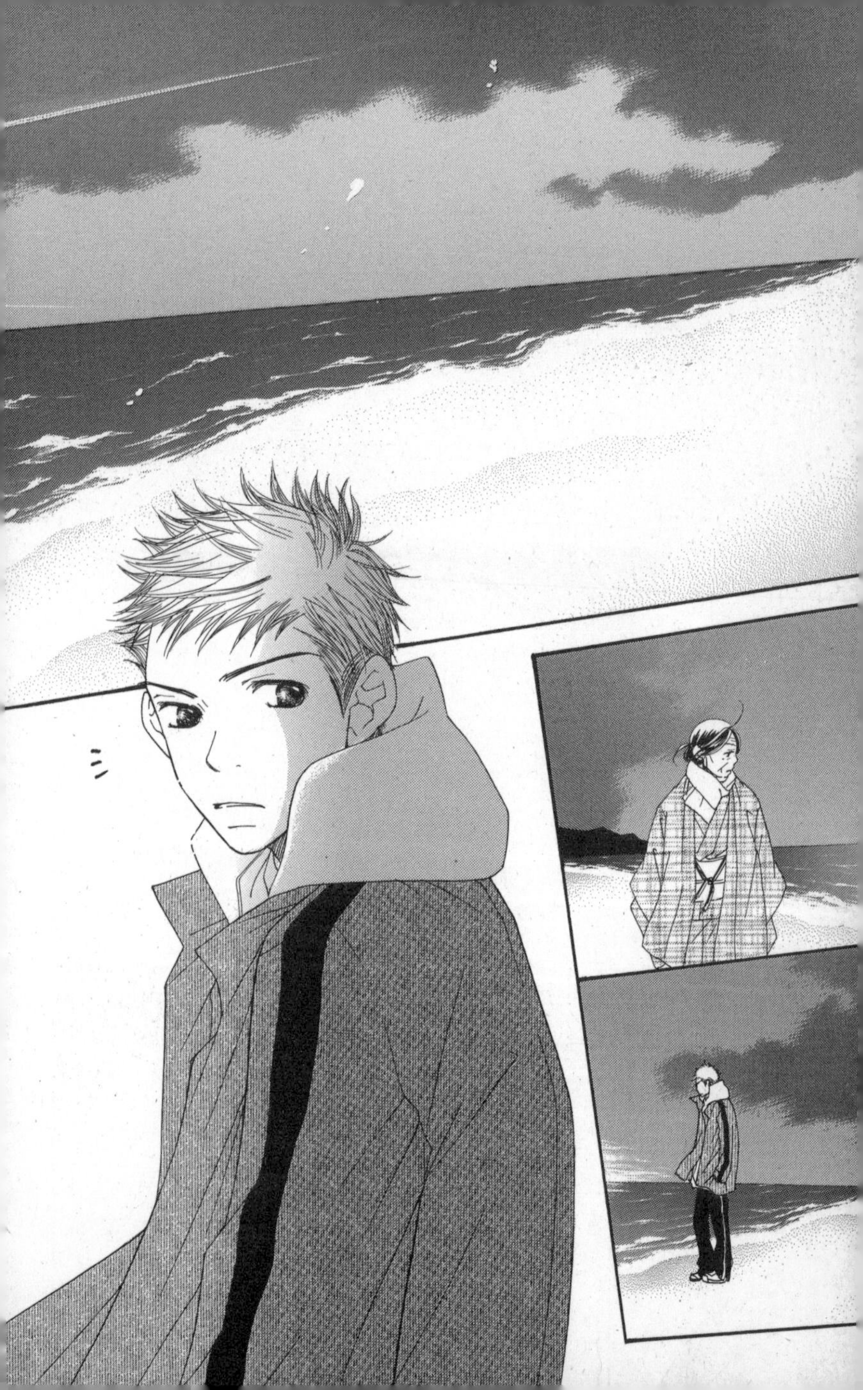

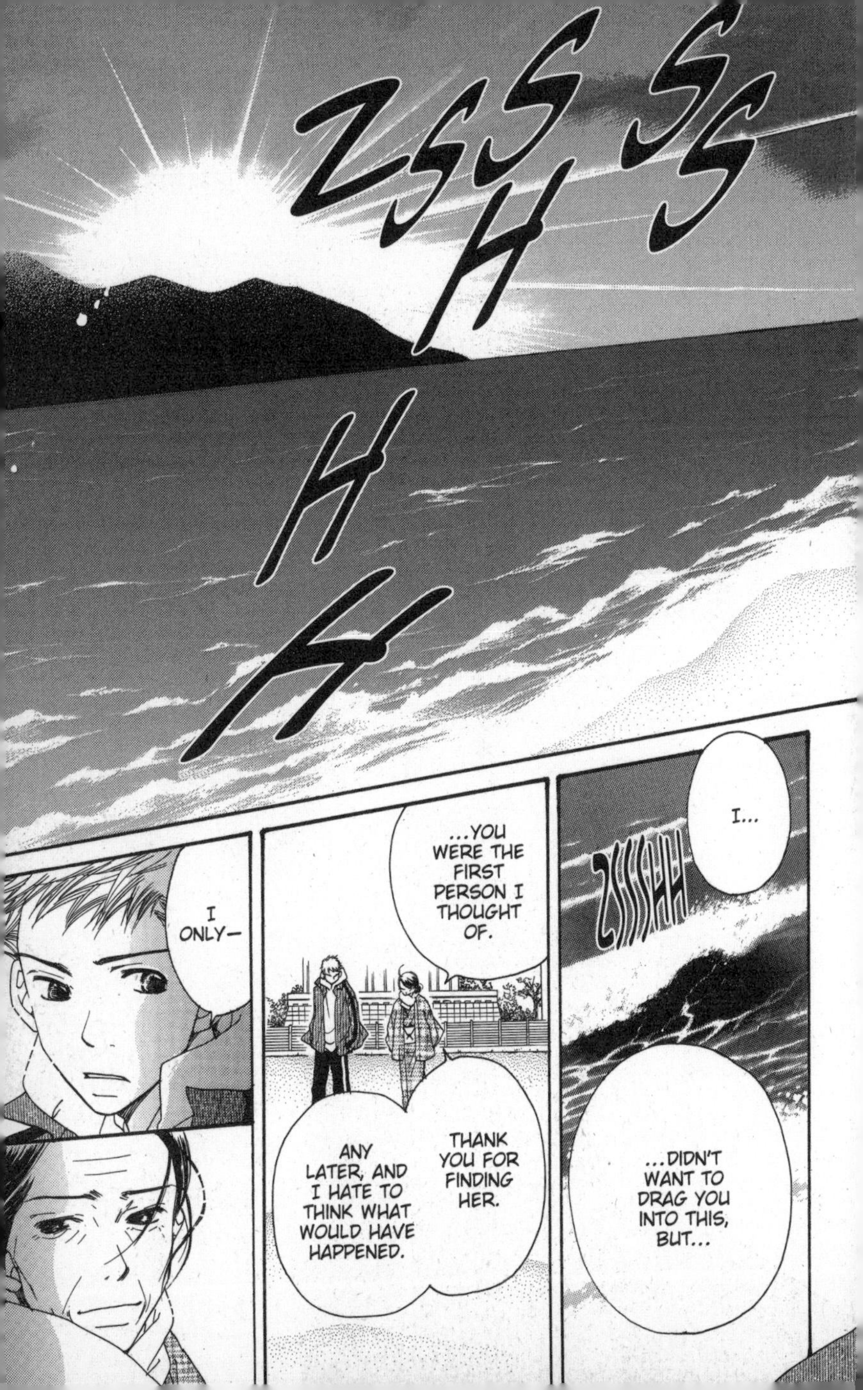
I...
...DIDN'T WANT TO DRAG YOU INTO THIS, BUT...
...YOU WERE THE FIRST PERSON I THOUGHT OF.
THANK YOU FOR FINDING HER.
ANY LATER, AND I HATE TO THINK WHAT WOULD HAVE HAPPENED.
I ONLY—

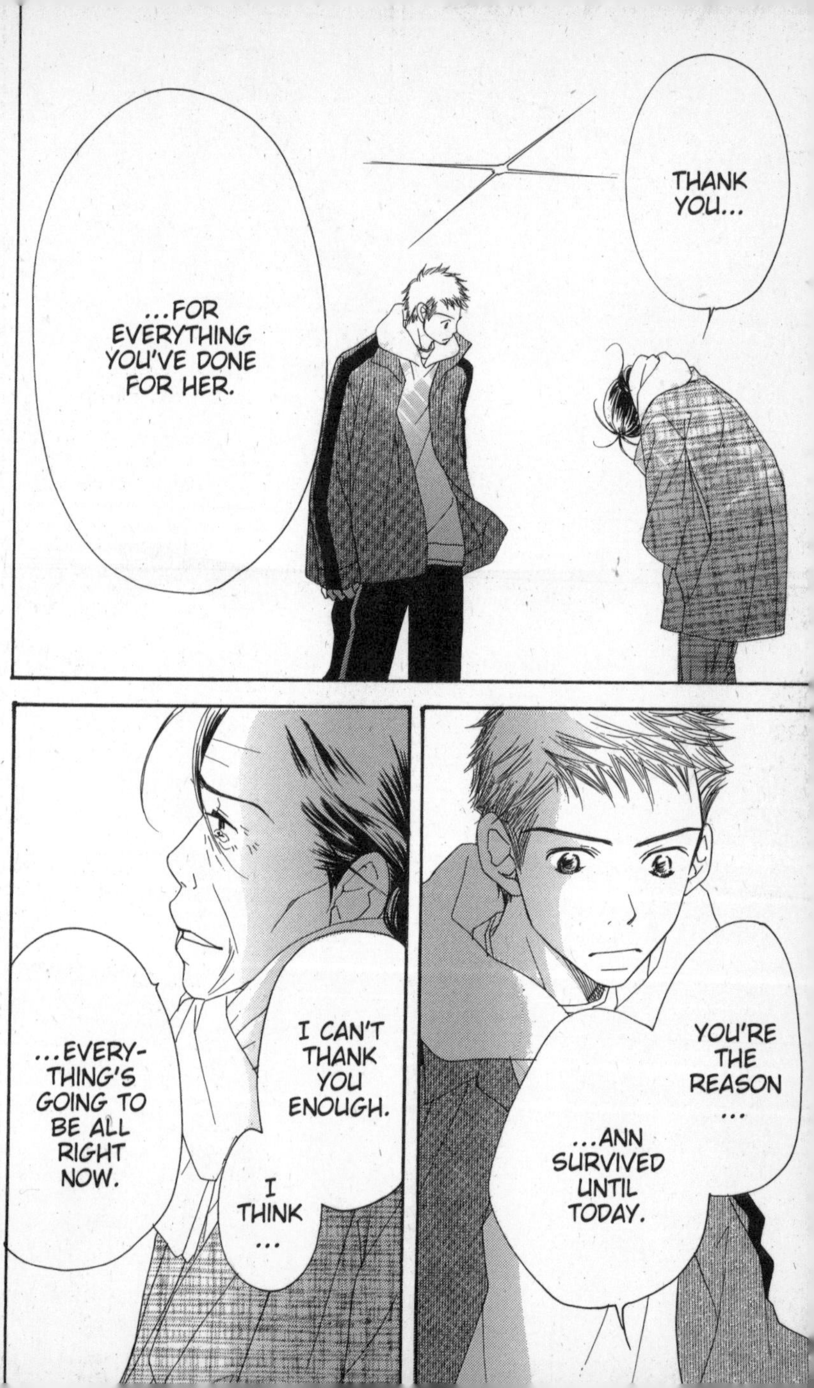
THANK YOU...
...FOR EVERYTHING YOU'VE DONE FOR HER.
YOU'RE THE REASON ...
...ANN SURVIVED UNTIL TODAY.
I CAN'T THANK YOU ENOUGH.
I THINK ...
...EVERY-THING'S GOING TO BE ALL RIGHT NOW.

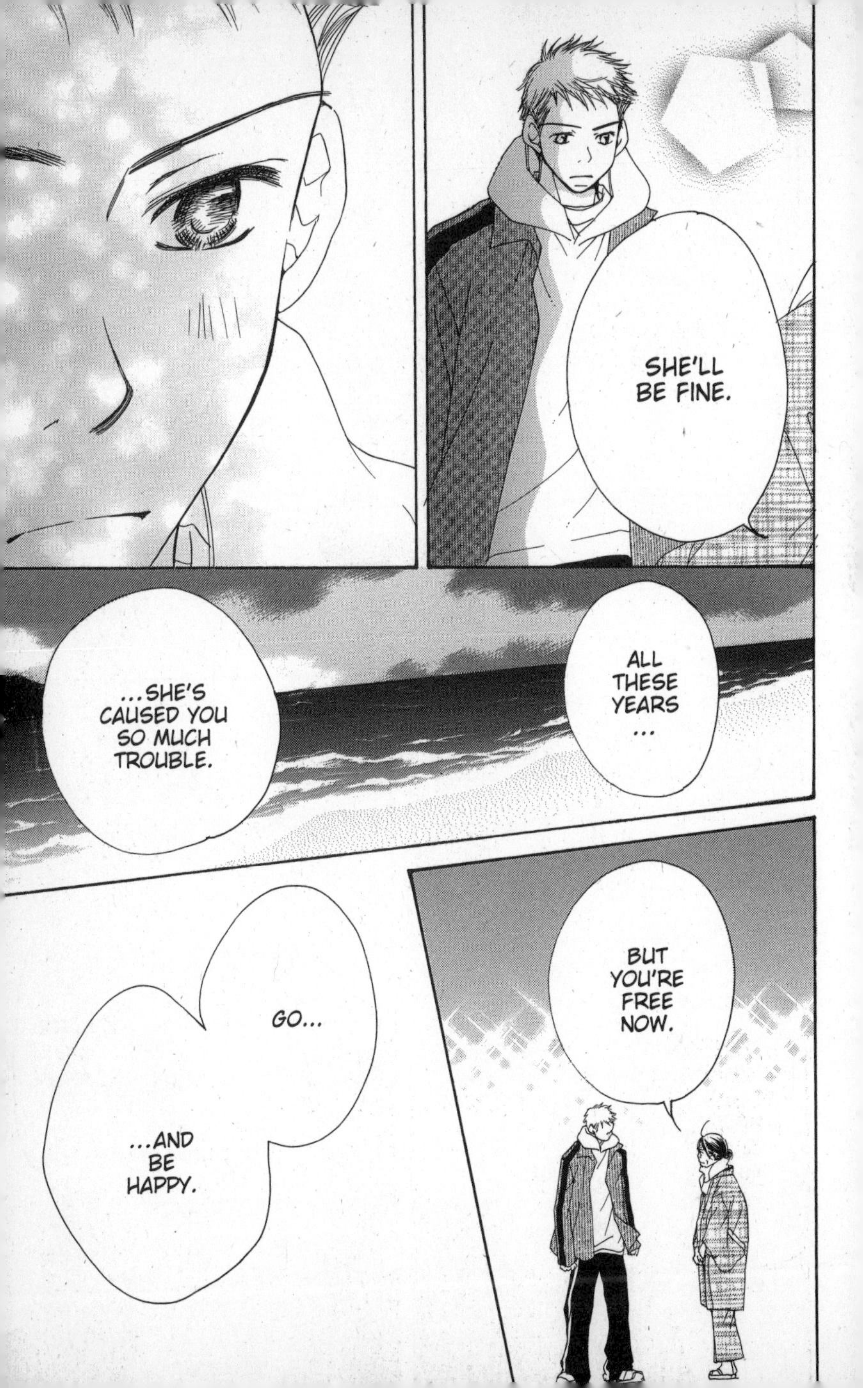
SHE'LL BE FINE.
ALL THESE YEARS ...
...SHE'S CAUSED YOU SO MUCH TROUBLE.
BUT YOU'RE FREE NOW.
GO...
...AND BE HAPPY.

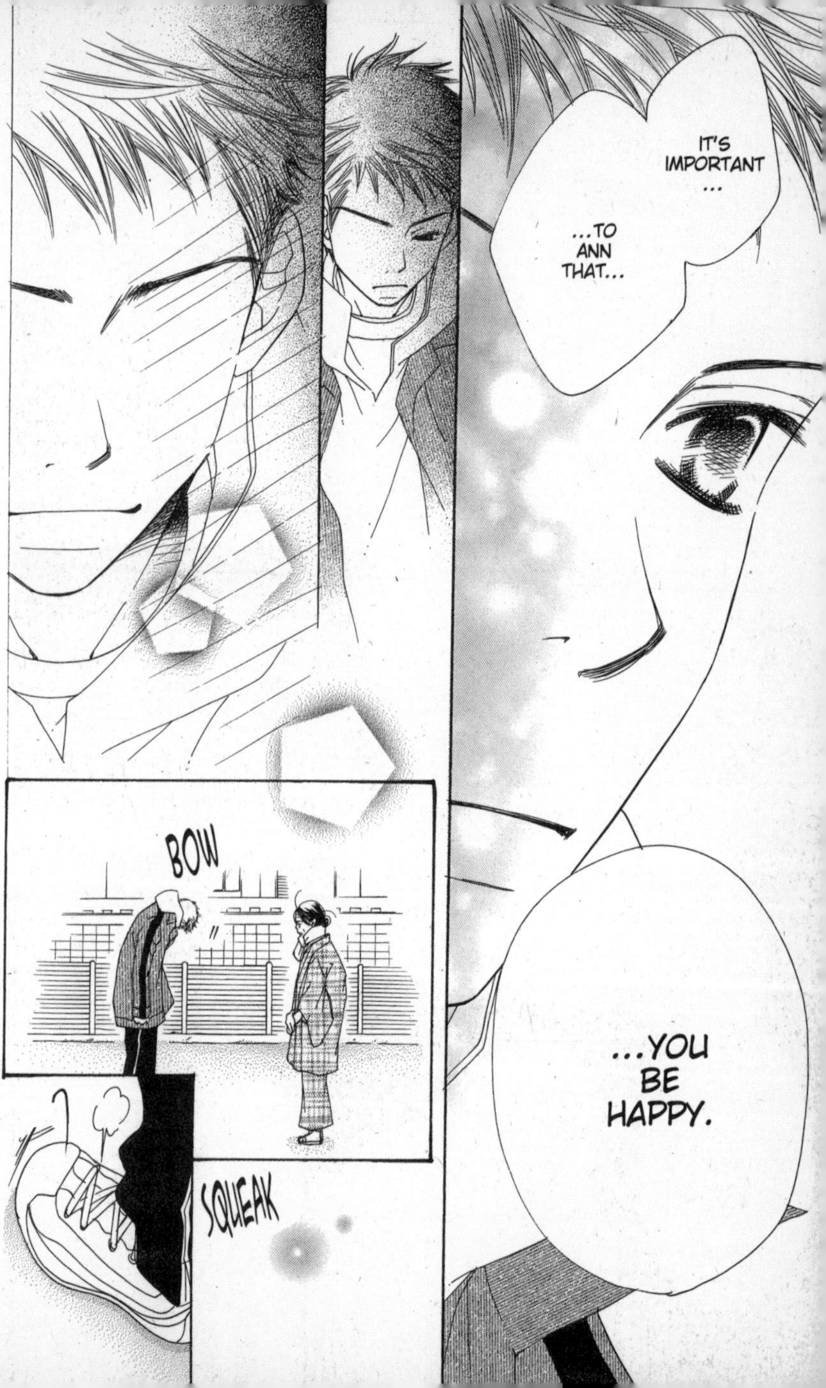
IT'S IMPORTANT ...
...TO ANN THAT...
...YOU BE HAPPY.
BOW
SQUEAK

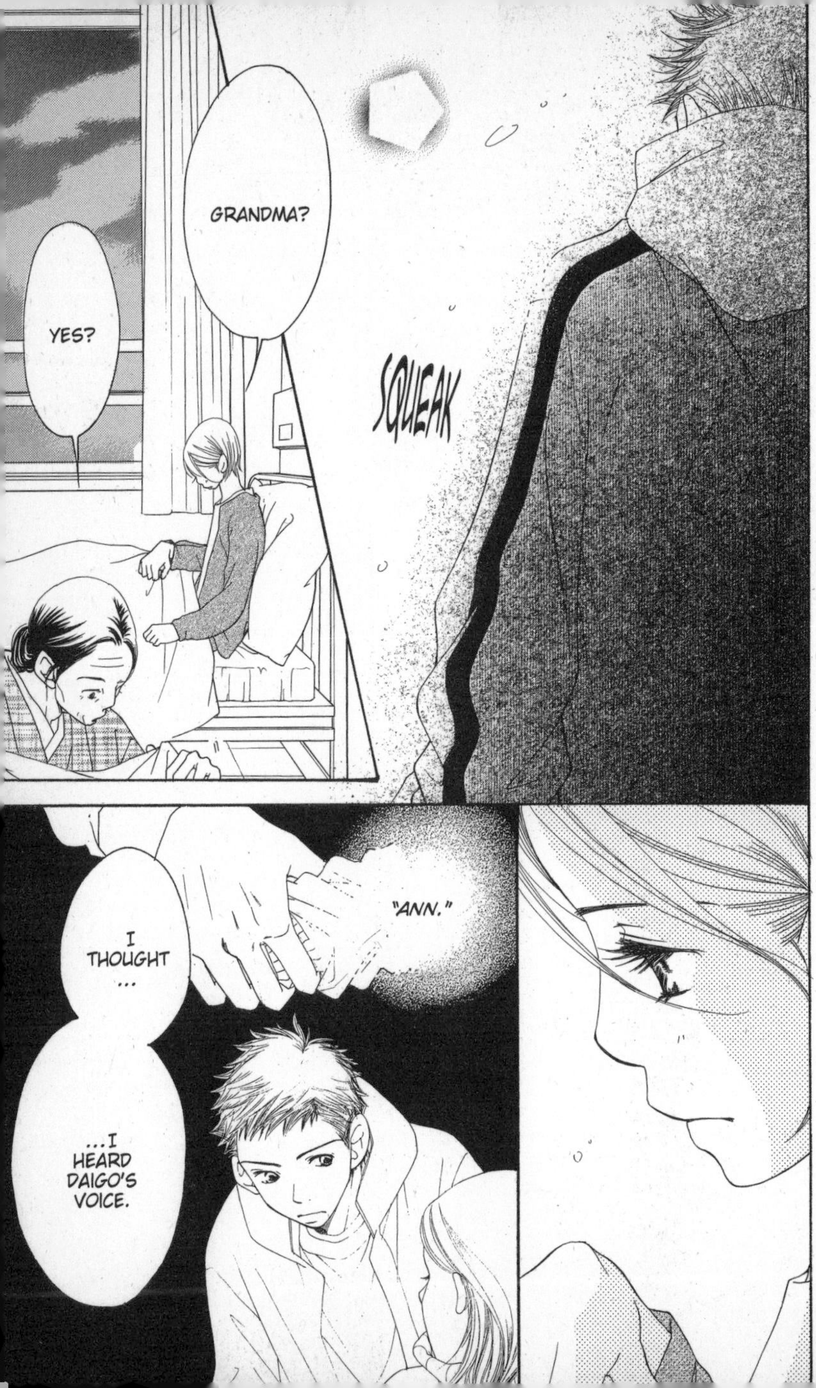
SQUEAK
GRANDMA?
YES?
"ANN."
I THOUGHT ...
...I HEARD DAIGO'S VOICE.

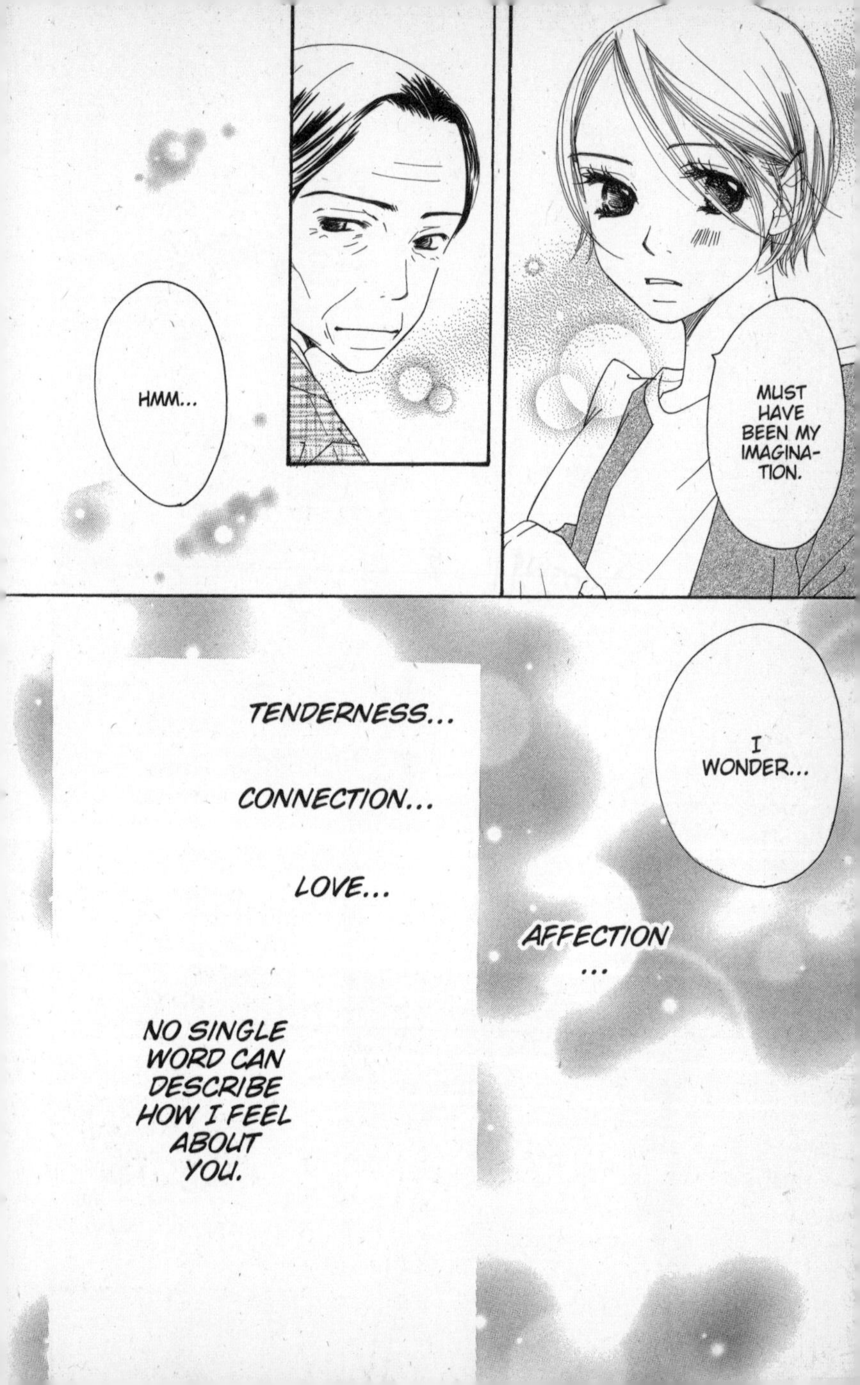
MUST HAVE BEEN MY IMAGINATION.
HMM...
I WONDER...
TENDERNESS...
CONNECTION...
LOVE...
AFFECTION ...
NO SINGLE WORD CAN DESCRIBE HOW I FEEL ABOUT YOU.

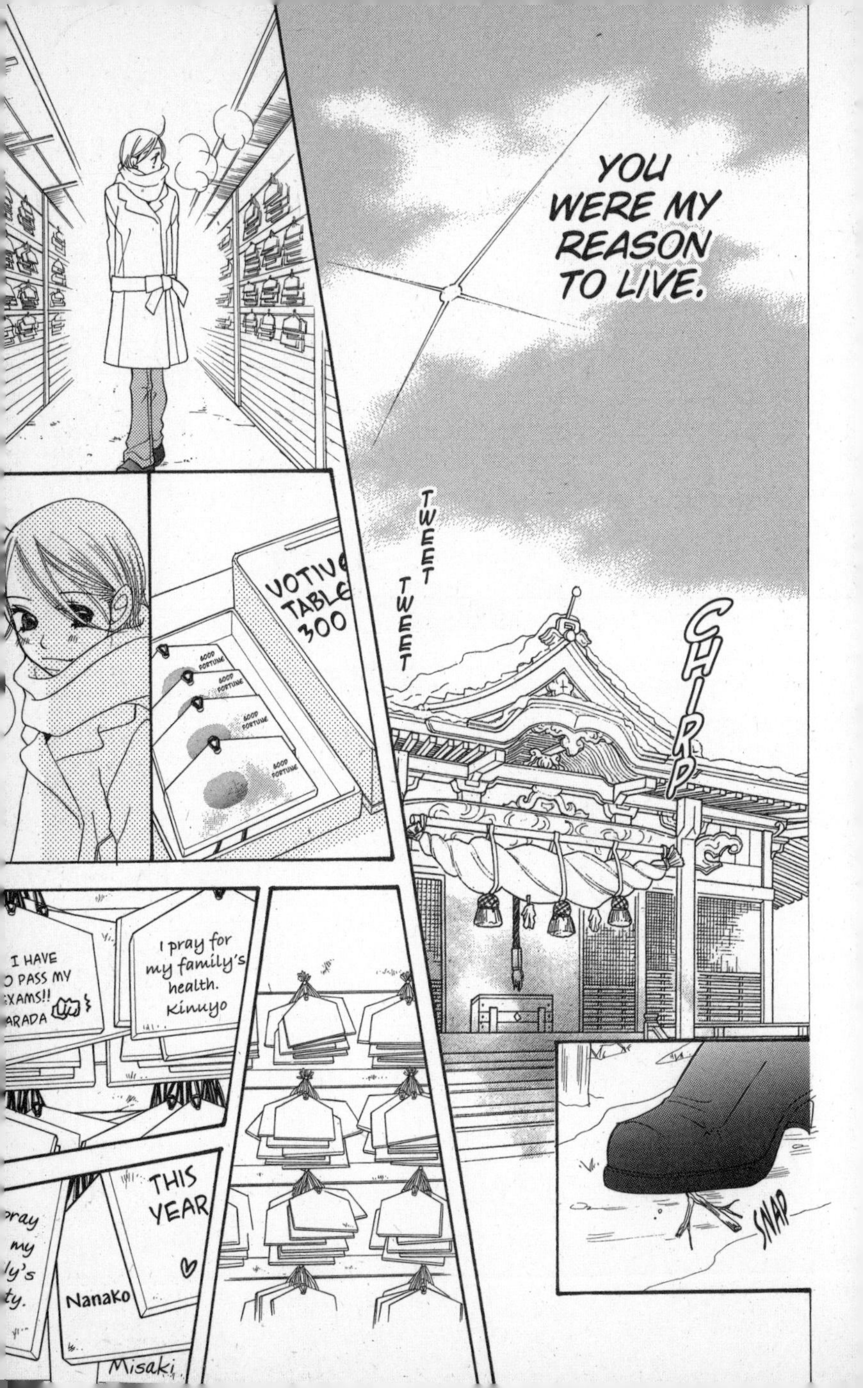
YOU WERE MY REASON TO LIVE.
TWEET TWEET
CHIRP
SNAP
VOTIVE TABLE 300
GOOD FORTUNE
GOOD FORTUNE
GOOD FORTUNE
GOOD FORTUNE
I pray for my family's health. Kinuyo
I HAVE
O PASS MY
EXAMS!!
ARADA
THIS YEAR
Nanako
Misaki

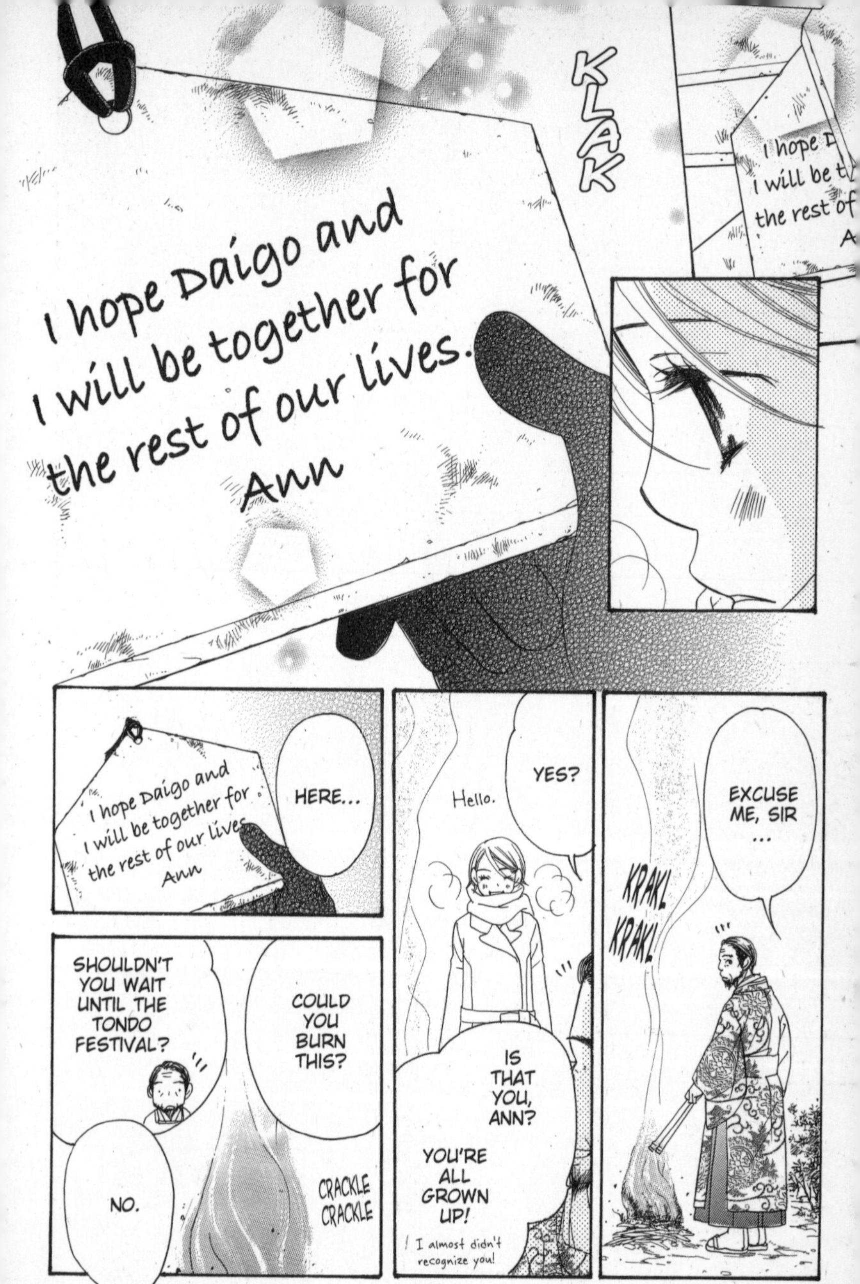
KLAK
I hope Daigo and I will be together for the rest of our lives.
Ann
EXCUSE ME, SIR ...
KRAKL KRAKL
YES?
Hello.
IS THAT YOU, ANN?
YOU'RE ALL GROWN UP!
I almost didn't recognize you!
HERE...
I hope Daigo and I will be together for the rest of our lives.
Ann
COULD YOU BURN THIS?
SHOULDN'T YOU WAIT UNTIL THE TONDO FESTIVAL?
NO.
CRACKLE CRACKLE

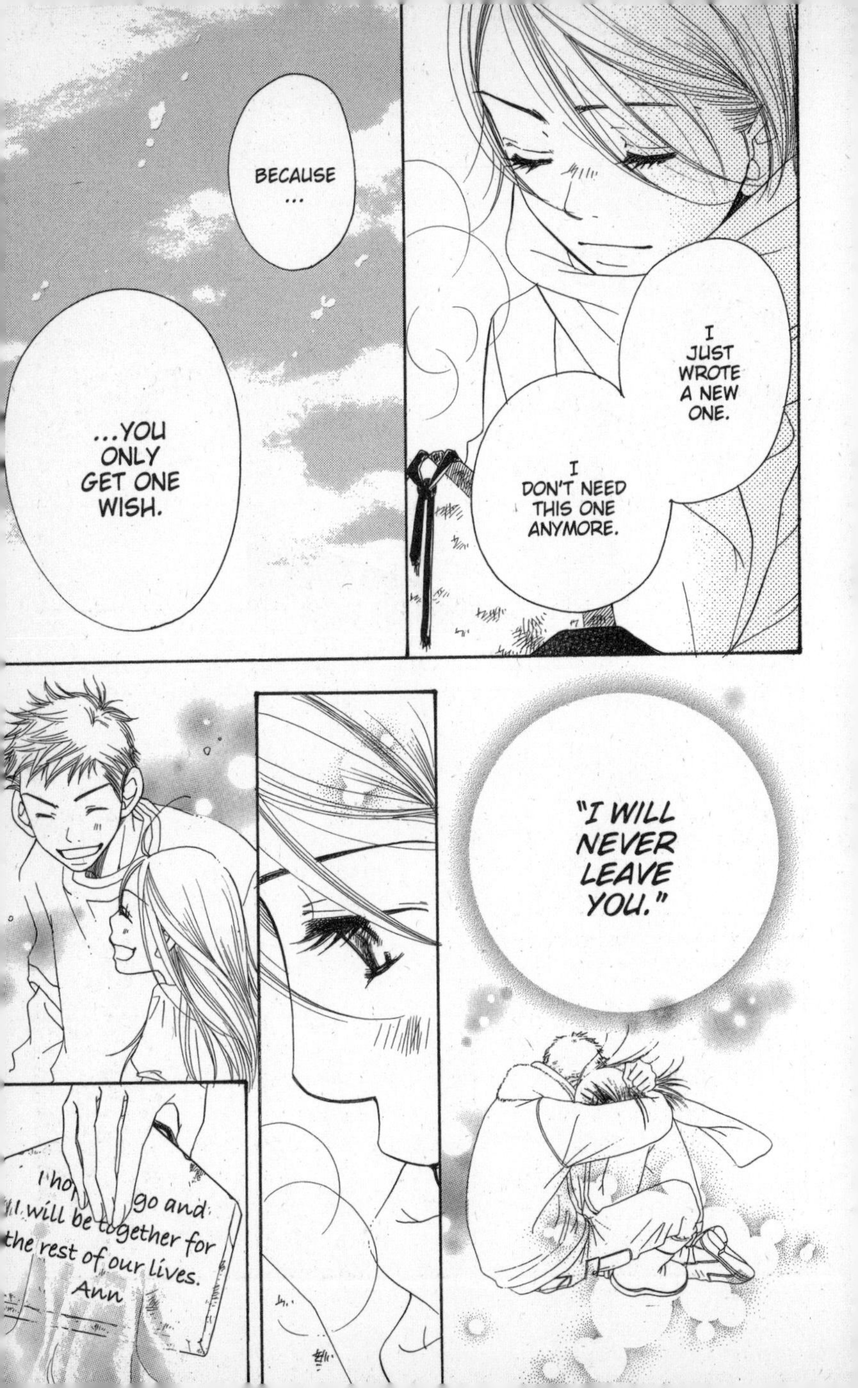
I JUST WROTE A NEW ONE.
I DON'T NEED THIS ONE ANYMORE.
BECAUSE ...
...YOU ONLY GET ONE WISH.
"I WILL NEVER LEAVE YOU."
go and
will be together for
the rest of our lives.
Ann

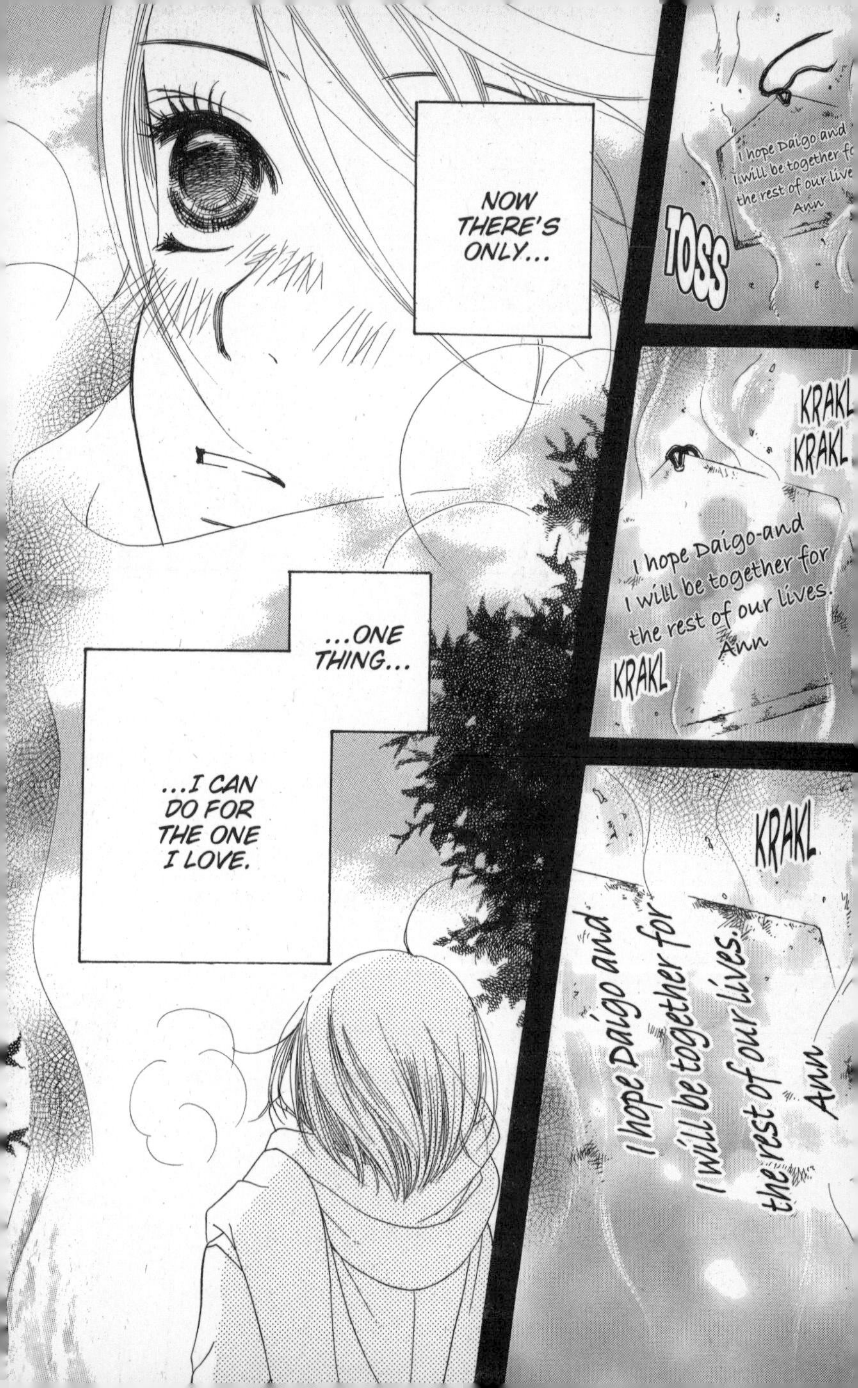
I hope Daigo and I will be together fo the rest of our live Ann
TOSS
KRAKL KRAKL
I hope Daigo-and I will be together for the rest of our lives. Ann
KRAKL
KRAKL
I hope Daigo and I will be together for the rest of our lives. Ann
NOW THERE'S ONLY...
...ONE THING...
...I CAN DO FOR THE ONE I LOVE.

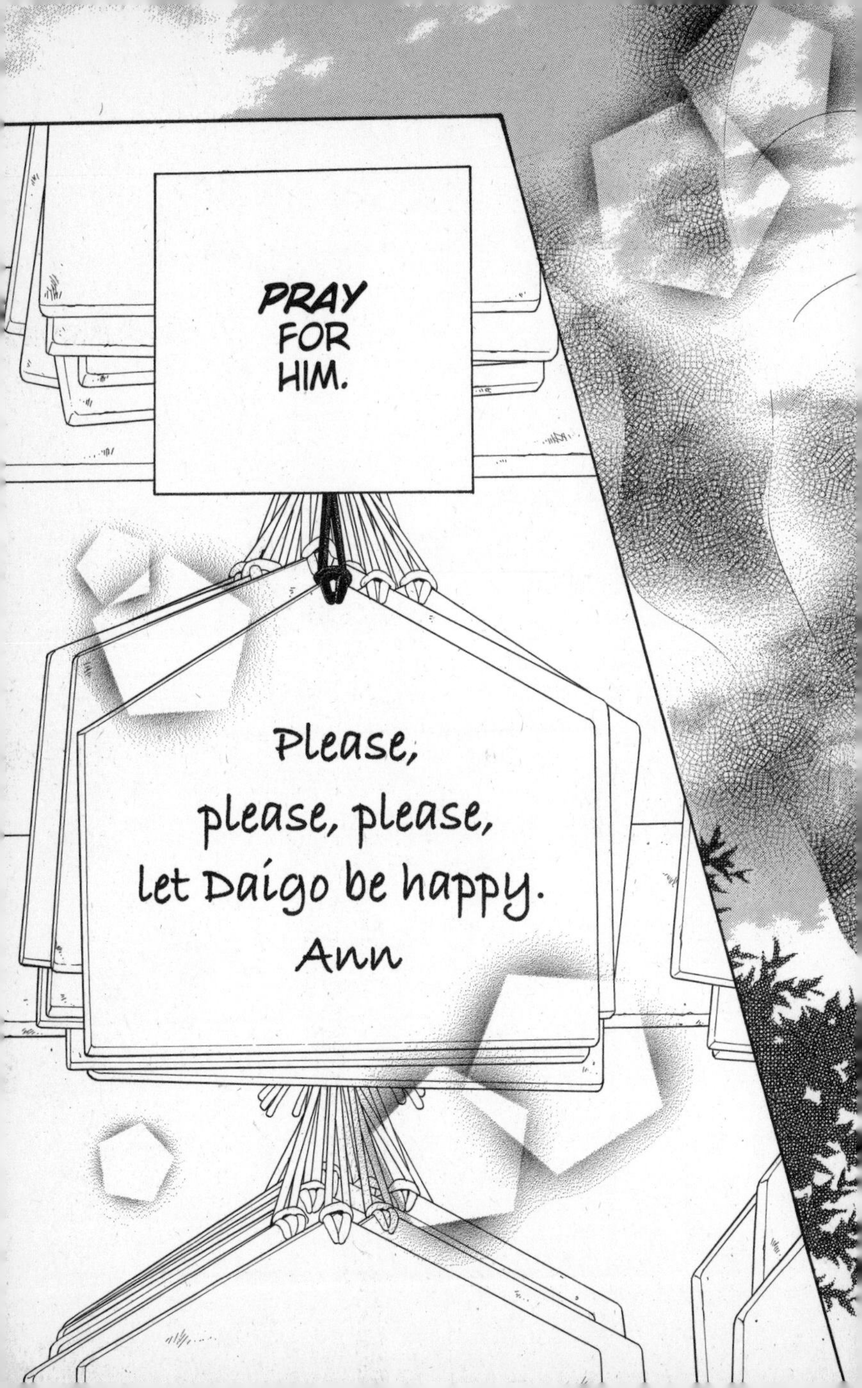
PRAY FOR HIM.
Please, please, please, let Daigo be happy. Ann

SAND CHRONICLES: EPILOGUE

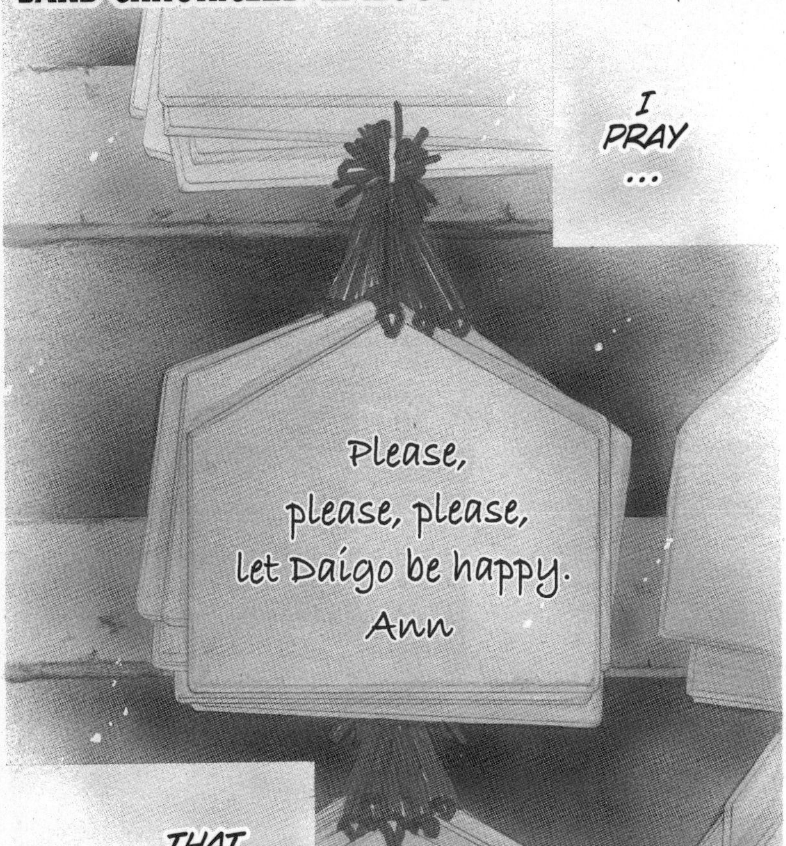

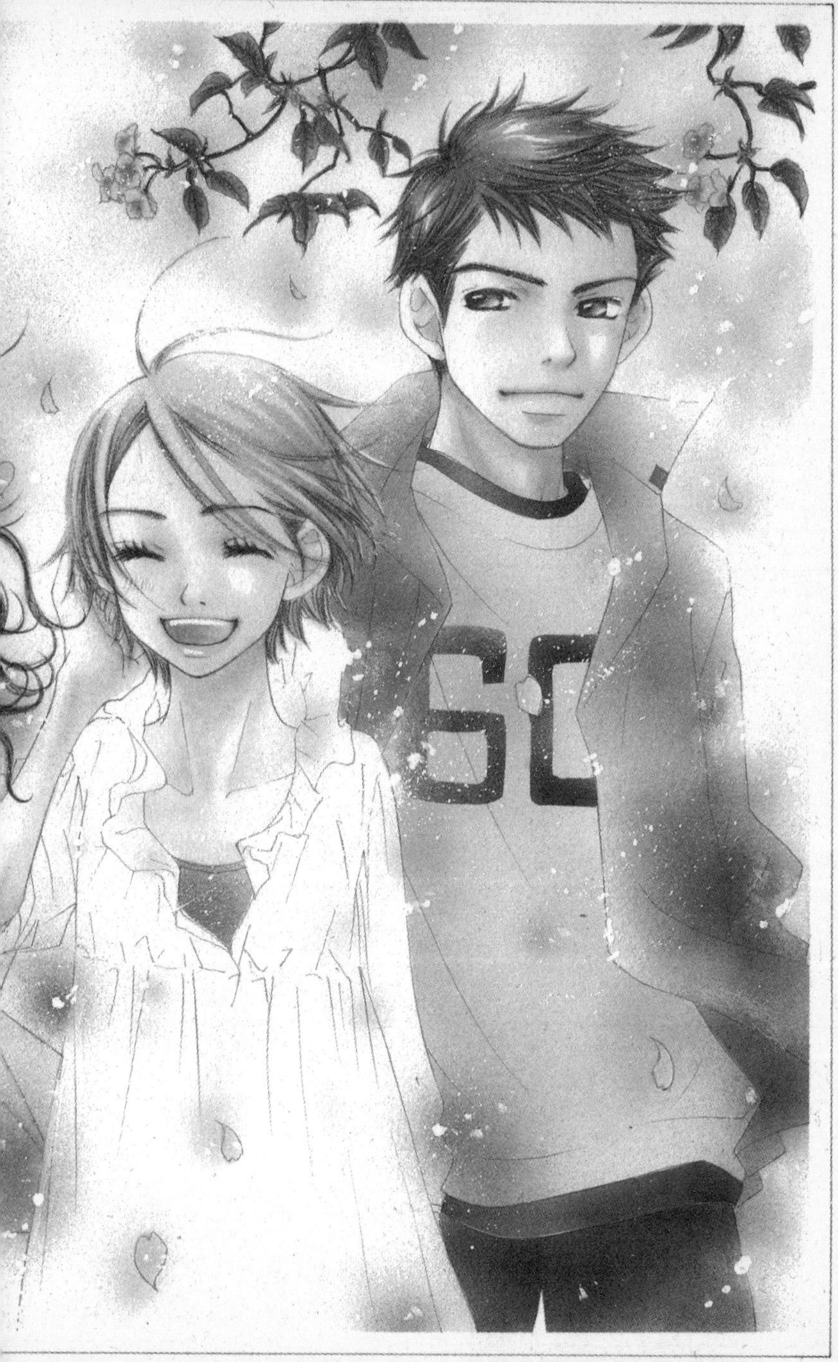

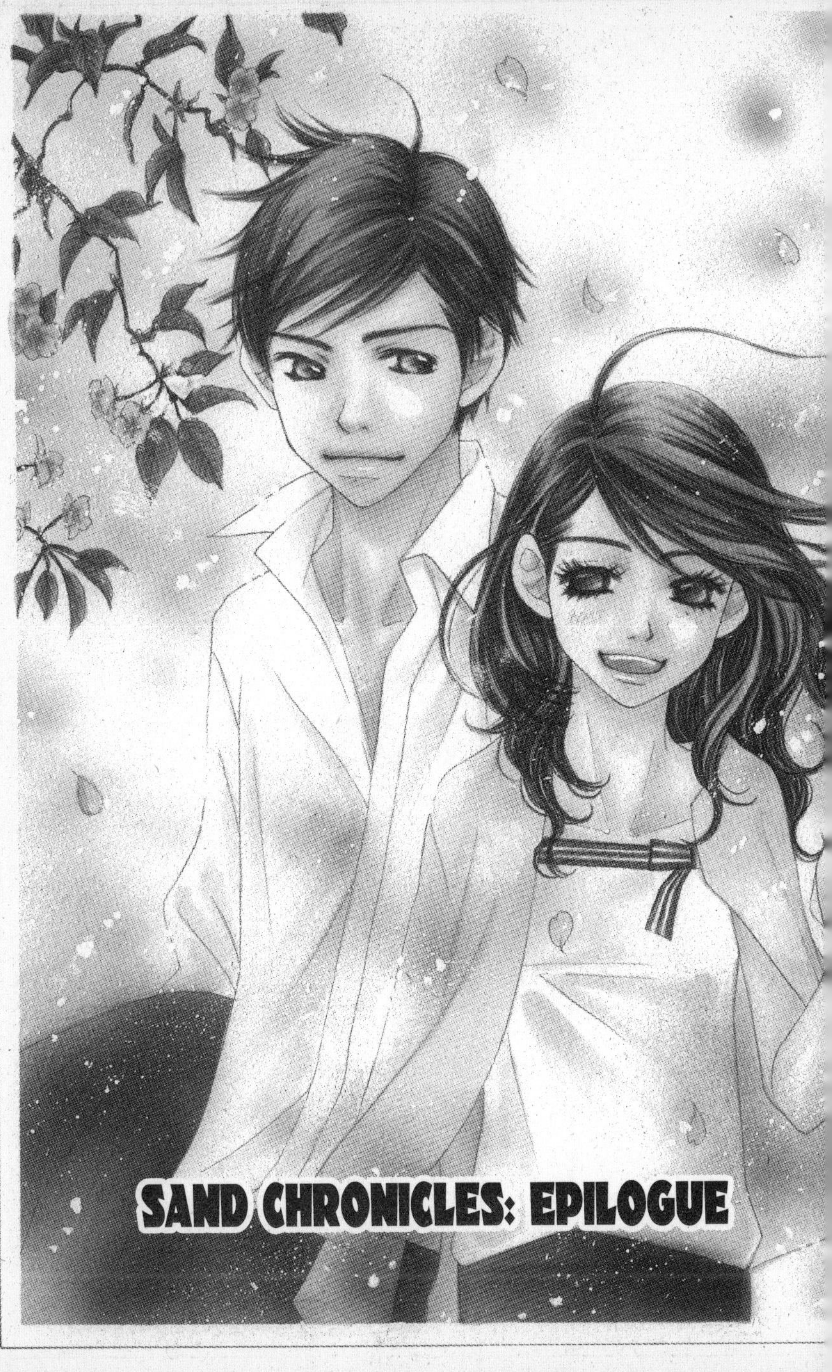
SAND CHRONICLES: EPILOGUE

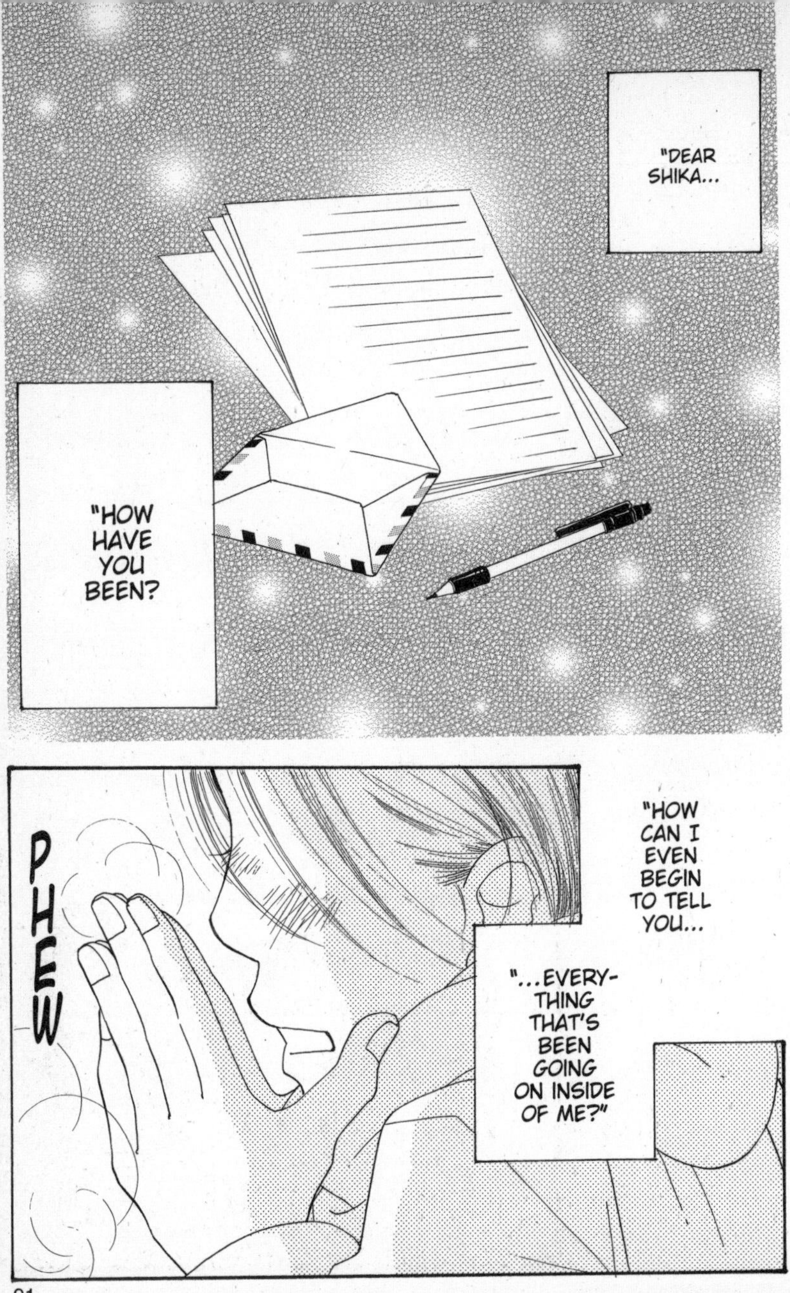
"DEAR SHIKA...
"HOW HAVE YOU BEEN?
"HOW CAN I EVEN BEGIN TO TELL YOU...
"...EVERY-THING THAT'S BEEN GOING ON INSIDE OF ME?"
PHEW

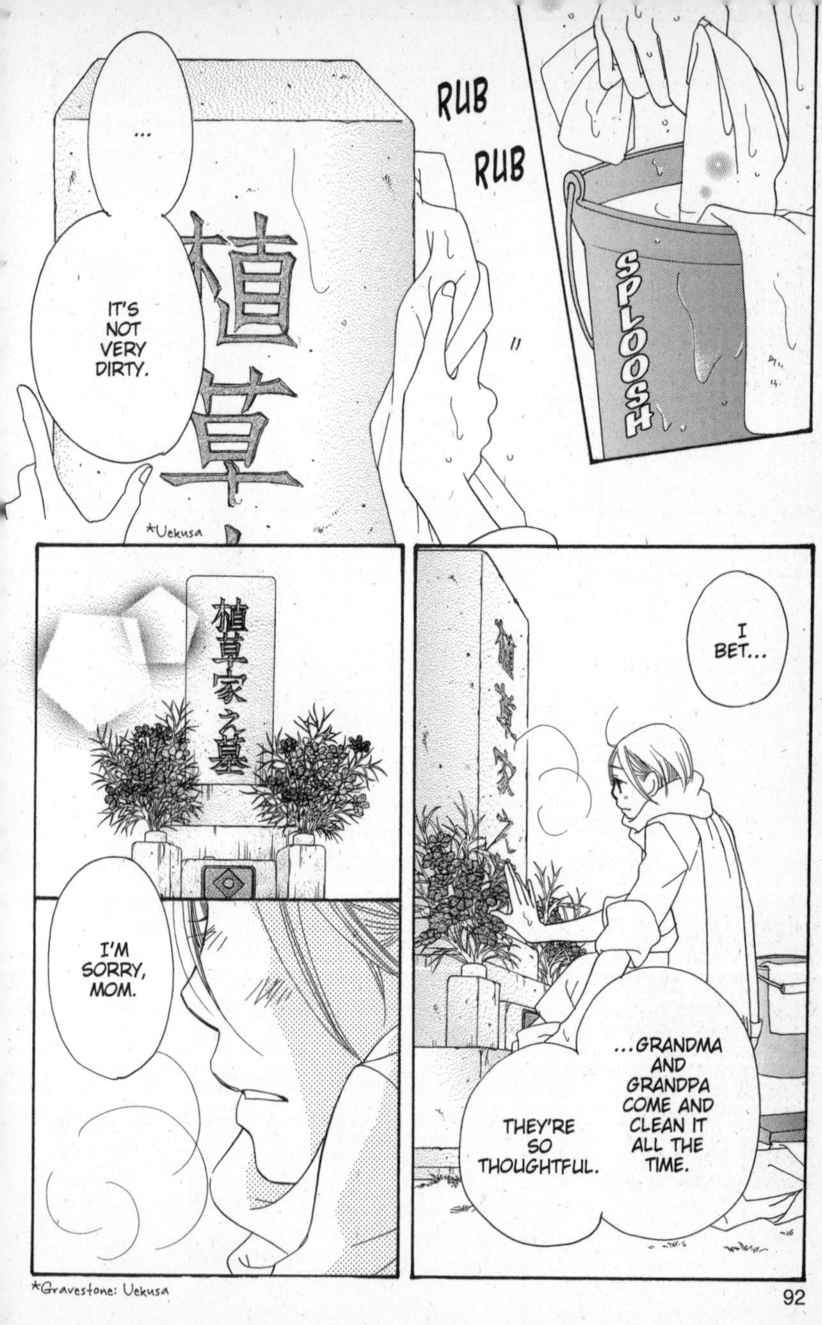
SPLOOSH
RUB
RUB
...
IT'S NOT VERY DIRTY.
植草
*Uekusa
I BET...
...GRANDMA AND GRANDPA COME AND CLEAN IT ALL THE TIME.
THEY'RE SO THOUGHTFUL.
植草家之墓
I'M SORRY, MOM.

*Gravestone: Uekusa

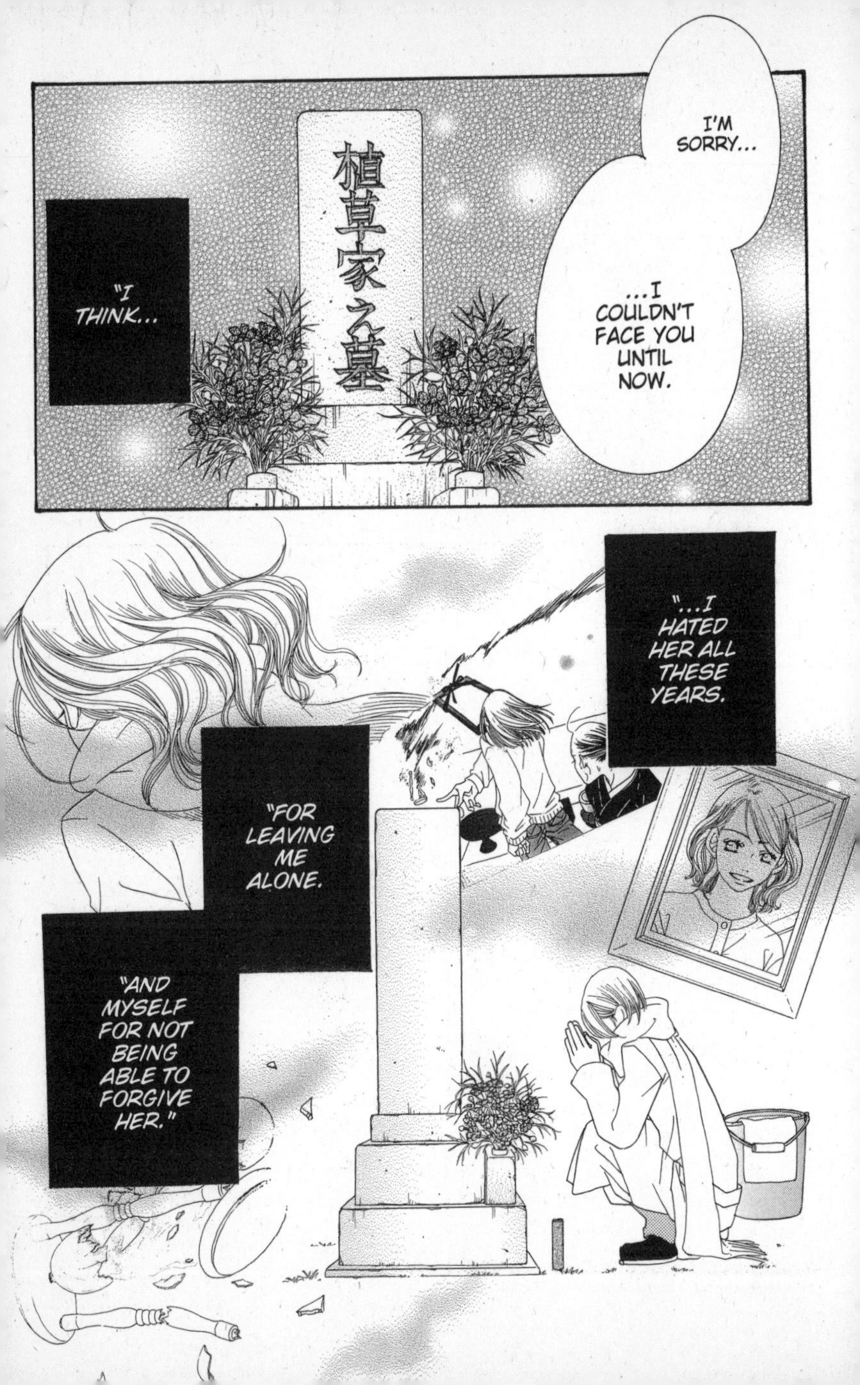
I'M SORRY...
...I COULDN'T FACE YOU UNTIL NOW.
植草家之墓
"I THINK...
"...I HATED HER ALL THESE YEARS.
"FOR LEAVING ME ALONE.
"AND MYSELF FOR NOT BEING ABLE TO FORGIVE HER."

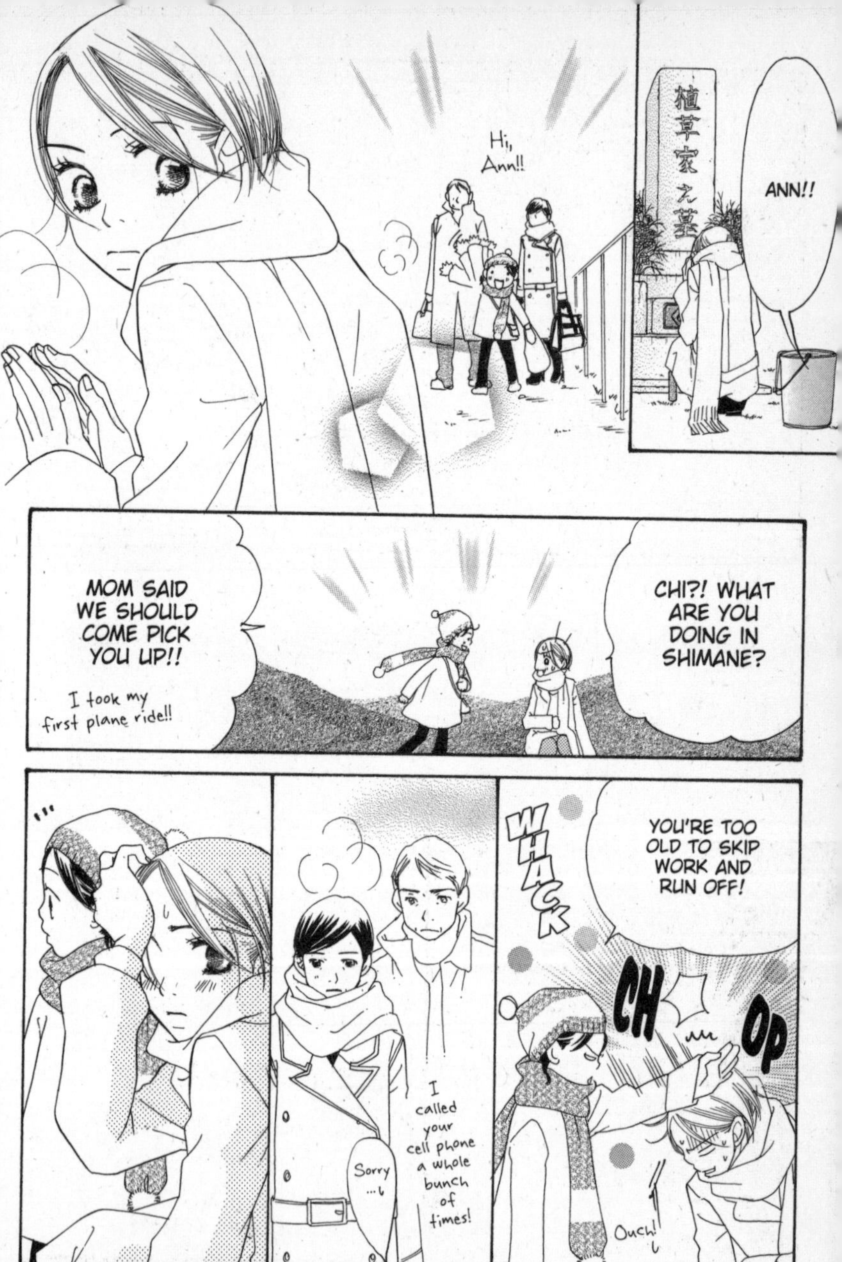
植草家之墓
ANN!!
Hi, Ann!!
CHI?! WHAT ARE YOU DOING IN SHIMANE?
MOM SAID WE SHOULD COME PICK YOU UP!!
I took my first plane ride!!
WHACK
YOU'RE TOO OLD TO SKIP WORK AND RUN OFF!
CH OP
Ouch!
I called your cell phone a whole bunch of times!
Sorry...
...

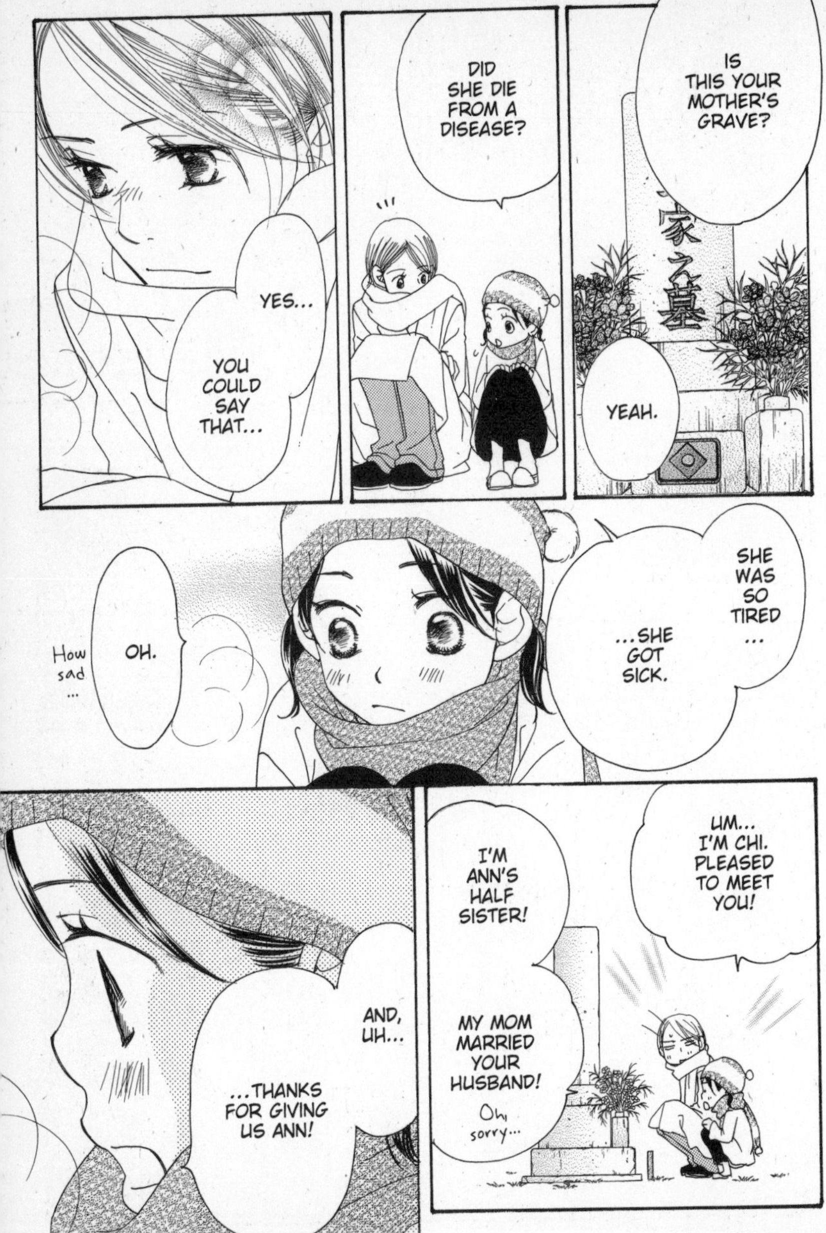
IS THIS YOUR MOTHER'S GRAVE?
YEAH.
DID SHE DIE FROM A DISEASE?
YES...
YOU COULD SAY THAT...
SHE WAS SO TIRED...
...SHE GOT SICK.
OH.
How sad...
UM... I'M CHI. PLEASED TO MEET YOU!
I'M ANN'S HALF SISTER!
MY MOM MARRIED YOUR HUSBAND!
Oh, sorry...
AND, UH...
...THANKS FOR GIVING US ANN!

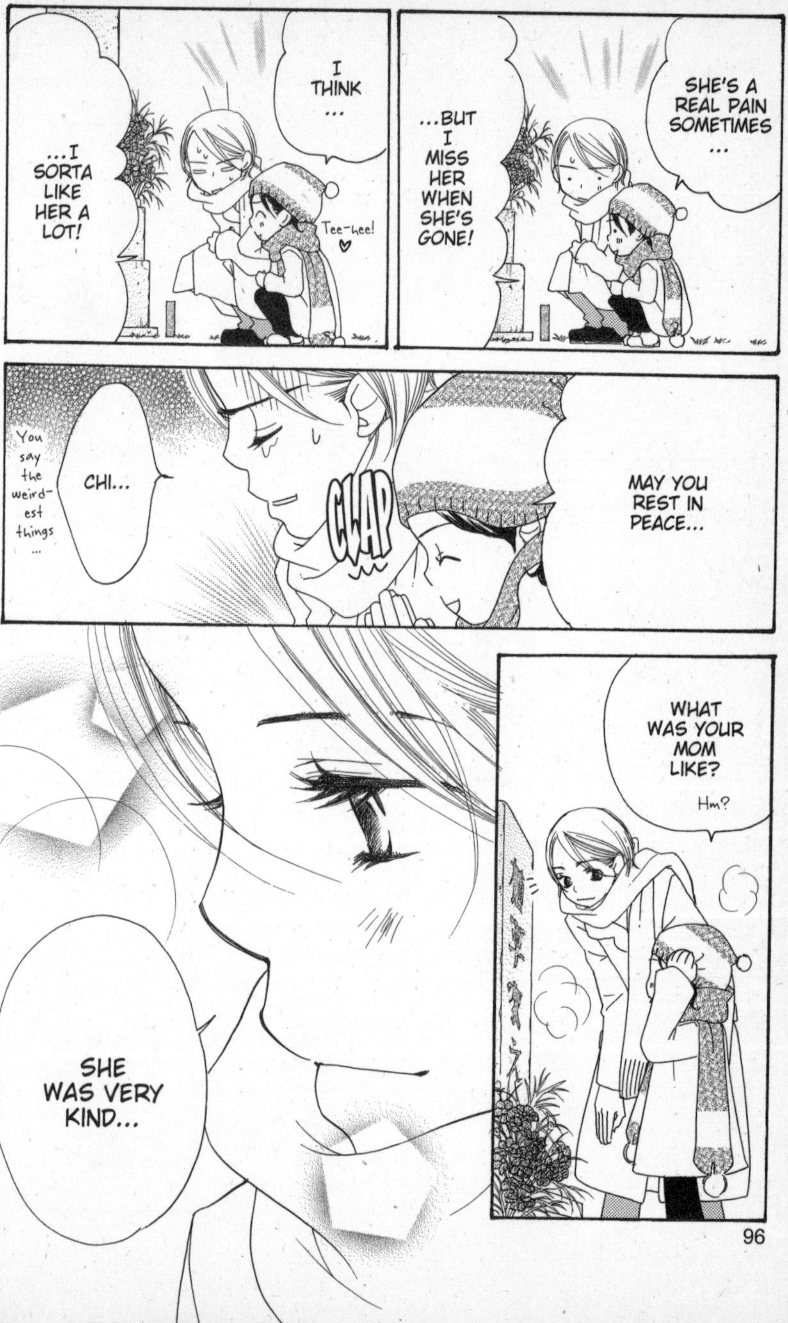
SHE'S A REAL PAIN SOMETIMES...
...BUT I MISS HER WHEN SHE'S GONE!
I THINK...
...I SORTA LIKE HER A LOT!
Tee-hee! ♡
MAY YOU REST IN PEACE...
CLAP
CHI...
You say the weird-est things...
WHAT WAS YOUR MOM LIKE?
Hm?
SHE WAS VERY KIND...

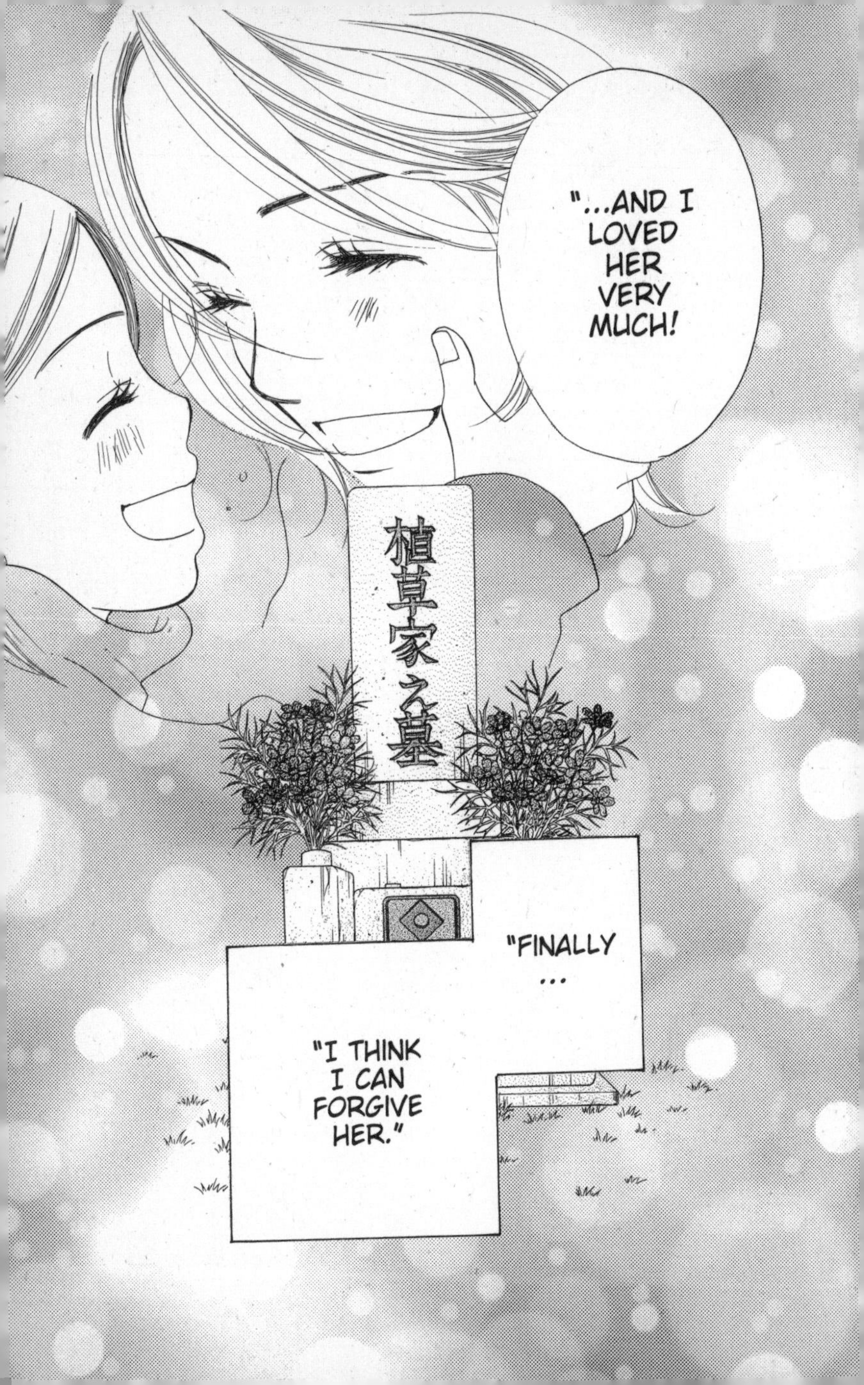
"...AND I LOVED HER VERY MUCH!
"FINALLY ...
"I THINK I CAN FORGIVE HER."

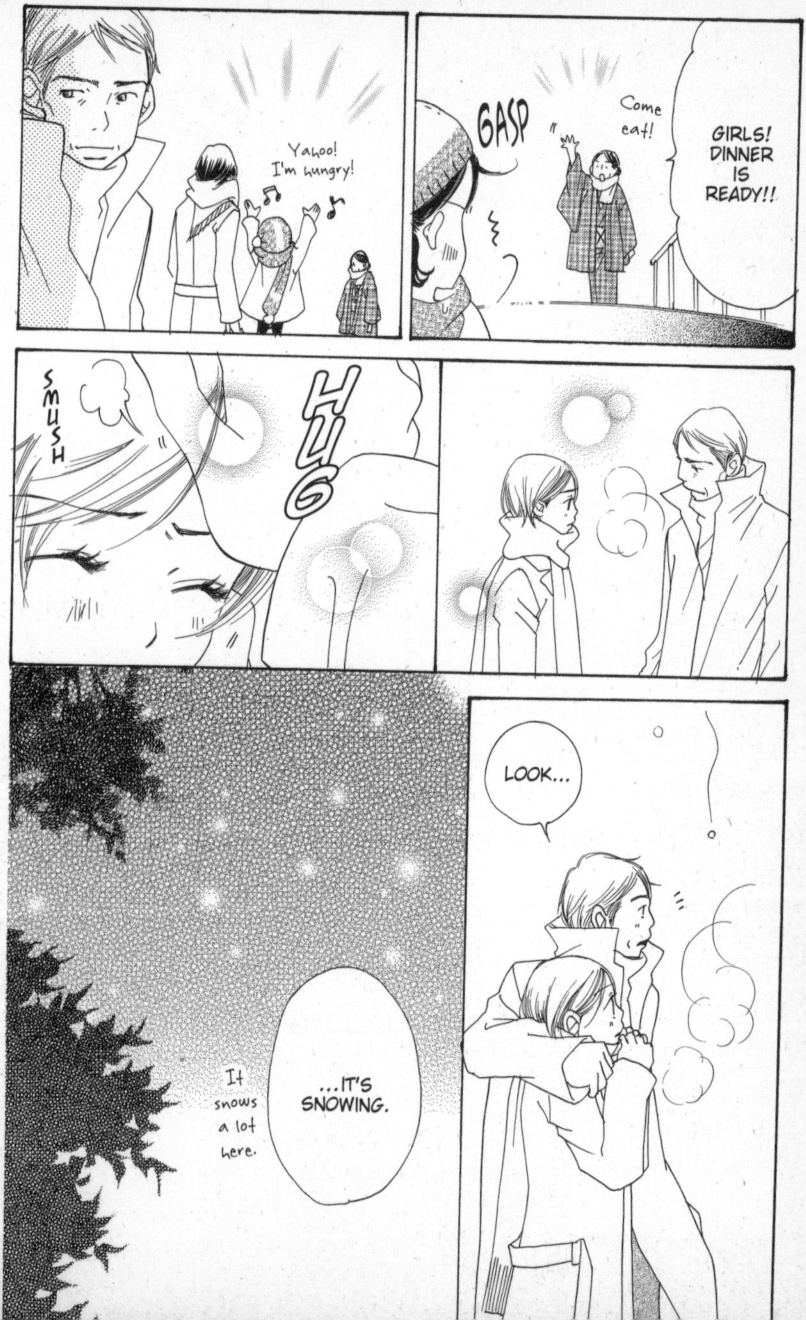
GIRLS! DINNER IS READY!!
Come eat!
GASP
Yahoo! I'm hungry!
HUG
SMUSH
LOOK...
...IT'S SNOWING.
It snows a lot here.

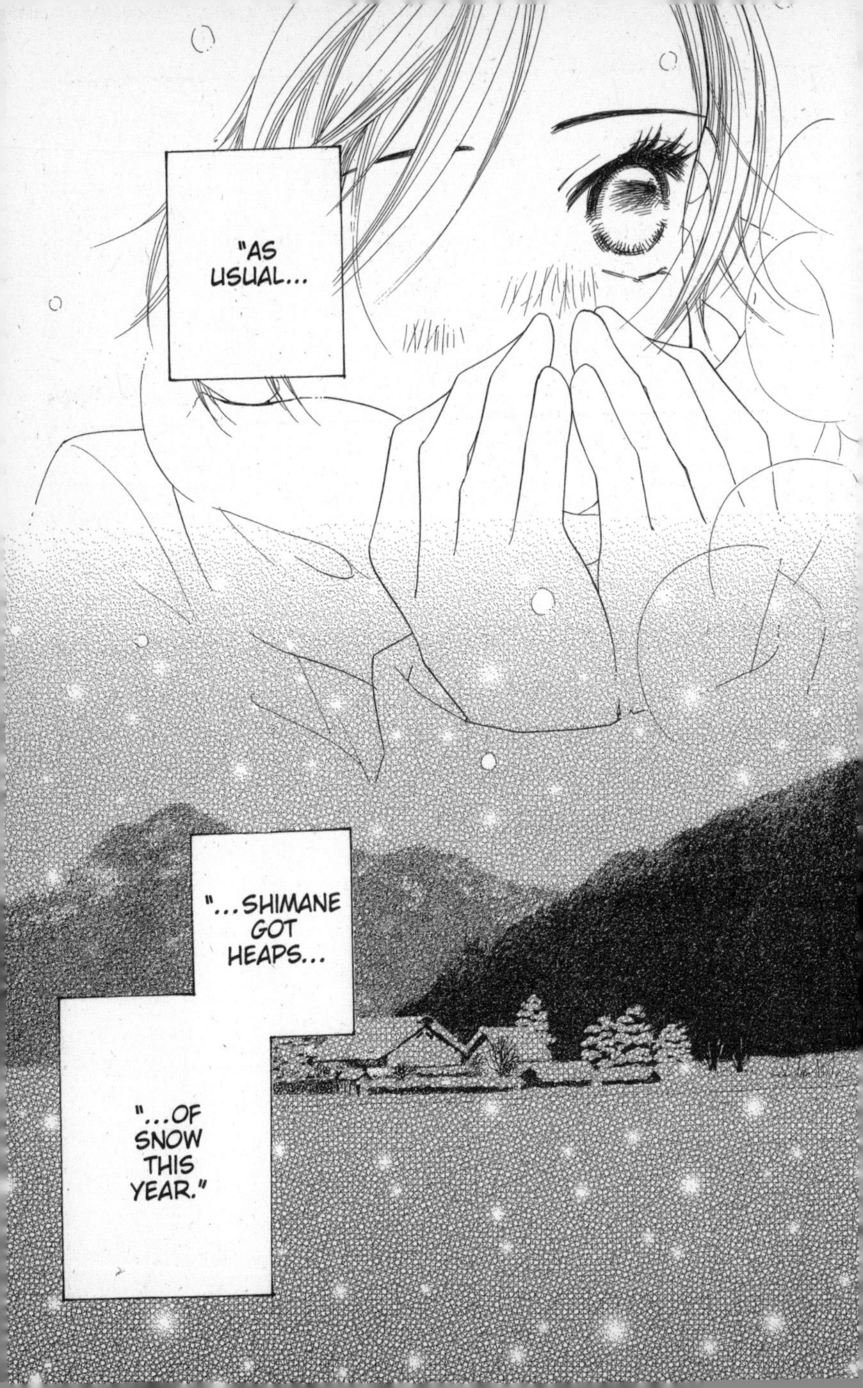
"AS USUAL...
"...SHIMANE GOT HEAPS...
"...OF SNOW THIS YEAR."

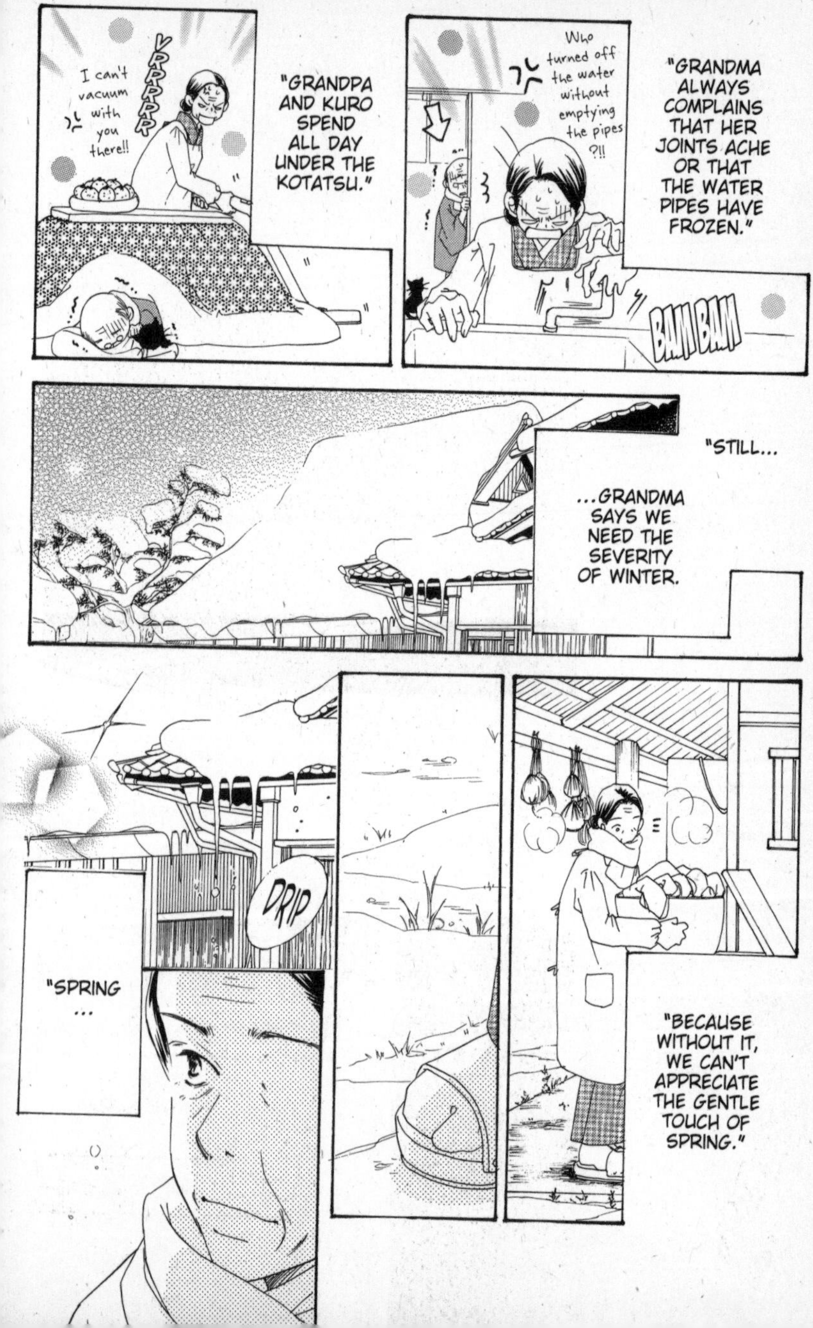
"GRANDMA ALWAYS COMPLAINS THAT HER JOINTS ACHE OR THAT THE WATER PIPES HAVE FROZEN."
Who turned off the water without emptying the pipes ?!!
BAM BAM
"GRANDPA AND KURO SPEND ALL DAY UNDER THE KOTATSU."
VRRRRR
I can't vacuum with you there!!
"STILL...
...GRANDMA SAYS WE NEED THE SEVERITY OF WINTER.
"BECAUSE WITHOUT IT, WE CAN'T APPRECIATE THE GENTLE TOUCH OF SPRING."
DRIP
"SPRING ...

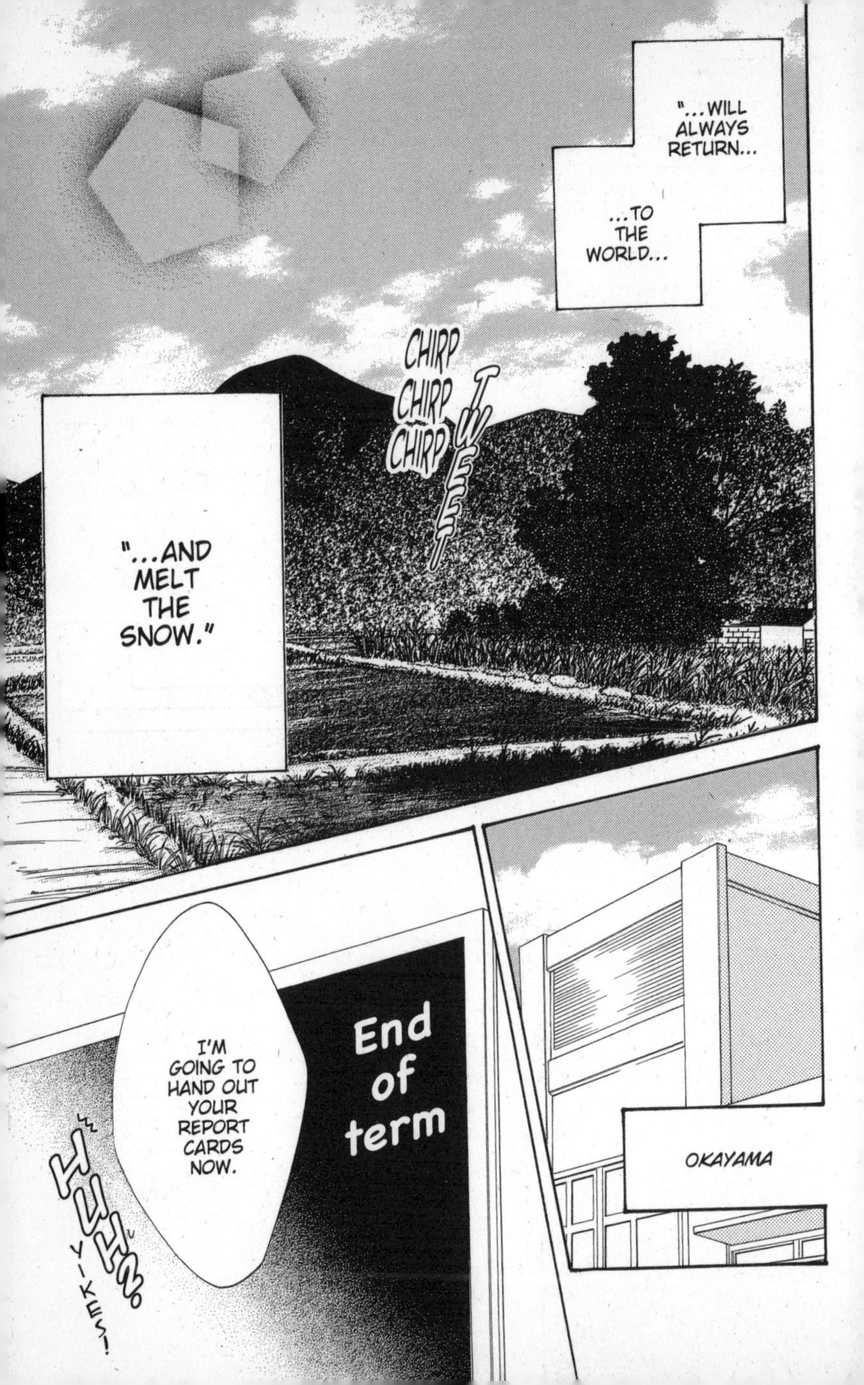
"...WILL ALWAYS RETURN...
...TO THE WORLD...
CHIRP CHIRP CHIRP
TWEET
"...AND MELT THE SNOW."
OKAYAMA
End of term
I'M GOING TO HAND OUT YOUR REPORT CARDS NOW.
YIKES!

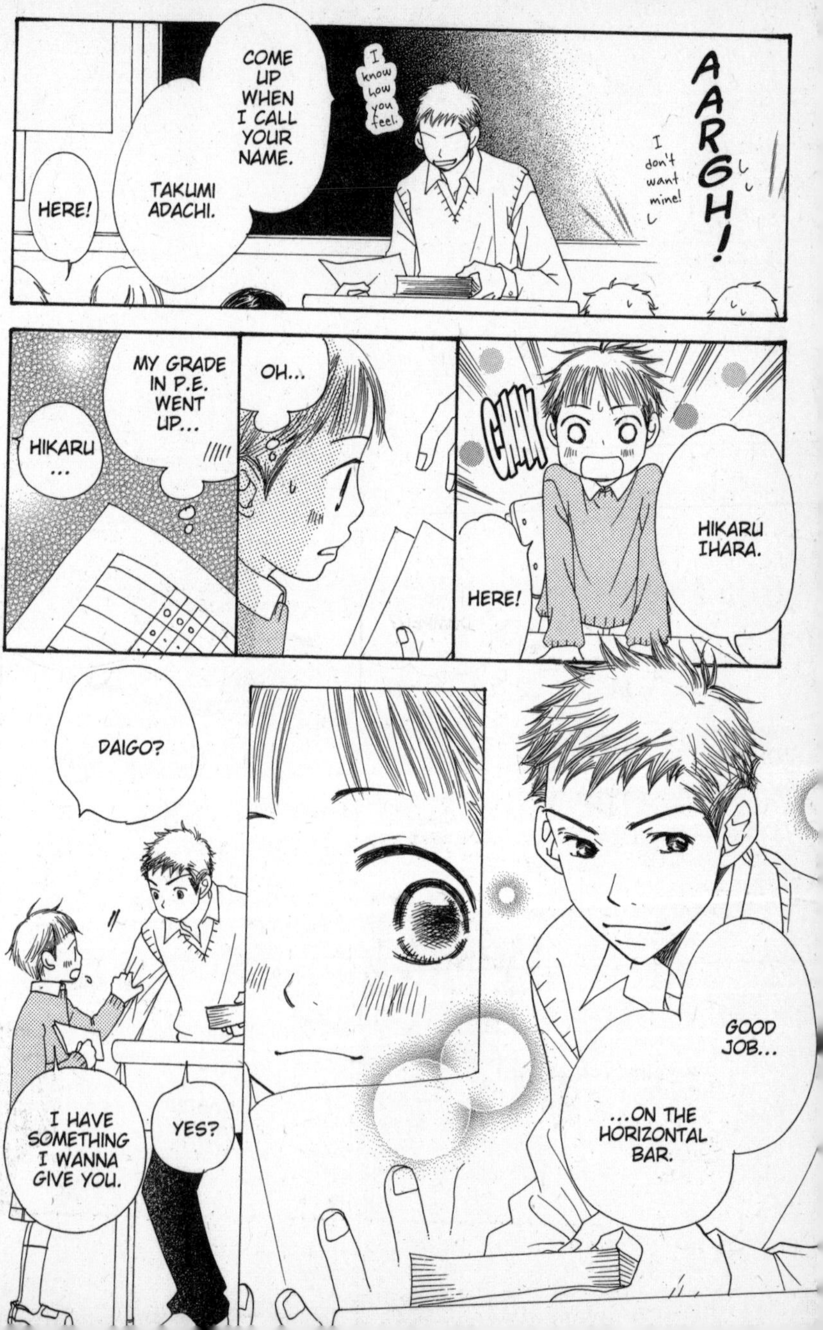
AARGH!
I don't want mine!
I know how you feel.
COME UP WHEN I CALL YOUR NAME.
TAKUMI ADACHI.
HERE!
HIKARU IHARA.
CHAK
HERE!
OH...
MY GRADE IN P.E. WENT UP...
HIKARU...
GOOD JOB...
...ON THE HORIZONTAL BAR.
DAIGO?
YES?
I HAVE SOMETHING I WANNA GIVE YOU.

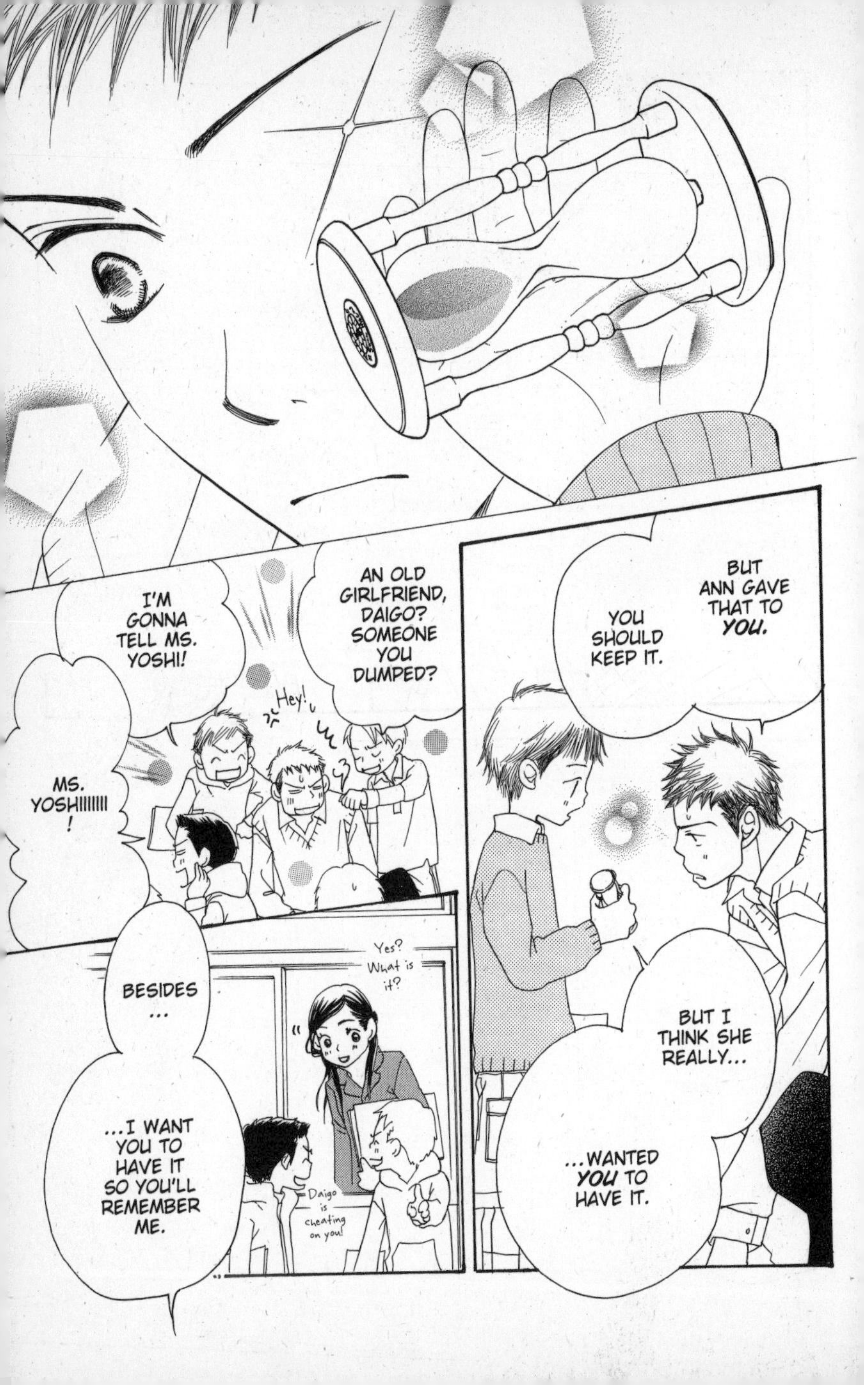
BUT ANN GAVE THAT TO *YOU.*
YOU SHOULD KEEP IT.
BUT I THINK SHE REALLY...
...WANTED *YOU* TO HAVE IT.
AN OLD GIRLFRIEND, DAIGO? SOMEONE YOU DUMPED?
Hey!
I'M GONNA TELL MS. YOSHI!
MS. YOSHIIIIIIIII!
Yes? What is it?
Daigo is cheating on you!
BESIDES...
...I WANT YOU TO HAVE IT SO YOU'LL REMEMBER ME.

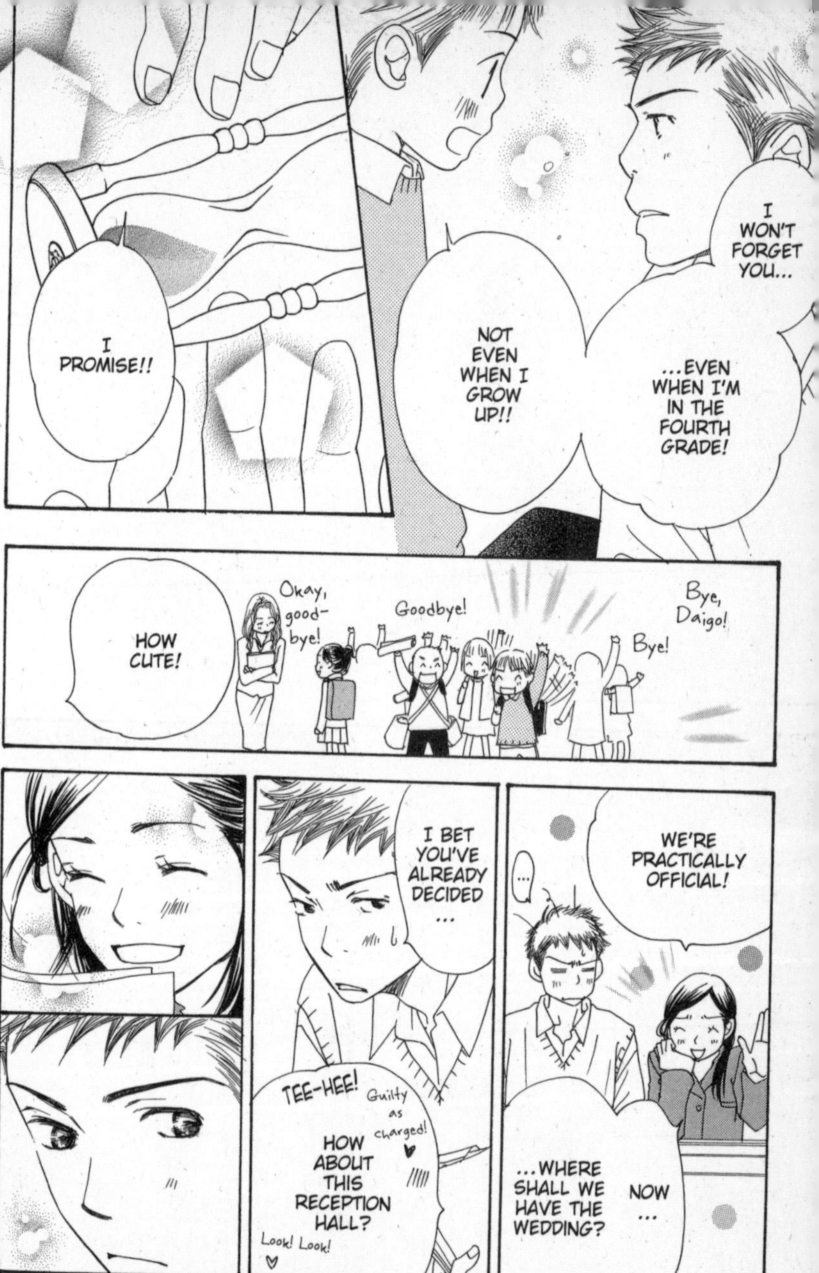
I WON'T FORGET YOU...
...EVEN WHEN I'M IN THE FOURTH GRADE!
NOT EVEN WHEN I GROW UP!!
I PROMISE!!
Bye, Daigo!
Bye!
Goodbye!
Okay, good-bye!
HOW CUTE!
WE'RE PRACTICALLY OFFICIAL!
...
NOW...
...WHERE SHALL WE HAVE THE WEDDING?
I BET YOU'VE ALREADY DECIDED...
TEE-HEE!
Guilty as charged!
HOW ABOUT THIS RECEPTION HALL?
Look! Look!

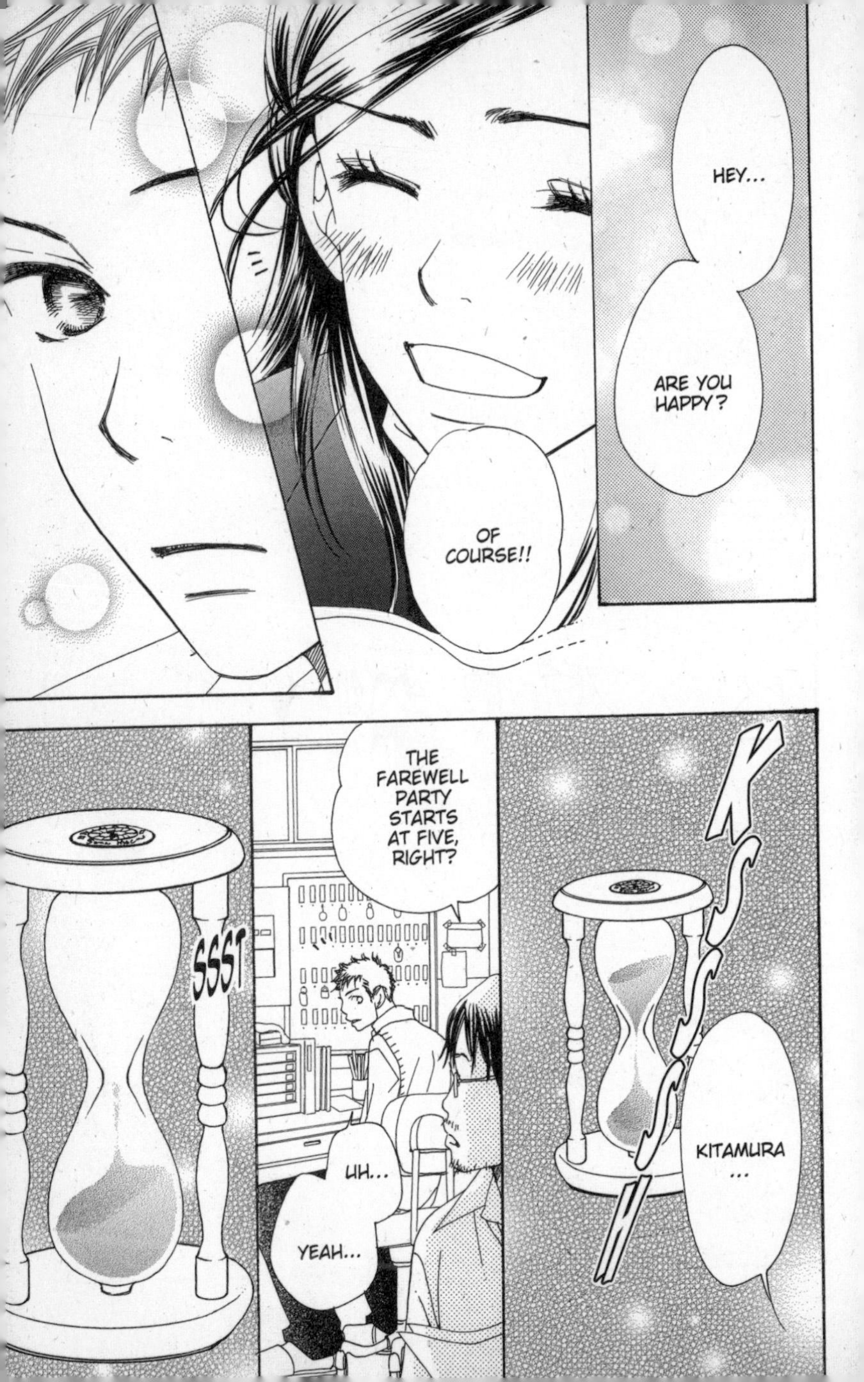
HEY...
ARE YOU HAPPY?
OF COURSE!!
KSSSH
KITAMURA...
THE FAREWELL PARTY STARTS AT FIVE, RIGHT?
UH...
YEAH...
SSST

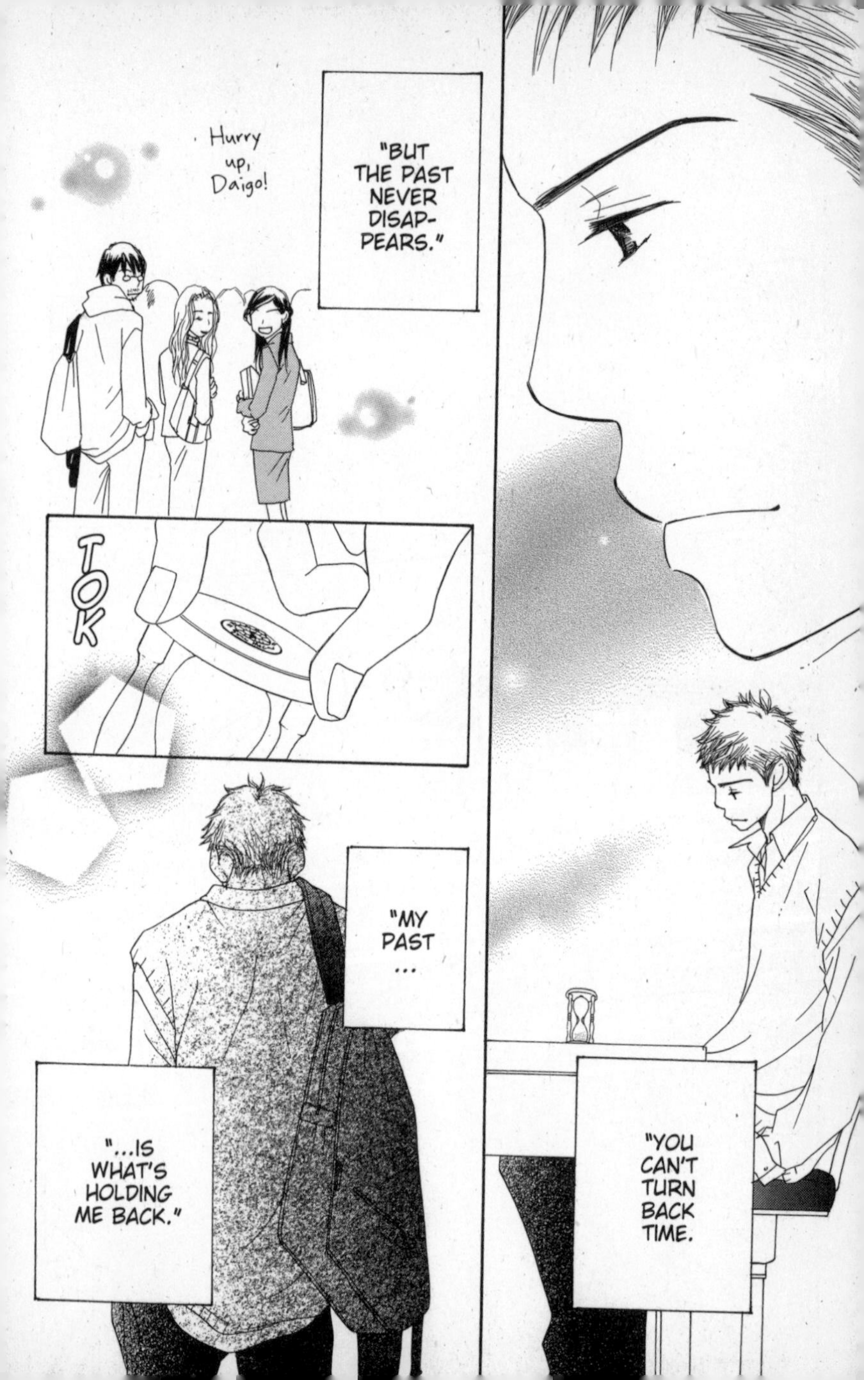
"YOU CAN'T TURN BACK TIME.
"BUT THE PAST NEVER DISAPPEARS."
Hurry up, Daigo!
TOK
"MY PAST ...
"...IS WHAT'S HOLDING ME BACK."

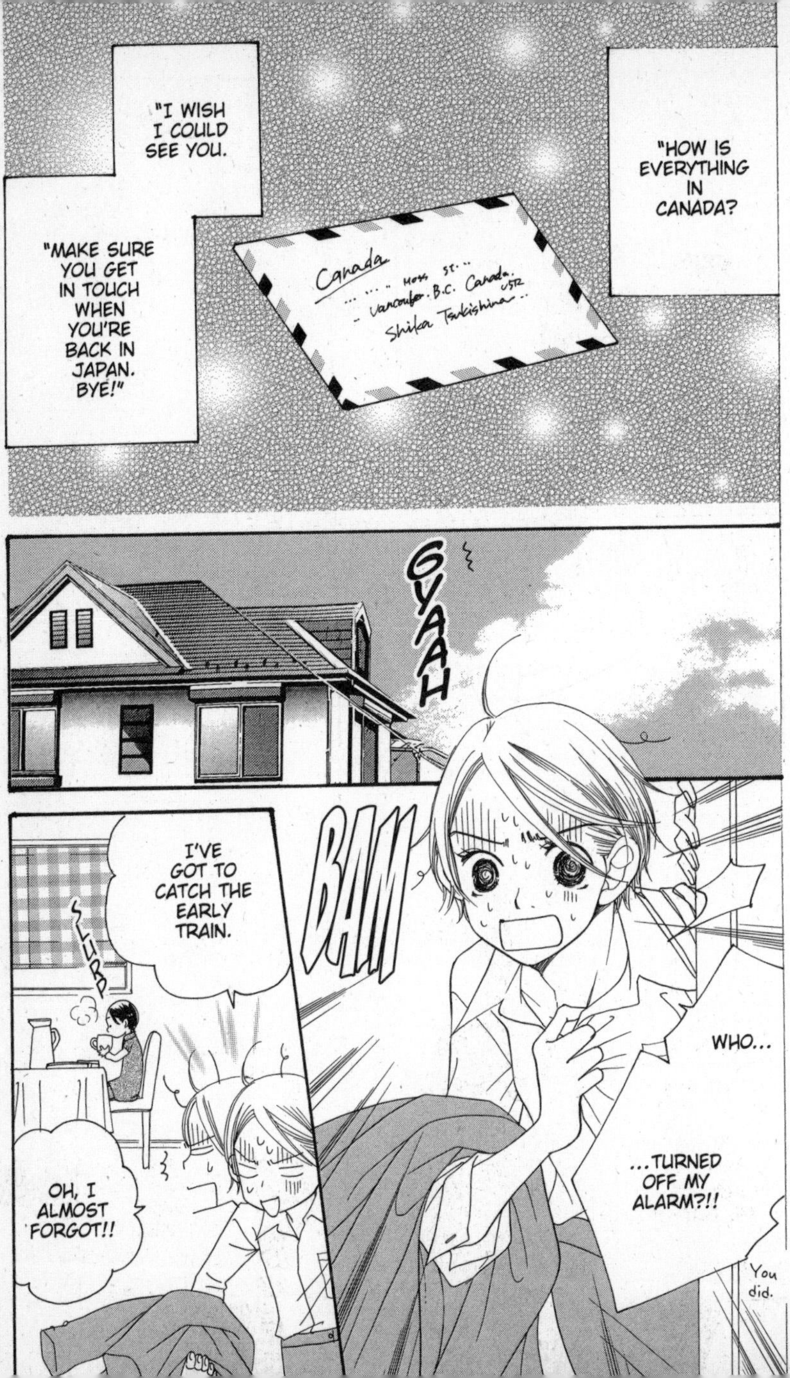
"HOW IS EVERYTHING IN CANADA?
"I WISH I COULD SEE YOU.
"MAKE SURE YOU GET IN TOUCH WHEN YOU'RE BACK IN JAPAN. BYE!"
Canada
Vancouver. B.C. Canada.
Shika Tsukishima
GYAAAH
BAM
WHO...
...TURNED OFF MY ALARM?!!
You did.
I'VE GOT TO CATCH THE EARLY TRAIN.
SLURP
OH, I ALMOST FORGOT!!

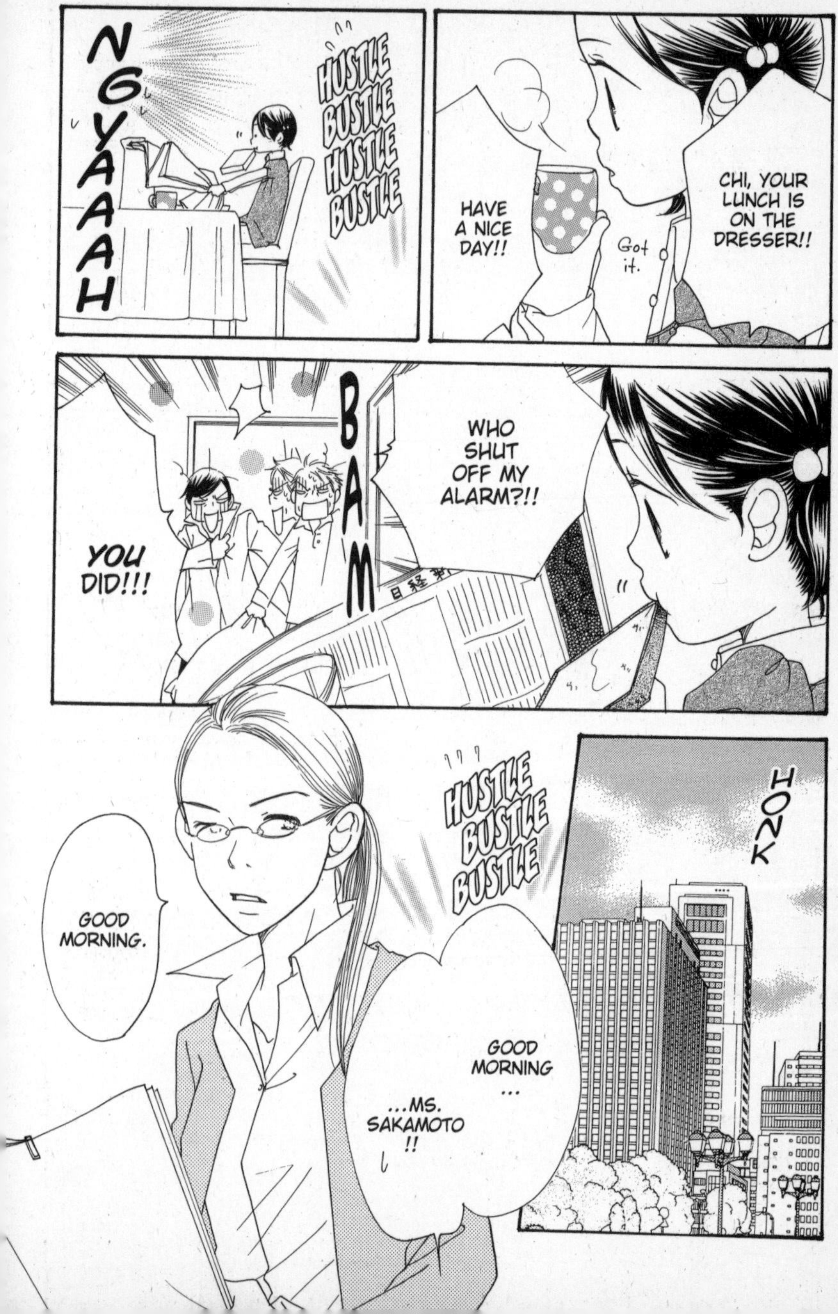
CHI, YOUR LUNCH IS ON THE DRESSER!!
Got it.
HAVE A NICE DAY!!
HUSTLE BUSTLE HUSTLE BUSTLE
NGYAAAAH
WHO SHUT OFF MY ALARM?!!
BAM
YOU DID!!!
HONK
HUSTLE BUSTLE BUSTLE
GOOD MORNING ...
...MS. SAKAMOTO !!
GOOD MORNING.

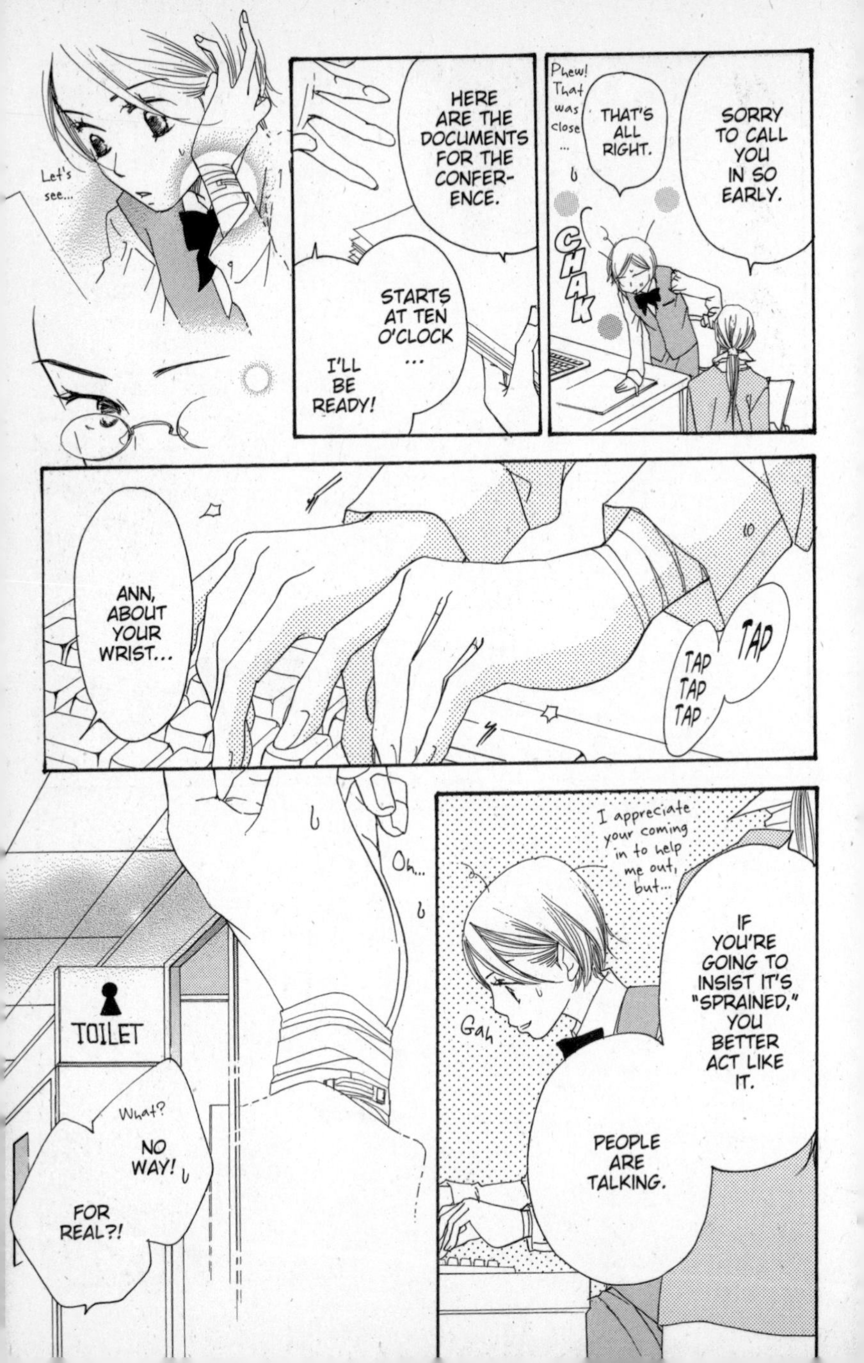
SORRY TO CALL YOU IN SO EARLY.
THAT'S ALL RIGHT.
Phew! That was close...
CHAK
HERE ARE THE DOCUMENTS FOR THE CONFERENCE.
STARTS AT TEN O'CLOCK...
I'LL BE READY!
Let's see...
TAP
TAP TAP TAP
ANN, ABOUT YOUR WRIST...
I appreciate your coming in to help me out, but...
IF YOU'RE GOING TO INSIST IT'S "SPRAINED," YOU BETTER ACT LIKE IT.
PEOPLE ARE TALKING.
Gah
Oh...
TOILET
What?
NO WAY!
FOR REAL?!

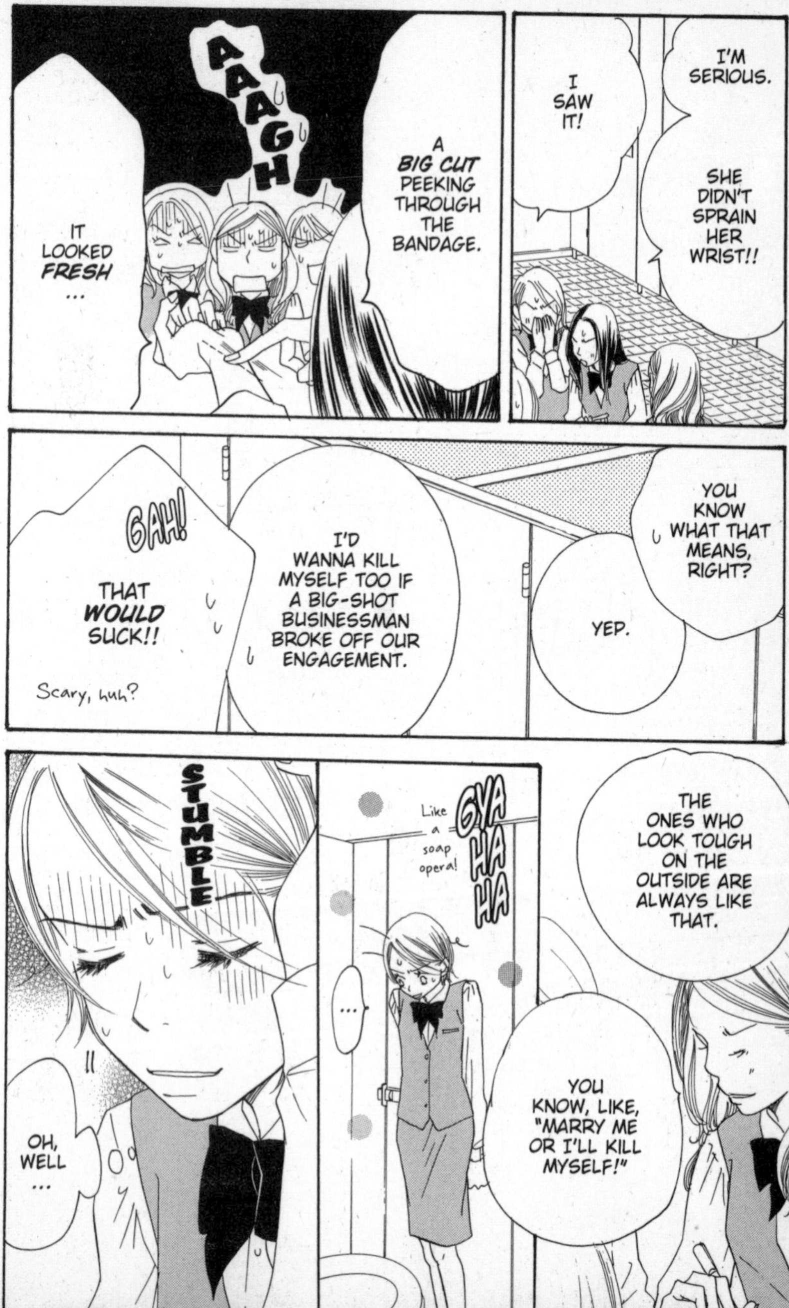
I'M SERIOUS.
I SAW IT!
SHE DIDN'T SPRAIN HER WRIST!!
A BIG CUT PEEKING THROUGH THE BANDAGE.
AAAGH
IT LOOKED FRESH ...
YOU KNOW WHAT THAT MEANS, RIGHT?
YEP.
I'D WANNA KILL MYSELF TOO IF A BIG-SHOT BUSINESSMAN BROKE OFF OUR ENGAGEMENT.
GAH!
THAT WOULD SUCK!!
Scary, huh?
THE ONES WHO LOOK TOUGH ON THE OUTSIDE ARE ALWAYS LIKE THAT.
YOU KNOW, LIKE, "MARRY ME OR I'LL KILL MYSELF!"
GYAHAHA
Like a soap opera!
...
STUMBLE
OH, WELL ...

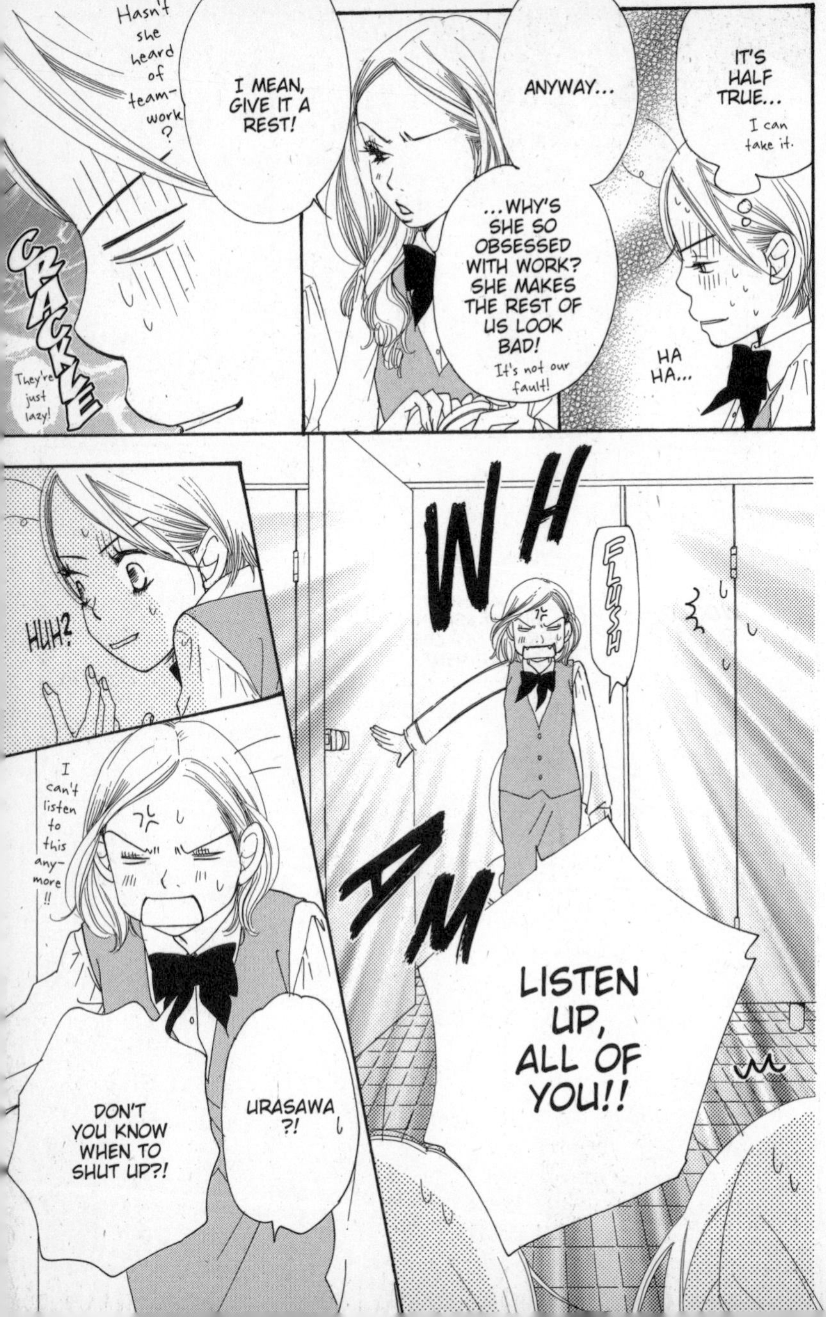
IT'S HALF TRUE...
I can take it.
HA HA...
ANYWAY...
...WHY'S SHE SO OBSESSED WITH WORK? SHE MAKES THE REST OF US LOOK BAD!
It's not our fault!
I MEAN, GIVE IT A REST!
Hasn't she heard of team-work?
CRACKLE
They're just lazy!
WHAM
FLUSH
LISTEN UP, ALL OF YOU!!
HUH?
I can't listen to this any-more!!
URASAWA?!
DON'T YOU KNOW WHEN TO SHUT UP?!

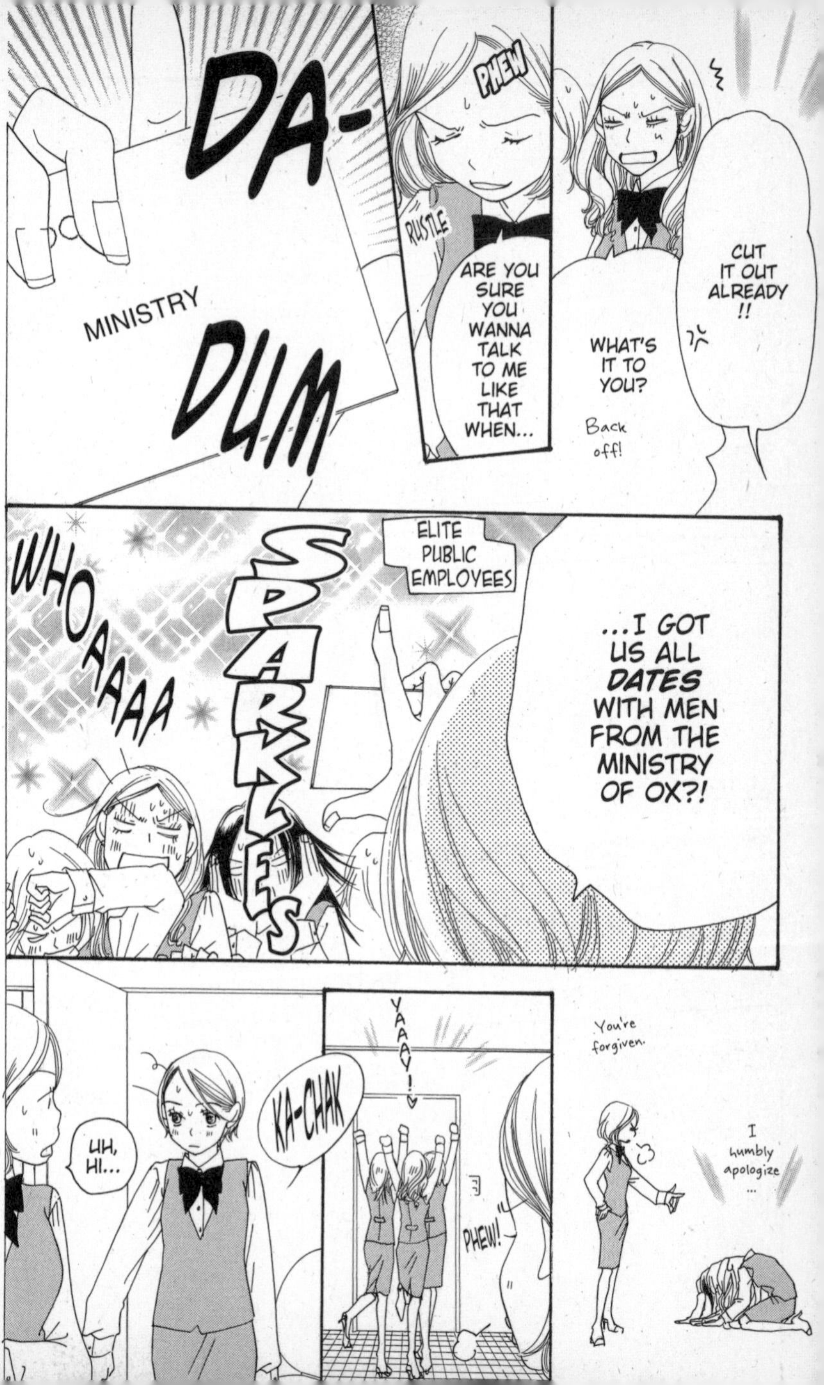
CUT IT OUT ALREADY!!
WHAT'S IT TO YOU?
Back off!
PHEW
RUSTLE
ARE YOU SURE YOU WANNA TALK TO ME LIKE THAT WHEN...
DA-
MINISTRY
DUM
ELITE PUBLIC EMPLOYEES
...I GOT US ALL DATES WITH MEN FROM THE MINISTRY OF OX?!
SPARKLES
WHOAAAAA
You're forgiven.
I humbly apologize ...
YAAAY!
PHEW!
KA-CHAK
UH, HI...

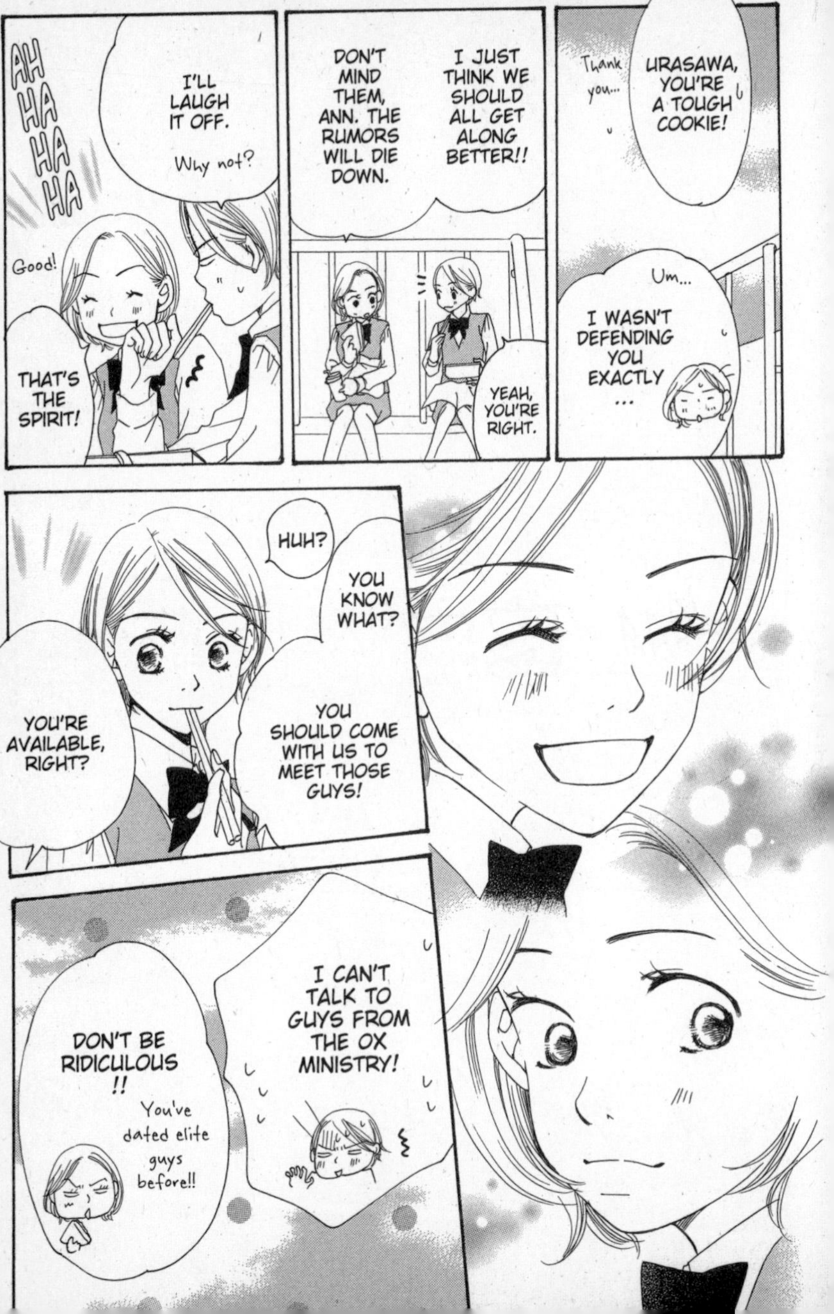
URASAWA, YOU'RE A TOUGH COOKIE!
Thank you...
Um...
I WASN'T DEFENDING YOU EXACTLY ...
DON'T MIND THEM, ANN. THE RUMORS WILL DIE DOWN.
I JUST THINK WE SHOULD ALL GET ALONG BETTER!!
YEAH, YOU'RE RIGHT.
I'LL LAUGH IT OFF.
Why not?
AH HA HA HA HA
Good!
THAT'S THE SPIRIT!
HUH?
YOU KNOW WHAT?
YOU SHOULD COME WITH US TO MEET THOSE GUYS!
YOU'RE AVAILABLE, RIGHT?
I CAN'T TALK TO GUYS FROM THE OX MINISTRY!
DON'T BE RIDICULOUS !!
You've dated elite guys before!!

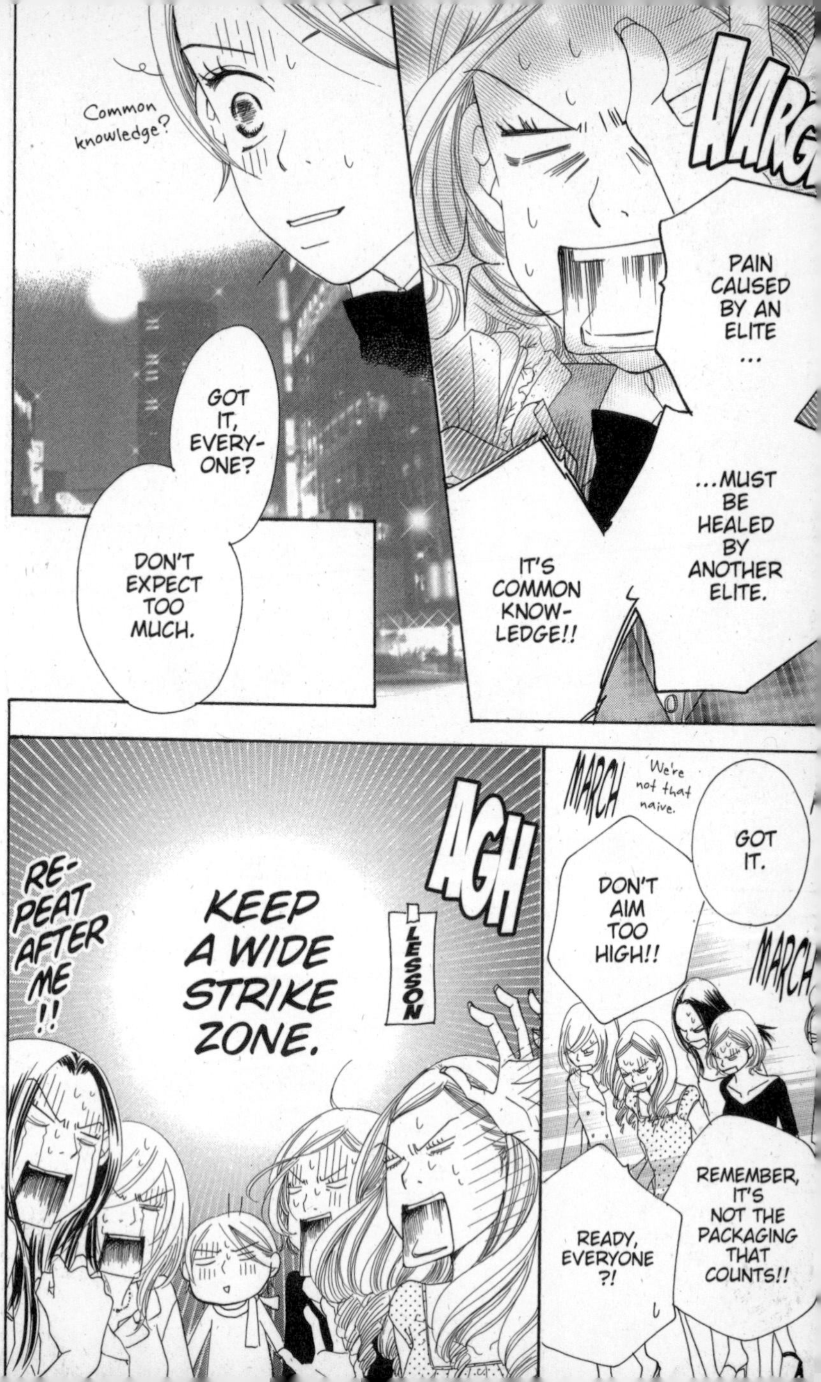
AARG
PAIN CAUSED BY AN ELITE...
...MUST BE HEALED BY ANOTHER ELITE.
IT'S COMMON KNOW-LEDGE!!
Common knowledge?
GOT IT, EVERY-ONE?
DON'T EXPECT TOO MUCH.
MARCH
We're not that naive.
GOT IT.
DON'T AIM TOO HIGH!!
MARCH
REMEMBER, IT'S NOT THE PACKAGING THAT COUNTS!!
READY, EVERYONE?!
AGH
LESSON
KEEP A WIDE STRIKE ZONE.
RE-PEAT AFTER ME!!

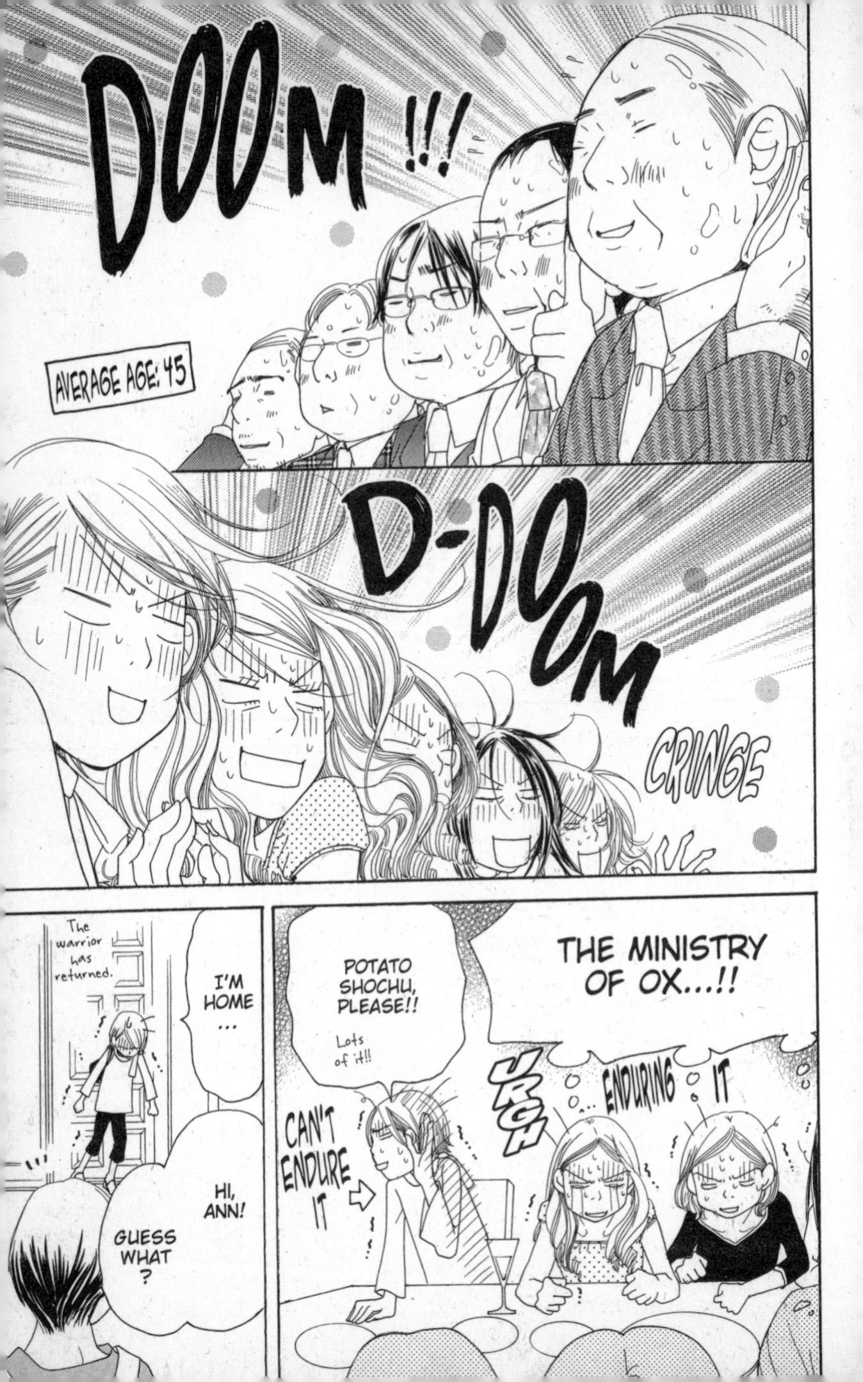
DOOM!!!
AVERAGE AGE: 45
D-DOOOM
CRINGE
THE MINISTRY OF OX...!!
ENDURING IT
URGH
POTATO SHOCHU, PLEASE!!
Lots of it!!
CAN'T ENDURE IT
The warrior has returned.
I'M HOME...
HI, ANN!
GUESS WHAT?

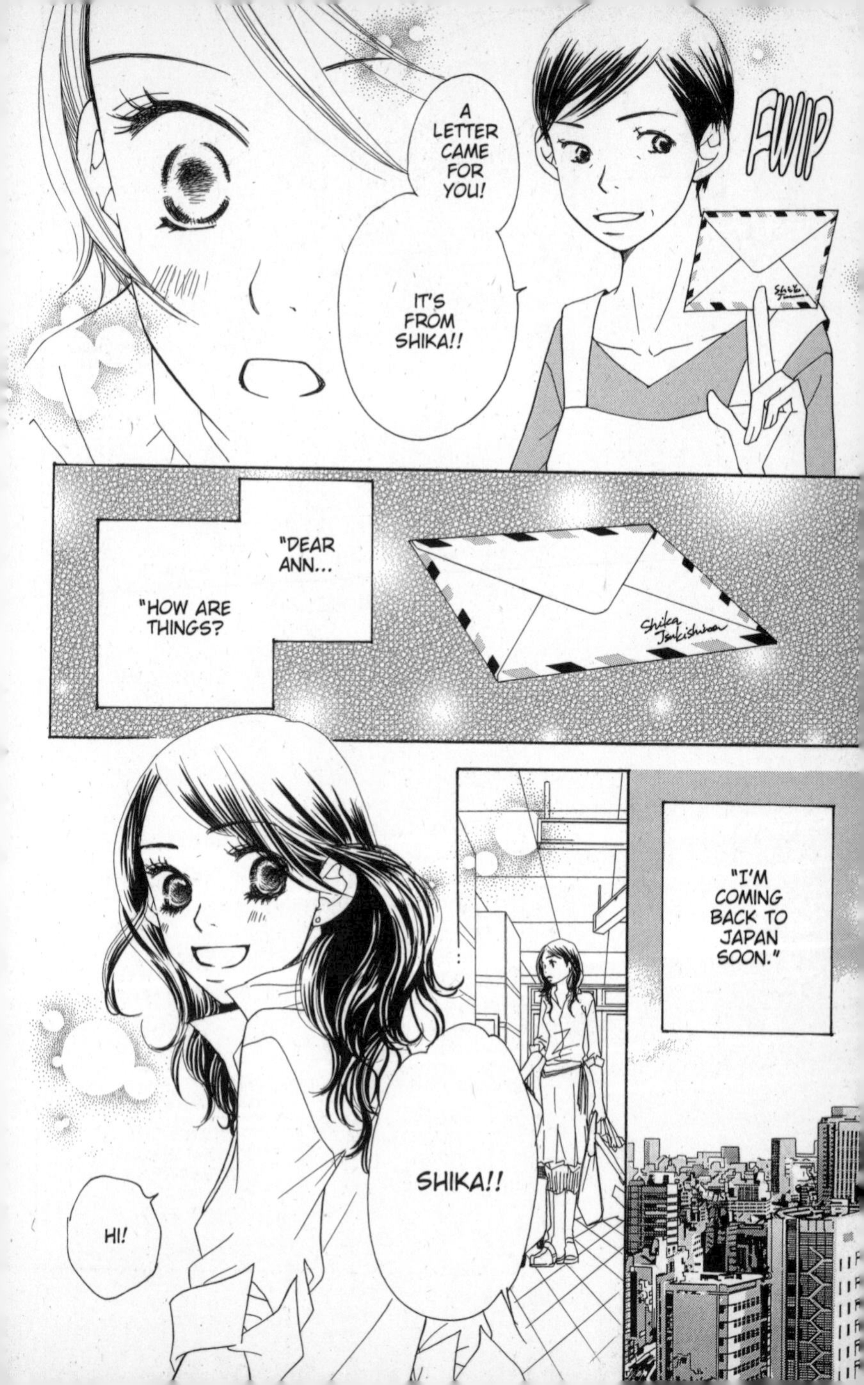
FWIP
A LETTER CAME FOR YOU!
IT'S FROM SHIKA!!
"DEAR ANN...
"HOW ARE THINGS?
"I'M COMING BACK TO JAPAN SOON."
SHIKA!!
HI!

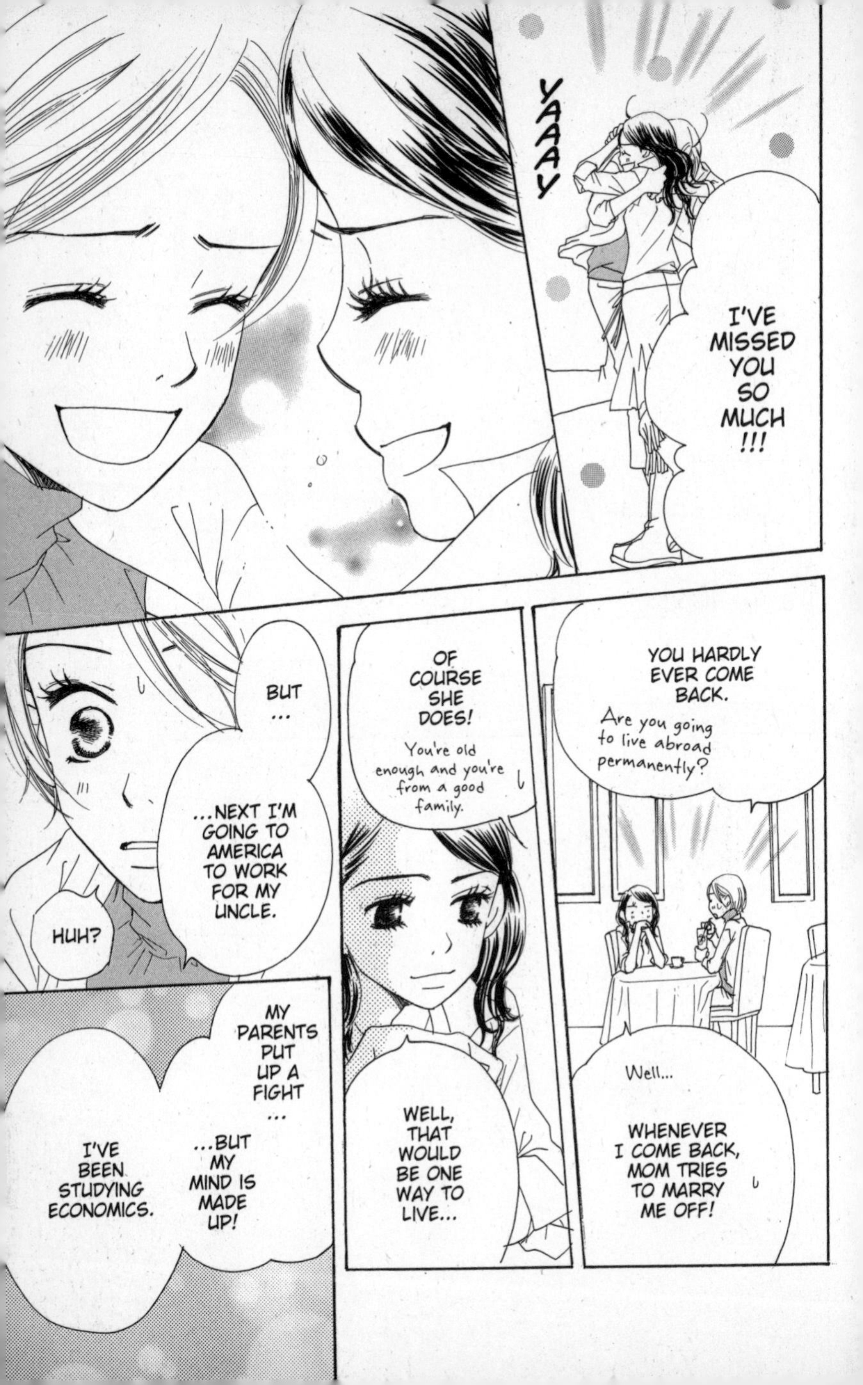
YAAAAY
I'VE MISSED YOU SO MUCH!!!
YOU HARDLY EVER COME BACK.
Are you going to live abroad permanently?
Well...
WHENEVER I COME BACK, MOM TRIES TO MARRY ME OFF!
OF COURSE SHE DOES!
You're old enough and you're from a good family.
WELL, THAT WOULD BE ONE WAY TO LIVE...
BUT...
...NEXT I'M GOING TO AMERICA TO WORK FOR MY UNCLE.
HUH?
MY PARENTS PUT UP A FIGHT...
...BUT MY MIND IS MADE UP!
I'VE BEEN STUDYING ECONOMICS.

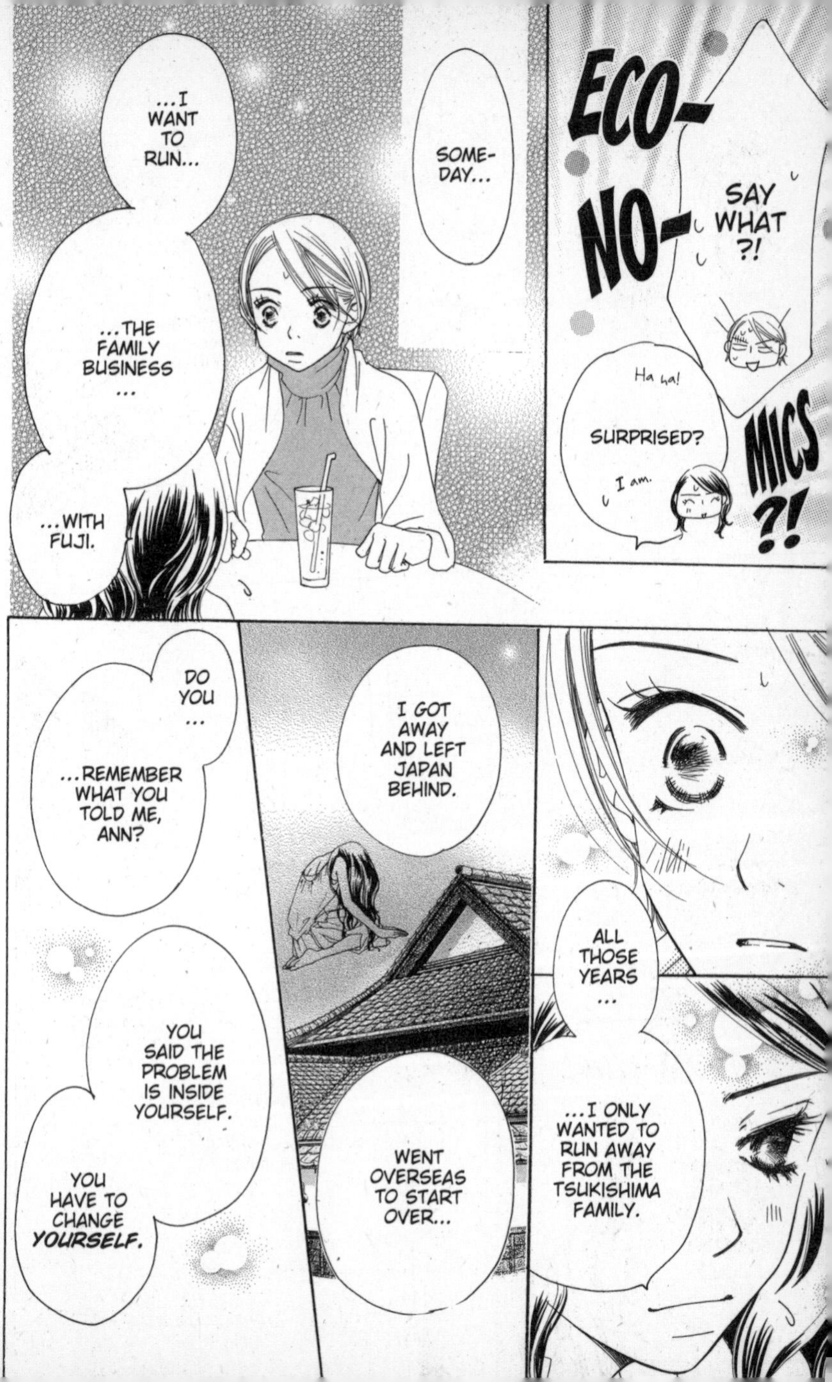
ECO-NO-MICS?!
SAY WHAT?!
Ha ha! SURPRISED? I am.
SOME-DAY...
...I WANT TO RUN...
...THE FAMILY BUSINESS...
...WITH FUJI.
ALL THOSE YEARS...
...I ONLY WANTED TO RUN AWAY FROM THE TSUKISHIMA FAMILY.
I GOT AWAY AND LEFT JAPAN BEHIND.
WENT OVERSEAS TO START OVER...
DO YOU...
...REMEMBER WHAT YOU TOLD ME, ANN?
YOU SAID THE PROBLEM IS INSIDE YOURSELF.
YOU HAVE TO CHANGE *YOURSELF*.

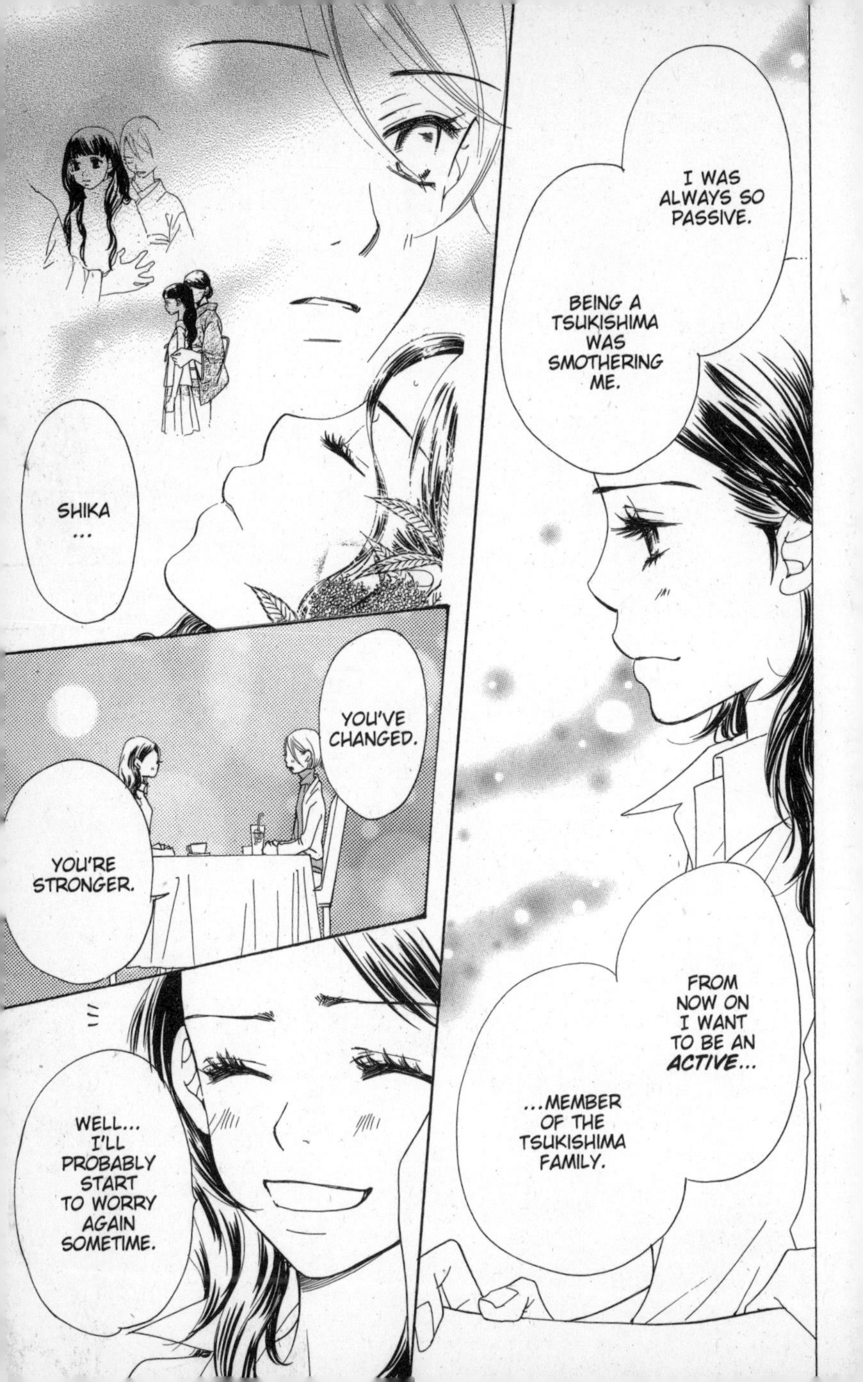
I WAS ALWAYS SO PASSIVE.
BEING A TSUKISHIMA WAS SMOTHERING ME.
FROM NOW ON I WANT TO BE AN ***ACTIVE***...
...MEMBER OF THE TSUKISHIMA FAMILY.
SHIKA...
YOU'VE CHANGED.
YOU'RE STRONGER.
WELL... I'LL PROBABLY START TO WORRY AGAIN SOMETIME.

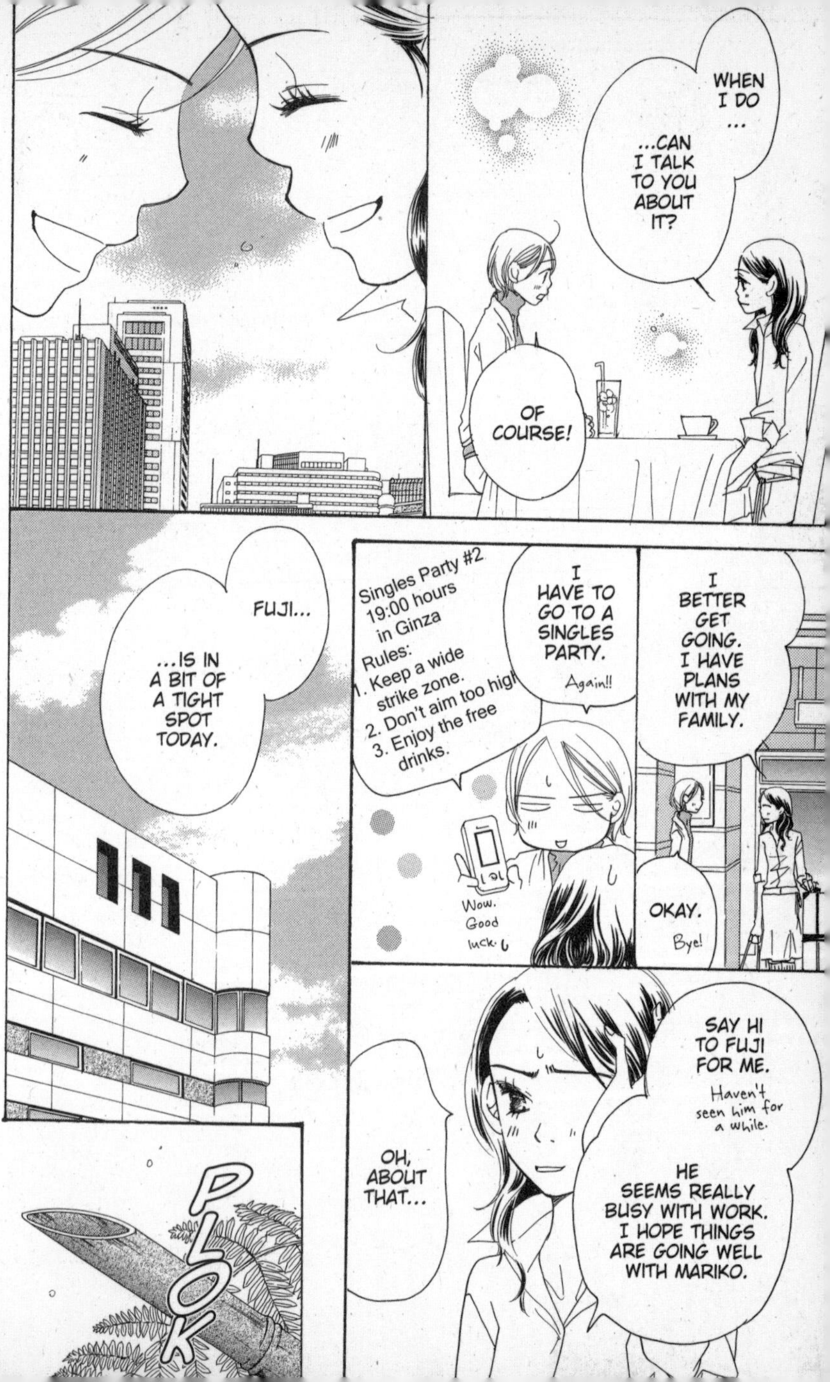
WHEN I DO ...
...CAN I TALK TO YOU ABOUT IT?
OF COURSE!
I BETTER GET GOING. I HAVE PLANS WITH MY FAMILY.
OKAY.
Bye!
I HAVE TO GO TO A SINGLES PARTY.
Again!!
Singles Party #2
19:00 hours
in Ginza
Rules:
1. Keep a wide strike zone.
2. Don't aim too high
3. Enjoy the free drinks.
Wow. Good luck.
SAY HI TO FUJI FOR ME.
Haven't seen him for a while.
HE SEEMS REALLY BUSY WITH WORK. I HOPE THINGS ARE GOING WELL WITH MARIKO.
OH, ABOUT THAT...
FUJI...
...IS IN A BIT OF A TIGHT SPOT TODAY.
PLOK

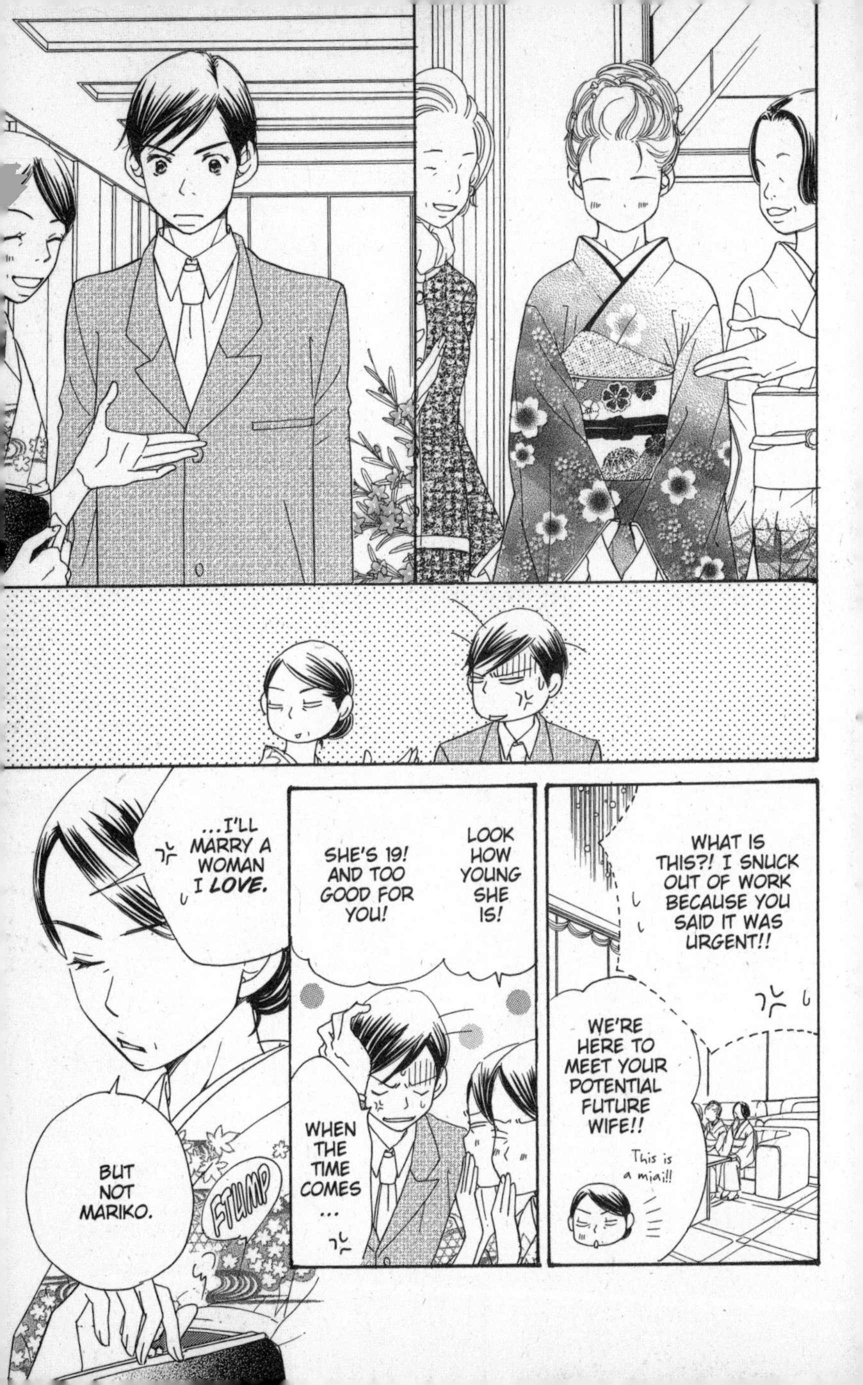
WHAT IS THIS?! I SNUCK OUT OF WORK BECAUSE YOU SAID IT WAS URGENT!!
WE'RE HERE TO MEET YOUR POTENTIAL FUTURE WIFE!!
This is a miai!!
LOOK HOW YOUNG SHE IS!
SHE'S 19! AND TOO GOOD FOR YOU!
WHEN THE TIME COMES...
...I'LL MARRY A WOMAN I LOVE.
BUT NOT MARIKO.
FTUMP

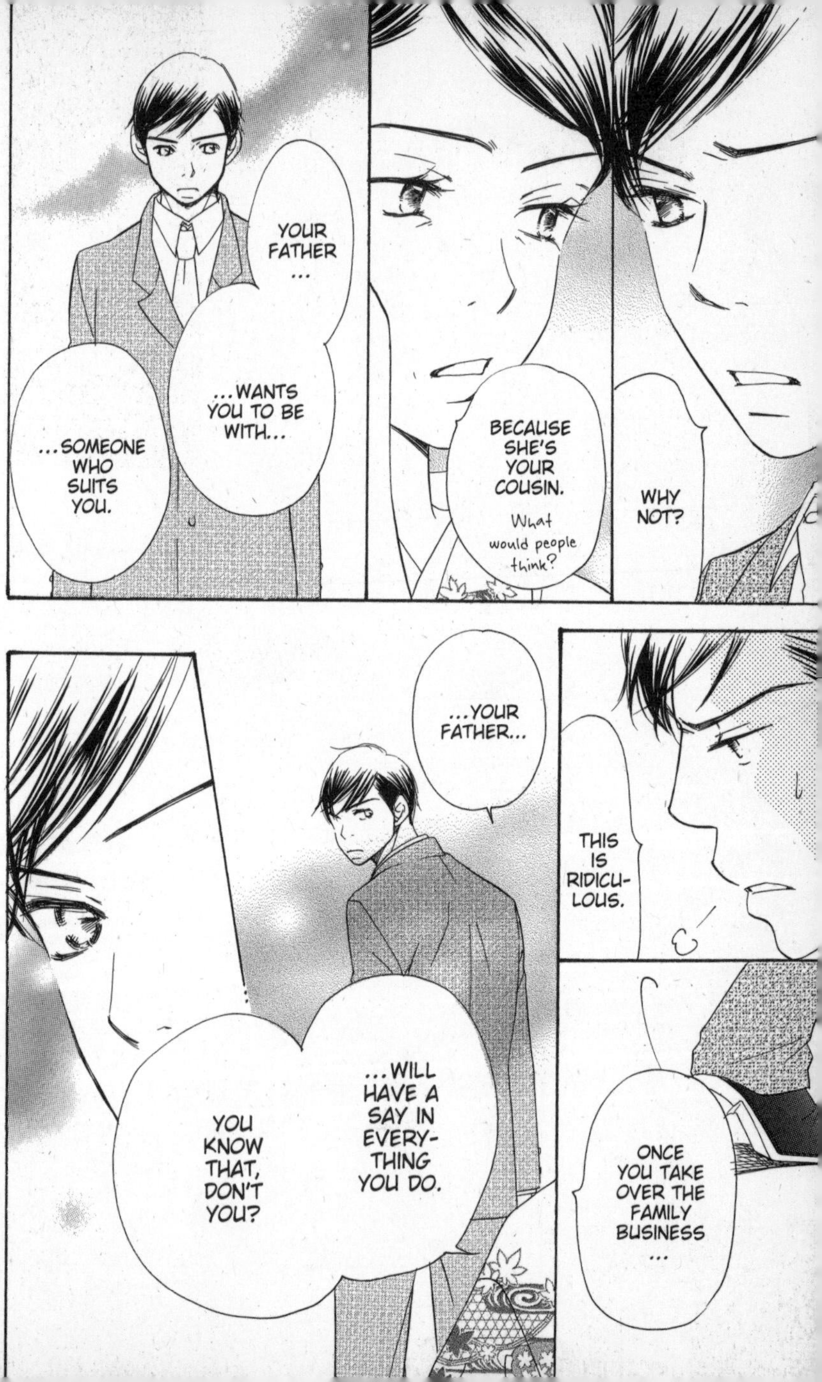
WHY NOT?
BECAUSE SHE'S YOUR COUSIN.
What would people think?
YOUR FATHER ...
...WANTS YOU TO BE WITH...
...SOMEONE WHO SUITS YOU.
THIS IS RIDICULOUS.
ONCE YOU TAKE OVER THE FAMILY BUSINESS ...
...YOUR FATHER...
...WILL HAVE A SAY IN EVERYTHING YOU DO.
YOU KNOW THAT, DON'T YOU?

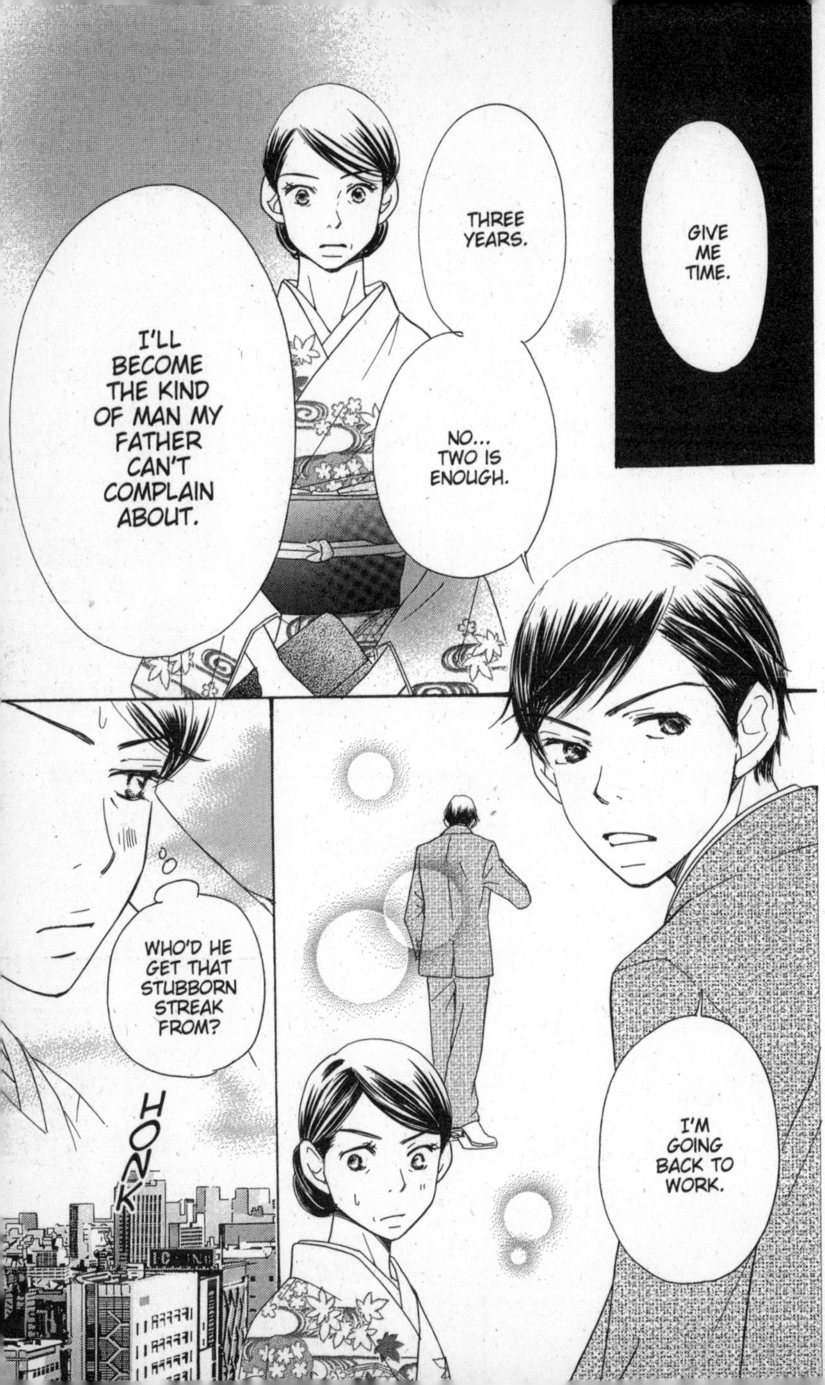
GIVE ME TIME.
THREE YEARS.
NO... TWO IS ENOUGH.
I'LL BECOME THE KIND OF MAN MY FATHER CAN'T COMPLAIN ABOUT.
I'M GOING BACK TO WORK.
WHO'D HE GET THAT STUBBORN STREAK FROM?
HONK

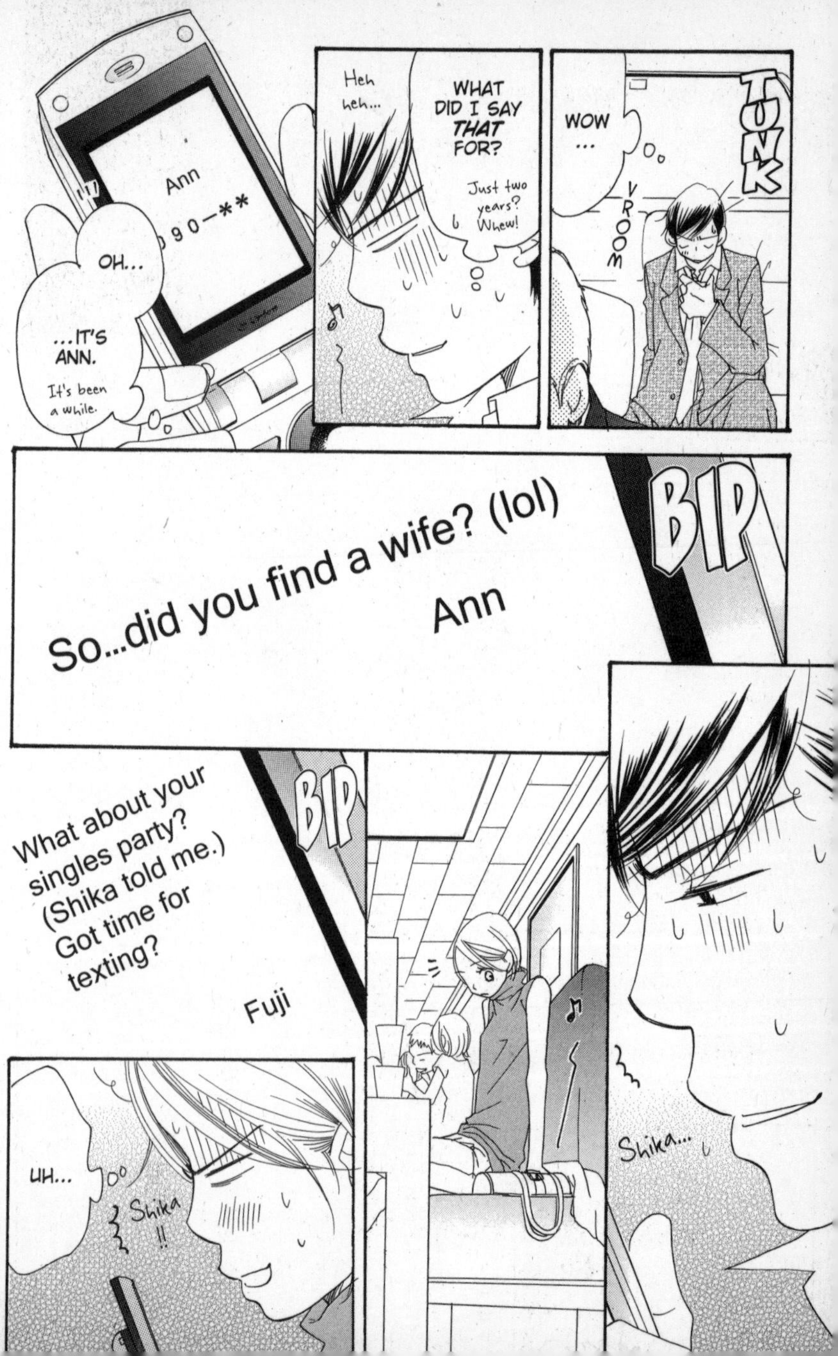

TUNK
WOW...
VROOM
Heh heh...
WHAT DID I SAY *THAT* FOR?
Just two years? Whew!
Ann
090-**
OH...
...IT'S ANN.
It's been a while.
BIP
So...did you find a wife? (lol)
Ann
Shika...
BIP
What about your singles party? (Shika told me.) Got time for texting?
Fuji
UH...
Shika!!

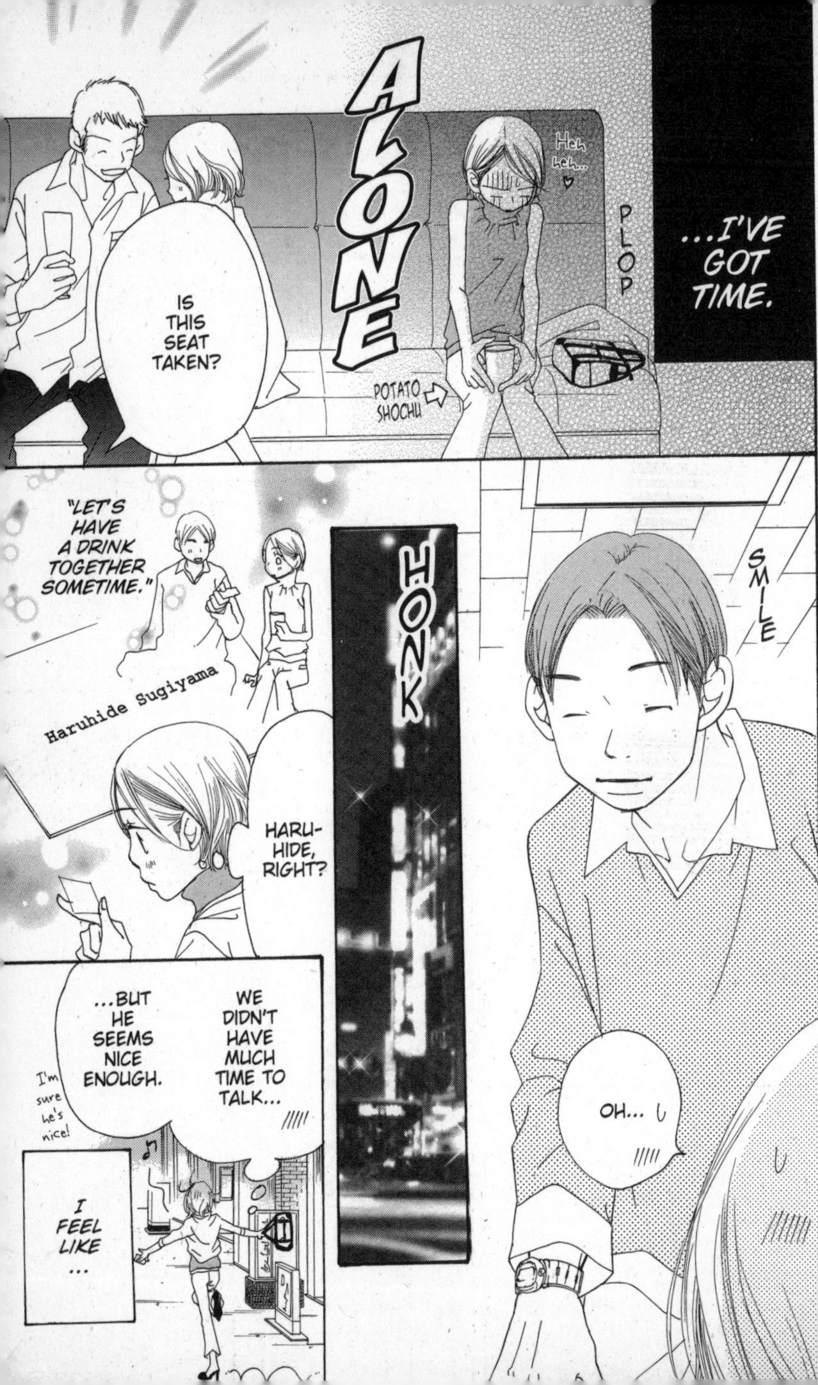
...I'VE GOT TIME.
PLOP
Heh heh...
ALONE
POTATO SHOCHU
IS THIS SEAT TAKEN?
SMILE
OH...
HONK
"LET'S HAVE A DRINK TOGETHER SOMETIME."
Haruhide Sugiyama
HARU-HIDE, RIGHT?
WE DIDN'T HAVE MUCH TIME TO TALK...
...BUT HE SEEMS NICE ENOUGH.
I'm sure he's nice!
I FEEL LIKE ...

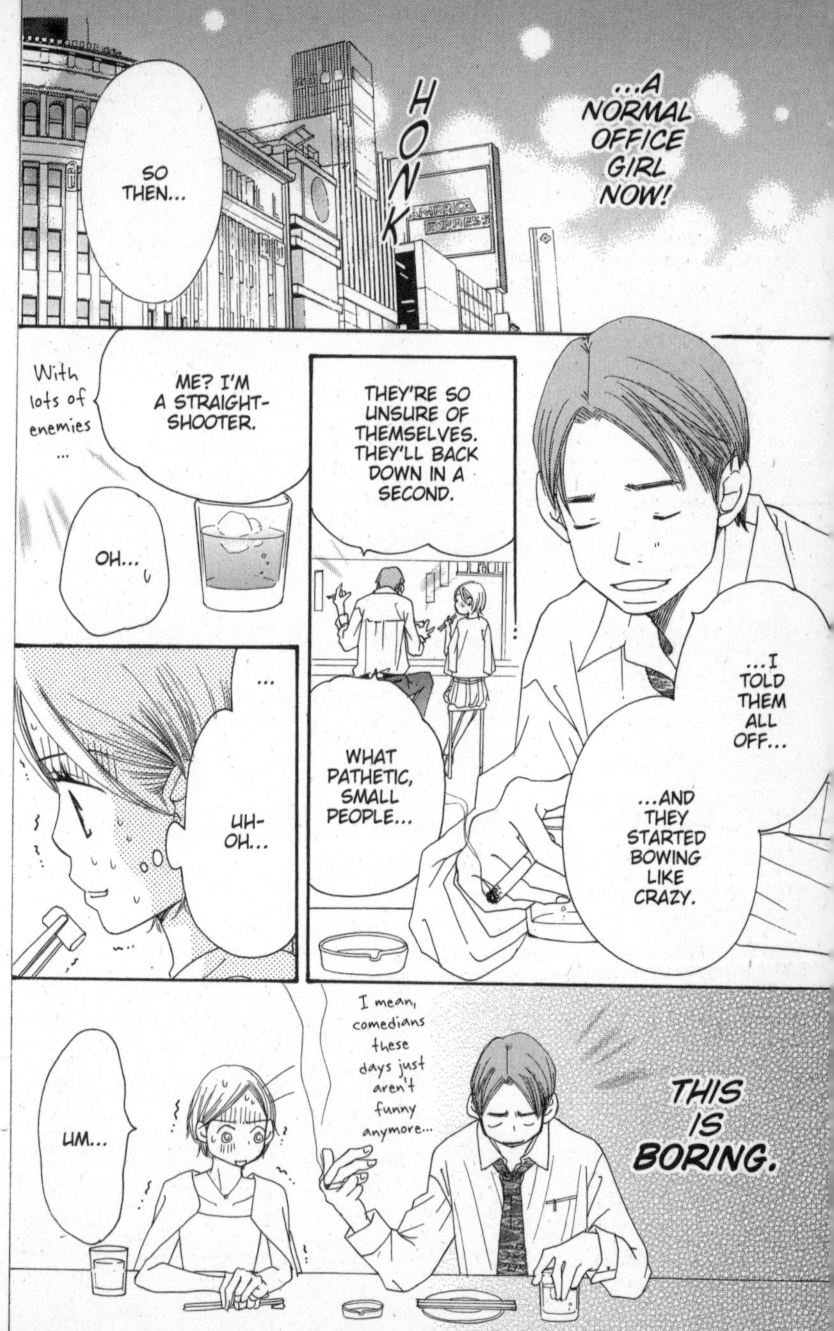
...A NORMAL OFFICE GIRL NOW!
HONK
SO THEN...
...I TOLD THEM ALL OFF...
...AND THEY STARTED BOWING LIKE CRAZY.
THEY'RE SO UNSURE OF THEMSELVES. THEY'LL BACK DOWN IN A SECOND.
WHAT PATHETIC, SMALL PEOPLE...
ME? I'M A STRAIGHT-SHOOTER.
With lots of enemies ...
OH...
...
UH-OH...
THIS IS BORING.
I mean, comedians these days just aren't funny anymore...
UM...

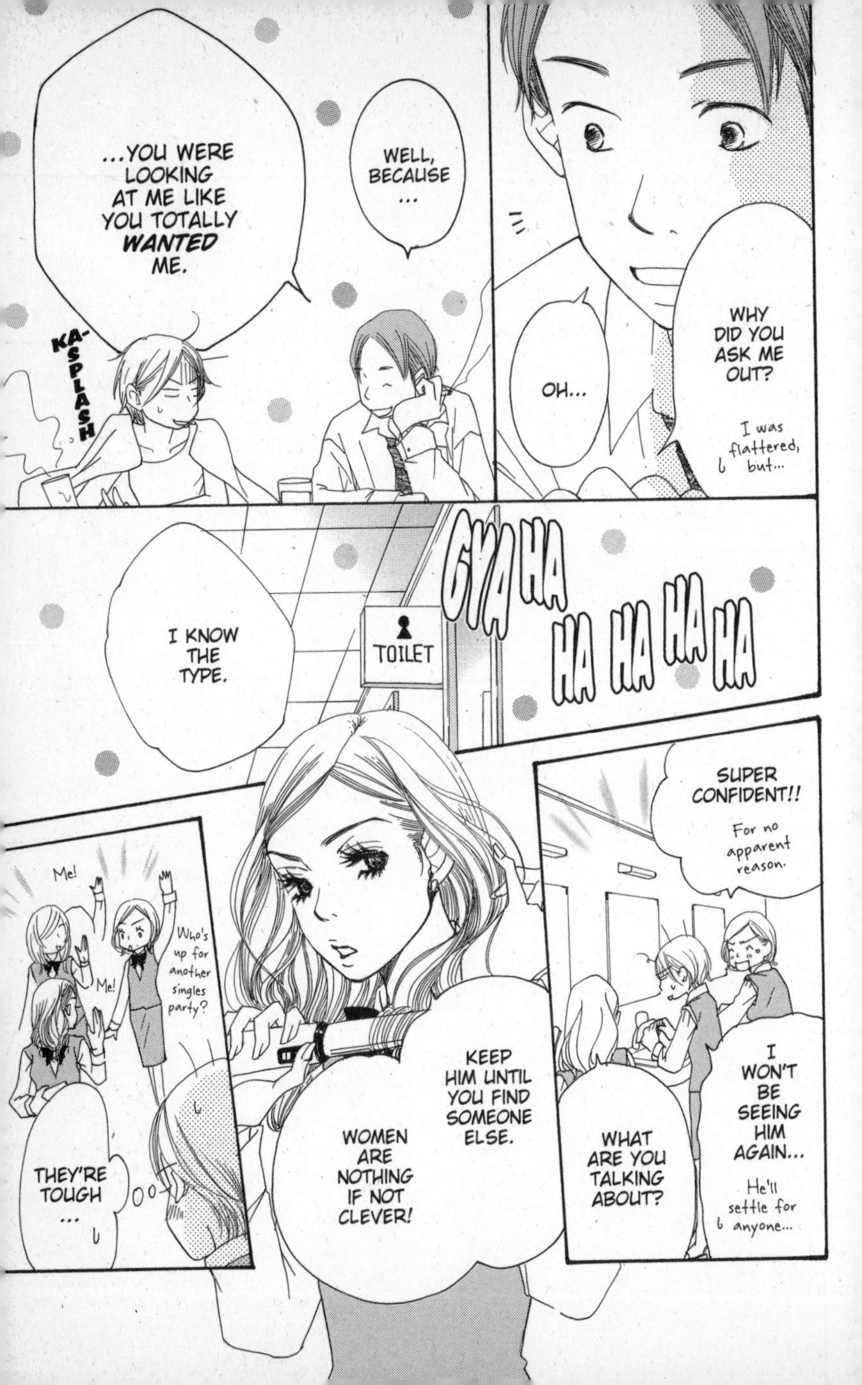
WHY DID YOU ASK ME OUT?
I was flattered, but...
OH...
WELL, BECAUSE ...
...YOU WERE LOOKING AT ME LIKE YOU TOTALLY **WANTED** ME.
KA-SPLASH
GYA HA HA HA HA HA
TOILET
I KNOW THE TYPE.
SUPER CONFIDENT!!
For no apparent reason.
I WON'T BE SEEING HIM AGAIN...
He'll settle for anyone...
WHAT ARE YOU TALKING ABOUT?
KEEP HIM UNTIL YOU FIND SOMEONE ELSE.
WOMEN ARE NOTHING IF NOT CLEVER!
Who's up for another singles party?
Me!
Me!
THEY'RE TOUGH ...

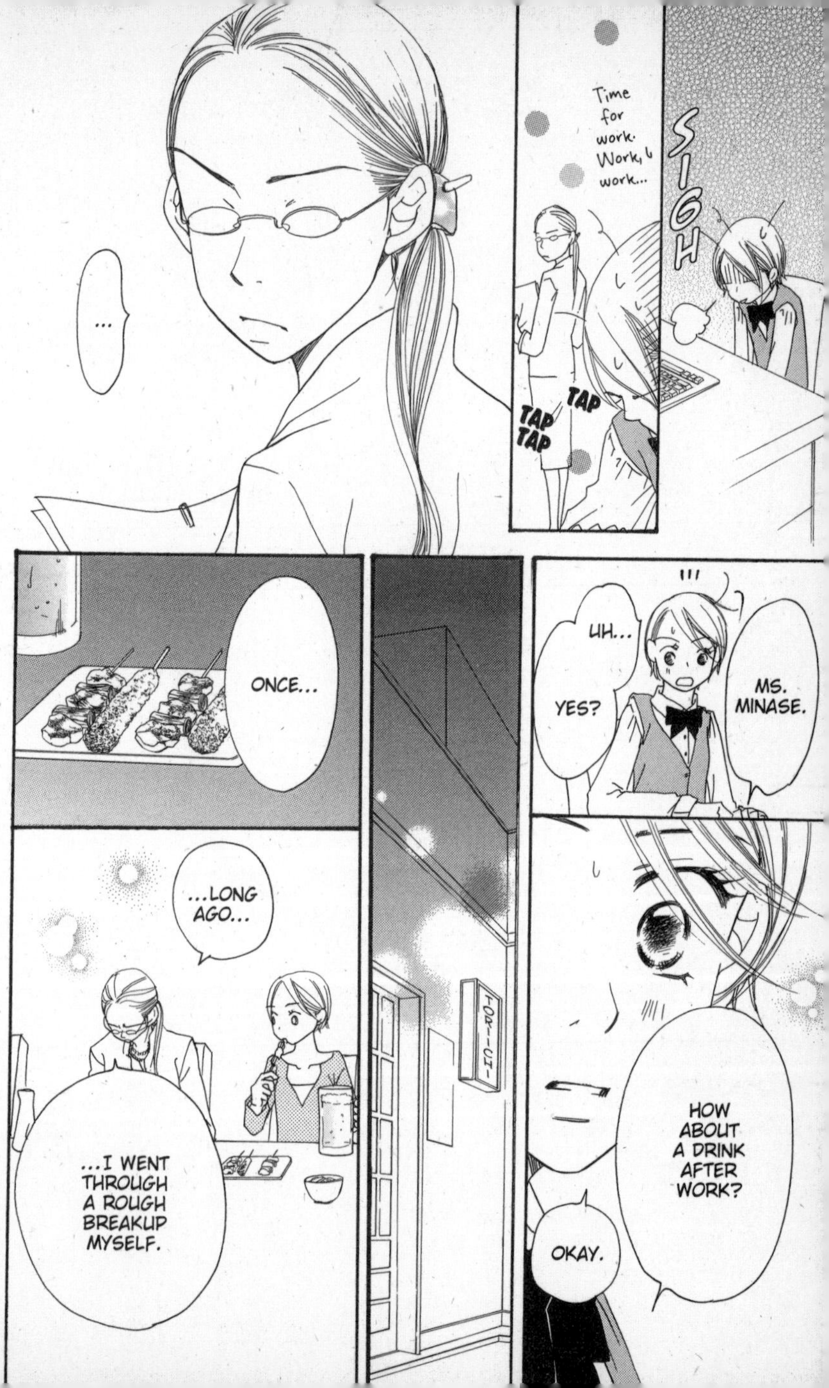
SIGH
Time for work. Work, work...
TAP
TAP TAP
...
MS. MINASE.
UH... YES?
HOW ABOUT A DRINK AFTER WORK?
OKAY.
TORICHI
ONCE...
...LONG AGO...
...I WENT THROUGH A ROUGH BREAKUP MYSELF.

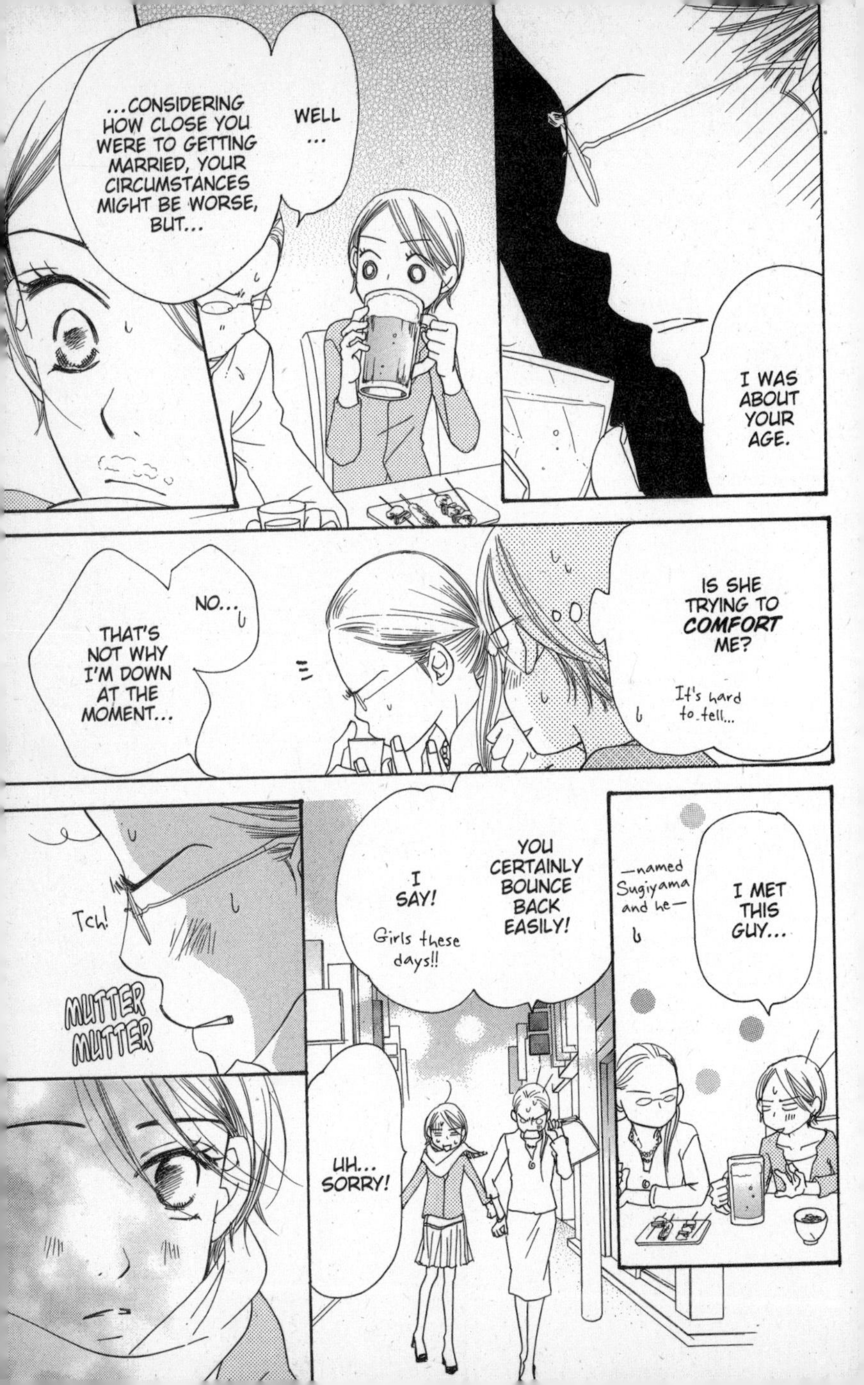
I WAS ABOUT YOUR AGE.
WELL...
...CONSIDERING HOW CLOSE YOU WERE TO GETTING MARRIED, YOUR CIRCUMSTANCES MIGHT BE WORSE, BUT...
IS SHE TRYING TO **COMFORT** ME?
It's hard to tell...
NO...
THAT'S NOT WHY I'M DOWN AT THE MOMENT...
I MET THIS GUY...
—named Sugiyama and he—
YOU CERTAINLY BOUNCE BACK EASILY!
I SAY!
Girls these days!!
UH... SORRY!
Tch!
MUTTER MUTTER

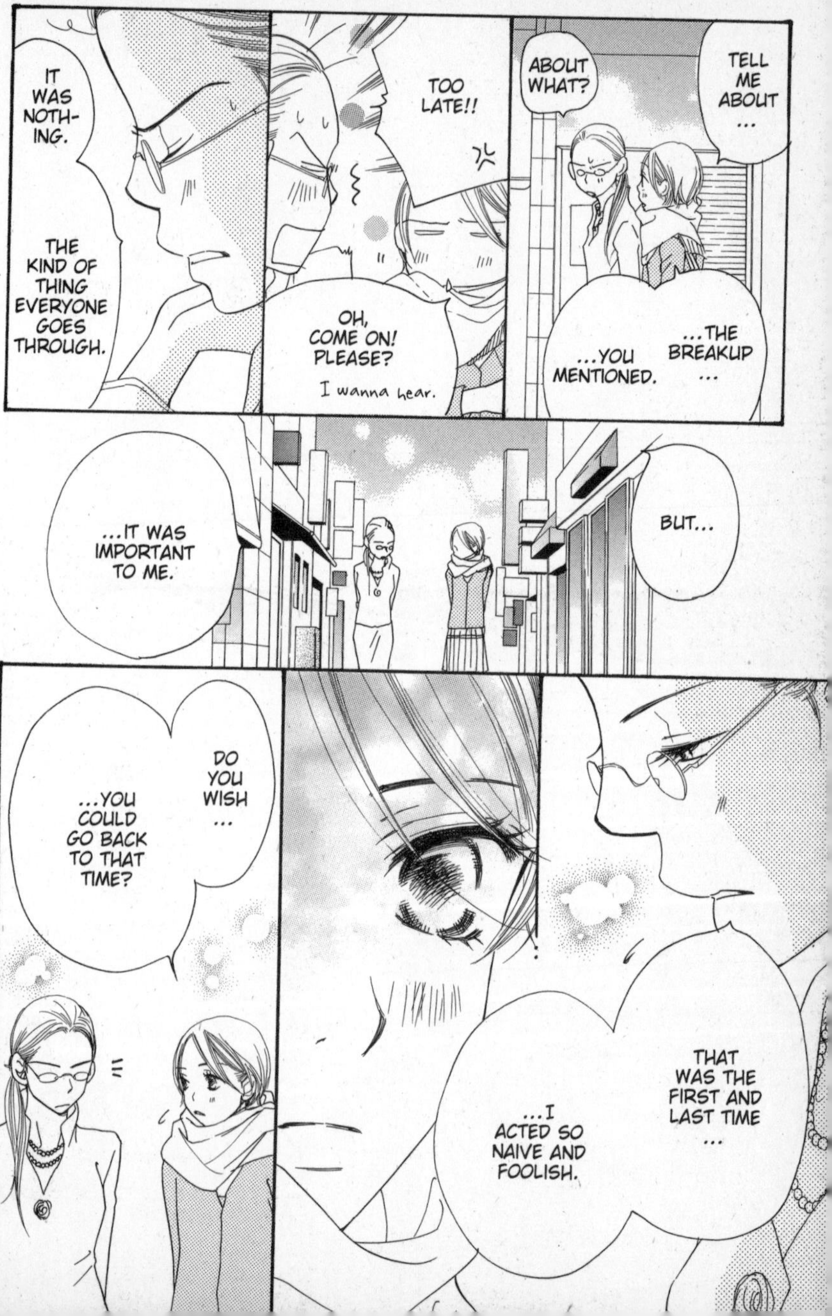
TELL ME ABOUT ...
ABOUT WHAT?
...THE BREAKUP ...
...YOU MENTIONED.
TOO LATE!!
OH, COME ON! PLEASE?
I wanna hear.
IT WAS NOTH-ING.
THE KIND OF THING EVERYONE GOES THROUGH.
BUT...
...IT WAS IMPORTANT TO ME.
THAT WAS THE FIRST AND LAST TIME ...
...I ACTED SO NAIVE AND FOOLISH.
DO YOU WISH ...
...YOU COULD GO BACK TO THAT TIME?

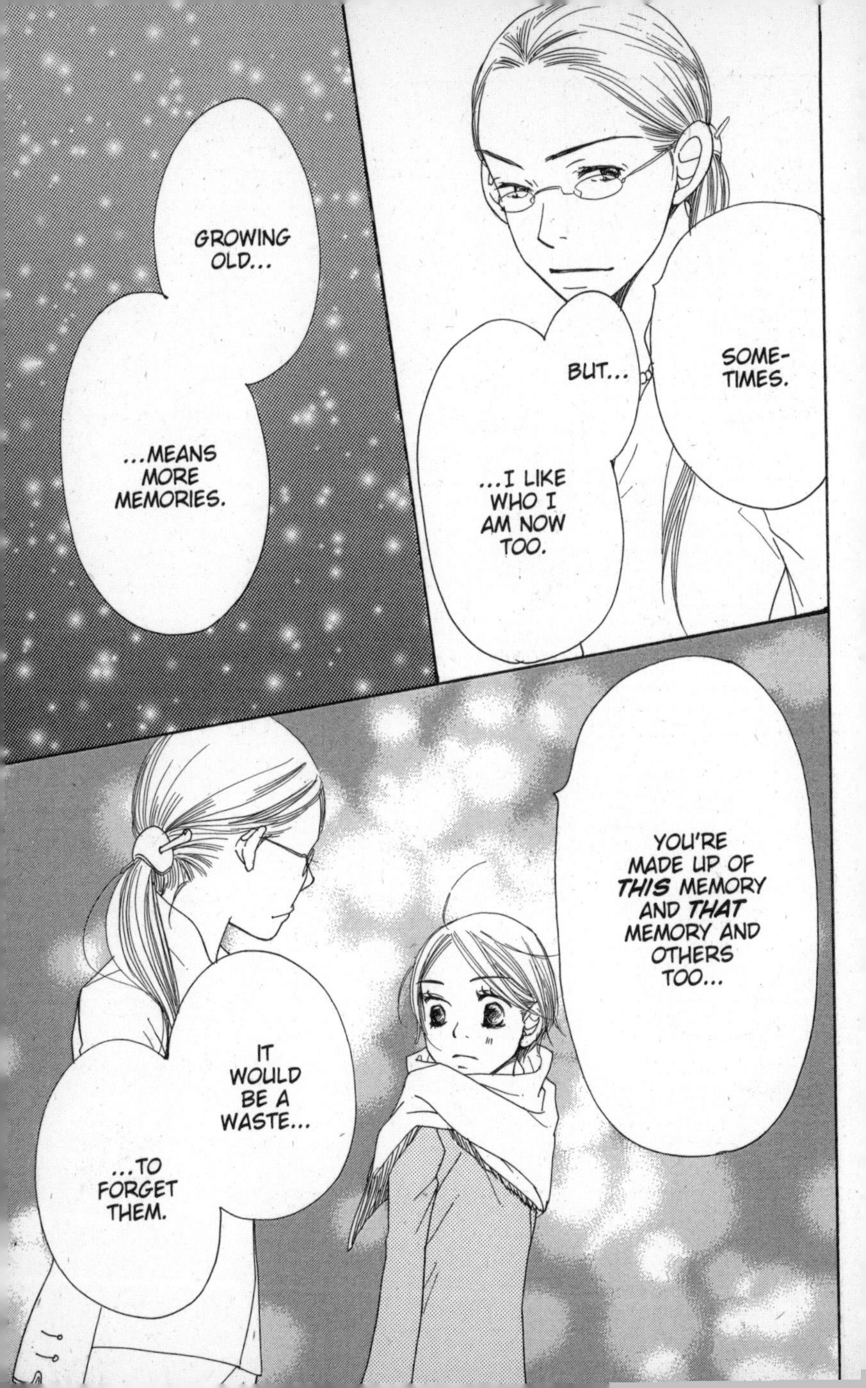
SOME-TIMES.
BUT...
...I LIKE WHO I AM NOW TOO.
GROWING OLD...
...MEANS MORE MEMORIES.
YOU'RE MADE UP OF *THIS* MEMORY AND *THAT* MEMORY AND OTHERS TOO...
IT WOULD BE A WASTE...
...TO FORGET THEM.

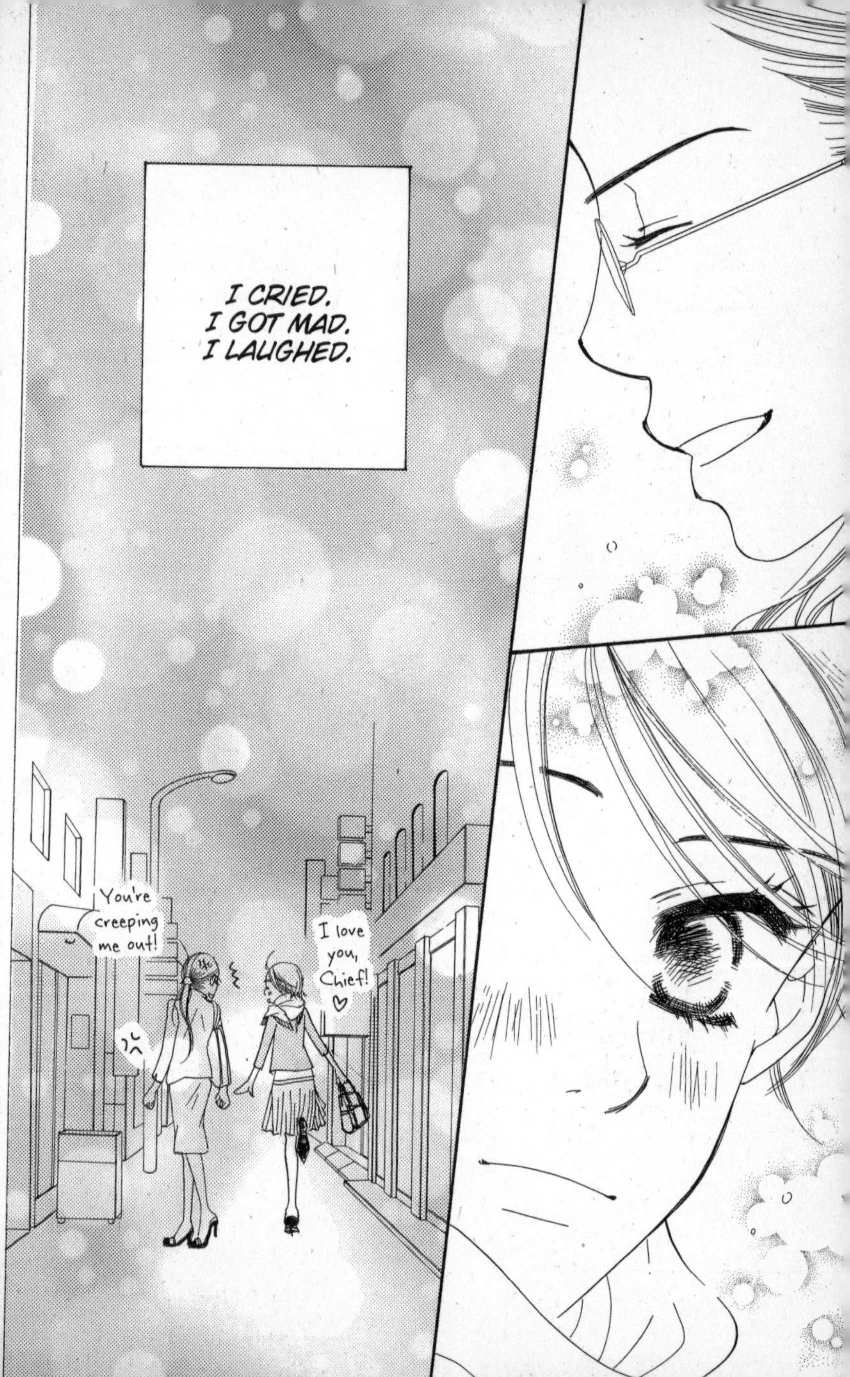
I CRIED.
I GOT MAD.
I LAUGHED.
I love you, Chief! ♡
You're creeping me out!

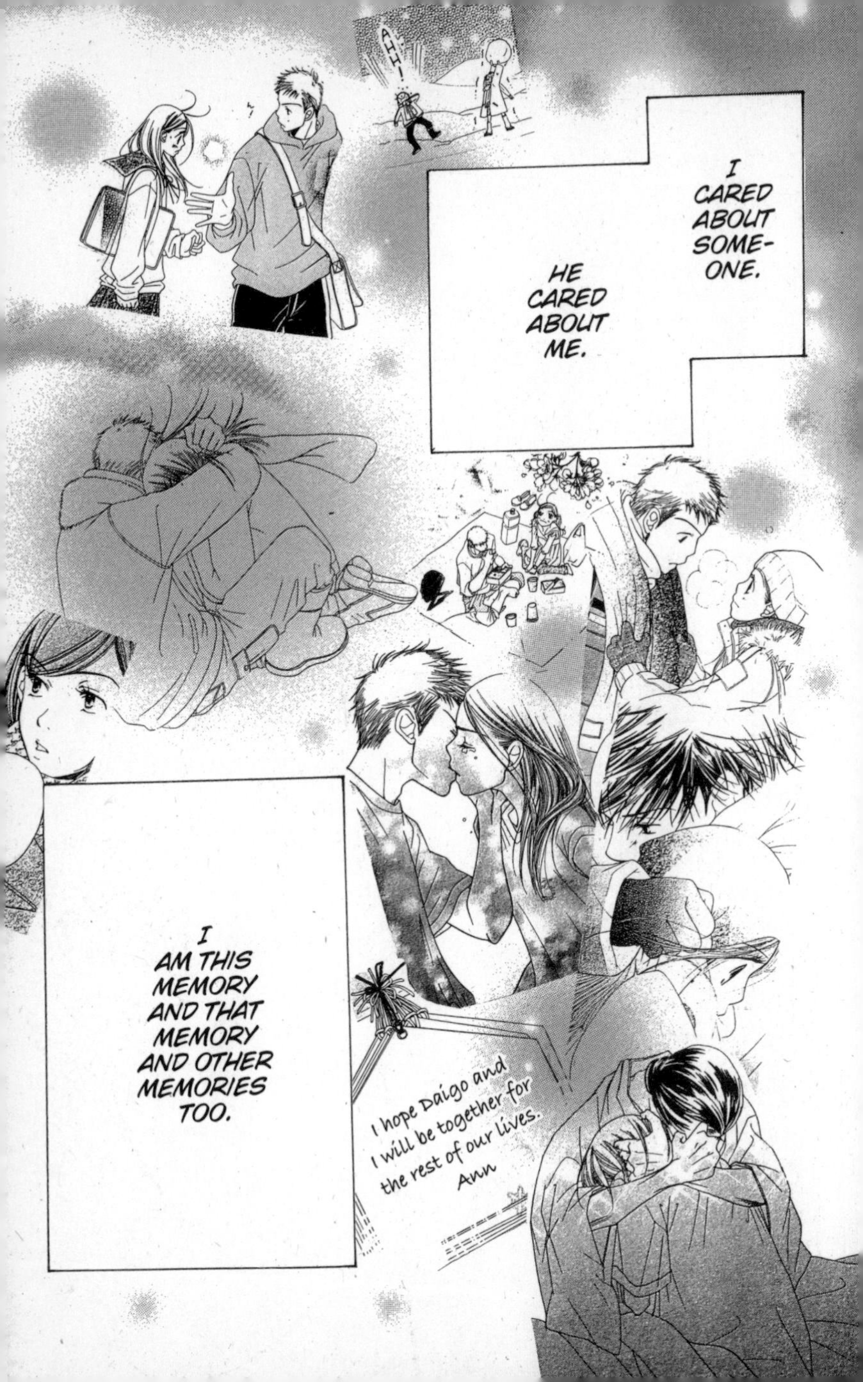
AHHH!
I CARED ABOUT SOMEONE.
HE CARED ABOUT ME.
I hope Daigo and I will be together for the rest of our lives.
Ann
I AM THIS MEMORY AND THAT MEMORY AND OTHER MEMORIES TOO.

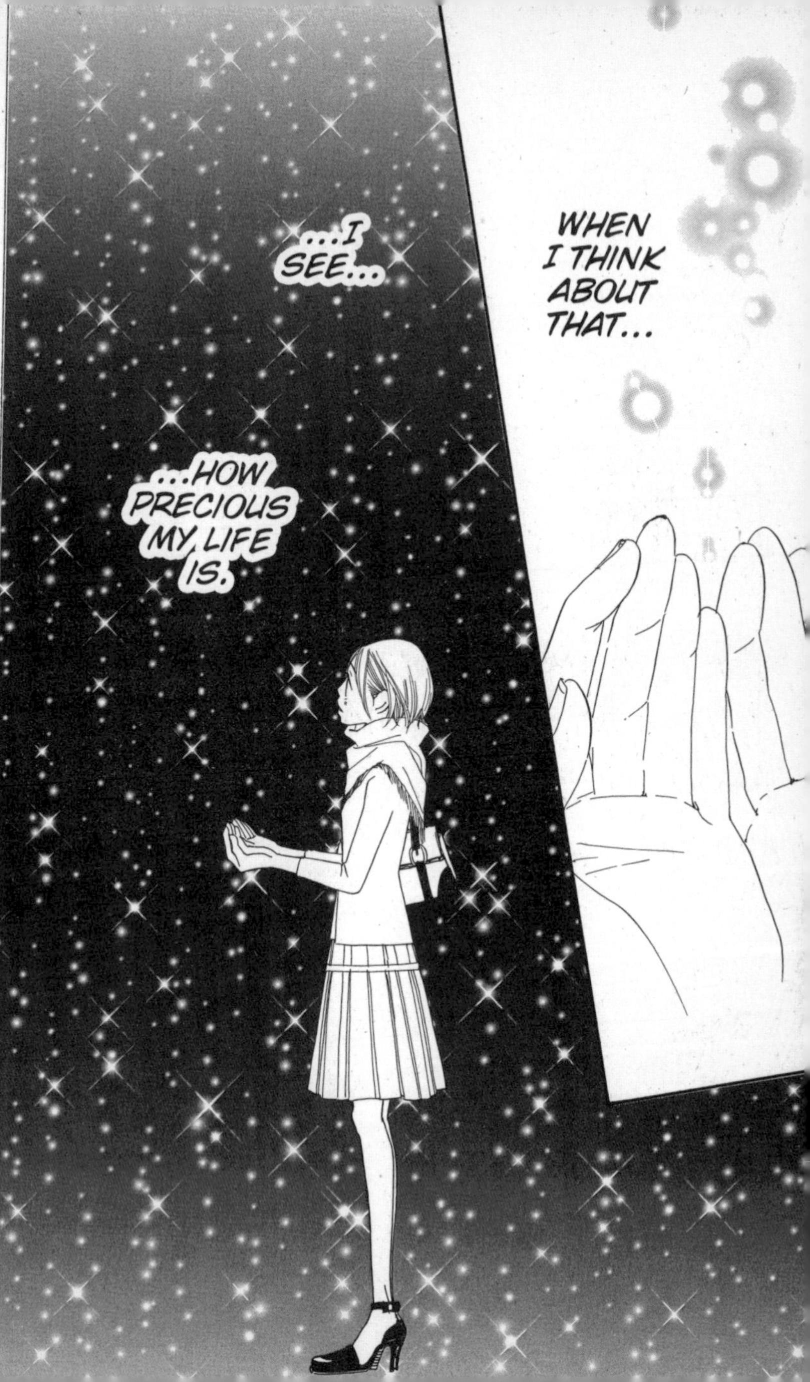
WHEN I THINK ABOUT THAT...
...I SEE...
...HOW PRECIOUS MY LIFE IS.

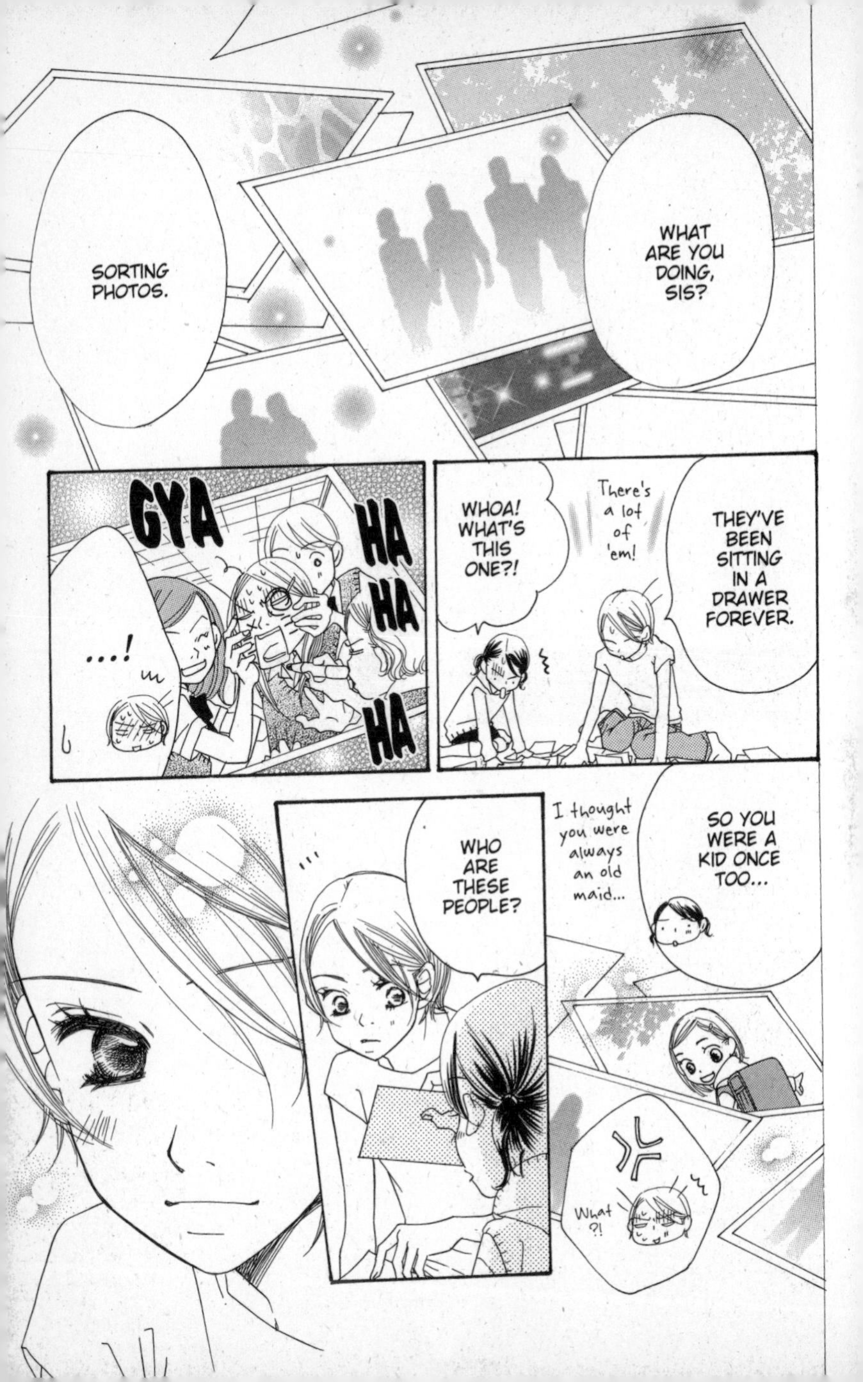
WHAT ARE YOU DOING, SIS?
SORTING PHOTOS.
THEY'VE BEEN SITTING IN A DRAWER FOREVER.
There's a lot of 'em!
WHOA! WHAT'S THIS ONE?!
HA HA HA
GYA
...!
SO YOU WERE A KID ONCE TOO...
I thought you were always an old maid...
What?!
WHO ARE THESE PEOPLE?
...

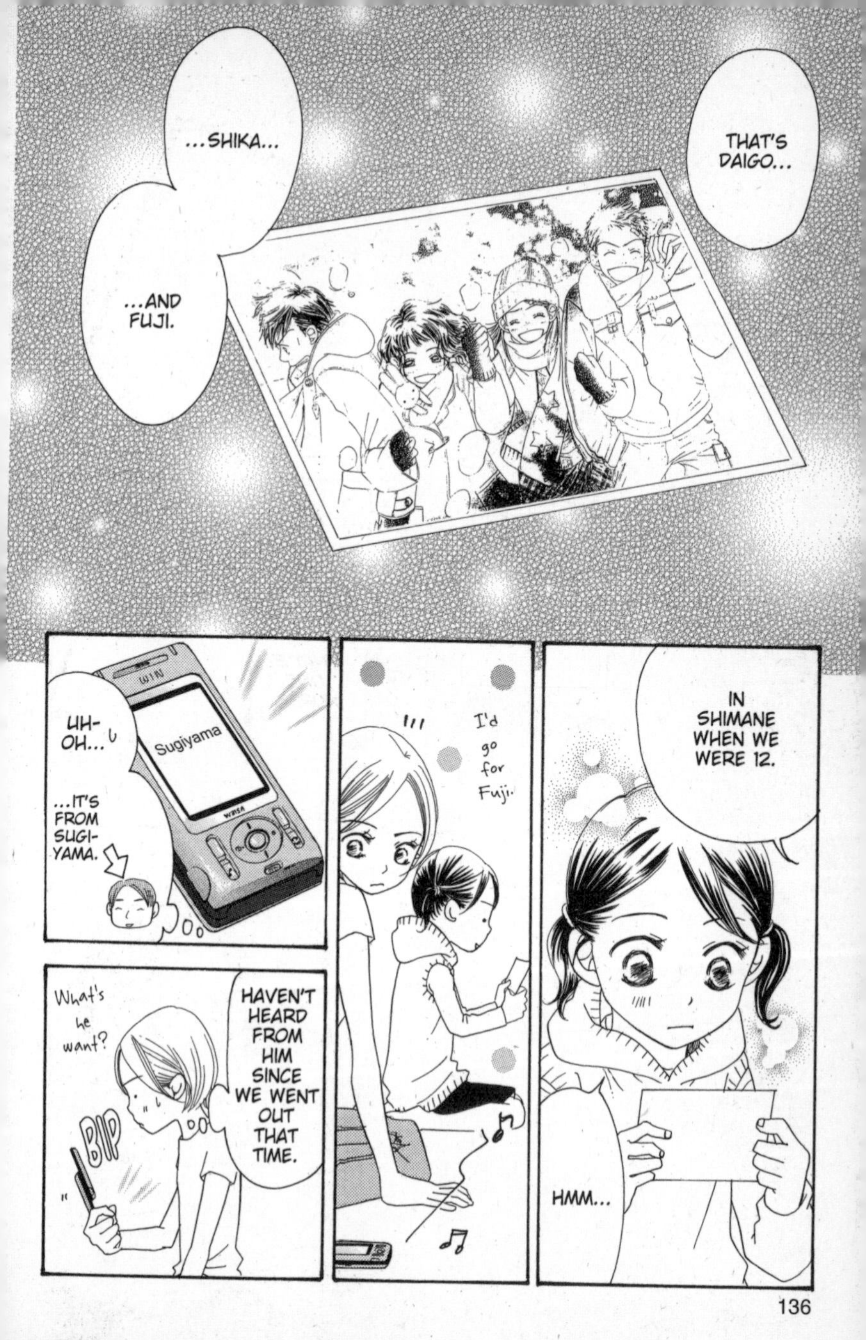
THAT'S DAIGO...
...SHIKA...
...AND FUJI.
IN SHIMANE WHEN WE WERE 12.
HMM...
I'd go for Fuji.
UH-OH...
Sugiyama
...IT'S FROM SUGI-YAMA.
HAVEN'T HEARD FROM HIM SINCE WE WENT OUT THAT TIME.
What's he want?
BIP

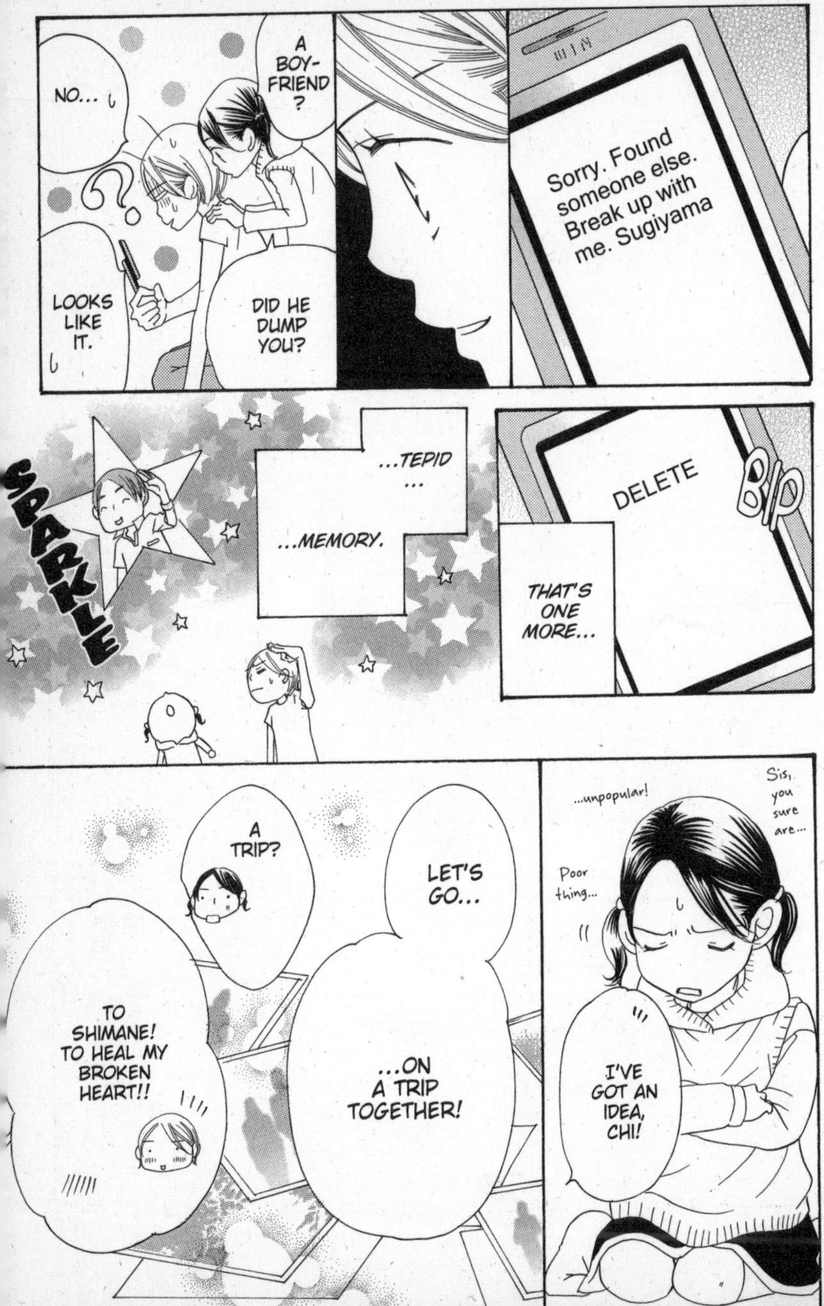
Sorry. Found someone else. Break up with me. Sugiyama
A BOY-FRIEND?
NO...
DID HE DUMP YOU?
LOOKS LIKE IT.
DELETE
BIP
THAT'S ONE MORE...
...TEPID ...
...MEMORY.
SPARKLE
Sis, you sure are...
...unpopular!
Poor thing...
I'VE GOT AN IDEA, CHI!
LET'S GO...
...ON A TRIP TOGETHER!
A TRIP?
TO SHIMANE! TO HEAL MY BROKEN HEART!!

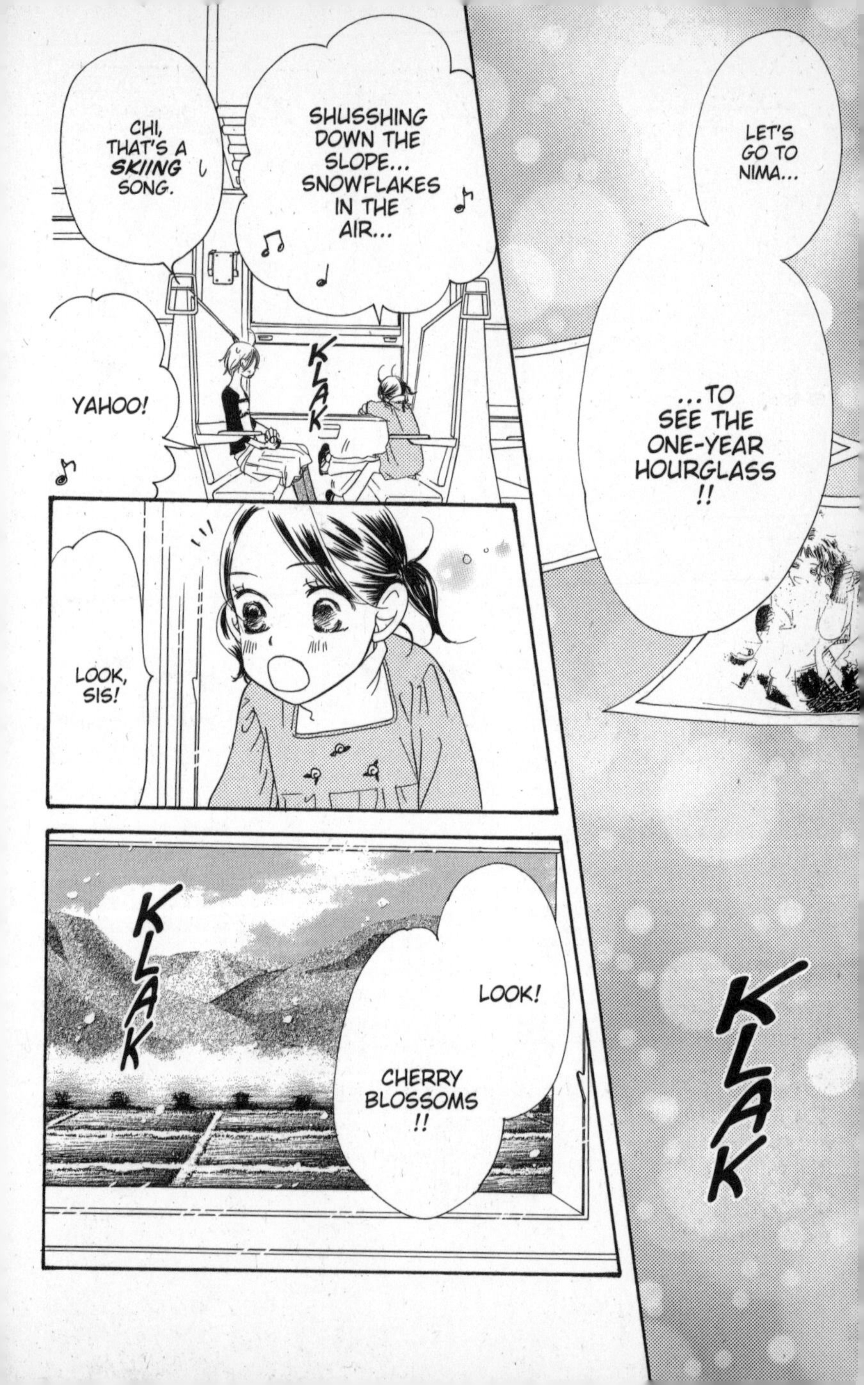
LET'S GO TO NIMA...
...TO SEE THE ONE-YEAR HOURGLASS!!
KLAK
SHUSSHING DOWN THE SLOPE... SNOWFLAKES IN THE AIR...
CHI, THAT'S A SKIING SONG.
KLAK
YAHOO!
LOOK, SIS!
LOOK!
CHERRY BLOSSOMS!!
KLAK

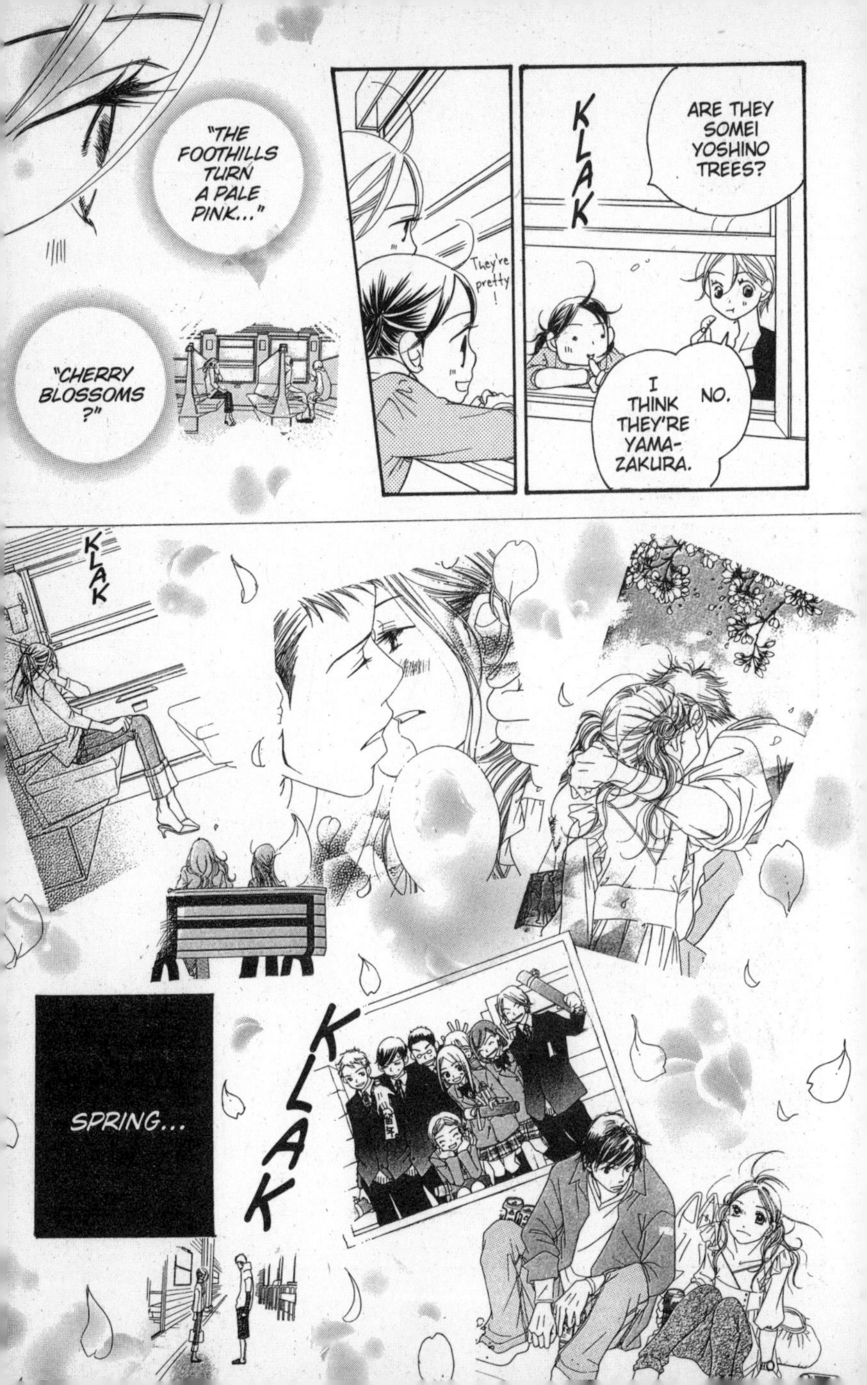
KLAK
ARE THEY SOMEI YOSHINO TREES?
NO.
I THINK THEY'RE YAMA-ZAKURA.
They're pretty!
"THE FOOTHILLS TURN A PALE PINK..."
"CHERRY BLOSSOMS?"
KLAK
KLAK
SPRING...

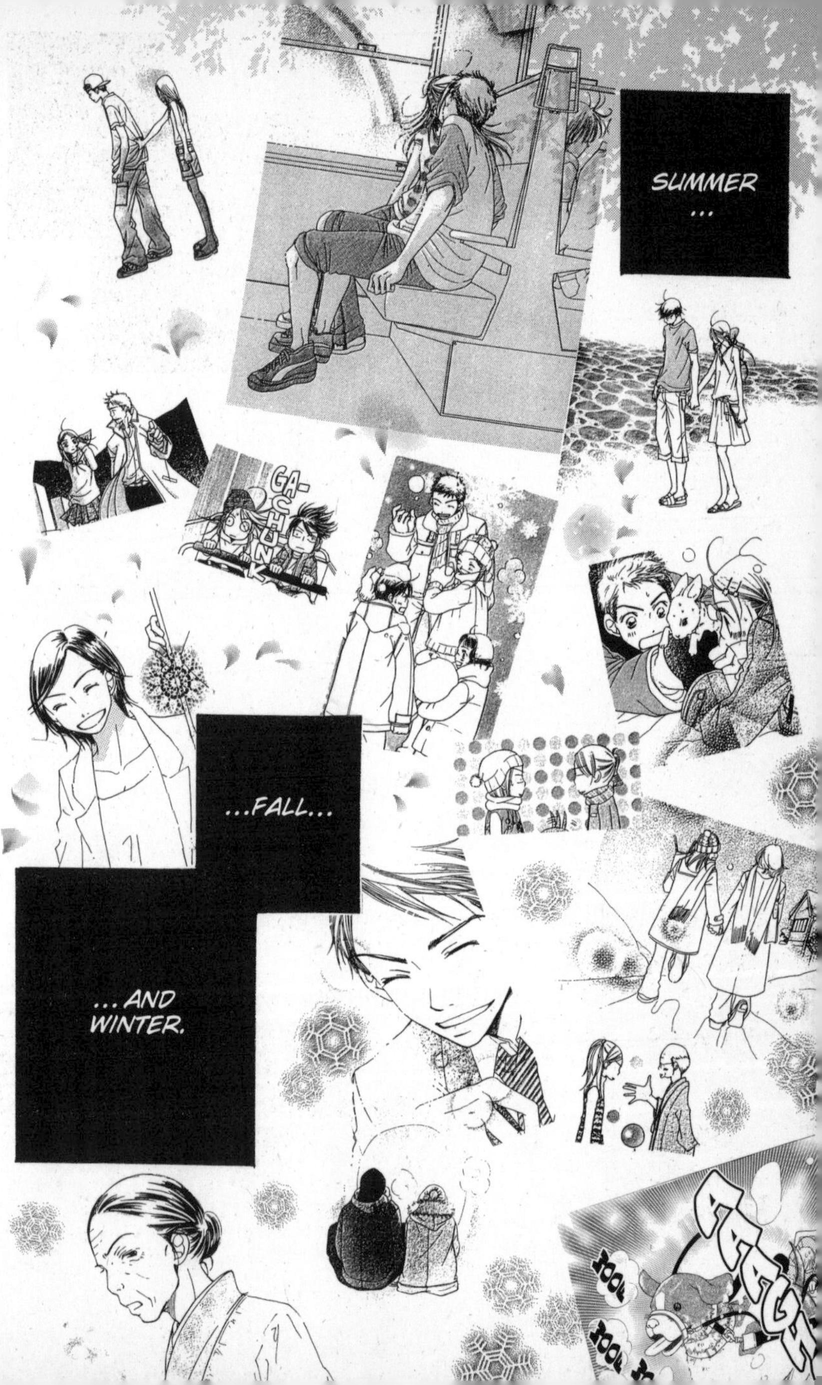
SUMMER …
GA-CHUNK
…FALL…
…AND WINTER.
AAAGH

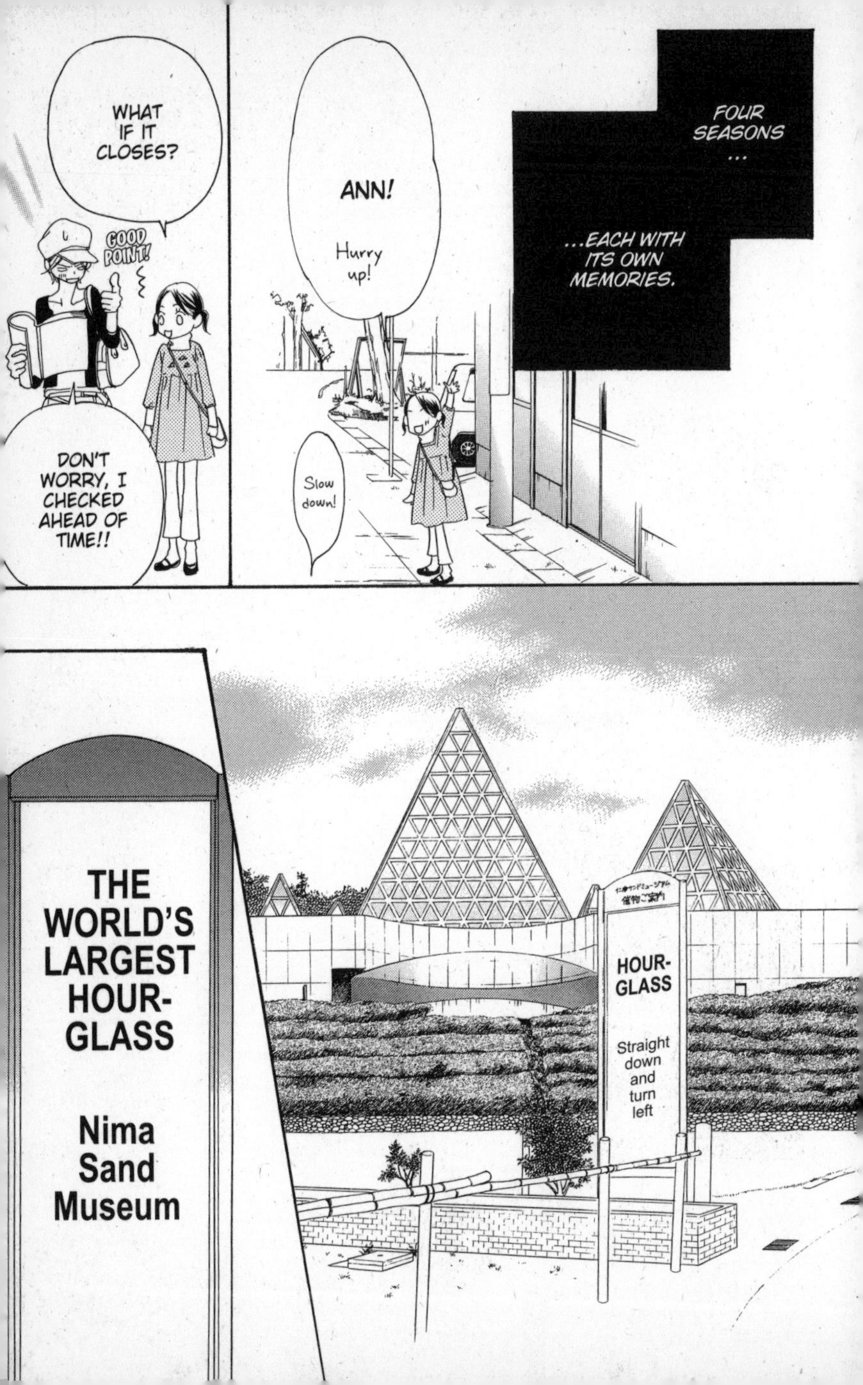
FOUR SEASONS...
...EACH WITH ITS OWN MEMORIES.
ANN!
Hurry up!
Slow down!
WHAT IF IT CLOSES?
GOOD POINT!
DON'T WORRY, I CHECKED AHEAD OF TIME!!
HOUR-GLASS
Straight down and turn left
THE WORLD'S LARGEST HOUR-GLASS
Nima Sand Museum

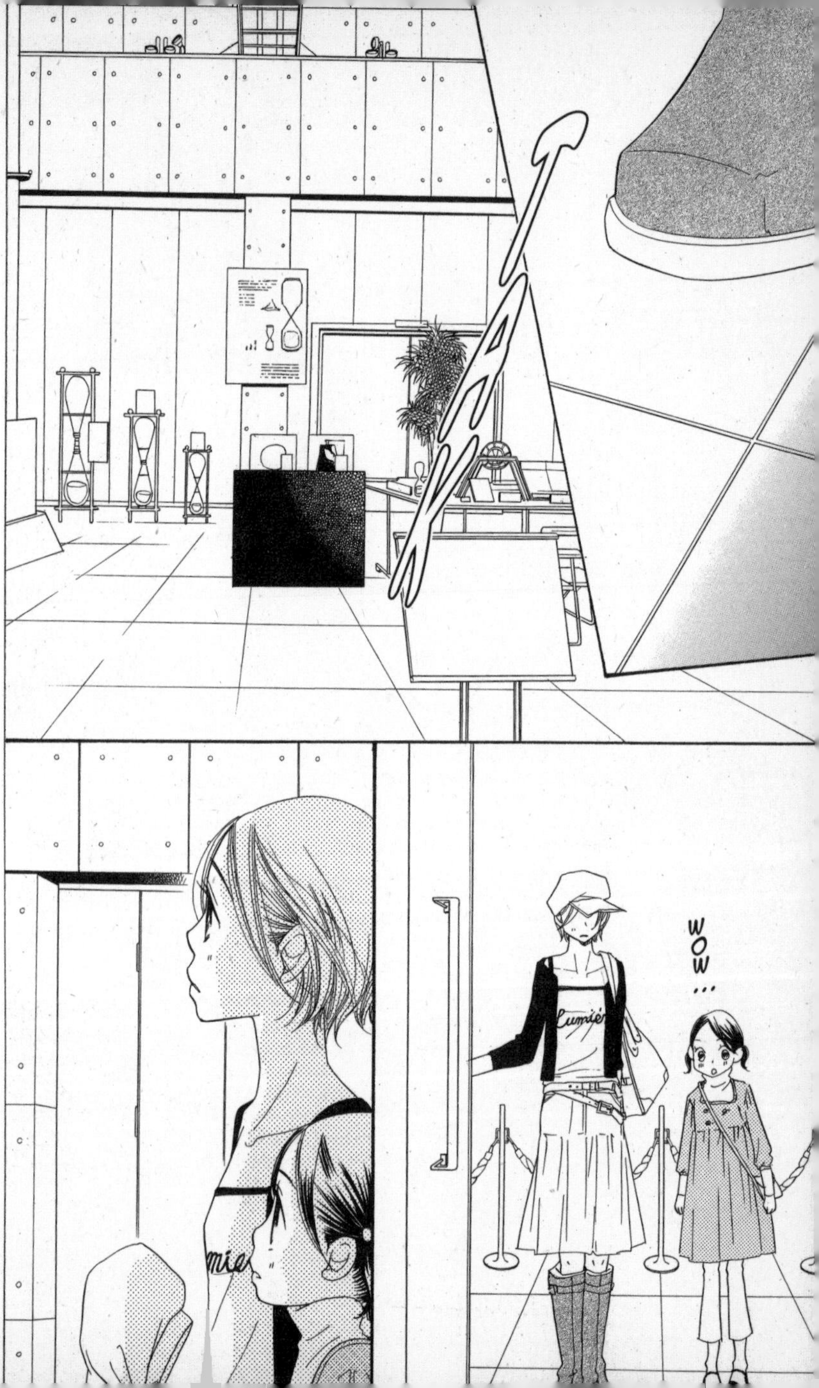
KAA
WOW...

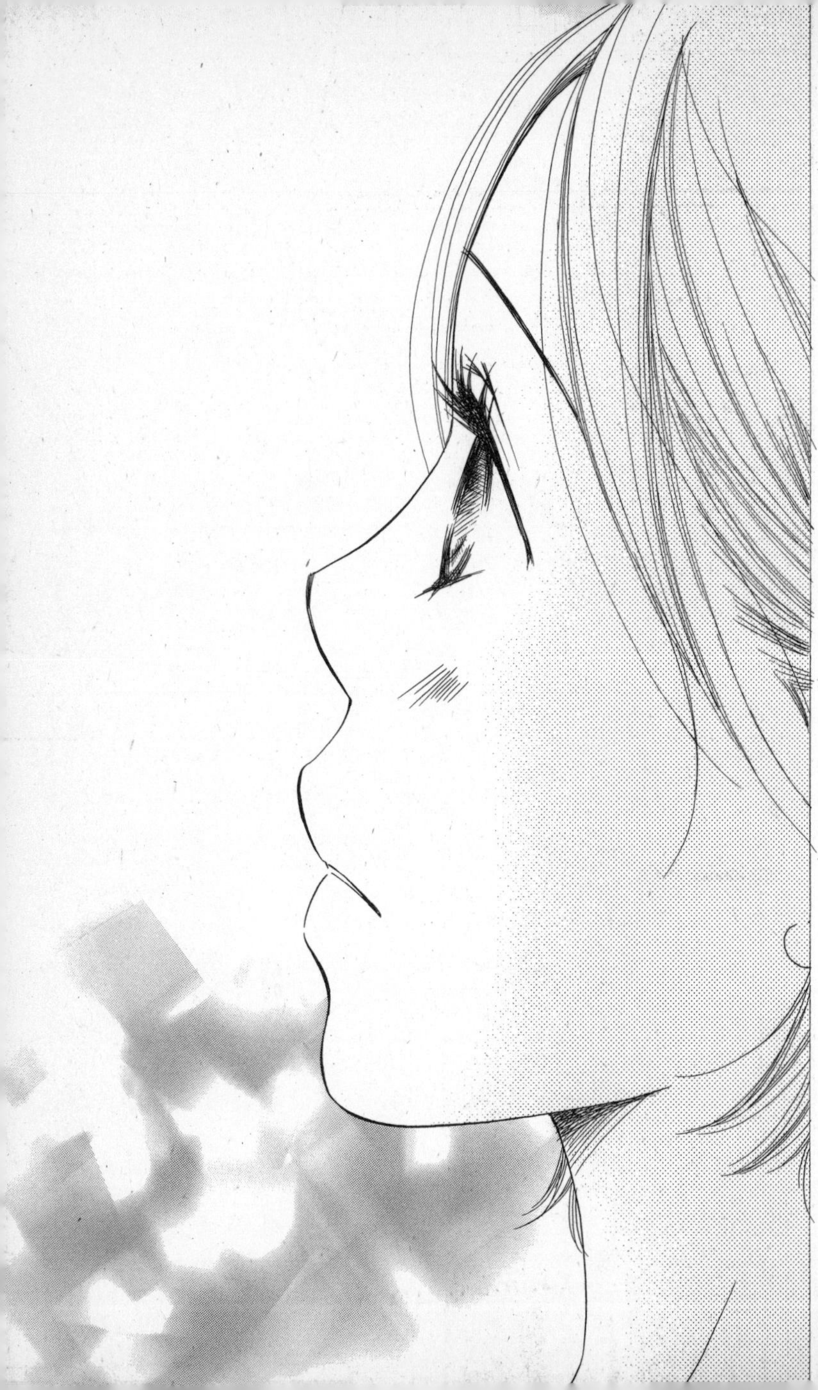

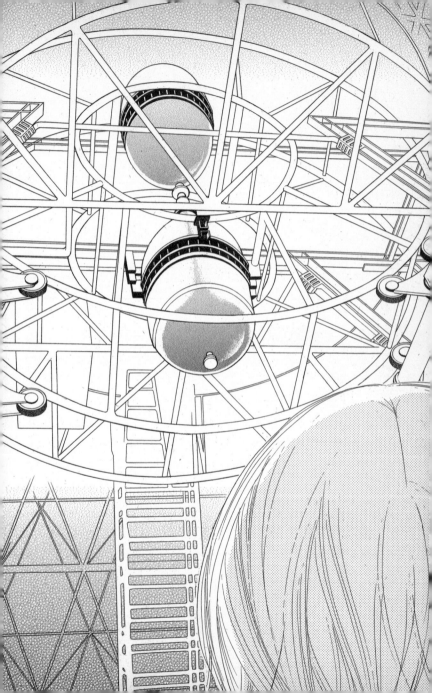

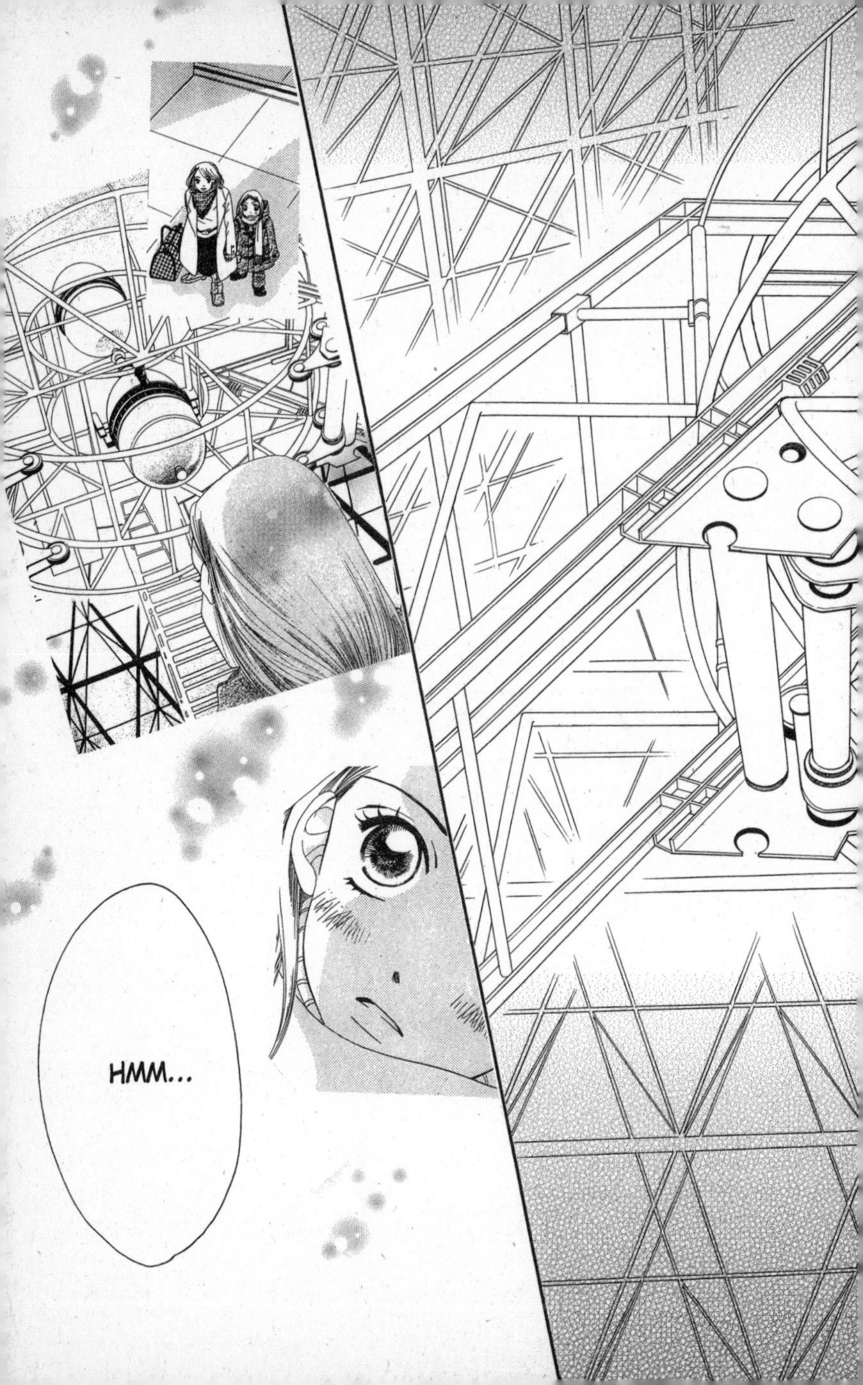
HMM...

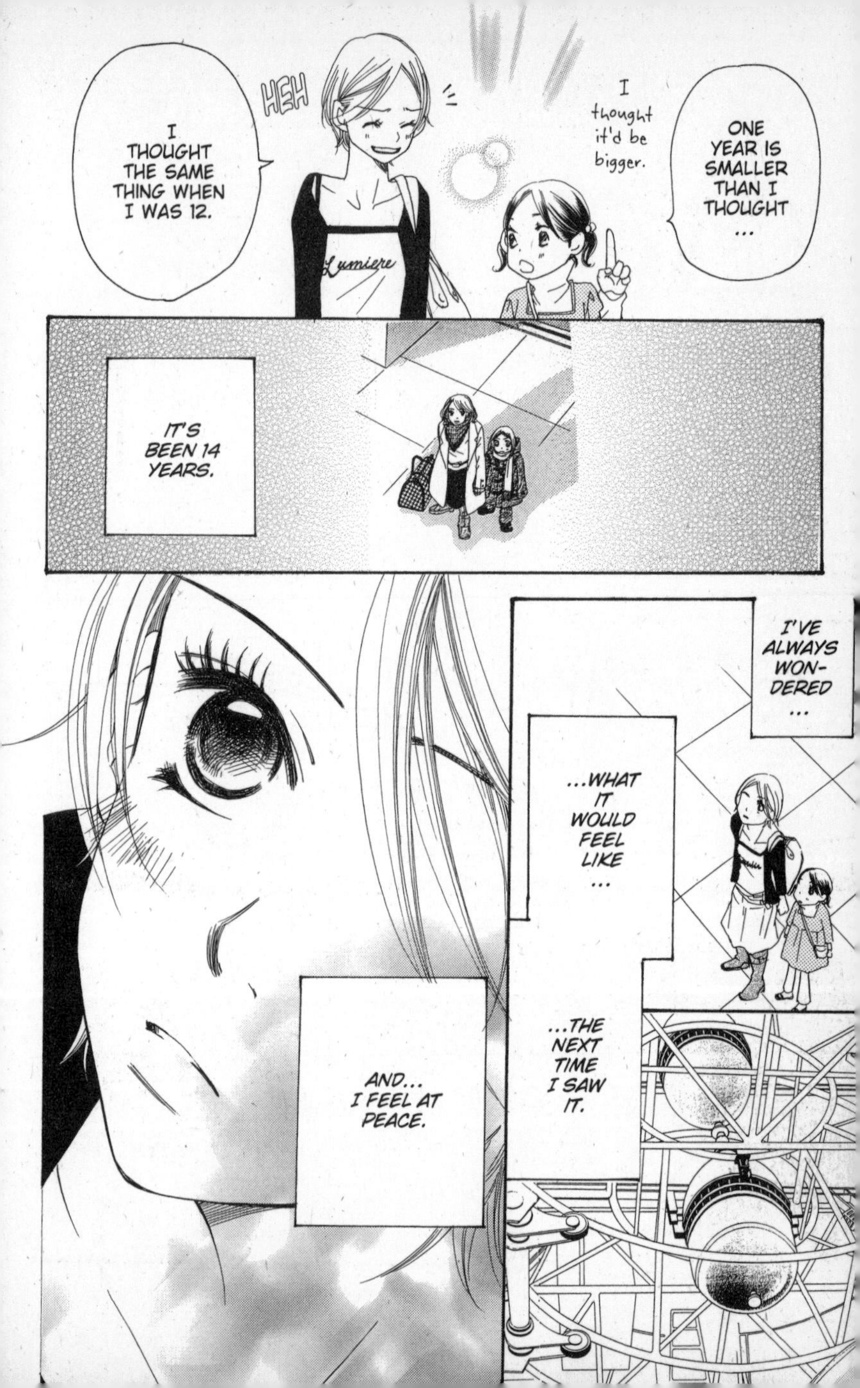
ONE YEAR IS SMALLER THAN I THOUGHT...
I thought it'd be bigger.
HEH
I THOUGHT THE SAME THING WHEN I WAS 12.
IT'S BEEN 14 YEARS.
I'VE ALWAYS WONDERED...
...WHAT IT WOULD FEEL LIKE...
...THE NEXT TIME I SAW IT.
AND... I FEEL AT PEACE.

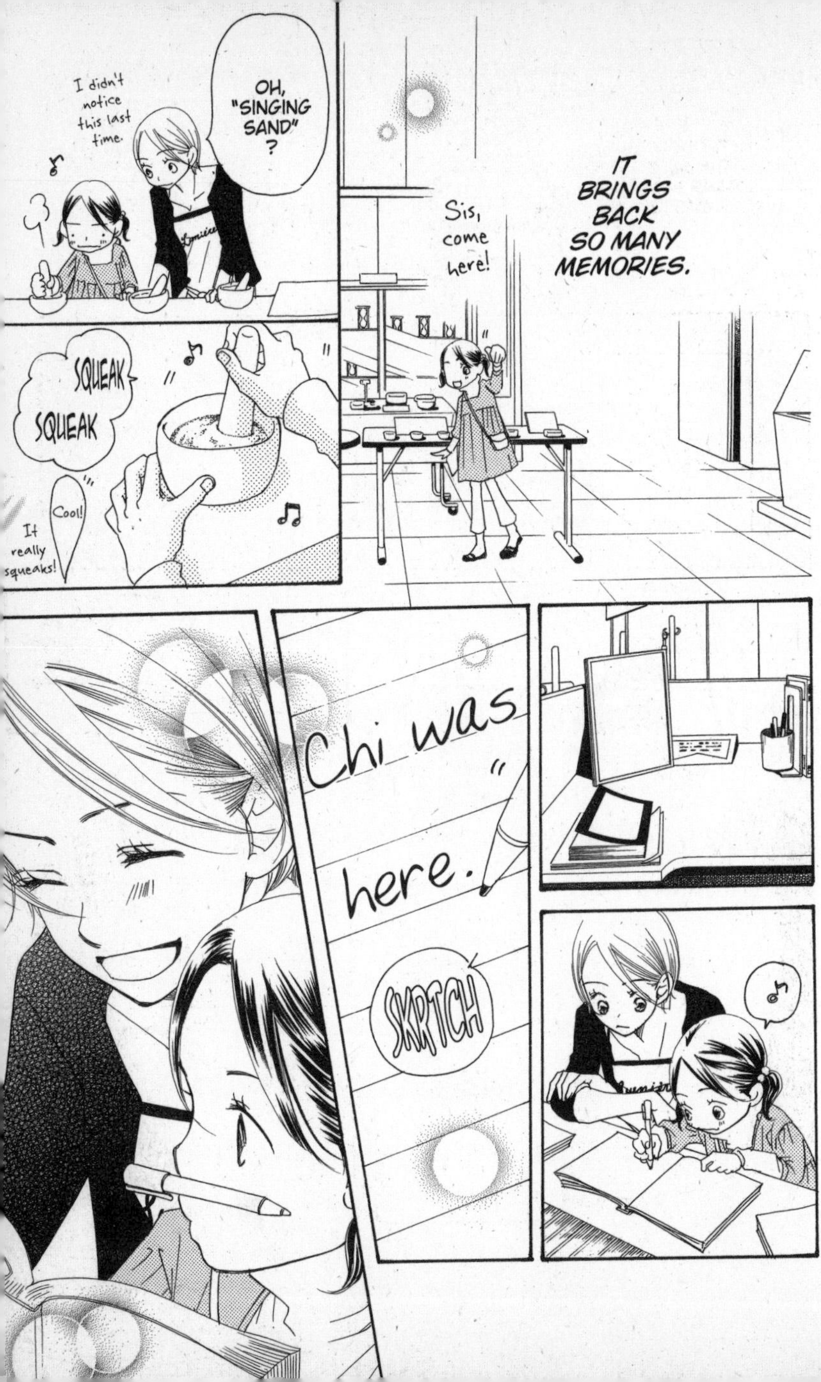
IT BRINGS BACK SO MANY MEMORIES.
Sis, come here!
OH, "SINGING SAND"?
I didn't notice this last time.
SQUEAK SQUEAK
Cool! It really squeaks!
Chi was here.
SKRTCH

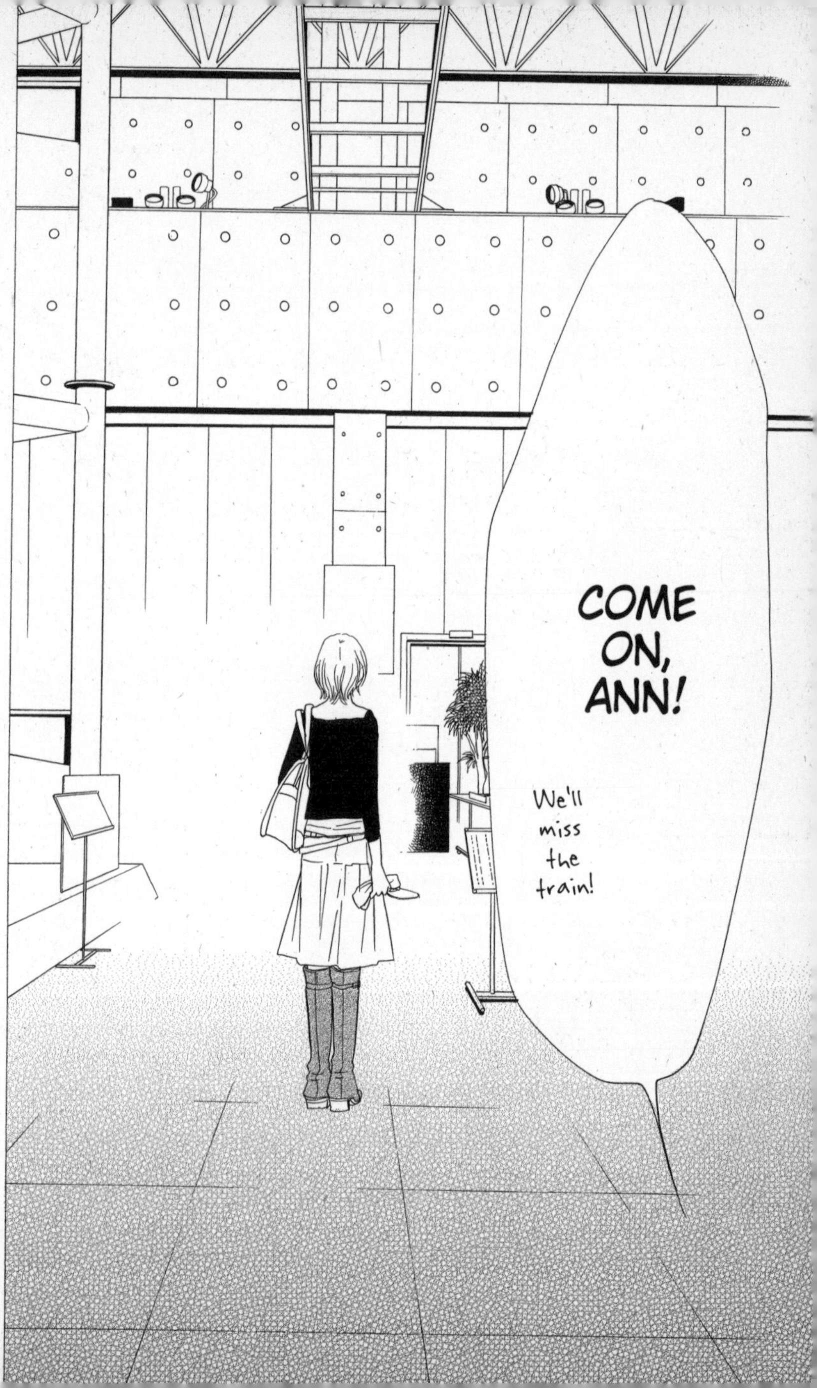
COME ON, ANN!
We'll miss the train!

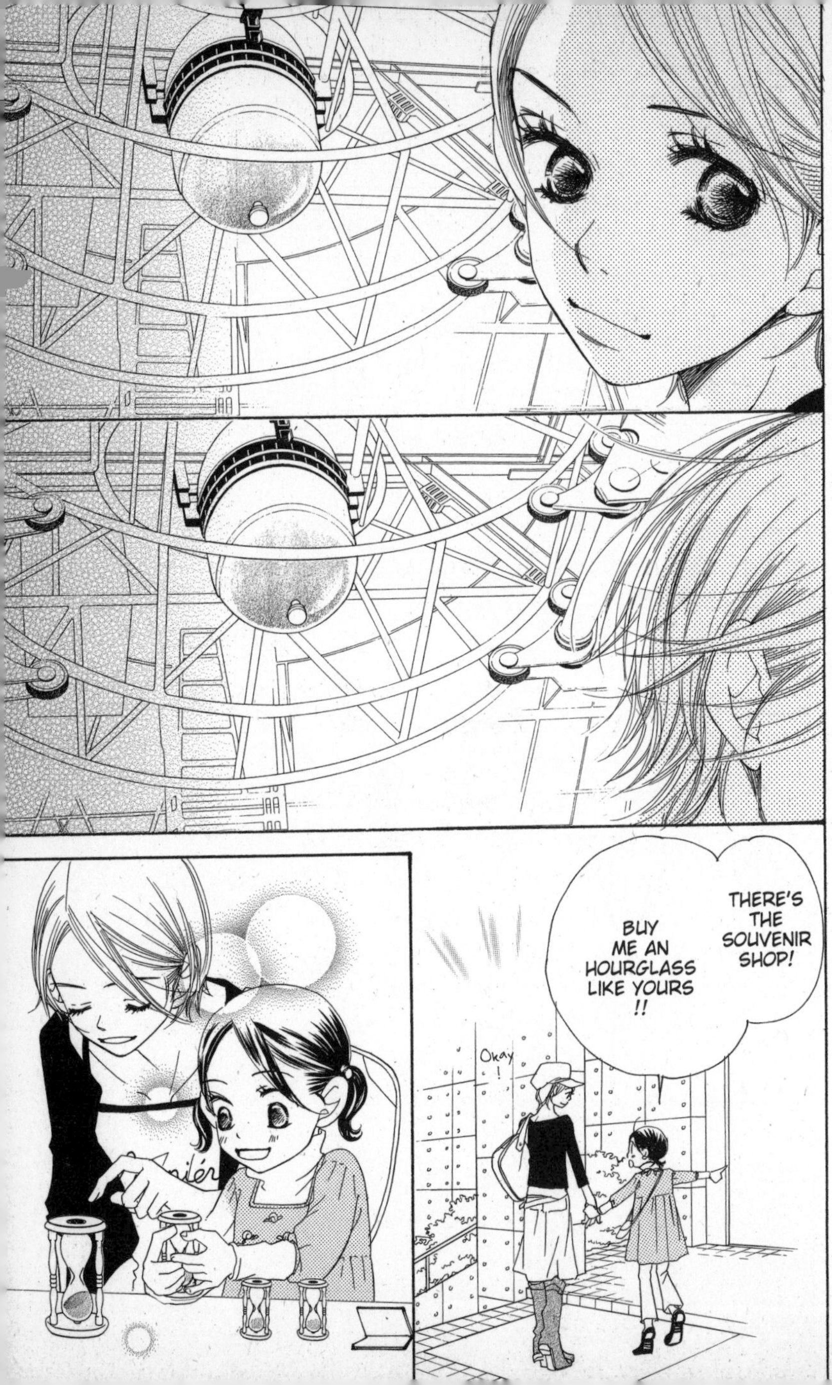
THERE'S THE SOUVENIR SHOP!
BUY ME AN HOURGLASS LIKE YOURS !!
Okay !
Aniér

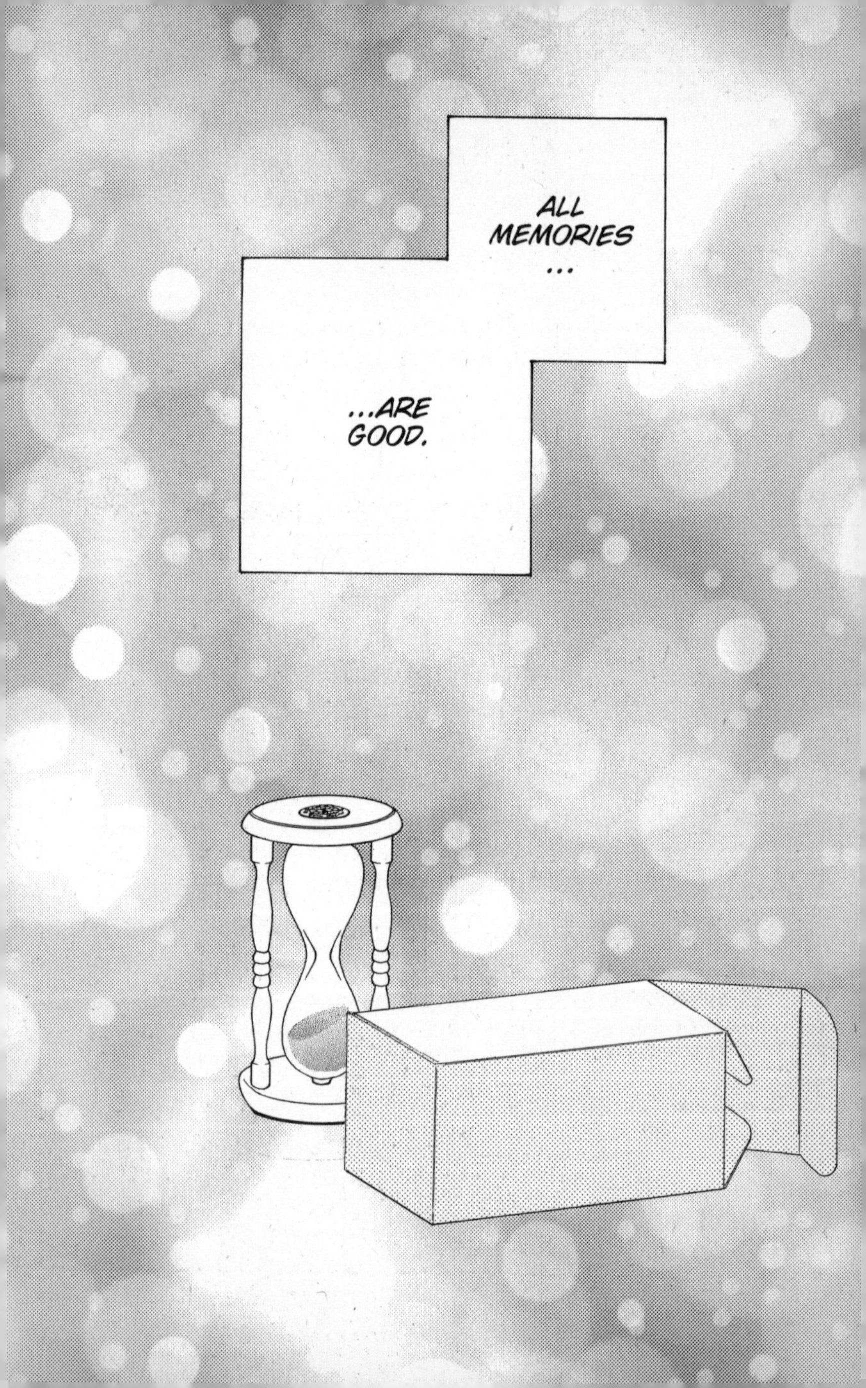
ALL MEMORIES ...
...ARE GOOD.

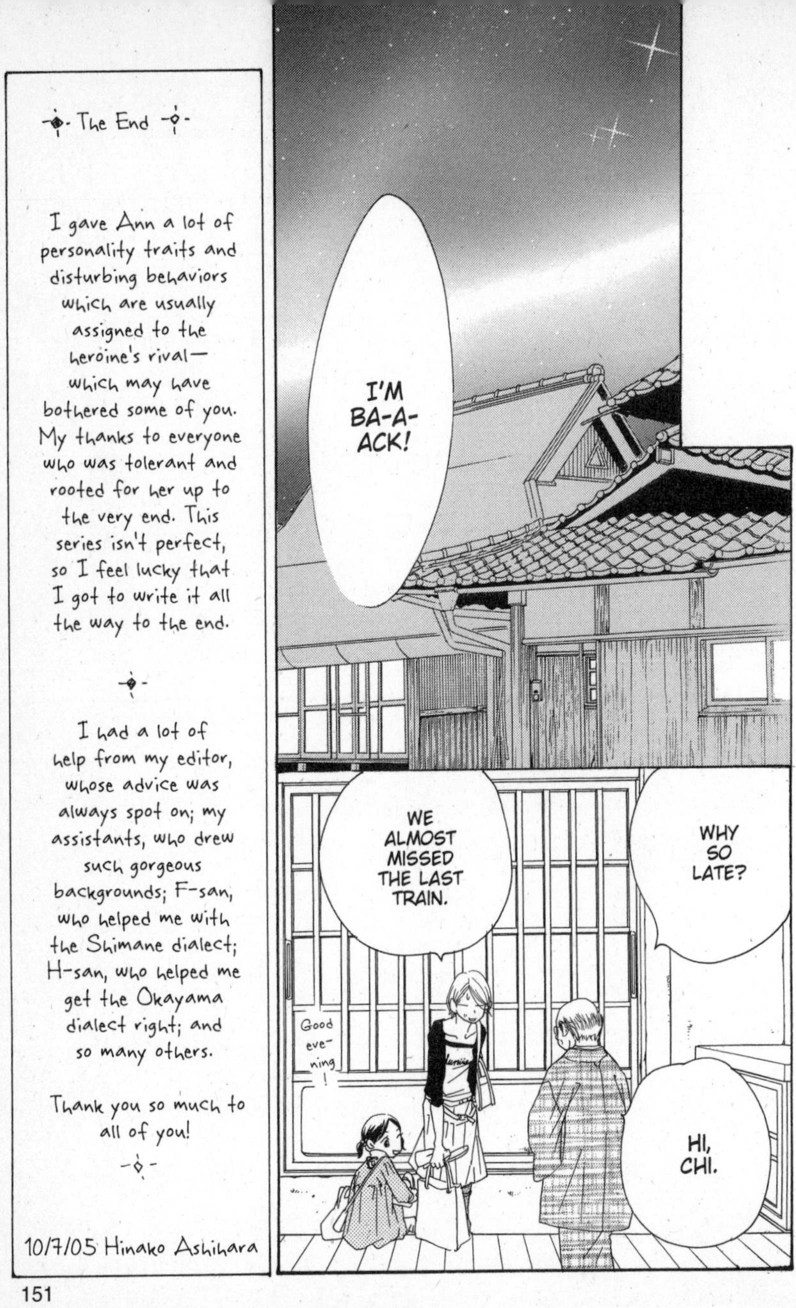
I'M BA-A-ACK!
WHY SO LATE?
WE ALMOST MISSED THE LAST TRAIN.
HI, CHI.
Good eve-ning!

-◆- The End -◆-

I gave Ann a lot of personality traits and disturbing behaviors which are usually assigned to the heroine's rival—which may have bothered some of you. My thanks to everyone who was tolerant and rooted for her up to the very end. This series isn't perfect, so I feel lucky that I got to write it all the way to the end.

-◆-

I had a lot of help from my editor, whose advice was always spot on; my assistants, who drew such gorgeous backgrounds; F-san, who helped me with the Shimane dialect; H-san, who helped me get the Okayama dialect right; and so many others.

Thank you so much to all of you!

-◇-

10/7/05 Hinako Ashihara

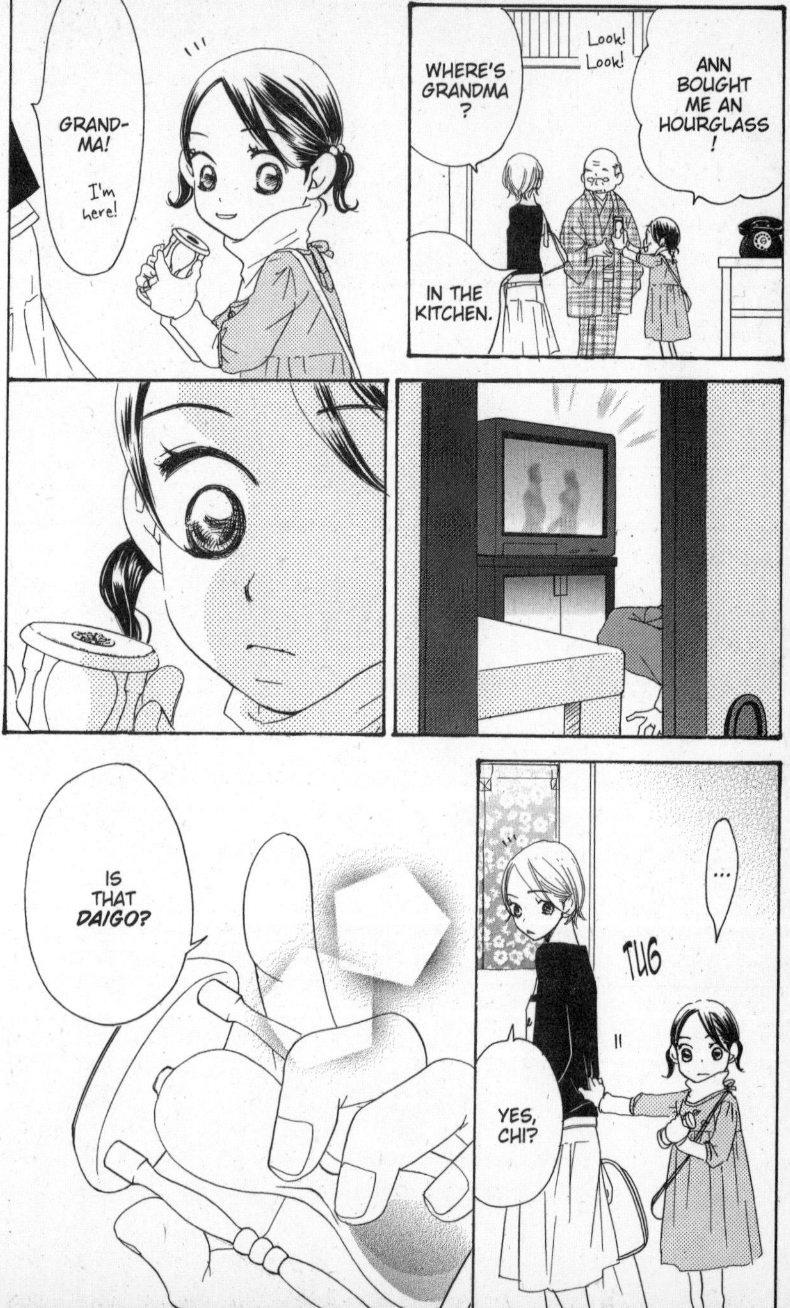
ANN BOUGHT ME AN HOURGLASS!
Look! Look!
WHERE'S GRANDMA?
IN THE KITCHEN.
GRAND-MA!
I'm here!
...
TUG
YES, CHI?
IS THAT DAIGO?

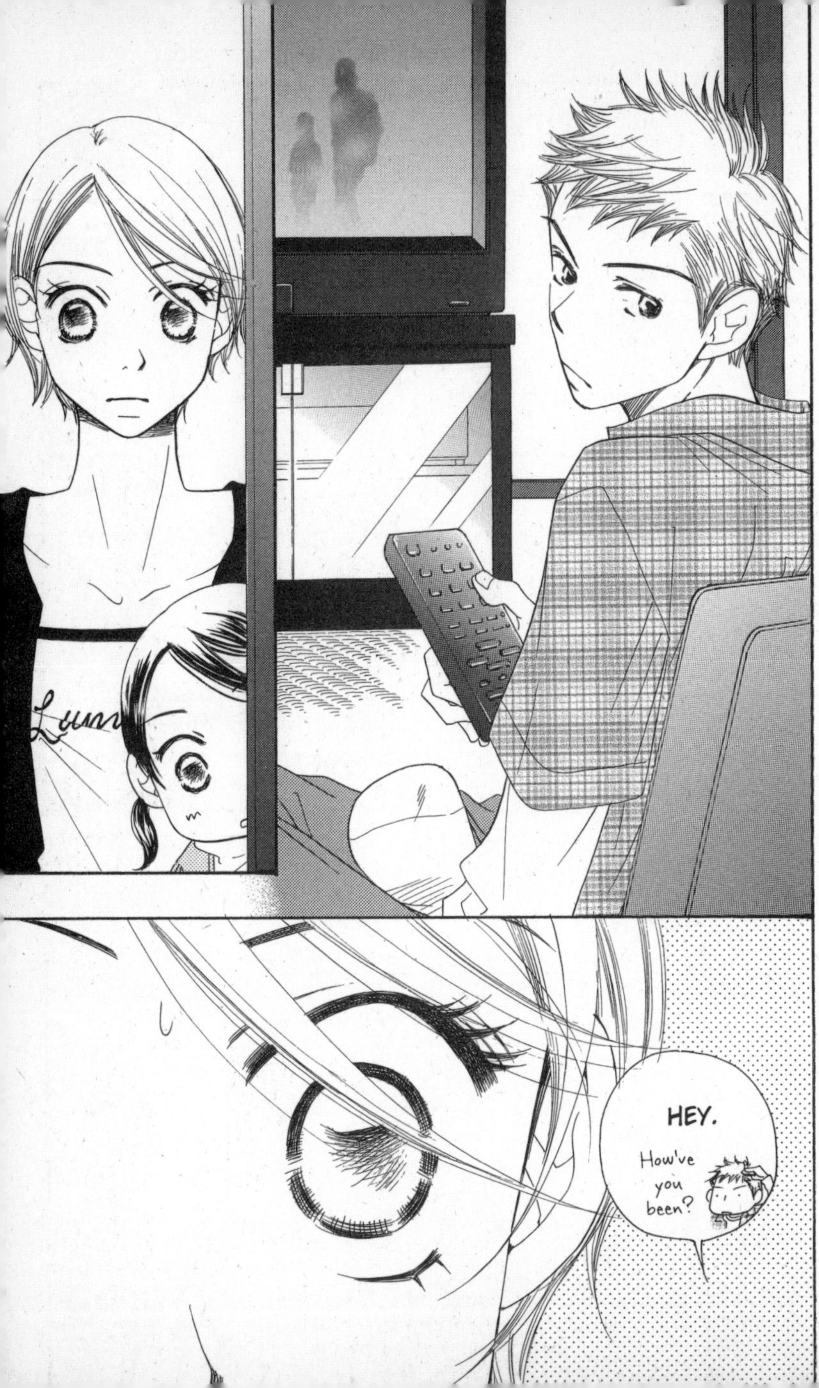
HEY.
How've you been?

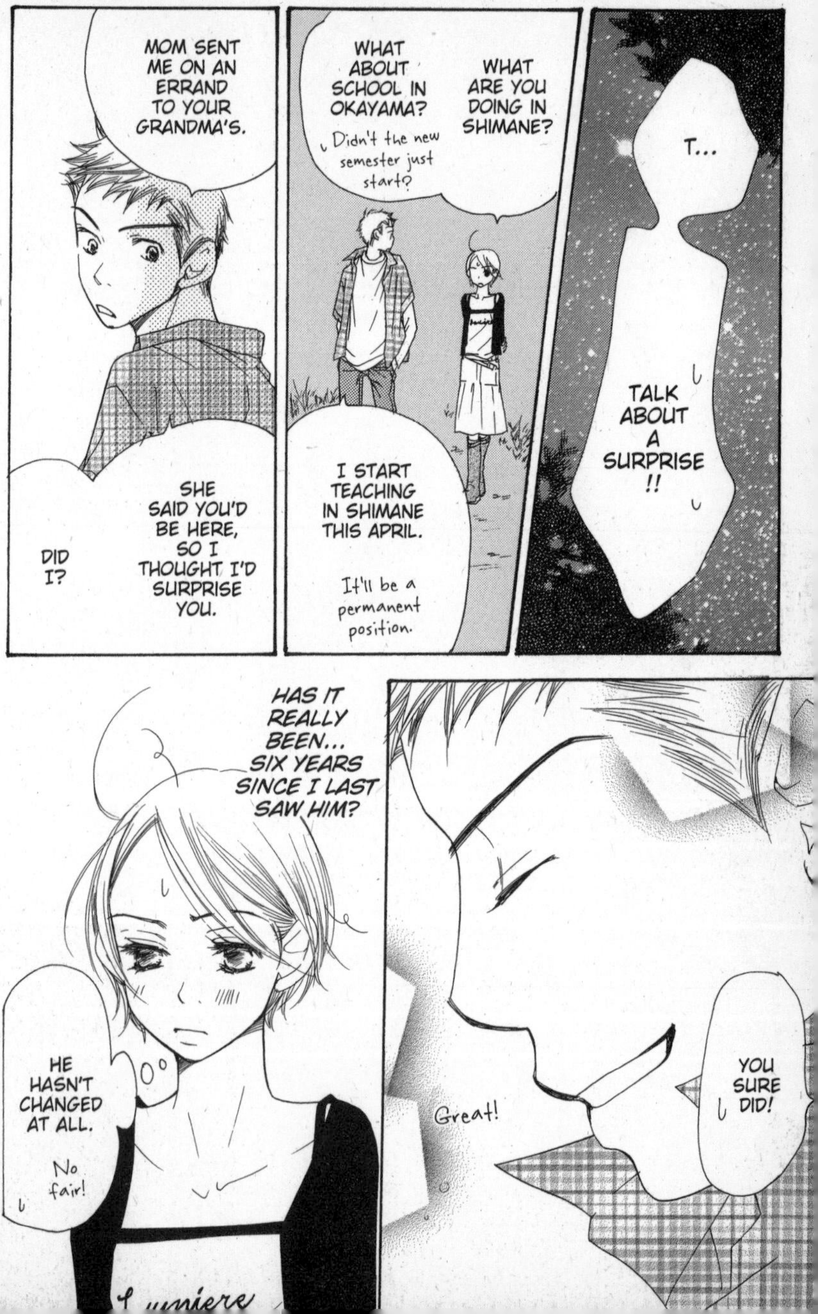
T...
TALK ABOUT A SURPRISE!!
WHAT ARE YOU DOING IN SHIMANE?
WHAT ABOUT SCHOOL IN OKAYAMA?
Didn't the new semester just start?
I START TEACHING IN SHIMANE THIS APRIL.
It'll be a permanent position.
MOM SENT ME ON AN ERRAND TO YOUR GRANDMA'S.
SHE SAID YOU'D BE HERE, SO I THOUGHT I'D SURPRISE YOU.
DID I?
YOU SURE DID!
Great!
HAS IT REALLY BEEN... SIX YEARS SINCE I LAST SAW HIM?
HE HASN'T CHANGED AT ALL.
No fair!

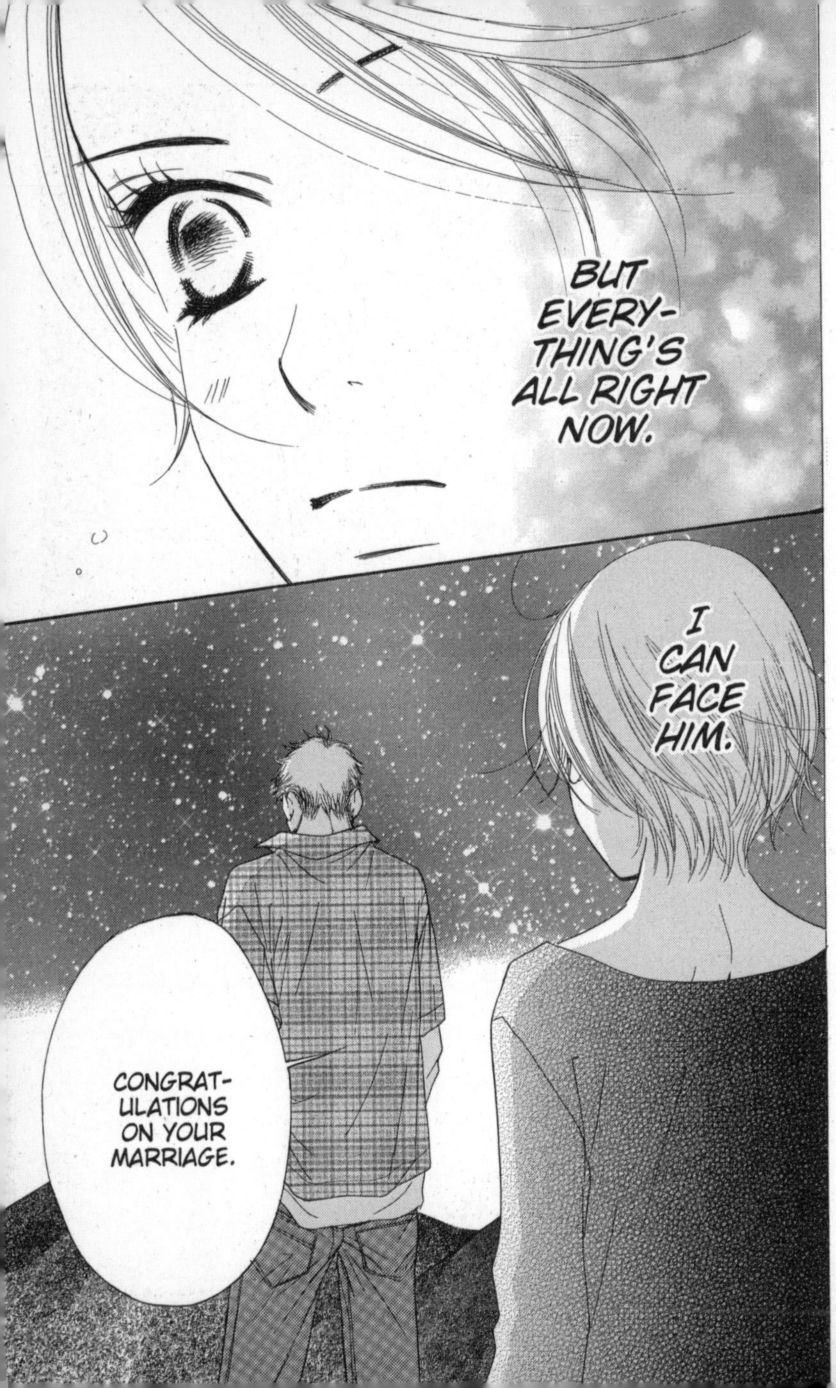
BUT EVERY-THING'S ALL RIGHT NOW.
I CAN FACE HIM.
CONGRAT-ULATIONS ON YOUR MARRIAGE.

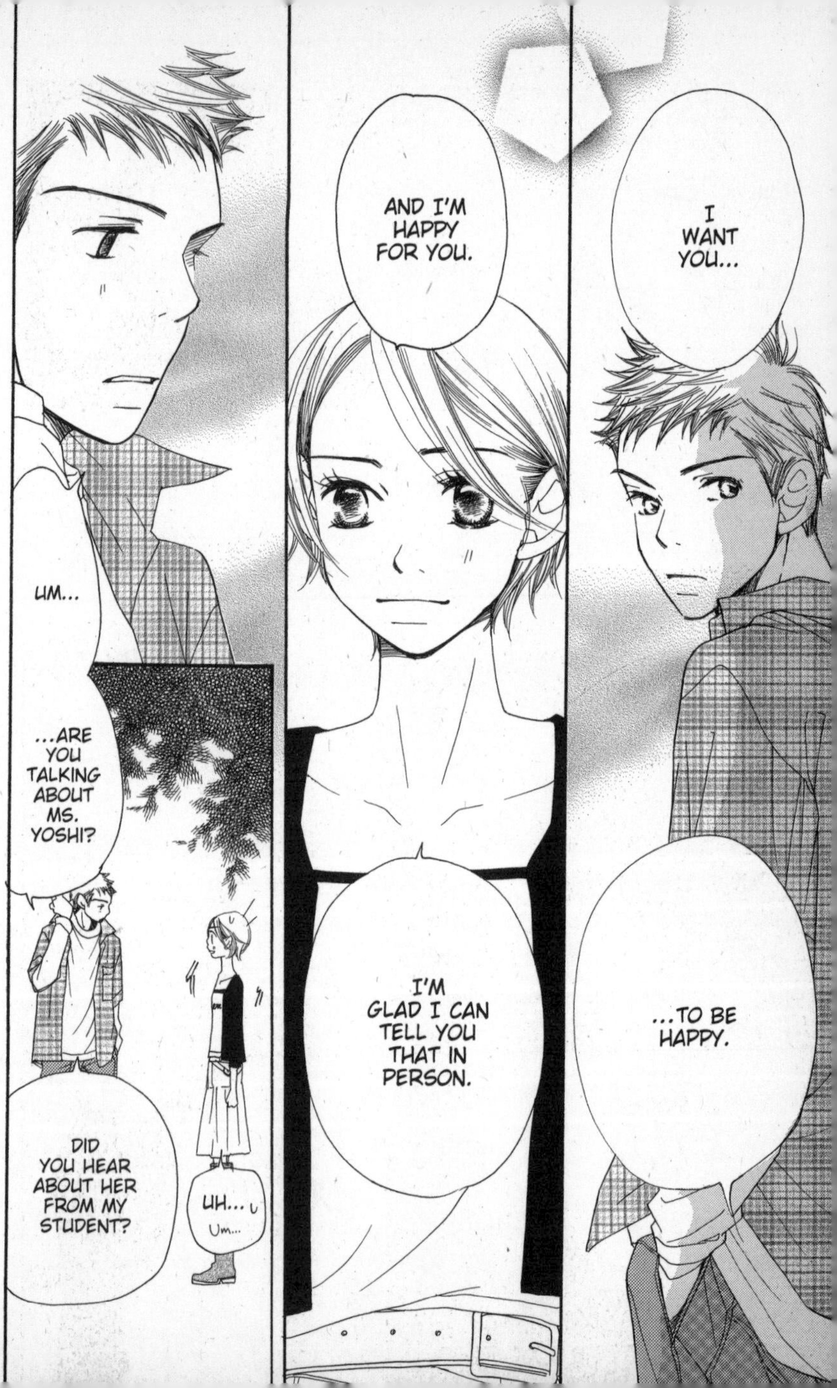

I WANT YOU...
...TO BE HAPPY.
AND I'M HAPPY FOR YOU.
I'M GLAD I CAN TELL YOU THAT IN PERSON.
UM...
...ARE YOU TALKING ABOUT MS. YOSHI?
DID YOU HEAR ABOUT HER FROM MY STUDENT?
UH...
Um...

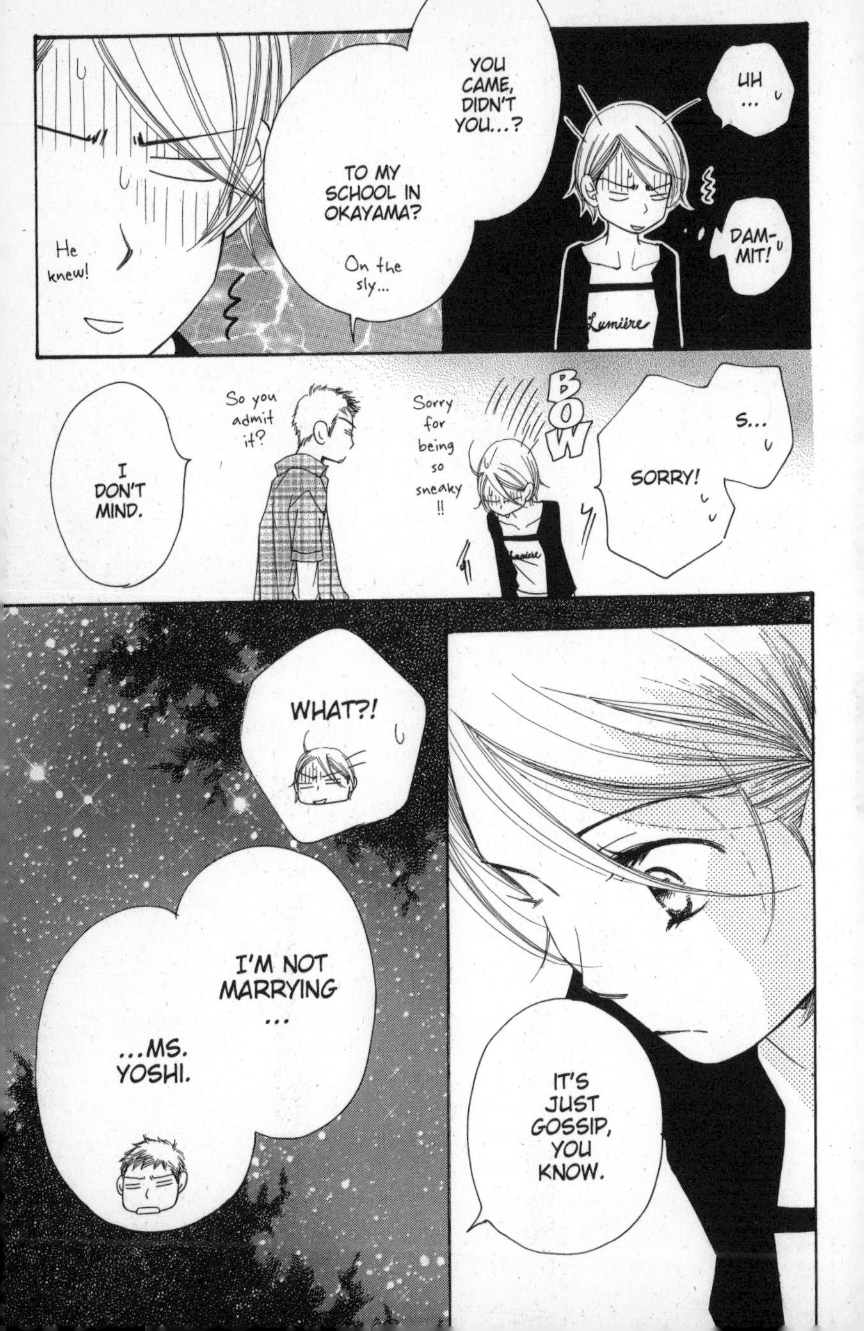
YOU CAME, DIDN'T YOU...?
TO MY SCHOOL IN OKAYAMA?
On the sly...
UH ...
DAM-MIT!
He knew!
S...
SORRY!
BOW
Sorry for being so sneaky!!
So you admit it?
I DON'T MIND.
I'M NOT MARRYING ...
...MS. YOSHI.
WHAT?!
IT'S JUST GOSSIP, YOU KNOW.

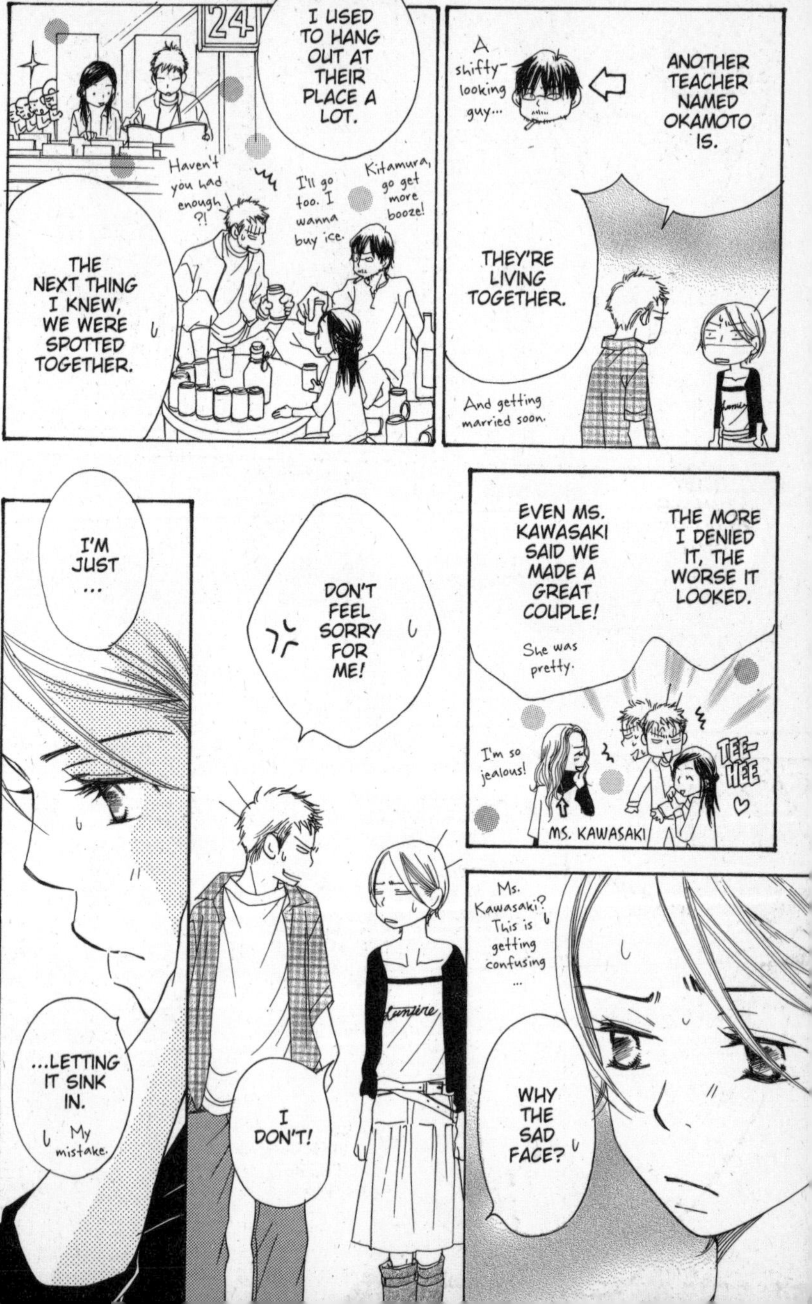
ANOTHER TEACHER NAMED OKAMOTO IS.
A shifty-looking guy...
THEY'RE LIVING TOGETHER.
And getting married soon.
I USED TO HANG OUT AT THEIR PLACE A LOT.
24
Kitamura, go get more booze!
I'll go too. I wanna buy ice.
Haven't you had enough?!
THE NEXT THING I KNEW, WE WERE SPOTTED TOGETHER.
THE MORE I DENIED IT, THE WORSE IT LOOKED.
EVEN MS. KAWASAKI SAID WE MADE A GREAT COUPLE!
She was pretty.
TEE-HEE
I'm so jealous!
MS. KAWASAKI
Ms. Kawasaki? This is getting confusing...
WHY THE SAD FACE?
DON'T FEEL SORRY FOR ME!
I DON'T!
I'M JUST...
...LETTING IT SINK IN.
My mistake.

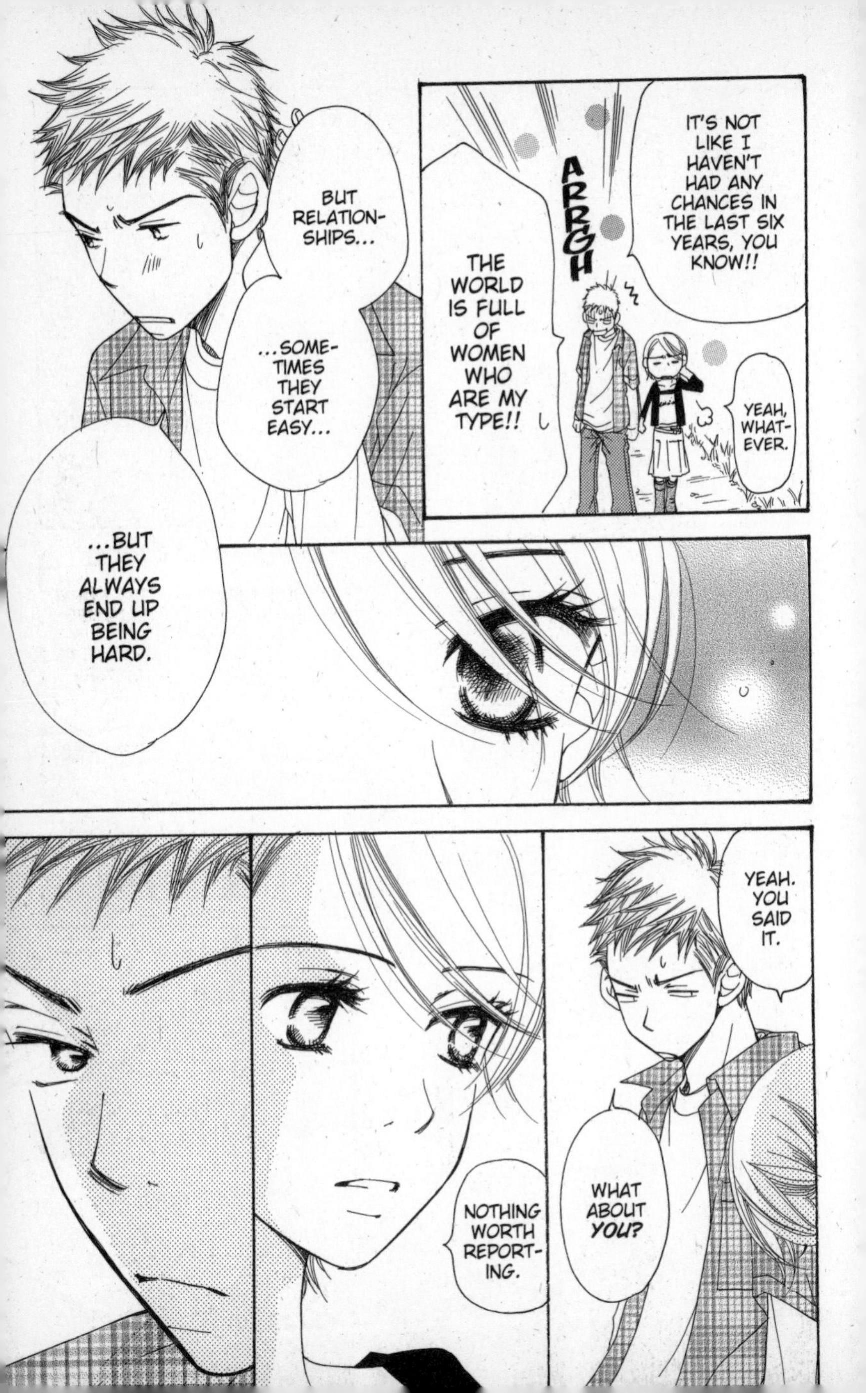
IT'S NOT LIKE I HAVEN'T HAD ANY CHANCES IN THE LAST SIX YEARS, YOU KNOW!!
ARRGH
THE WORLD IS FULL OF WOMEN WHO ARE MY TYPE!!
YEAH, WHATEVER.
BUT RELATIONSHIPS...
...SOMETIMES THEY START EASY...
...BUT THEY ALWAYS END UP BEING HARD.
YEAH. YOU SAID IT.
WHAT ABOUT *YOU*?
NOTHING WORTH REPORTING.

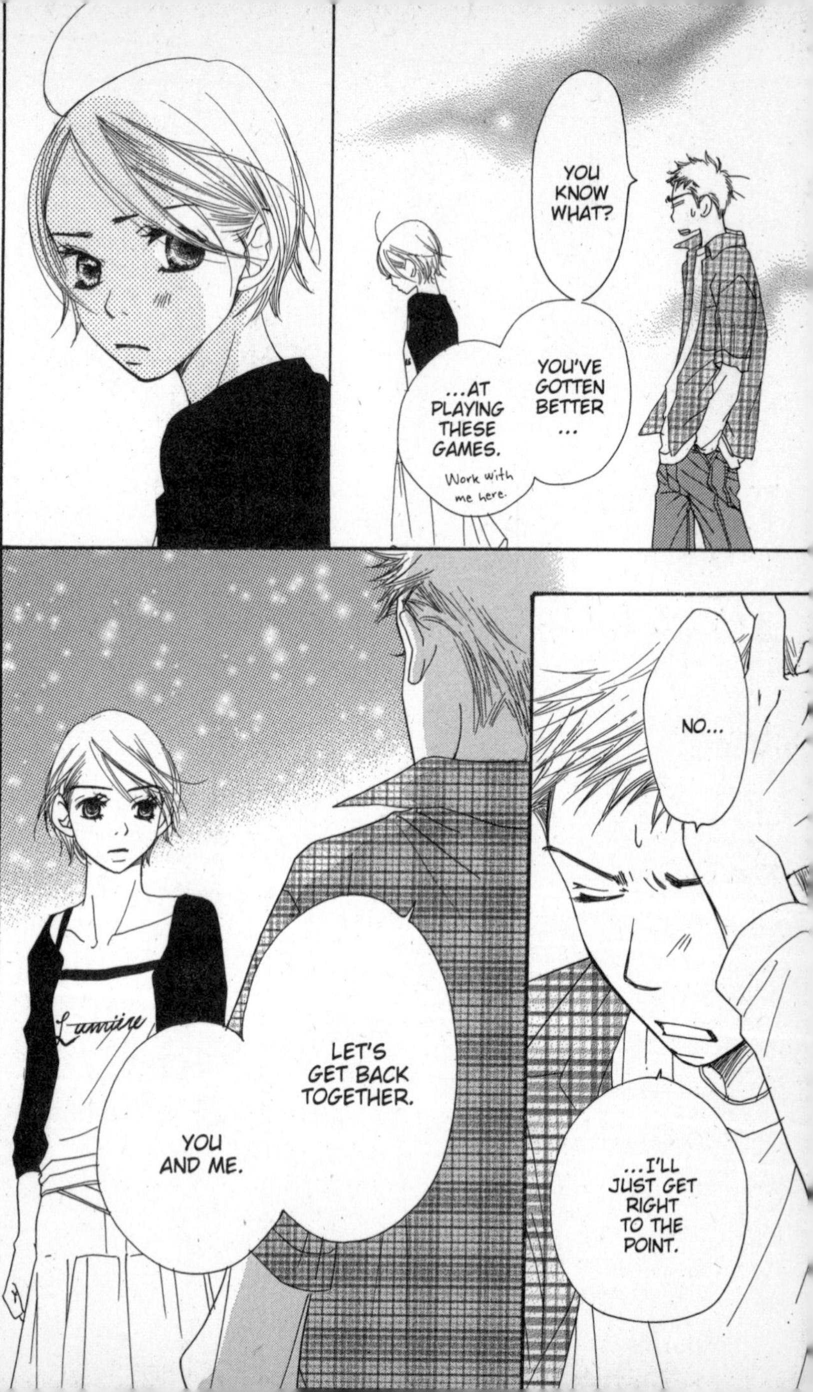
YOU KNOW WHAT?
YOU'VE GOTTEN BETTER...
...AT PLAYING THESE GAMES.
Work with me here.
NO...
...I'LL JUST GET RIGHT TO THE POINT.
LET'S GET BACK TOGETHER.
YOU AND ME.

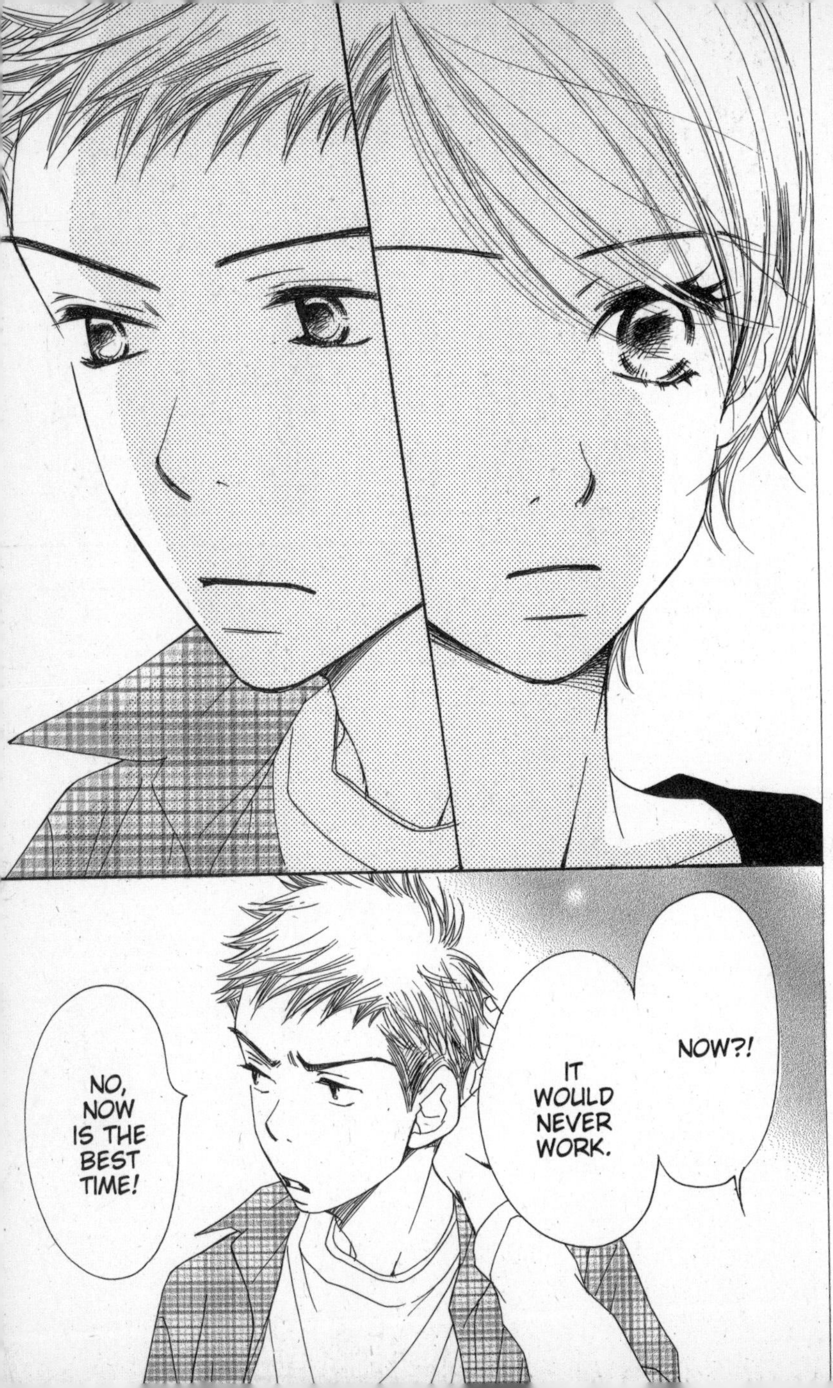
NOW?!
IT WOULD NEVER WORK.
NO, NOW IS THE BEST TIME!

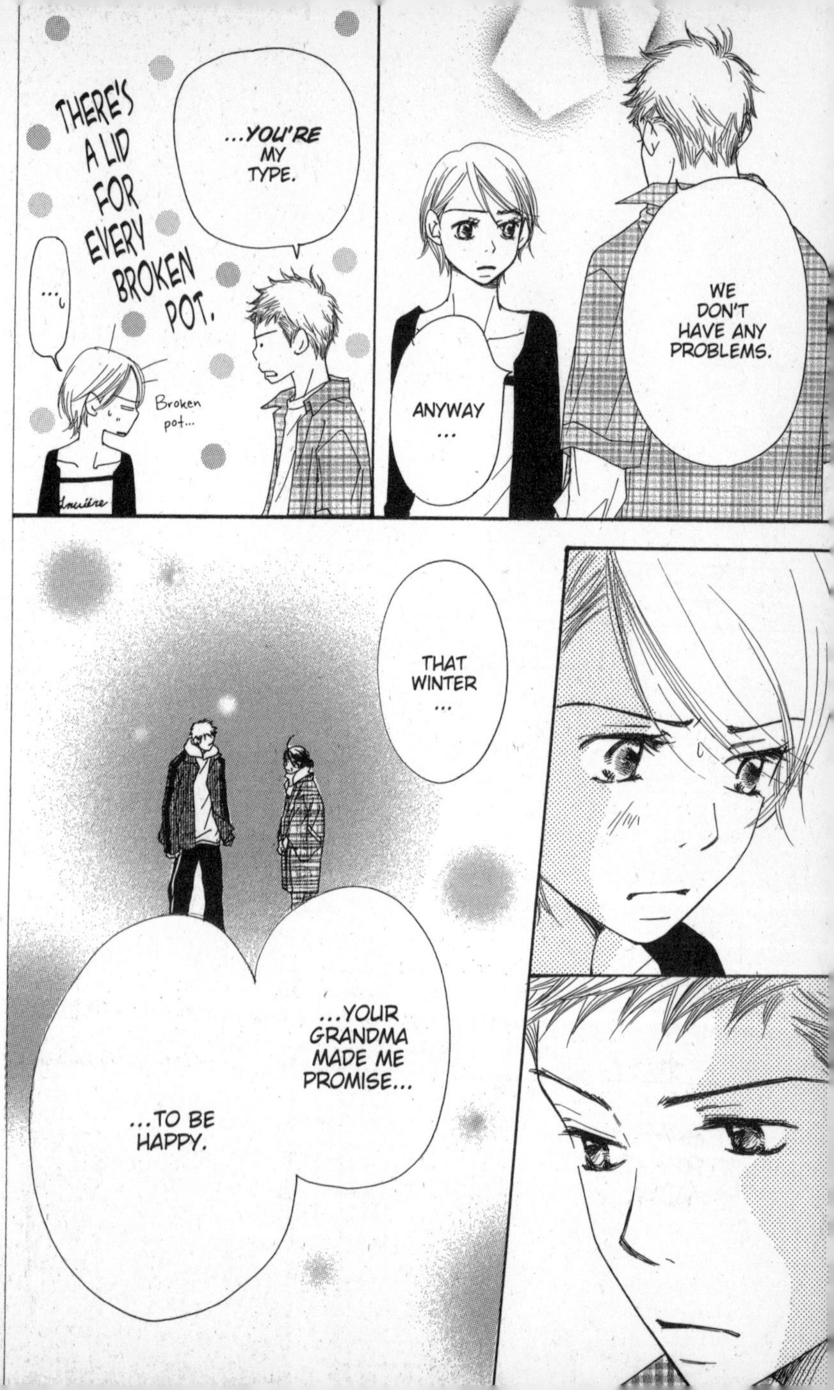
WE DON'T HAVE ANY PROBLEMS.
ANYWAY...
...YOU'RE MY TYPE.
THERE'S A LID FOR EVERY BROKEN POT.
...
Broken pot...
THAT WINTER...
...YOUR GRANDMA MADE ME PROMISE...
...TO BE HAPPY.

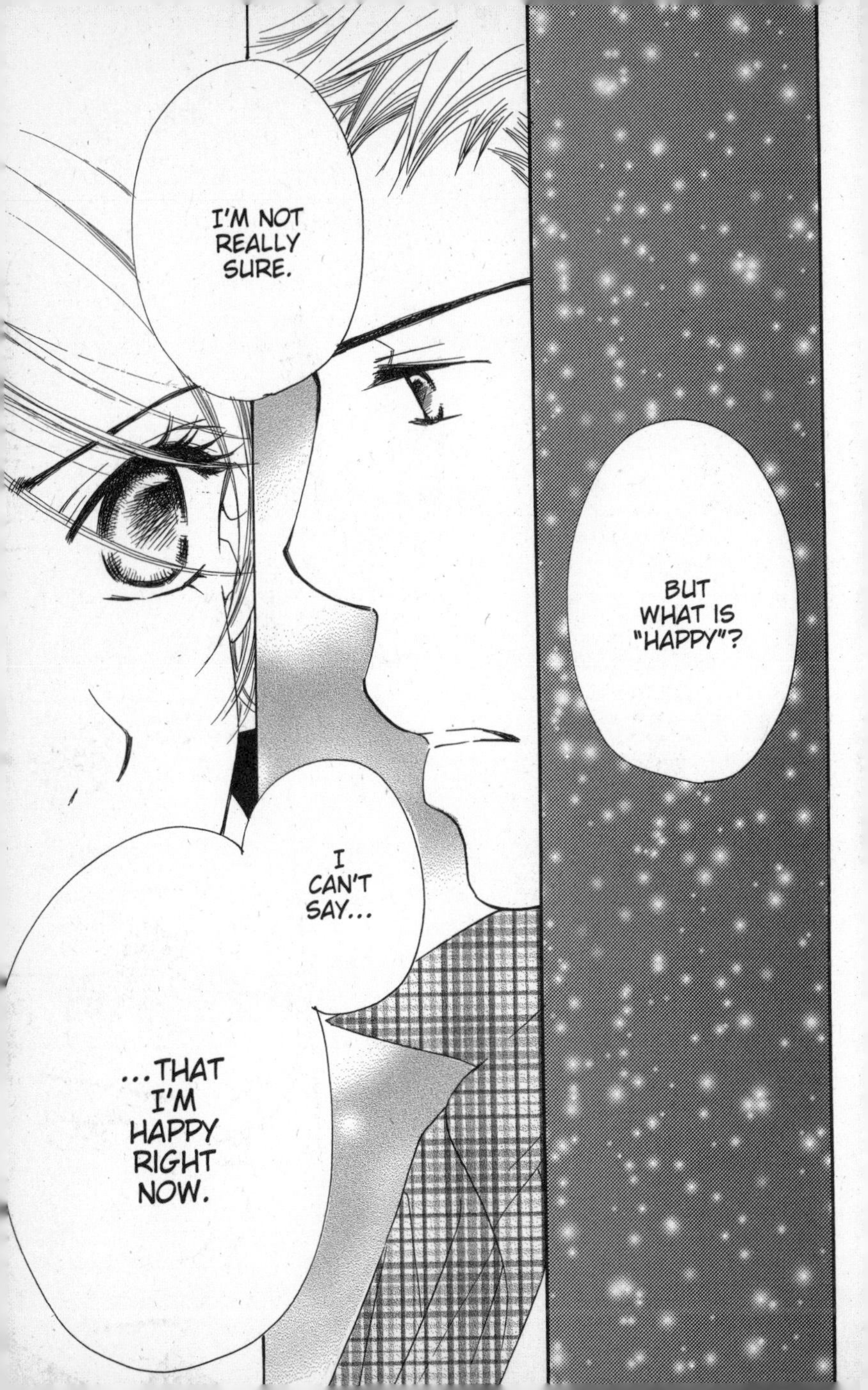
BUT WHAT IS "HAPPY"?
I'M NOT REALLY SURE.
I CAN'T SAY...
...THAT I'M HAPPY RIGHT NOW.

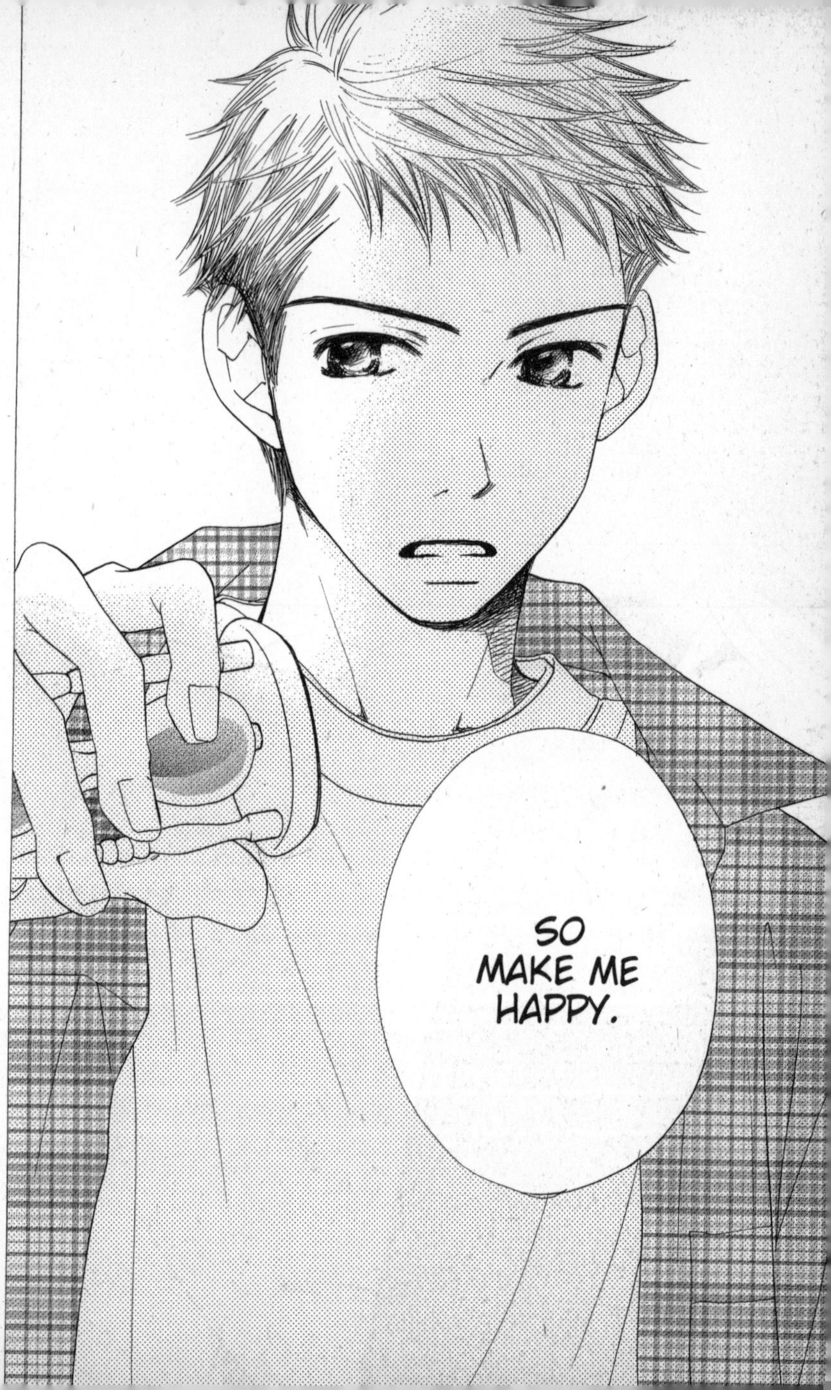
SO MAKE ME HAPPY.

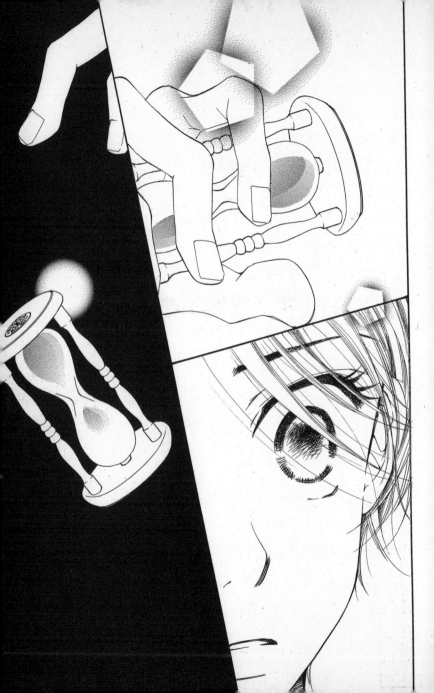

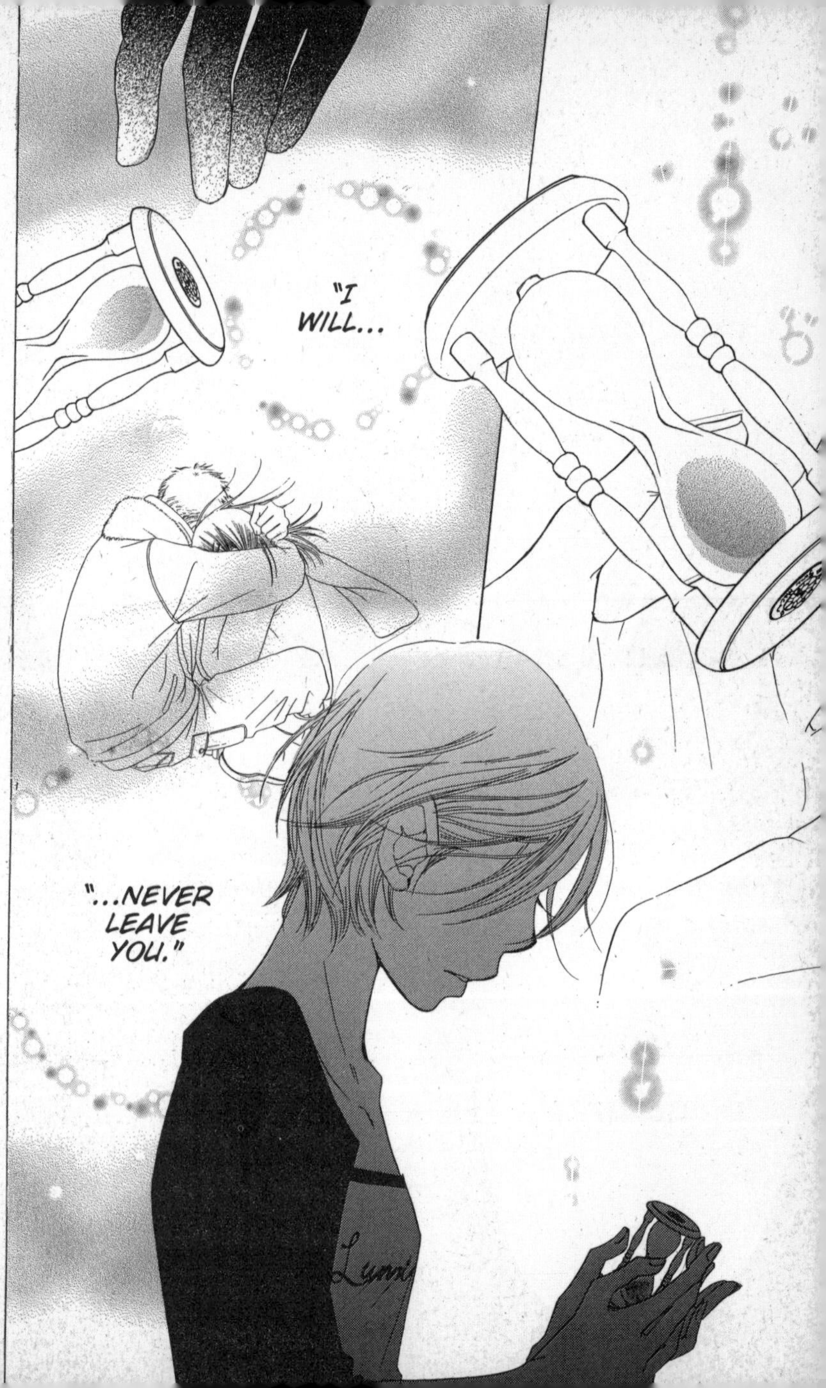
"I WILL...
"...NEVER LEAVE YOU."

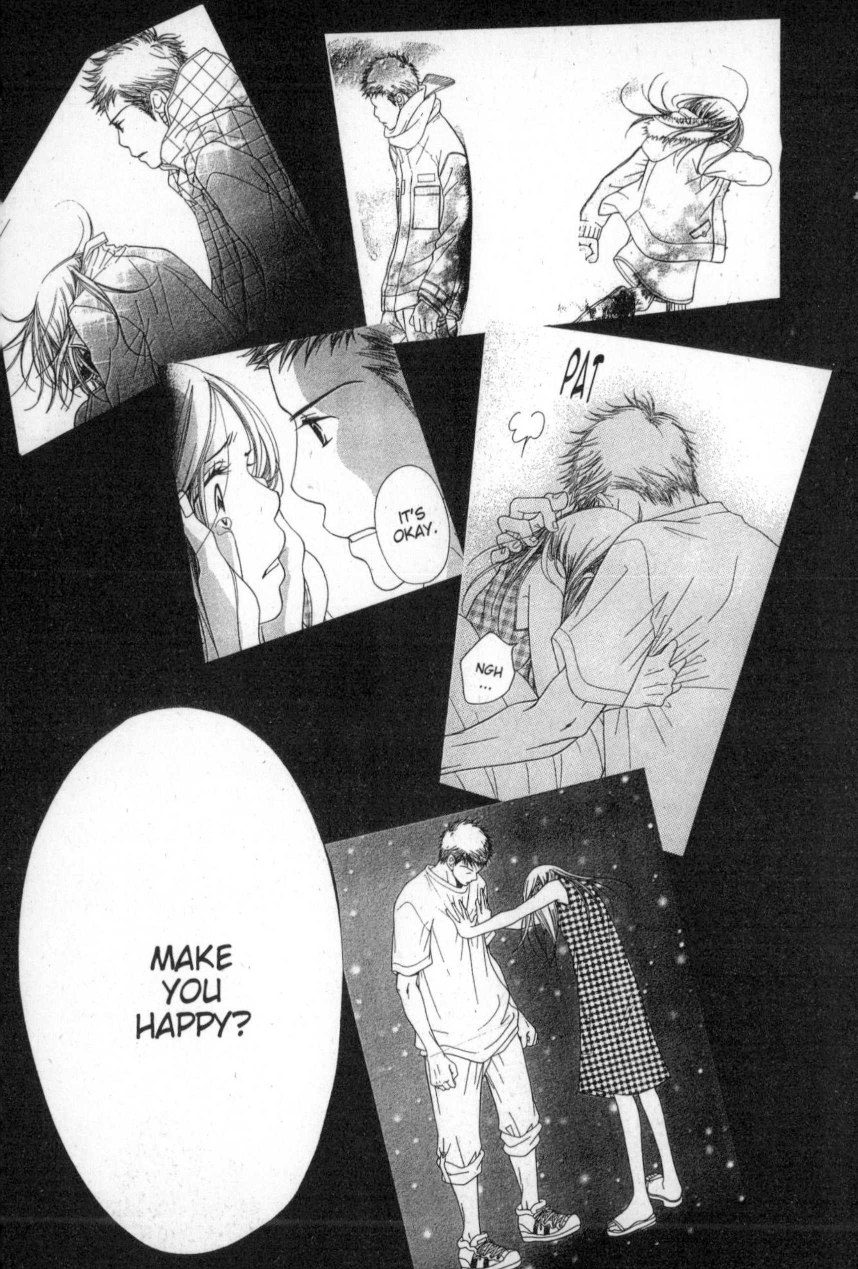
PAT
NGH ...
IT'S OKAY.
MAKE YOU HAPPY?

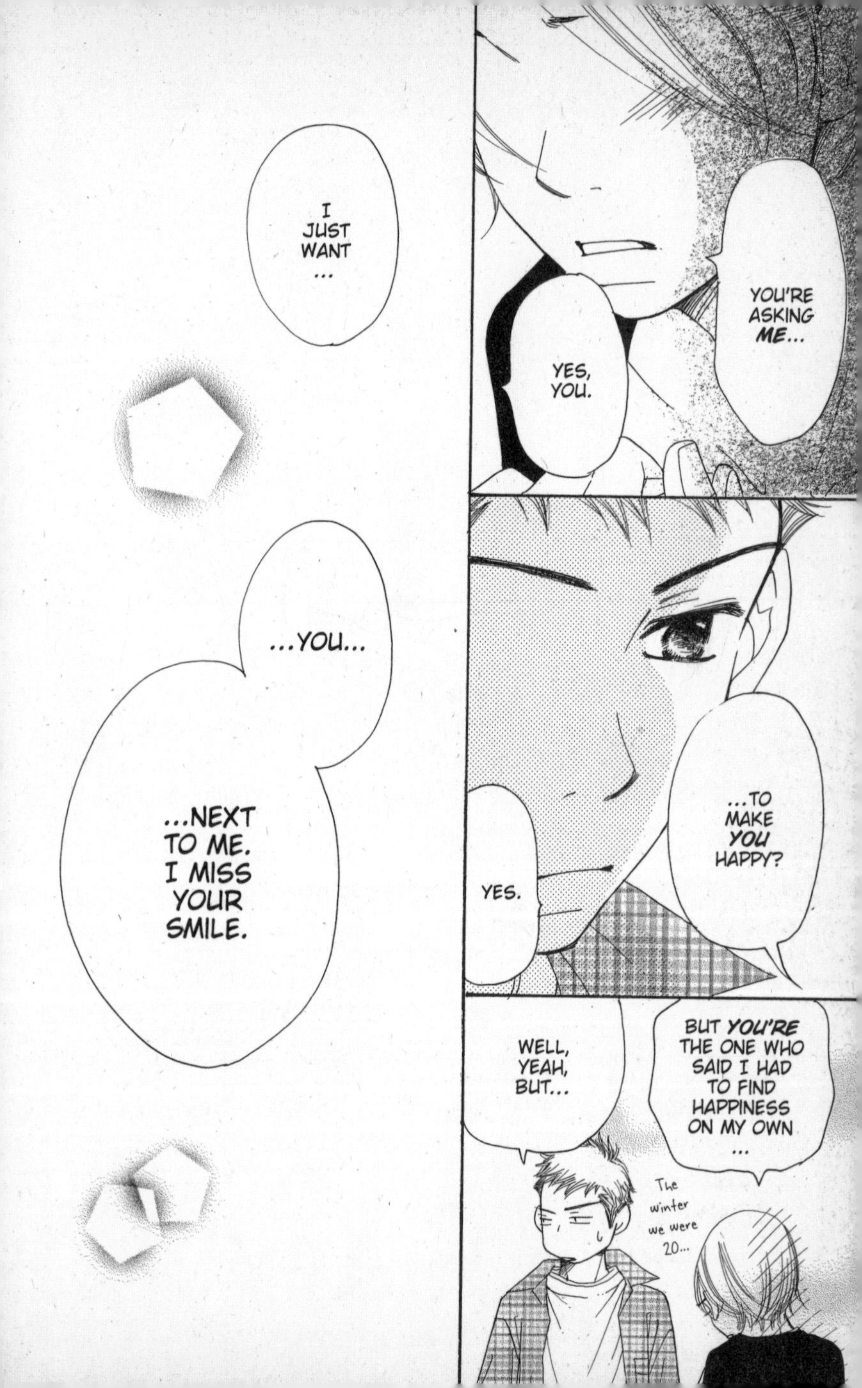
YOU'RE ASKING *ME*...
YES, YOU.
...TO MAKE *YOU* HAPPY?
YES.
BUT *YOU'RE* THE ONE WHO SAID I HAD TO FIND HAPPINESS ON MY OWN ...
WELL, YEAH, BUT...
The winter we were 20...
I JUST WANT ...
...YOU...
...NEXT TO ME. I MISS YOUR SMILE.

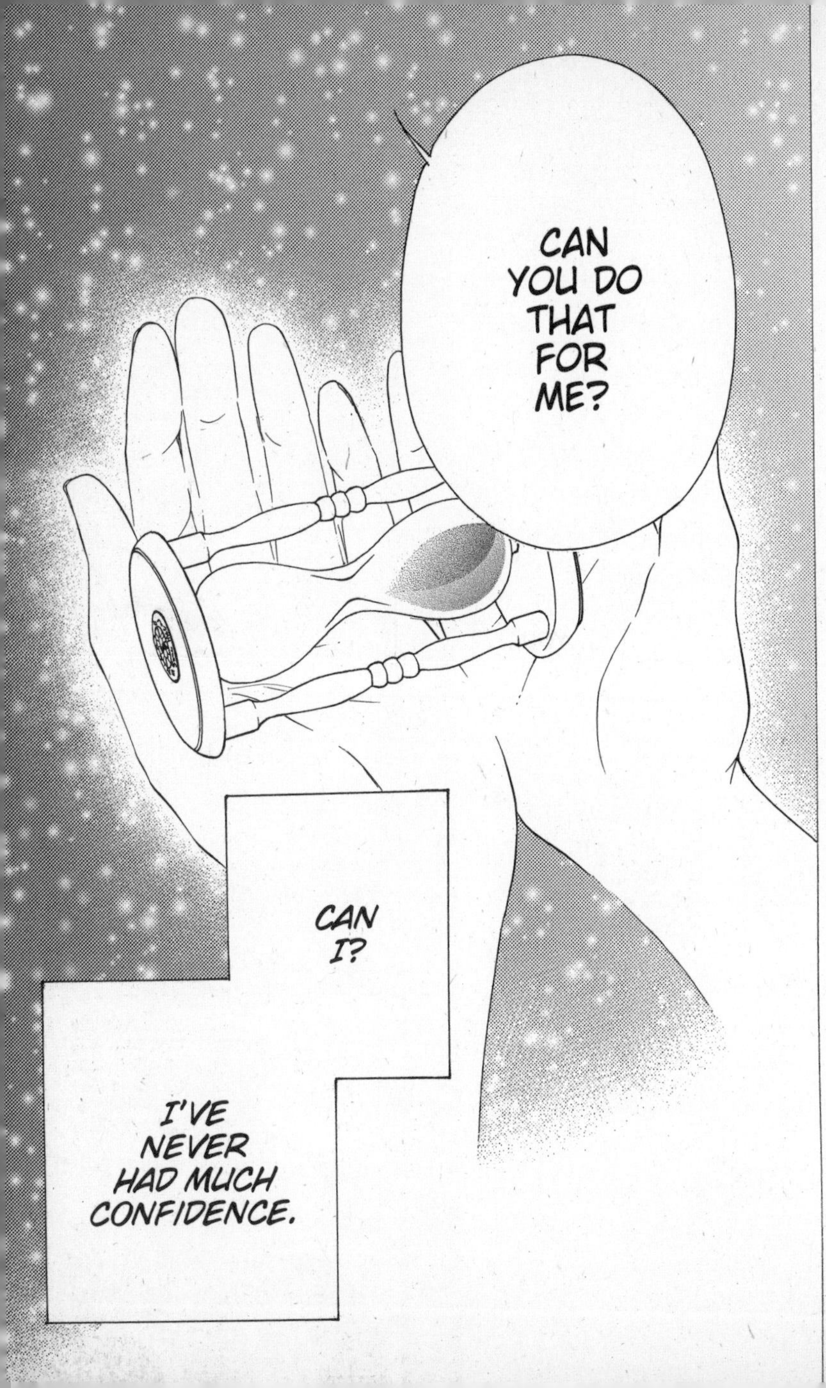
CAN YOU DO THAT FOR ME?
CAN I?
I'VE NEVER HAD MUCH CONFIDENCE.

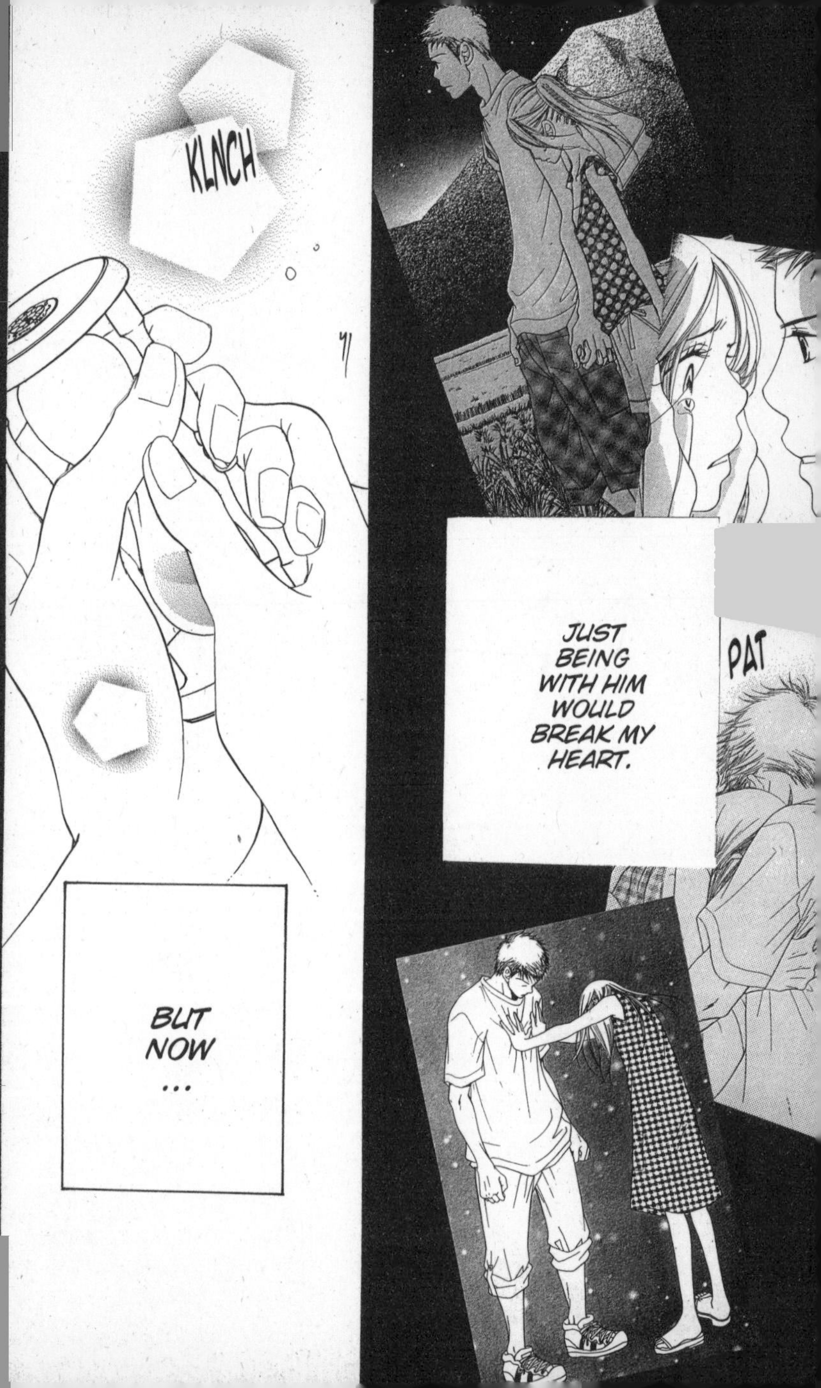
JUST BEING WITH HIM WOULD BREAK MY HEART.
PAT
KLNCH
BUT NOW ...

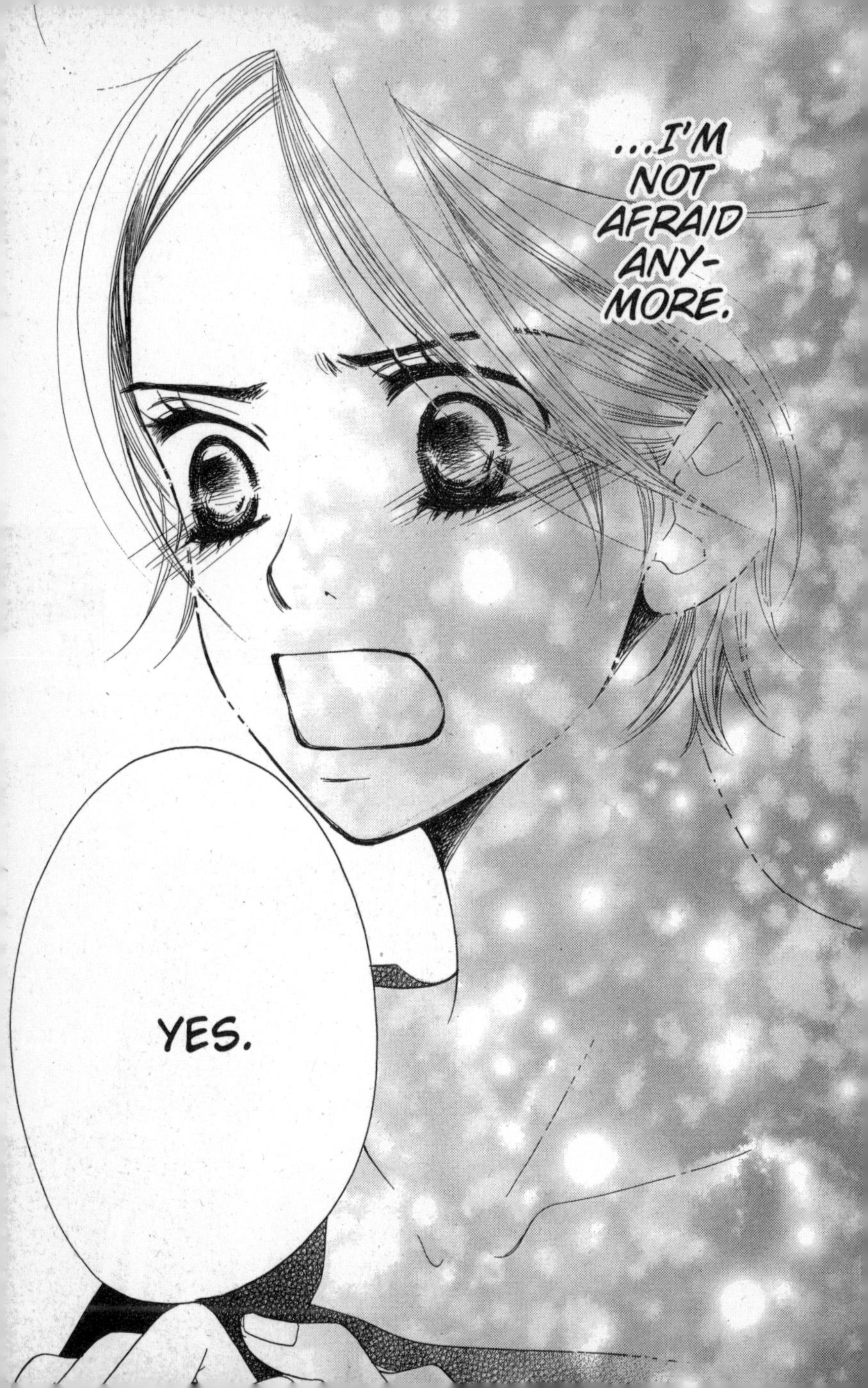
...I'M NOT AFRAID ANY-MORE.
YES.

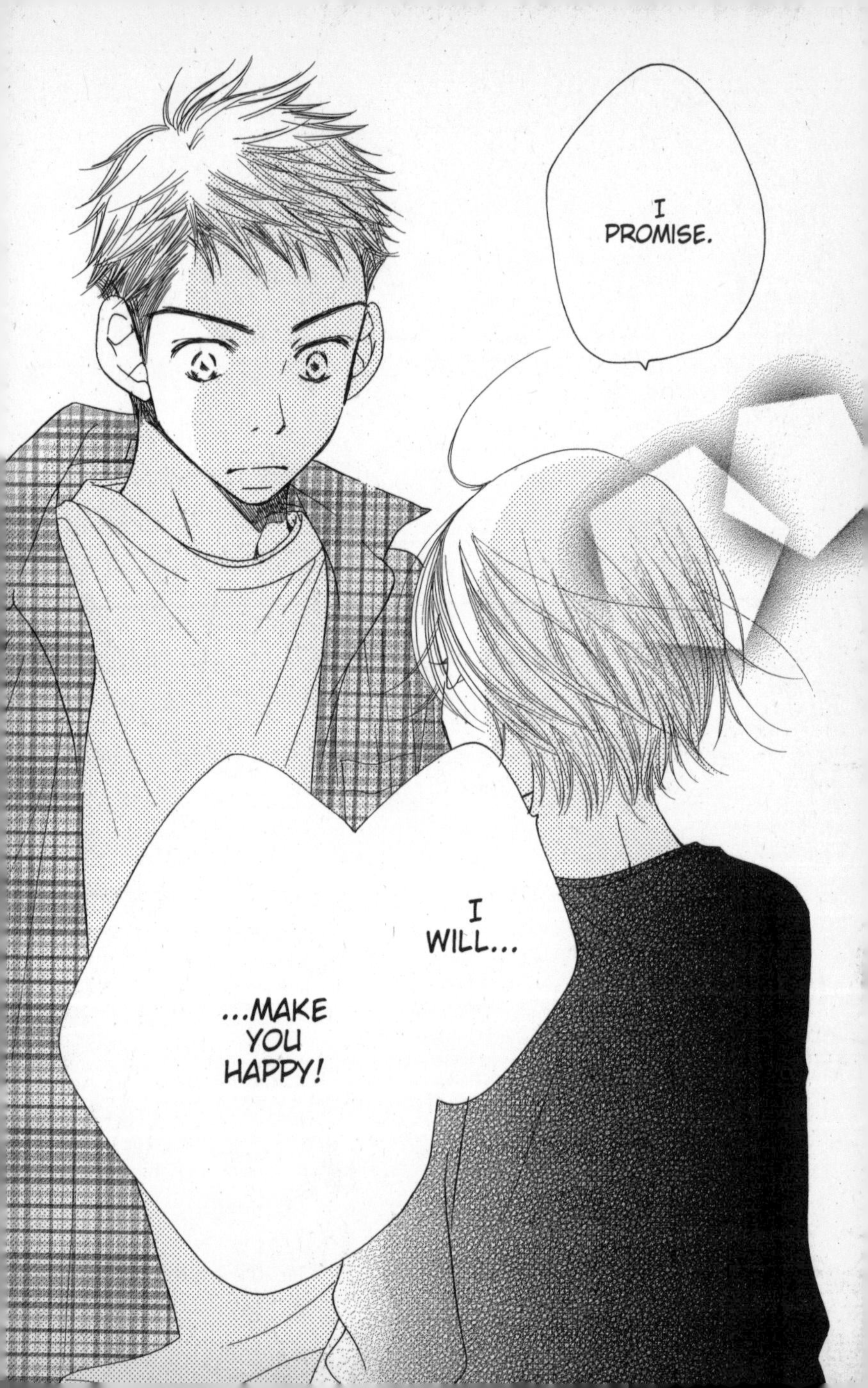
I PROMISE.
I WILL...
...MAKE YOU HAPPY!

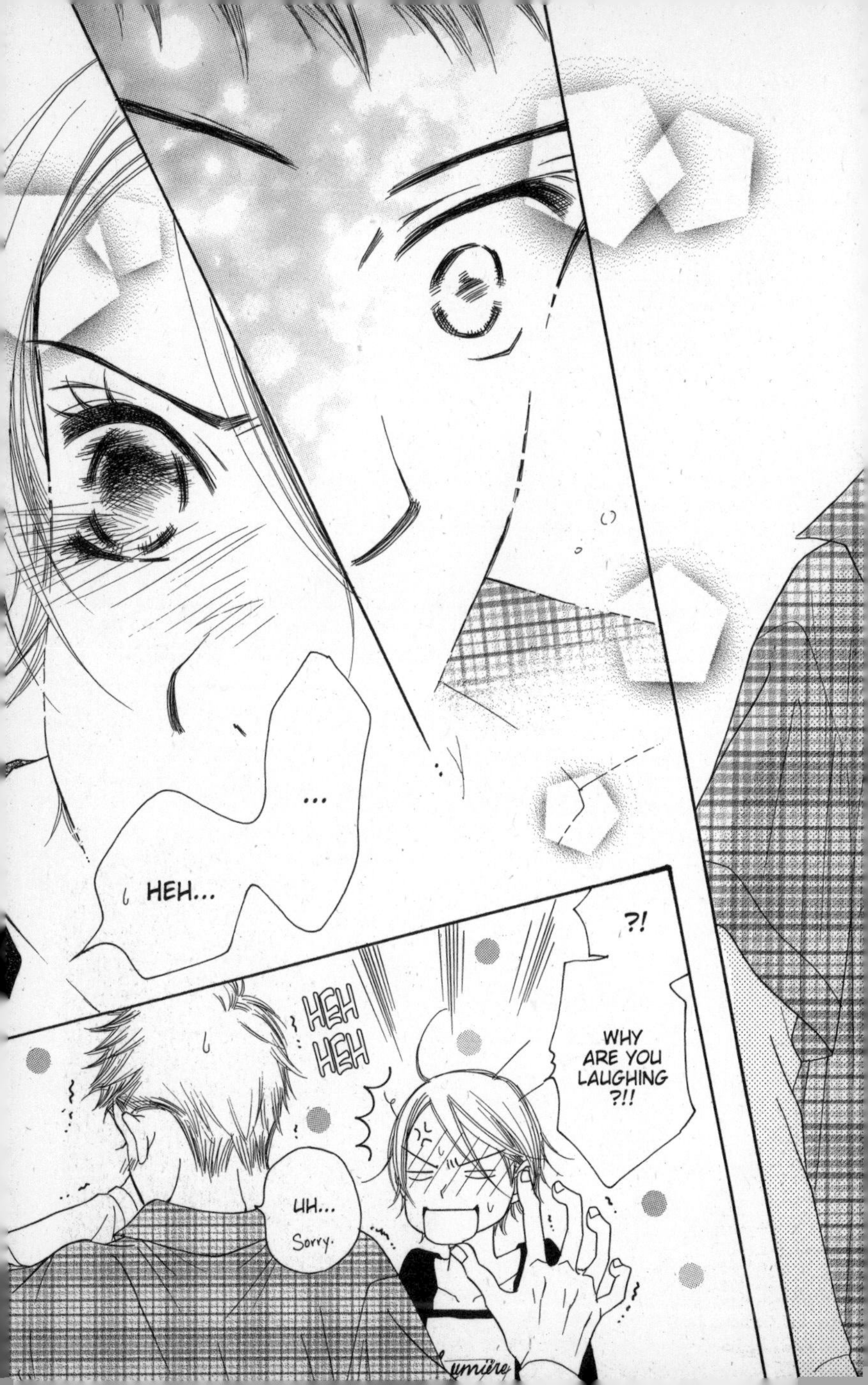
...
HEH...
?!
WHY ARE YOU LAUGHING ?!!
HEH HEH
UH...
Sorry.

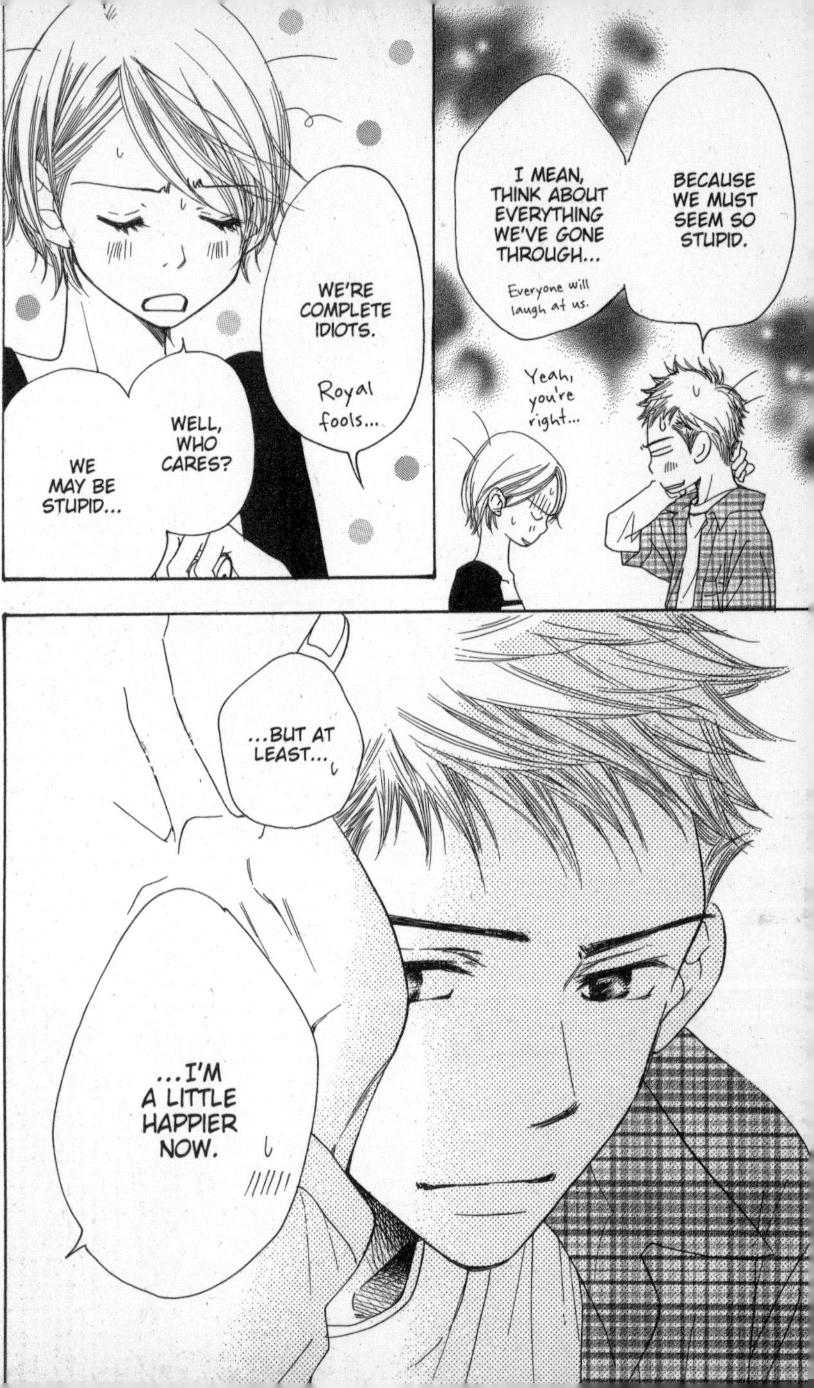
BECAUSE WE MUST SEEM SO STUPID.
I MEAN, THINK ABOUT EVERYTHING WE'VE GONE THROUGH...
Everyone will laugh at us.
Yeah, you're right...
WE'RE COMPLETE IDIOTS.
Royal fools...
WELL, WHO CARES?
WE MAY BE STUPID...
...BUT AT LEAST...
...I'M A LITTLE HAPPIER NOW.

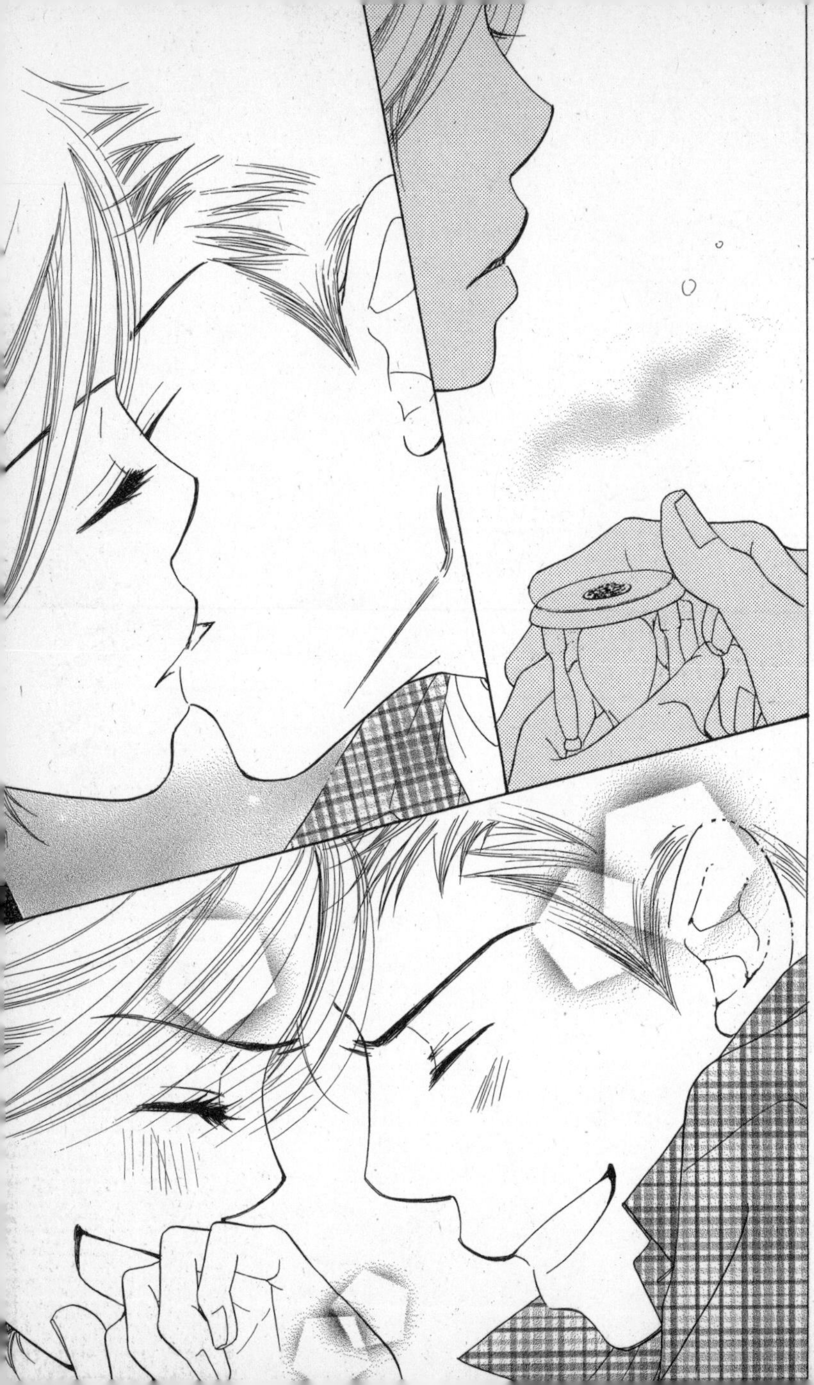

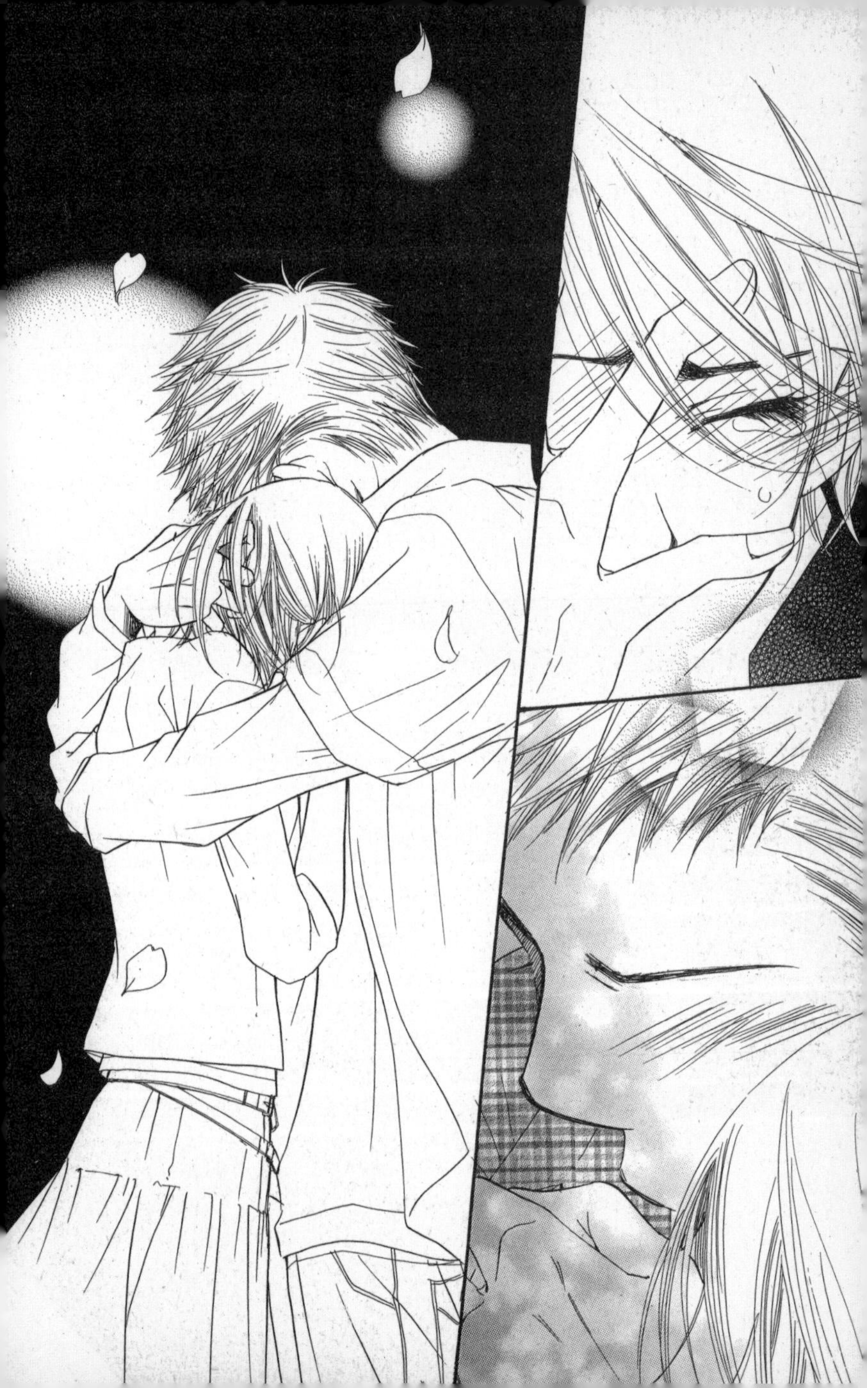

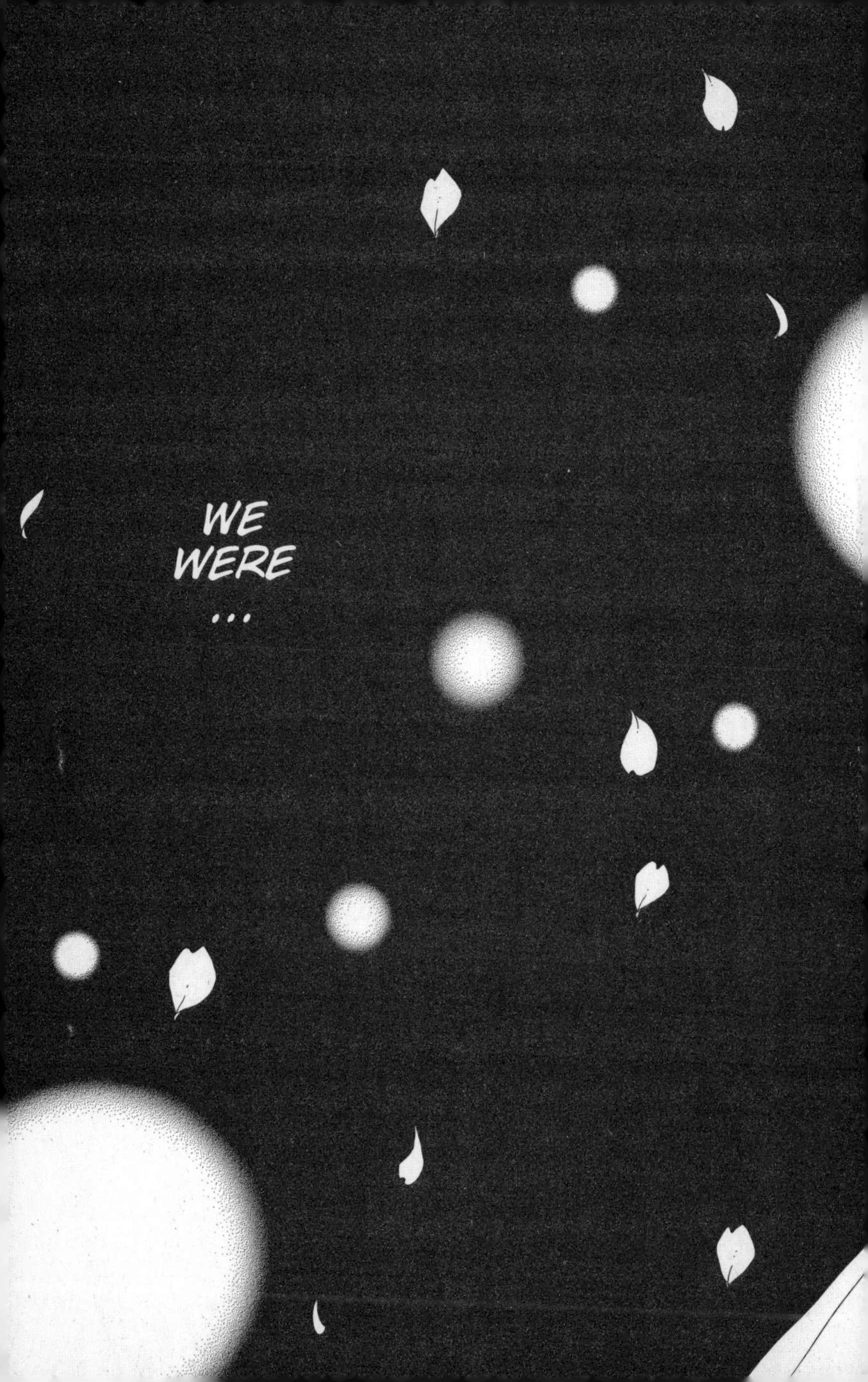
WE WERE ...

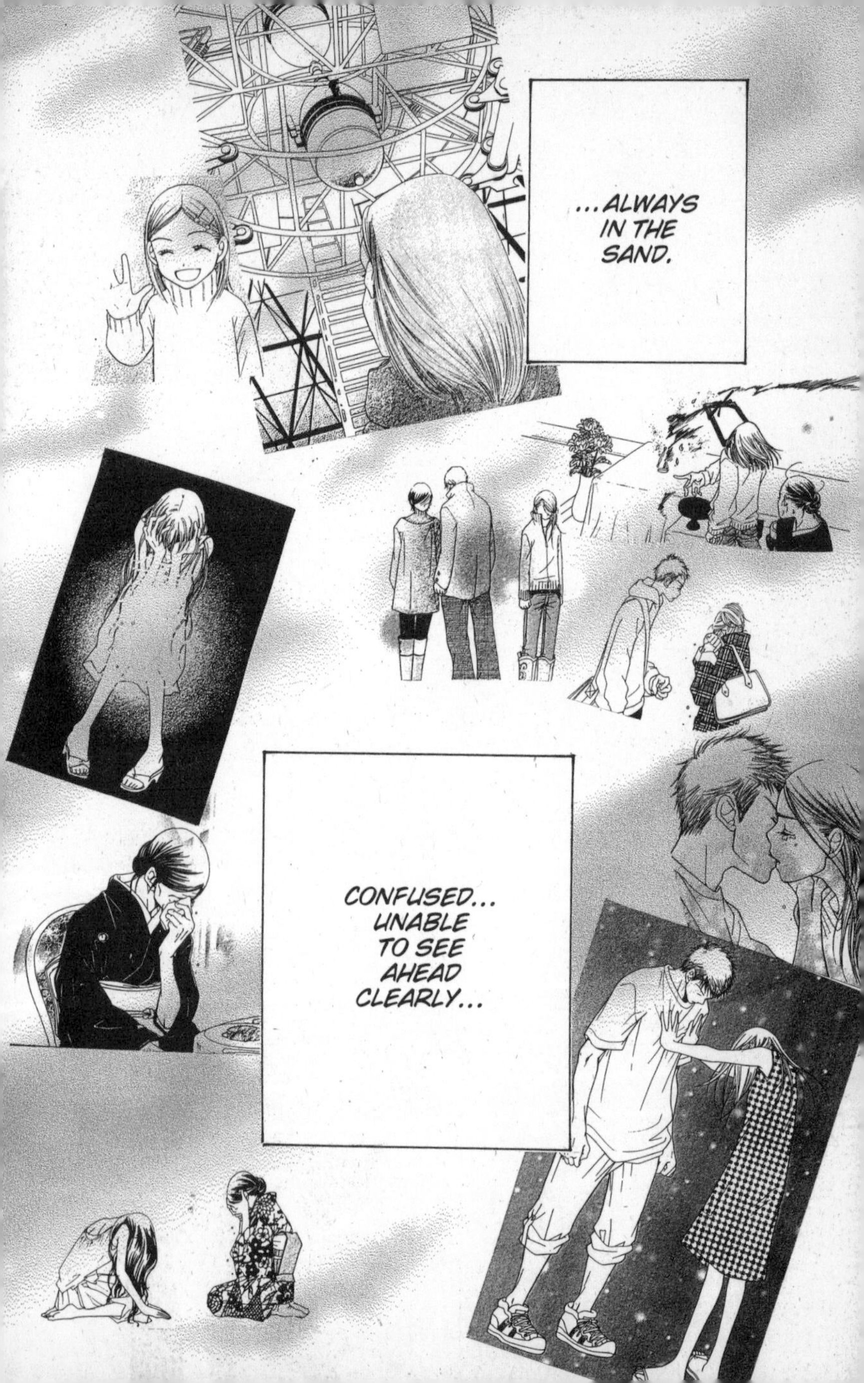
...ALWAYS IN THE SAND.
CONFUSED... UNABLE TO SEE AHEAD CLEARLY...

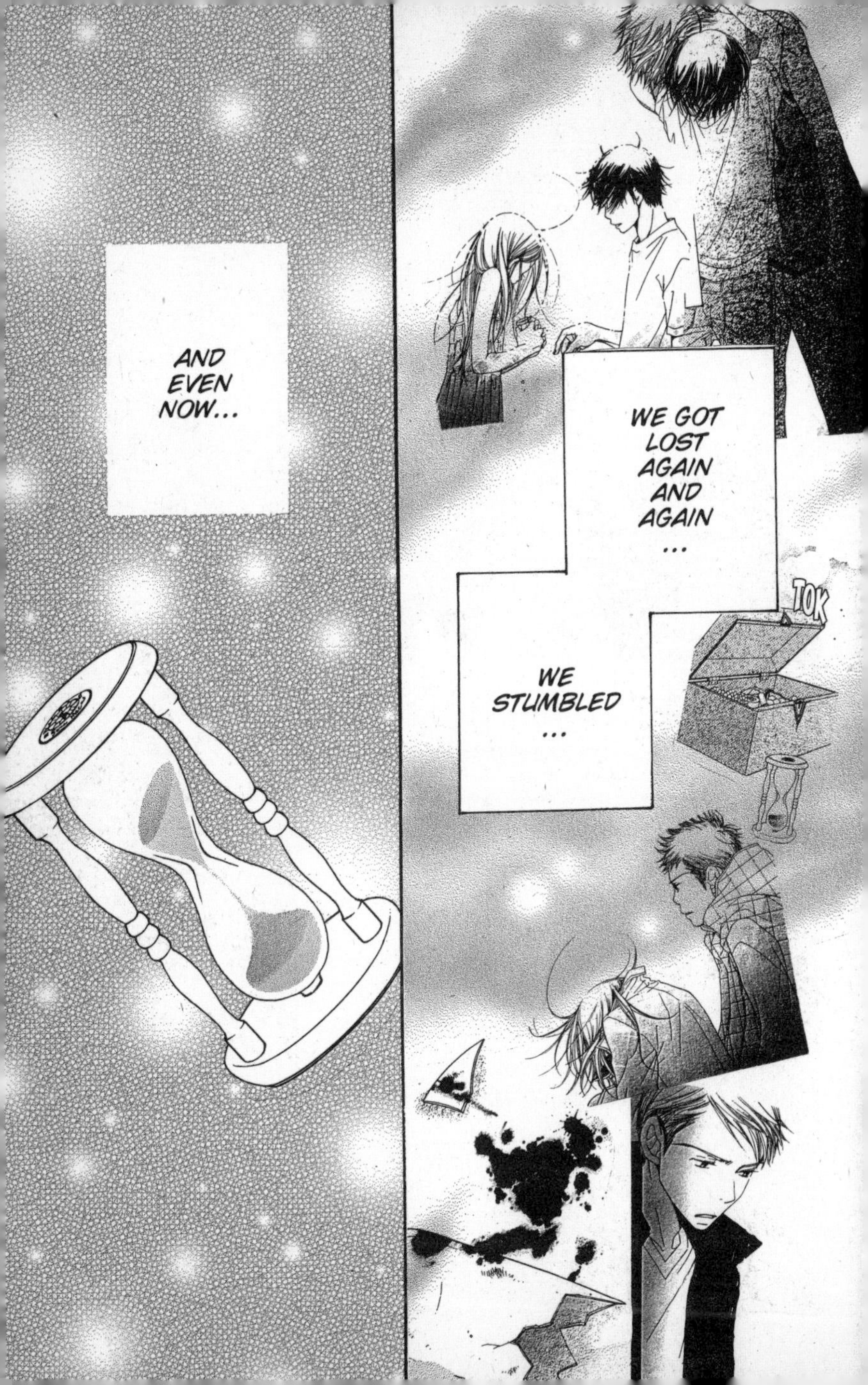
WE GOT LOST AGAIN AND AGAIN ...
TOK
WE STUMBLED ...
AND EVEN NOW...

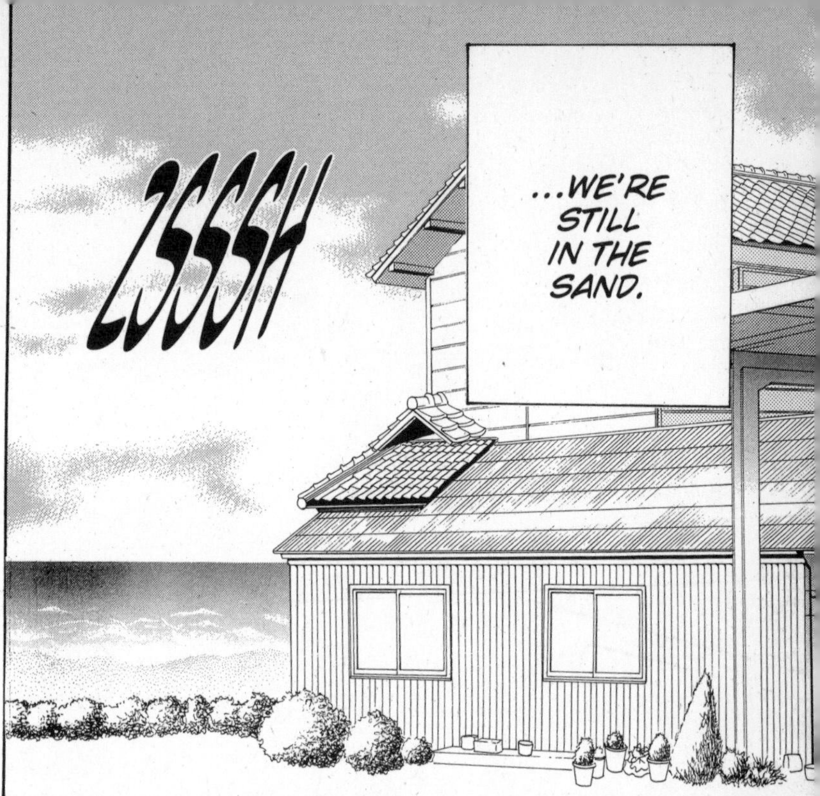
...WE'RE STILL IN THE SAND.
ZSSSH
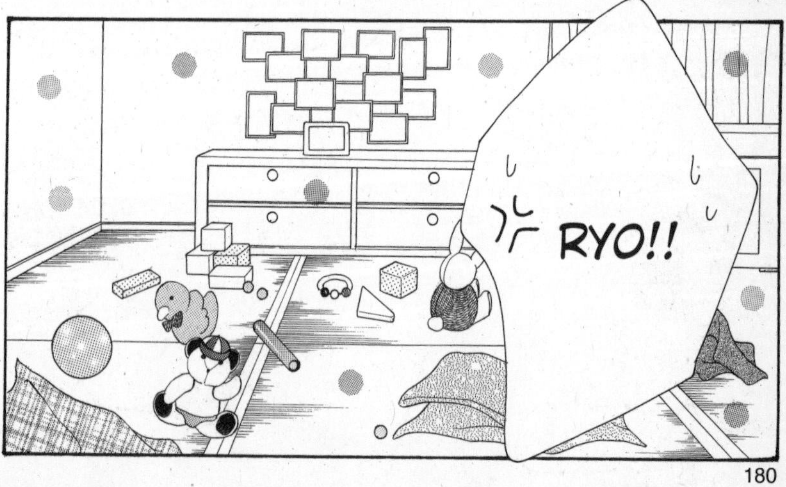
RYO!!

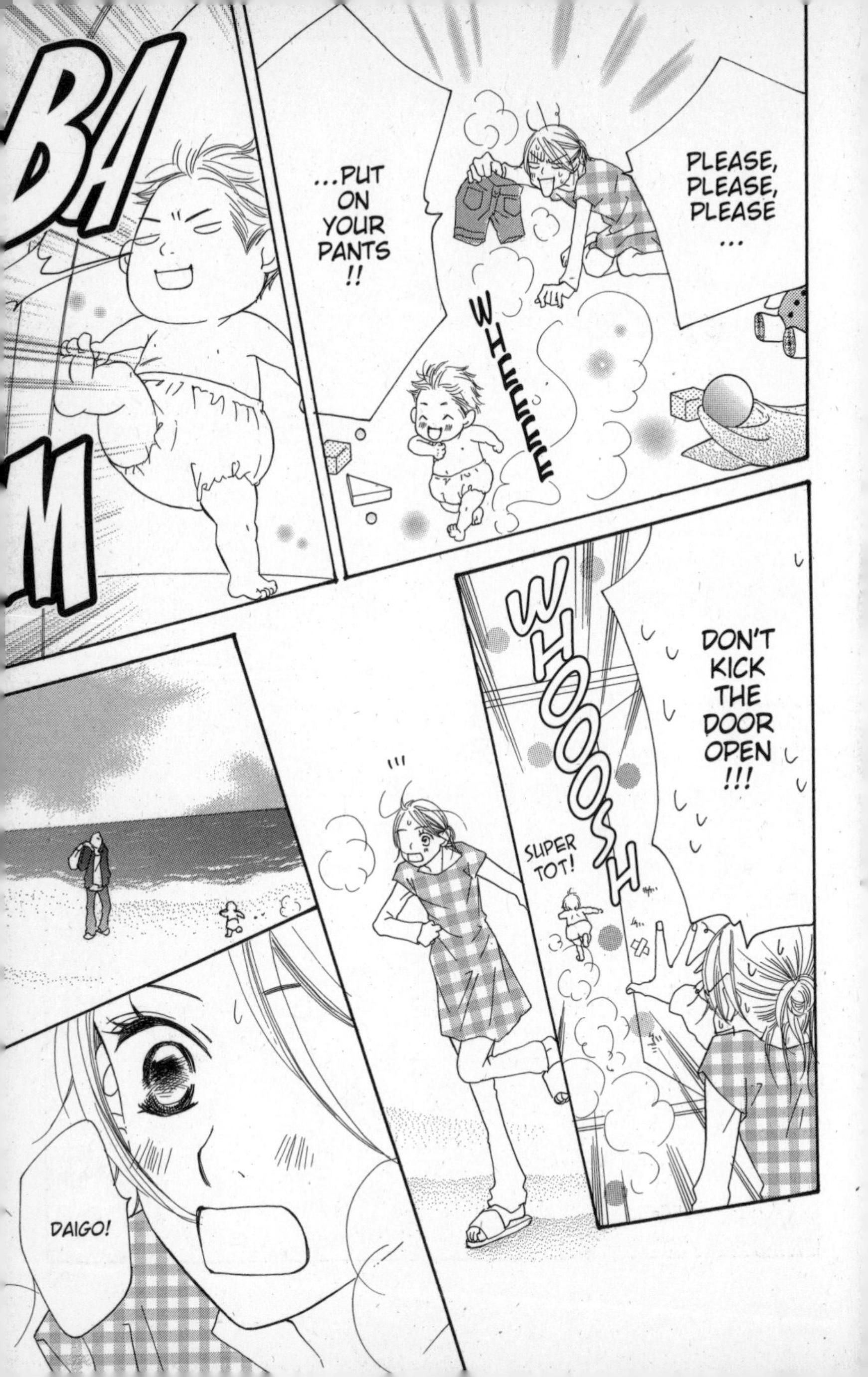
PLEASE, PLEASE, PLEASE ...
...PUT ON YOUR PANTS!!
WHEEEEE
BAM
DON'T KICK THE DOOR OPEN!!!
WHOOOOSH
SUPER TOT!
DAIGO!

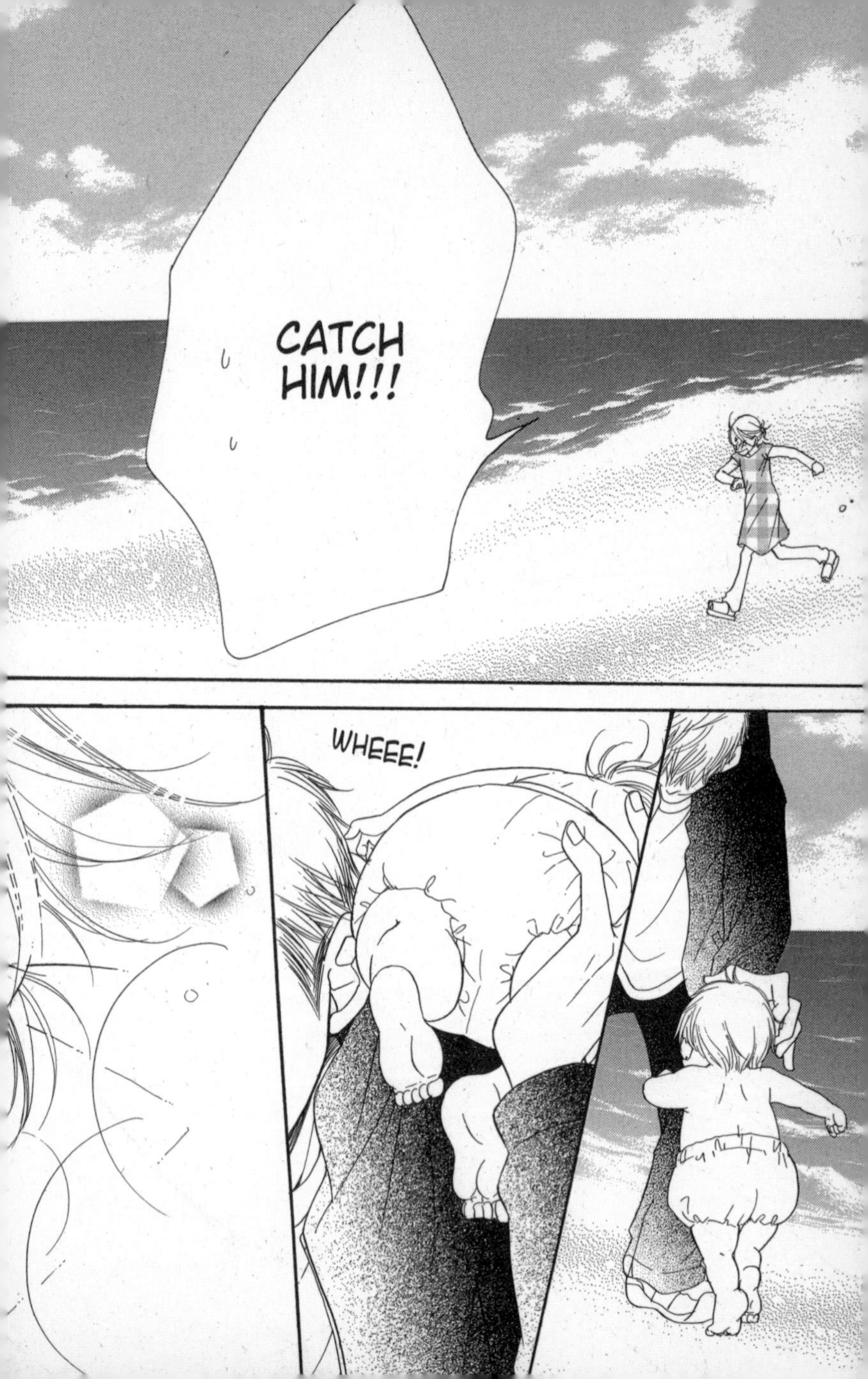
CATCH HIM!!!
WHEEE!

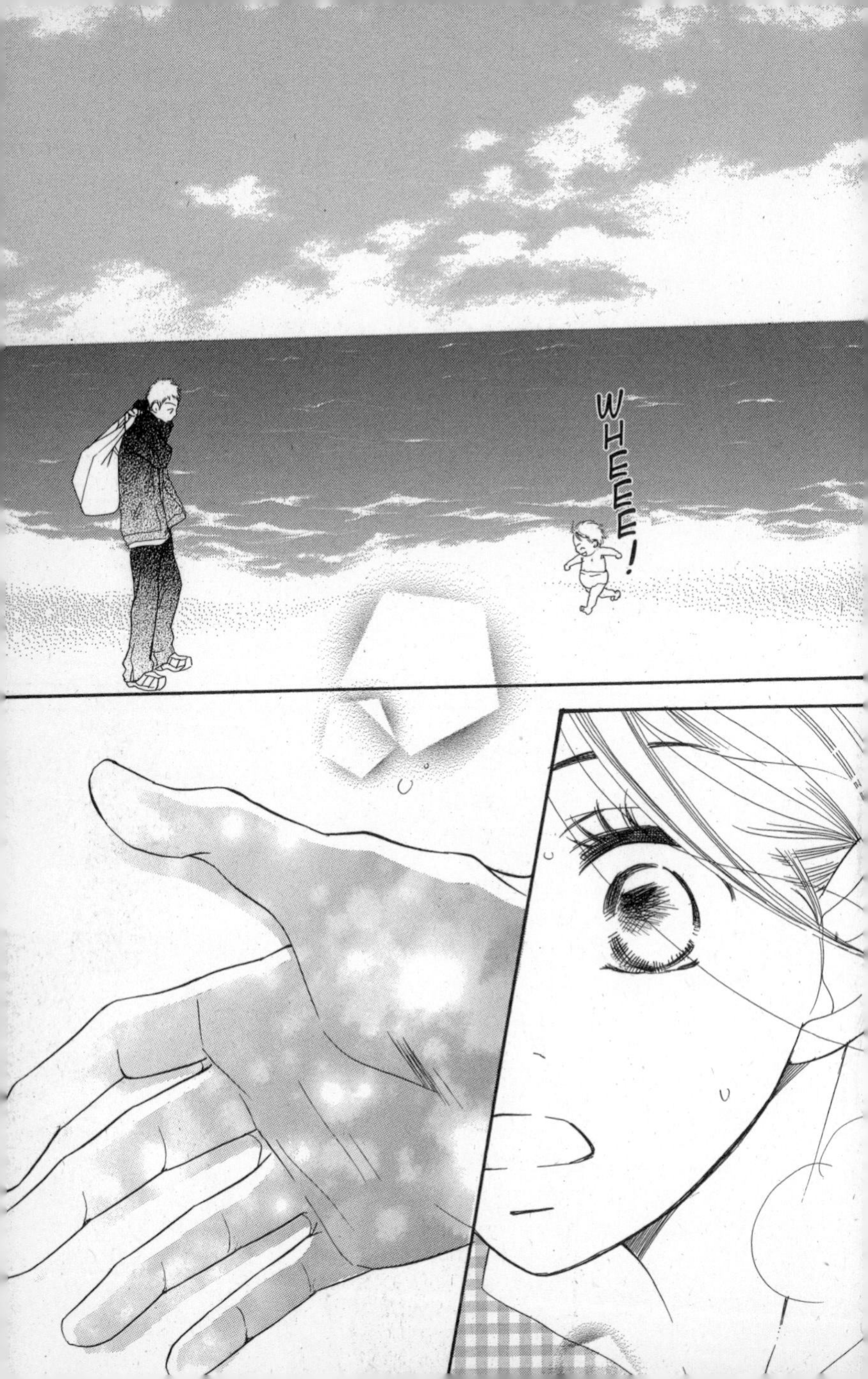
WHEEE!

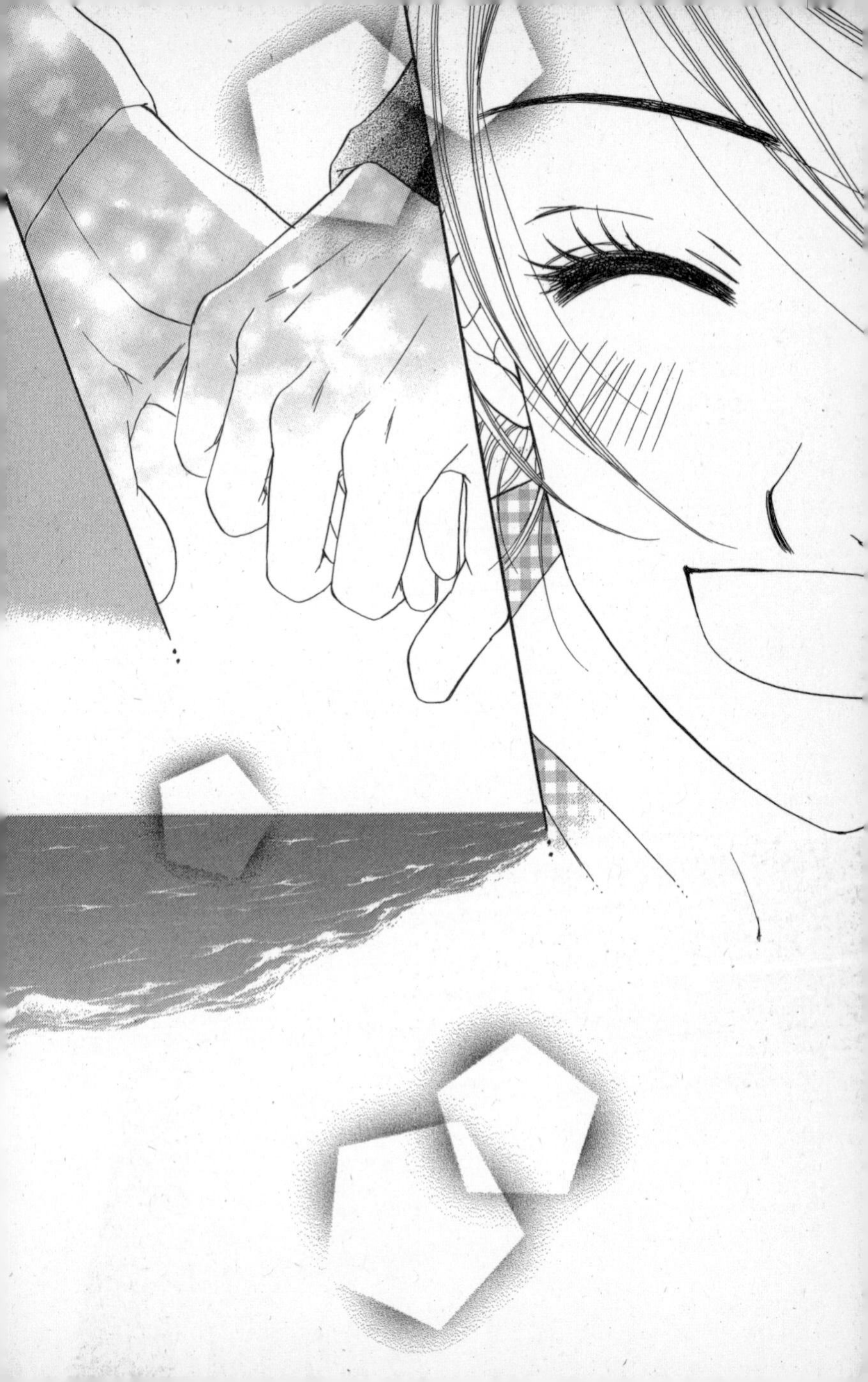

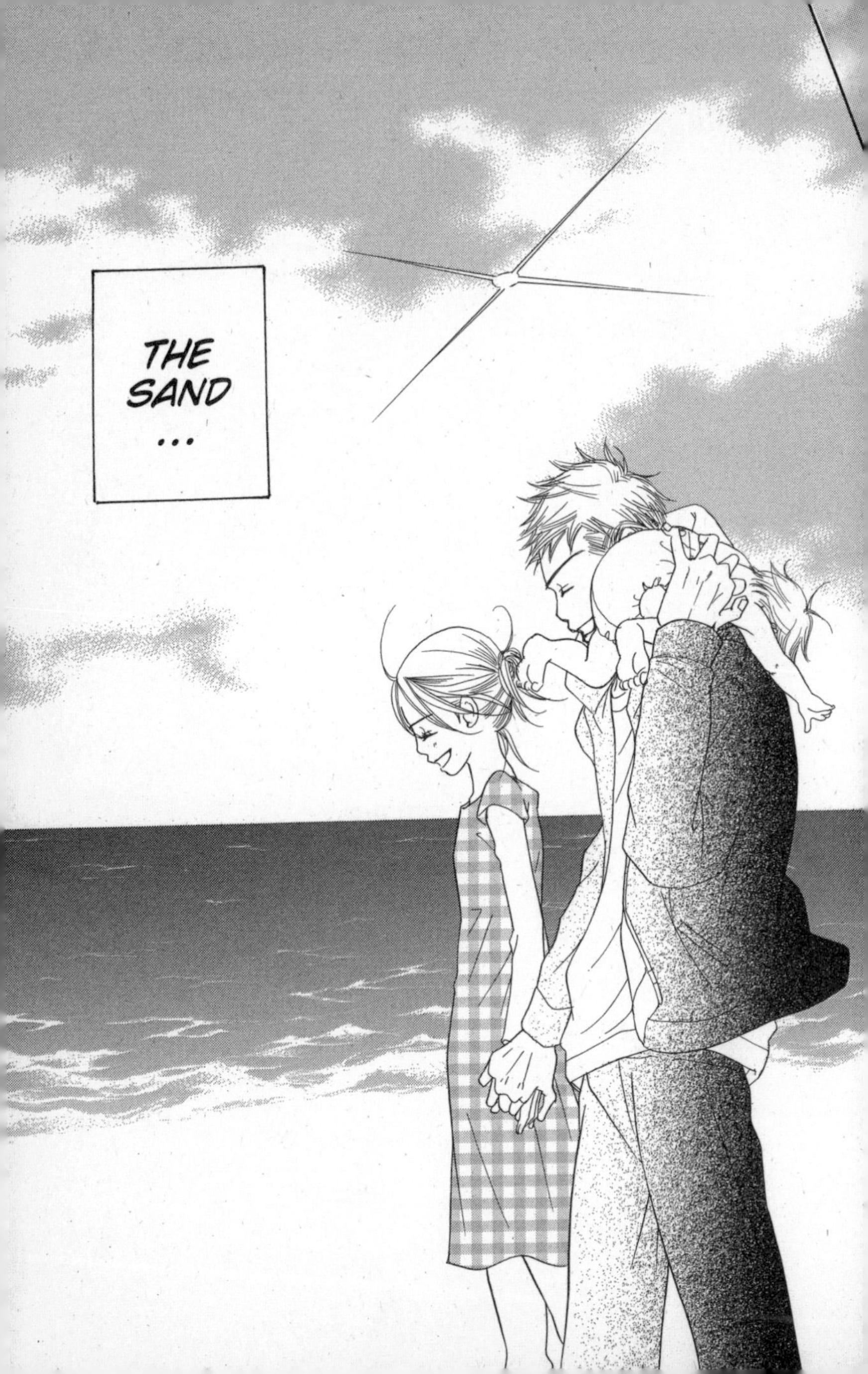
THE SAND ...

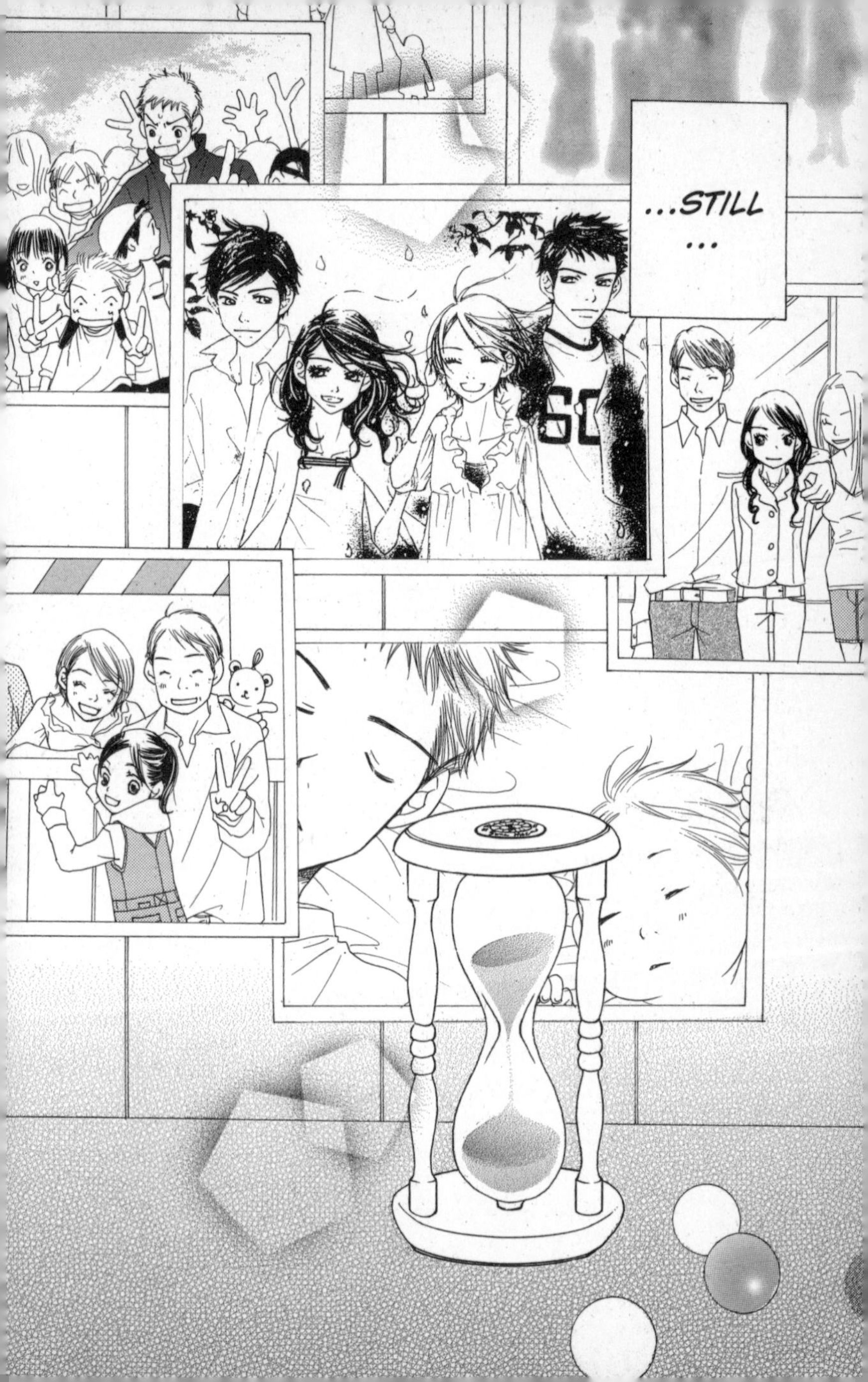
...STILL
...

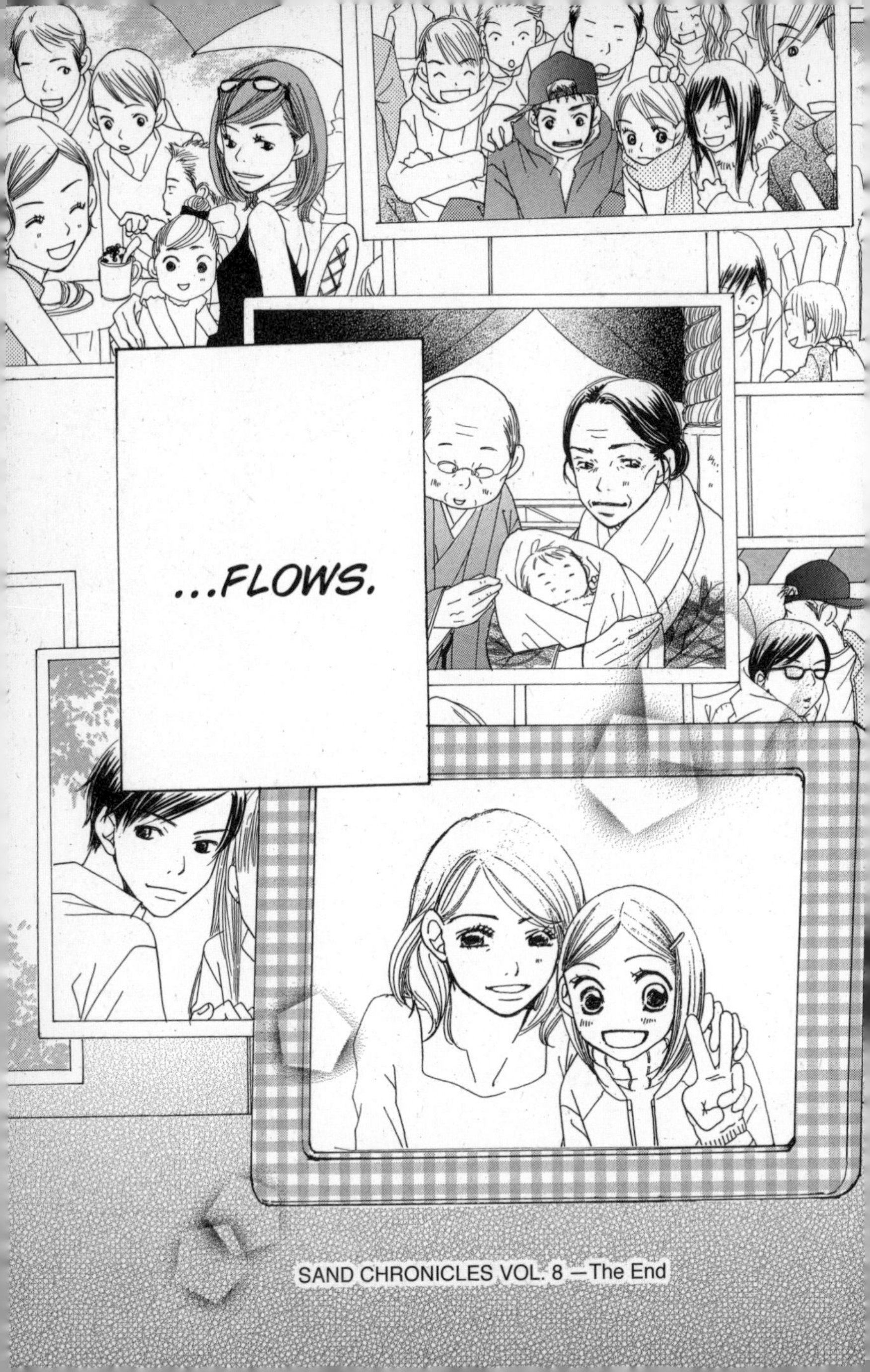
...FLOWS.
SAND CHRONICLES VOL. 8 —The End

Glossary

If only adolescence came with an instruction manual.
We can't give you that, but this glossary of terms
might prove useful for this volume.

Page 14, panel 1: *nimono*
Potatoes, vegetables, pork or root
vegetables simmered in a soy sauce broth.

Page 14, panel 2: *kinpira gobo*
Julienned burdock root that is sautéed and
simmered.

Page 22, panel 4: *kinako* bread
Bread made of soybean flour.

Page 82, panel 7: *Tondo*
A Shinto fire festival where votive tablets,
among other things, are ritually burned.

Page 100, panel 2: *kotatsu*
A table with a blanket and heater
underneath. In the colder months, people
sit or lie with their legs under the blanket.

Page 115, panel 3: *shochu*
An alcoholic drink sometimes made from
potatoes.

Page 121, panel 4: *miai*
A meeting between two individuals
seeking a spouse and their families. It's one
of the steps toward an arranged marriage.

Page 162, panel 2: a lid for every broken pot
A proverb meaning that for every person
out there, no matter how weird, there's a
fitting partner.

Profile of Hinako Ashihara

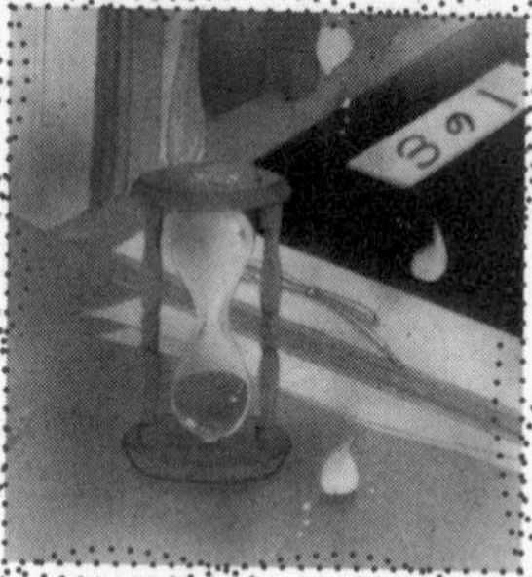

This is the final volume! No, not really. The series will continue until volume 10. After this one, though, the stories will be bonus stories.

Now you're in the know!
—Hinako Ashihara

Hinako Ashihara won the 50th Shogakukan Manga Award for *Sunadokei*. She debuted with *Sono Hanashi Okotowari Shimasu* in *Bessatsu Shojo Comics* in 1994. Her other works include *SOS*, *Forbidden Dance*, and *Tennen Bitter Chocolate*.

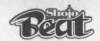

SAND CHRONICLES
Vol. 8
Shojo Beat Edition

STORY AND ART BY HINAKO ASHIHARA

Original Japanese edition "SUNADOKEI" published by SHOGAKUKAN Inc.

English Adaptation/John Werry
Translation/Kinami Watabe, HC Language Solutions Inc.
Touch-up Art & Lettering/Rina Mapa
Additional Touch-up/Rachel Lightfoot
Design/Izumi Evers
Interior/Deirdre Shiozawa
Editor/Annette Roman

VP, Production/Alvin Lu
VP, Sales & Product Marketing/Gonzalo Ferreyra
VP, Creative/Linda Espinosa
Publisher/Hyoe Narita

A CIP catalogue record for this book is available from the British Library.

Printed in Canada

www.viz.com www.shojobeat.com

Published by VIZ Media, LLC
P.O. Box 77010
San Francisco, CA 94107

10 9 8 7 6 5 4 3 2 1
First printing, May 2010

RATED T+ FOR OLDER TEEN

PARENTAL ADVISORY
SAND CHRONICLES is rated T+ for Older Teen and is recommended for ages 16 and up. This volume contains mature themes.
ratings.viz.com

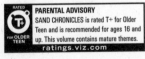

MANGA from the HEART

OTOMEN
STORY AND ART BY AYA KANNO

VAMPIRE KNIGHT
STORY AND ART BY MATSURI HINO

Natsume's BOOK of FRIENDS
STORY AND ART BY YUKI MIDORIKAWA

Want to see more of what you're looking for?

Let your voice be heard!

shojobeat.com/mangasurvey

Help us give you more manga from the heart!

www.viz.com